# TRAINING
# FOR
# PERFORMANCE

# Wiley Series
# Human Performance and Cognition

## Acquisition and Performance of Cognitive Skills
*Edited by Ann M. Colley and John R. Beech*

## Stress and Performance in Sport
*Edited by J. Graham Jones and Lew Hardy*

## Training for Performance: Principles of Applied Human Learning
*Edited by John E. Morrison*

*Further titles in preparation*

# TRAINING FOR PERFORMANCE

## Principles of Applied Human Learning

*Edited by*
**John E. Morrison**
*Human Resources Research Organization,*
*Fort Knox, Kentucky, USA*

**JOHN WILEY & SONS**
Chichester · New York · Brisbane · Toronto · Singapore

*Other Wiley Editorial Offices*

John Wiley & Sons, Inc., 605 Third Avenue,
New York, NY 10158-0012, USA.

Jacaranda Wiley Ltd, G.P.O. Box 859, Brisbane,
Queensland 4001, Australia.

John Wiley & Sons (Canada) Ltd, 22 Worcester Road,
Rexdale, Ontario M9W 1L1, Canada.

John Wiley & Sons (SEA) Pte Ltd, 37 Jalan Pemimpin #05-04,
Block B, Union Industrial Building, Singapore 2057.

*Library of Congress Cataloging-in-Publication Data:*

Training for performance : principles of applied human learning /
   edited by John E. Morrison.
        p.   cm. — (Wiley series, human performance and cognition)
   Includes bibliographical references and indexes.
   ISBN 0-471-92248-X
   1. Learning, Psychology of.   2. Cognition.   I. Morrison, John E.
   II. Series: Wiley series in human performance and cognition.
   LB1051.T664   1991
   370.15′23—dc20                                         90–22211
                                                              CIP

*British Library Cataloguing in Publication Data:*

Training for performance.
   1. Personnel. Training
   I. Morrison, John E. II. Series
   658.3124

   ISBN 0-471-92248-X

Typeset in 10/12 Times by Inforum Typesetting, Portsmouth
Printed and bound in Great Britain by Courier International, Tiptree, Essex

# Contents

# List of Contributors

**Phillip L. Ackerman**      Associate Professor, Department of Psychology, University of Minnesota, USA

**John Annett**      Professor of Psychology, University of Warwick, UK

**Susan R. Crandall**      Graduate Student of Human Resource Management, Graduate School of Business, University of Washington, USA

**Joseph D. Hagman**      Senior Research Psychologist, US Army Research Institute for the Behavioral and Social Sciences, Boise, Idaho, USA

**Dennis H. Holding**      Professor, Department of Psychology, University of Louisville, USA

**Greg Kearsley**      Associate Professor, School of Education and Human Development, The George Washington University, USA

**Patrick C. Kyllonen**      Senior Scientist, US Air Force Human Resources Laboratory, Brooks Air Force Base, Texas, USA

**Gary P. Latham**      Professor, Faculty of Management, University of Toronto, Toronto, Ontario, Canada

**Gavan Lintern**      Assistant Professor, Aviation Research Laboratory, University of Illinois, USA

**John E. Morrison**      Senior Staff Scientist, Human Resources Research Organization, Fort Knox, Kentucky, USA

**John Patrick**      Senior Lecturer, School of Psychology, University of Wales College of Cardiff, UK

**Joel D. Schendel**      Area Coordinator, Hay Systems, Inc., Orlando, Florida, USA

# Series Preface

Books in the original Series on Human Performance were designed to provide clear explanations of the main issues affecting human performance, based on a broad range of experimental research. The earlier volumes dealt with such topics as the analysis of human skills, the effects of sleep and biological rhythms, the sustainment of attention during vigilance performance, the effects of noise on human efficiency, the changes resulting from aging, and the consequences of sex differences in performance. In each of these volumes it became evident that it was necessary to take account of the cognitive mechanisms that underlie the overt expression of human performance variables. It was clearly desirable to devote more explicit attention to such mechanisms, and to the research findings concerning the relevant cognitive processes. These considerations have found expression in the most recent volumes, on the acquisition of cognitive skills, and on the effects of stress in sport, that began the new Series in Human Performance and Cognition.

As indicated by the revised title, the extended series now has a broader scope. One advantage of the change in title is to give explicit recognition to what had hitherto been implicit, thus making clear that human performance is regulated by cognitive processes. However, the change is not merely an improvement in nomenclature. Rather, it provides an opportunity to offer books dealing with a much wider spectrum of topics, ranging from cognitive science to cognitive ergonomics. The new series will shortly include volumes concerning such issues as decision-making, and circadian variations in arousal. Despite the new format, the series will preserve those distinguishing features, such as clarity of expression, that have accounted for its present measure of success. These characteristics will be carried into further extensions of the series that are to include selected undergraduate texts.

Until now, many of the books in the series have taken the form of edited volumes rather than monographs. However, the end products of the editing process are not haphazard collections of papers, but systematically organized texts that utilize the advantages of multiple authorship. Although writing a monograph is often regarded as the more difficult assignment, the task of producing an edited volume presents a considerable challenge. On one hand, it provides an opportunity to bring to bear on the subject matter a concentration of expertise that would otherwise be unavailable; on the other hand, the need for a multiplicity of contributors carries with it the risk that the overall result might lack coherence. In the present series, every effort has been made to counter the potential disadvantages of the edited format while preserving the positive advantages that stem from the opportunity to draw on specialized knowledge. The individual chapters have been commissioned in accordance with an integrated plan for each volume, information about chapter content has been circulated among the contributors to ensure cohesiveness, and editorial control has been extended to the level of difficulty as well as to the format of each text. The books have thus been designed to combine readability with high standards of scholarship.

The present volume continues these traditions, providing a readily assimilable but carefully researched description of the factors that must be taken into account in providing training for skills. It should be noted that the volume successfully integrates performance with cognition, in accordance with the current designation of the series. In fact, the introductory chapter by Dr Morrison documents the transition toward the use of cognitive explanations that has taken place in training theory during recent decades, thus establishing a framework for the later contributions. Like many of the earlier books, the *Training for Performance* volume also manages to satisfy two other related objectives, integrating both theoretical and practical issues. As the subtitle to the book implies, the main theoretical issues are those concerned with the principles of human learning. These are perhaps best represented in the early chapters on the acquisition of skill, the retention of skill, and the transfer of skill. However, it is clear that theoretical issues of many kinds also arise in the chapters more directly concerned with training problems, beginning with the consideration of task analysis as a prelude to designing training schemes. The subsequent chapters on instructional strategies, on individual differences among trainees, on the characteristics of training media, and on organizational variables, all provide their contributions to theoretical debate.

Although the book is in no sense a training manual, it has much to offer that is of practical value, often in the form of direct recommendations for training practice. It is particularly noteworthy that many of its findings are broadly applicable to all of the training contexts from which supporting evidence was derived, which include many kinds of industrial settings, and a wide range of military and defense applications, in addition to more traditional academic backgrounds. Its breadth of coverage, combined with careful documentation and a high standard of exposition, ensure that *Training for Performance* fully complies with the objectives outlined above. The book clearly reflects the wide experience and competence of the volume editor, while at the same time drawing on the technical expertise of a representative group of training researchers. As a consequence, this volume constitutes a very welcome addition to the Series in Human Performance and Cognition.

*Dennis Holding*
*University of Louisville*

# Chapter 1

# Introduction

### John E. Morrison
Human Resources Research Organization

The purpose of the present text is to present current psychological research on human learning, memory, and performance as it relates to the practice of training. Thus, the purpose of the present text is similar to that espoused in Holding's (1965) *Principles of Training*, which for years has provided an authoritative reference book for the training practitioner and researcher. Since the publication of that book, however, the inevitable progress in learning theory and training technology has made it necessary to examine the topic of training reserarch once again. This re-examination with its emphasis on recent scientific and technological developments provides, in essence, the focus for the remaining chapters in this text.

Whereas the remaining chapters examine specific issues for training research and practice, the first two sections of the present chapter briefly describe two general historical trends that have occurred between the publication of Holding's (1965) book and the present volume, and that have important implications for training research and practice. One relates to changes in the theoretical *Zeitgeist* that provides the foundation for training research, while the other pertains to changes in the nature of work itself. The third and final section of this chapter more specifically identifies the training research issues to which the present text is addressed.

## CHANGES TO CONCEPTUAL UNDERPINNINGS

Some of the basic theoretical concepts that underlie training research and practice have changed drastically since the publication of Holding's (1965) textbook on training. Two of the more important developments are discussed below.

### The fall of behavioral learning theory and the rise of cognitive theory

In 1965, the implicit theoretical basis for most training research was behavioral learning theory, which existed in several guises. Hull's (1943) theory, later elaborated on and revised by Spence (1956), perhaps serves as the prototypical example of behavioristic learning theories that sought to develop complete and formal analyses of learning in terms of behavioral changes. According to strict behaviorism, performance can be explained by the relationships between external stimuli and overt responses. One of the basic tenets of this theory is that a performer's internal processes are either unknowable or irrelevant to the explanation of learning, retention, and transfer of skills. Behaviorism has been criticized continuously starting with its inception provided by Watson's (1913) manifesto. For instance, critics disparagingly characterized the learner depicted in behavioristic theories as being reduced to simply a 'black box' between stimulus input and response output.

Despite the criticisms, the impact of behaviorism on training research was significant in the 1950s and 1960s and is still being felt in the practice of training today. One of the more influential applications of behavioristic learning theory to training technology was Mager's (1962) concept of behavioral objectives. Mager argued that training development should begin with the identification of training objectives, which provide a clear description of instructional intent (Pipe, 1975). Furthermore, training objectives should be behaviorally defined so that the to-be-learned task(s) are completely specified and objectively measurable. By 'behaviorally defined' Mager maintained that a well-stated objective must describe the to-be-learned task in terms of three essential components: (a) the *observable behavior* that the learner must perform to demonstrate mastery of the objective; (b) the *stimulus conditions* under which the behavior should be observed; and (c) the objective *criteria* of success that define competent performance. The specification of training content by behavioral objectives is now regarded as a 'core' concept in training development and practice.

Just as behavioral learning theory had its peak influence on training practice and research in the late 1960s and early 1970s, learning theorists were becoming increasingly dissatisfied with behavioral conceptions of learning and increasingly more interested in the study of internal knowledge structures and cognitive processes that underlie task performance. Some researchers have characterized this shift in focus as a revolution in theoretical models and research paradigms (e.g. Neisser, 1967), while others have viewed this change as a less dramatic evolutionary shift from *how* learning occurs to *what* is learned (e.g. Greeno, 1980). Fokkema (1978) noted that rise of cognitive psychology was resisted in the United States because of its strong behaviorist tradition, whereas the shift to cognitive theory was less revolutionary in Great Britain where mental concepts such as Bartlett's (1932) schema were widely accepted. Regardless of the perceived extent of change, it is undeniable that cognitive theory is now the predominant theoretical viewpoint in research on learning and memory.

One of the benefits of the recent shift from the study of behavior to the study of cognition is that researchers have shown less interest in simple knowledge-lean tasks (e.g. paired associate learning, free recall) as performed under artificial laboratory conditions in favor of knowledge-rich tasks (e.g. chess, algebra, reading) as performed in realistic contexts. This approach has significantly increased our knowledge of how such complex tasks are performed. Glaser (1990) noted that, as our knowledge of complex performances has increased, researchers are starting to tackle the more difficult problem of how they are learned. Glaser reviewed recent learning research from a cognitive perspective, and lamented that the learning processes and instructional implications show very few commonalities across the task domains. He remained confident, however, that an integrated theory can and must be designed that prescribes a mix of instructional approaches for specific training purposes. Clearly, this is a formidable objective for research, but one that must be met for cognitive psychology to have a significant and lasting impact on training practice and research.

Although the thread of cognitive theorizing is recognizable throughout the present volume, the authors differ with respect to the degree to which they embrace its tenets. Most of the authors implicitly accept the cognitive viewpoint while focusing on more narrow models of learning and performance to explain training phenomena. In contrast, Lintern (Chapter 6) is skeptical of cognitive theory, arguing that its theories are so ill-defined that one can often accommodate competing findings with only minor adjustments in theoretical assumptions. He does agree with Glaser (1990), however, that research on instruction and training should focus on complex, real-world tasks. Still others actively extol cognitive theorizing for its new insights into the problems of training, such as those related to the analysis of tasks (Patrick, Chapter 5), the prediction of training and job success (Ackerman and Kyllonen, Chapter 7), and the explanation of the effects of social factors in the context of training (Latham and Crandall, Chapter 9).

Perhaps the value of a theoretical basis for training research is not determined primarily by its ultimate rectitude, but rather by the usefulness of its by-products and technologies for the practice of training. This view is reminiscent of the assertion, in theoretical circles, that the value of a theory is determined by its heuristic utility to explain existing findings and to stimulate new research. This point of view would lead to the conclusion that, even though behaviorism has been eclipsed theoretically, it continues to have utility to training research and development. For instance, the concept of behavioral objectives, an outgrowth of behavioral learning theory, is still serving trainers well. In addition to helping to define the content of training, research indicates that the use of behavioral objectives has a positive effect on learning at the individual level (Wells and Hagman, 1989). However, it is interesting to note that the theoretical interpretation of this effect invokes a more cognitive explanation of learning. For instance, Gagné (1965) speculated that one way that behavioral objectives enhance learning is by giving the learner a goal to which he can actively aspire and judge his own learning progress. Hartley and Davies (1976) pointed out that this argument assumes that the learner fully understands the goal (a cognitive concept), and knows how to use the goal for learning purposes (a metacognitive concept). Thus, behavioral objectives—a direct outgrowth of behaviorism—has proven itself to be a robust concept whose effects can be interpreted with both cognitive as well as behavioristic theories.

## The rise of systems approaches to training

The process of developing and implementing training requires the coordination and integration of media, equipment, methods, and personnel required to meet an explicitly stated purpose—that is, to train people for jobs. Partly due to this complexity, researchers in the 1960s and 1970s started to use the concept of systems analysis to describe this multifaceted process (Crawford, 1962; Smith, 1971). A systems approach to training is one that views each component of training as influencing and interacting with the other components in the system. Careful analysis of the system leads to better definitions of the system's purpose and to prescriptions for changes should the system not accomplish its objectives. The starting point for this analysis is the explicit identification of the system's objectives. Thus, Mager's concept of behavioral objectives was a natural fit and was quickly adopted in most systems approaches. In the training literature, the systems approach to training became a subject unto itself under the rubric of Instructional Systems Development (or ISD).

One of the early proponents of the systems approach to training was the Human Resources Research Organization (HumRRO). Smith (1971) described HumRRO's model of the systems engineering of training as a seven-step process (see Figure 1.1). In Step 1, the analyst focuses on the job situation and identifies all the people and equipment that interact to produce work output. In Step 2, the analyst changes focus to the individual trainee, identifying all tasks that he is expected to perform. At this point, the system splits into parallel processes. One path (Steps 3, 4 and 5) describes the process of instructional development whereas the other path (Step 6) is concerned exclusively with development of proficiency tests. Following the instructional path, the analyst identifies the knowledge and skills required to perform the tasks (Step 3). The next process on this branch (Step 4) is to identify which skills and knowledge need training and which do not; the result is a complete inventory of objectives for the systems. The final process in this branch (Step 5) is to select media and configure instruction as needed. The process of developing proficiency tests (Step 6) is parallel to the instructional branch to ensure that proficiency tests are closely allied with the performance goals of the system and are not more narrowly defined by specific instructional aims. The final step (Step 7) is to evaluate the training program itself to test whether or not the system is performing its goals, that is, producing proficient students. Crawford (1985) argued that the HumRRO systems approach has provided a useful framework with which others in both the military and industrial training arenas have elaborated and refined into a useful technology for training.

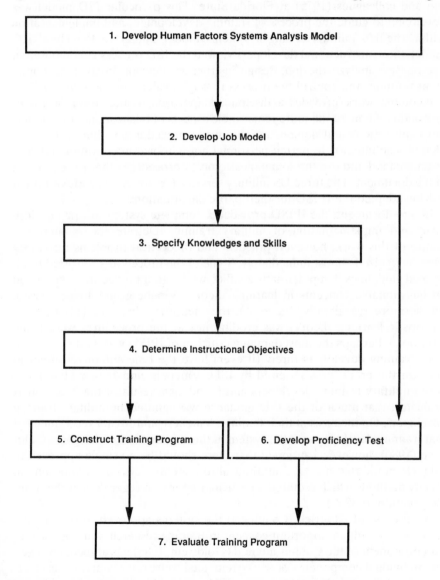

**Figure 1.1.** HumRRO's seven-step approach to developing training.

Since HumRRO's systems approach was developed, many other systems approaches to training have been introduced. Ten years ago, Goldstein (1980) commented that '. . . there are almost as many systems approaches as there are authors on the subject' (p. 231). However, perhaps the zenith of the systems approach to training was the publication of the *Interservice Procedures for Instructional Systems Development (IPISD)* developed by Branson and colleagues (1975) at Florida State. This particular ISD model was developed to guide the process of training development and implementation within the US military. Using a systems model similar to the HumRRO model, these instructional developers viewed the ISD process as composed of five phases: analyze the job, design instruction, develop instruction, implement training, and control the process through evaluation and revision. This five-volume work provides a disciplined approach to the development of instruction. Some of the more remarkable aspects of this work are the numerous explanations and demonstrations of the procedures within each of the phases. The intent is to permit personnel not schooled in educational theory to understand and use the sometimes complex procedures that are described in the document. The three US military services (Army, Navy, and Air Force) quickly adapted the IPISD for their particular situations.

In one document, the IPISD provided a complete system for the development and implementation of military training. Despite the monumental nature of this work, however, practical and theoretical problems for IPISD were recognized almost immediately. Some of the procedures consisted of ill-defined guidelines that potentially conflict, while other procedures were based on questionable concepts in learning theory (Vineberg and Joyner, 1980). Furthermore (as already discussed), the theoretical basis of ISD (i.e. behavioristic learning theory) was eroding just at the procedures were being developed. Perhaps the most damning criticism of IPISD was its sheer magnitude: training developers rarely (if ever) have the time and/or resources to perform the procedures required by ISD. Vineberg and Joyner (1980) surveyed military training developers and found, as a result of these and other problems, that much of the ISD guidance was ignored by military training developers. On the basis of their findings, Vineberg and Joyner recommended that training developers use the system in the way that it was designed. Goldstein (1980), however, cautioned that there should be no single approach to ISD. He noted that it is '. . . antithetical to the entire system's philosophy to specify methods which required a particular approach regardless of the training situation' (p. 232).

As discussed by Patrick (Chapter 5) the systems approach to training development is still an important concept in training research. Another significant proponent of the systems method (Goldstein, 1986) has argued, however, that individual components of the system need to be rethought. For instance, Kearsley (Chapter 8) contends that ISD media selection models that are based primarily on pedagogical factors should consider other variables such as cost effectiveness and ergonomic factors. Another area for reform is in the development of short-cuts to streamline the process wherever possible. Morrison (1985) presented a shortened version of a training development process that is appropriate for revising existing courses. Finally, another needed change to the systems approach is to interject theoretical concepts from cognitive psychology. Halff, Hollan and Hutchins (1986) suggested that traditional ISD methods are suitable for courses that address behavioral training objectives, but not for the increasing number of courses that address cognitive skills. In that regard, real progress has been made in codifying procedures for analyzing and developing instruction for complex tasks such as electronics troubleshooting (Glaser et al., 1986; E. Gagné, 1988). The problem is that the ISD models tend to be appropriate to one or the other type of training. A comprehensive model is needed to integrate the variety of tasks that are being trained in the workplace today. In that regard, training developers need to be aware of recent changes to the workplace described below and their implications for training.

## CHANGES TO THE NATURE OF WORK

The period from publication of Holding's book to the present (25 years) is quite brief in terms of the development of industrial society. Nevertheless there have been some recent changes over that comparatively short period that have an impact on the sorts of issues that are relevant to training research. Goldstein and Gilliam (1990) listed some changes that have recently happened or will soon happen to affect the workplace such as changes in demographics, the shift from manufacturing to service jobs, and the influence of international markets. These changes create important social and organization issues for training research, some of which are discussed by Latham and Crandall in this volume (Chapter 9). In addition to these societal changes, Goldstein and Gilliam also discussed the increase in task automation made possible by computer technology. This latter change is particularly important in that it actually has changed the nature of work for many job incumbents.

Whereas automation has undeniably changed the manner in which people perform their jobs, it has not (as some have argued) made job tasks uniformly easier or more difficult. In fact, at least three types of effects can be detected. The first effect that automation has had is to increase the procedural component of tasks. For instance, the job of maintenance troubleshooting was originally a task predominated by problem-solving and decision-making skills. With the advent of electronic computerized job aids and test equipment built into operational equipment, the job incumbent's task is to follow the clearly defined procedures and occasionally test the results. These aids are designed to lead the incumbent systematically to some resolution such as replacing some component or (if beyond a simple replacement) referring the problem to a supervisor or to another maintenance unit. Relevant to this sort of change one consistent finding from the literature is that procedural tasks, such as this troubleshooting task, are more easily forgotten compared to psychomotor tasks (e.g. Mengelkoch, Adams and Gainer, 1971). As a consequence, this shift toward procedural tasks has renewed interest in skill retention (Johnson, 1981) and in the effects of procedural job aids (Hagman and Schendel, 1981). Another research issue relating to increased proceduralization is the role of understanding in learning and retention of tasks. In an oft-cited study, Kieras and Bovair (1984) demonstrated that learning and retention of procedures to operate a device is greatly enhanced by instruction on how the device works.

The second effect that automation can have on job performance has been called 'paradoxical' in that automation actually increases the cognitive complexity of some jobs (Goldstein and Gilliam 1990). That is, whereas automation can make jobs less routine, it can also make the incumbent responsible for new tasks or task components that require more complex problem-solving skills. One personally familiar example is the secretary's job in research organizations. In bygone years the secretary's primary task was to type manuscripts from handwritten documents produced by the researchers. The critical components of their job were the perceptual requirement of decoding the handwriting and manual requirement of typing. With the advent of word processing, researchers now provide secretaries with floppy diskettes containing their 'pretyped' work. The secretary's job now includes tasks such as proofing the document and formatting it for printing. (With the advent of laser printing, the aesthetic standards for reports have increased dramatically.) To perform these new tasks, the secretary must have internalized at least two sources of information: word processing software documentation and guidance for manuscript publication. Using these complex sources of information and the raw typed input, the objective is to produce a document that is free from grammatical and spelling errors, adheres to accepted publication guidelines, and is aesthetically pleasing. This change has meant that 'typing' involves less traditional decoding and manual skills and more in the way of problem-solving skills. Compared to the previous tasks, these new fuzzily defined tasks require more reading (of both the manuscript and the supporting documentation) and solving the problems that inevitably occur while trying to output printed documents. For training purposes, the essential problem is to define precisely what these new cognitive job requirements are in order to deterine what should be trained. Patrick (Chapter 5, this text), in agreement with Gagné (1962), argues that the identification of training requirements remains a paramount issue in training development.

The third possible effect of automation on job performance is to add new components to already complex tasks that must be performed simultaneously with other task activities. For example, in air-to-air combat, pilots are required to perform the difficult psychomotor task of engaging an evasive target while monitoring the constantly updated information on that target automatically provided by the aircraft's avionics (e.g. the target's aspect angle and range). The less expert pilot typically concentrates on one aspect of this task to the detriment of the other aspects. To perform the task successfully, pilots must learn effectively to time-share their attention between the simultaneously performed components. Pilots commonly call the subjective feeling of exceeding one's span of attention as being 'task saturated'. The phenomenon is not limited to flight tasks. Similar problems have been noted in research on air traffic controllers (Means *et al.*, 1988) and on tank commanders (Quinkert, 1987). As a result, the theory related to attention and multi-task phenomena has had an increasingly important role in training research (e.g. Wickens, 1989).

## ISSUES IN TRAINING RESEARCH

Despite these important developments in training theory and changes to the nature of work, training research continues to be organized around major 'issues' that define the major subject-matter areas for training research and practice. In the following chapters, authoritative researchers from the United States and the United Kingdom provide in-depth discussions of these issues.

Some of the venerable issues treated in Holding's (1966) textbook and even earlier works on training remain important topics for training research and practice. These include the topics of acquisition, retention, and transfer of job skills. Because these are learning phenomena that must be explained and predicted by any theory, they are just as relevant to cognitive theories as they were to behavioral theories of learning. Because of the fundamental nature of these issues, the next three chapters (2–4) by Annett, by Schendel and Hagman, and by Holding are devoted to summarizing the theories and research findings related to these three important and basic issues.

Two other issues have also traditionally been treated in textbooks on training. Unlike the more basic topics discussed above, these two issues concern more practical issues related to the development and implementation of training. The first of these two (Patrick, Chapter 5) concerns analysis of tasks to identify the objectives for training. Patrick describes task analysis as the first step in the training development process. He then provides a detailed discussion of the various types of methods that are currently in use for analyzing tasks. Once the objectives have been identified, the trainer must be concerned with the arrangement of practice events and other aspects of the learning environment to facilitate learning and retention. In the second of these two chapters, Lintern (Chapter 6) discusses these issues in the context of the instructional strategies that are appropriate for training. Later chapters are concerned with issues that have only more recently emerged. For the most part, research on training has been conducted within the framework of 'experimental' psychology and ignored the psychology of individual differences. As far back as 1957, Cronbach called for the integration of these two realms of research. In the spirit of this integration, Ackerman and Kyllonen (Chapter 7) discuss the role of individual differences in training research. They discuss the fact that the concept of individual differences is often depicted as competing with the process of training. In contrast to this opinion, these authors maintain that an understanding of basic learning phenomena will aid in the integration of both processes. Another new issue is the rise of training technology. Technology has changed not only the nature of work but also the way we train. Kearsley (Chapter 8) provides a discussion of how training media and technology can be used to amplify the trainee's ability to learn his or her job. Kearsley describes not only the advantages and disadvantages that are inherent in the different categories of training technologies but also the problems of their implementation in the workplace. Latham and Crandall (Chapter 9) examine the role of social and organizational factors in training. They argue that the failure of training to transfer to improved work performance can be attributed to the ignorance of organization and social factors such as the organizational culture, pay and promotion policies, the financial health of the organization, and trainee interactions with others. Finally, Morrison and Holding (Chapter 10) review the entire text and identify fruitful topics for future research in training.

## REFERENCES

Bartlett, F. C. (1932). *Remembering.* Cambridge: Cambridge University Press.

Branson, R. K., Rayner, G. T., Cox, J. L., Furman, J. P., King, F. J. and Hannum, W. H. (1975). *Interservice Procedures for Instructional Systems Development* (ADA 019 486). Center for Educational Technology, The Florida State University.

Crawford, M. P. (1962). Concepts of training. In R. M. Gagné (ed.). *Psychological Principles in System Development.* New York: Holt, Rinehart, and Winston.

Crawford, M. P. (1985). Psychology, technology, and professional service, *American Psychologist,* **40**, 415–422.

Cronbach, L. (1957). The two disciplines of scientific psychology, *American Psychologist,* **12**, 671–684.

Fokkema, S. D. (1978). In A. M. Lesgold, J. W. Pellegrino, S. D. Fokkema and R. Glaser (eds). *Cognitive Psychology and Instruction.* New York: Plenum Press.

Gagné, E. D. (1988). *A Cognitive Approach to Defining Job Proficiency.* Paper presented at the 96th Annual Convention of the American Psychological Association, Atlanta, GA.

Gagné, R. M. (1962). Military training and principles of learning, *American Psychologist*, **17**, 83–91.

Gagné, R. M. (1965). *The Conditions of Learning*. New York: Holt, Rinehart and Winston.

Glaser, R. (1990). The emergence of learning theory within instructional research, *American Psychologist*, **45**, 29–39.

Glaser, R., Lesgold, A., Lajoie, S., Eastman, R., Greenberg, L., Logan, D., Magone, M., Weiner, A., Wolf, R. and Yengo, L. (1986). *Cognitive Task Analysis to Enhance Technical Skills Training and Assessment* (Contract No. F418689-83-C-0029). Learning Research and Development Center, University of Pittsburgh.

Goldstein, I. L. (1980). Training in work organizations, *Annual Review of Psychology*, **31**, 229–272.

Goldstein, I. L. (1986). *Training in Organizations: Needs Assessment, Development and Evaluation*. Monterey, CA: Brooks/Cole.

Goldstein, I. L. and Gilliam, P. (1990). Training system issues in the year 200, *American Psychologist*, **45**, 134–143.

Greeno, J. G. (1980). Psychology of learning, 1960–1980, *American Psychologist*, **35**, 713–728.

Hagman, J. D. and Schendel, J. D. (1981). Effects of refresher training on job-task performance, *JSAS Catalog of Selected Documents in Psychology*, **11**, 91. (Ms. No. 2391.)

Hartley, J. and Davies, I. K. (1976). Preinstructional strategies: The role of pretests, behavioral objectives, overviews and advance organizers, *Review of Educational Research*, **46**, 239–265.

Halff, H. M., Hollan, J. D. and Hutchins, E. L. (1986) Cognitive science and military training, *American Psychologist*, **41**, 1131–1139.

Holding, D. H. (1965). *Principles of Training*. London: Pergamon Press.

Hull, C. L. (1943). *Principles of Behavior*. New York: Appleton-Century-Crofts.

Johnson, S. L. (1981). Effect of training device on retention and transfer of a procedural task, *Human Factors*, **23**, 257–272.

Kieras, D. E. and Bovair, S. (1984). The role of a mental model in learning to operate a device, *Cognitive Science*, **8**, 255–273.

Mager, R. F. (1962). *Preparing Instructional Objectives*. Belmont, CA: Fearon Publishers.

Means, B., Mumaw, R., Roth, C., Schlager, M., McWilliams, E., Gagné, E., Rice, V., Rosenthal, D. and Heon, S. (1988). *ATC Training Analysis Study: Design of the Next-Generation ATC Training System* (OPM Work Order 342–036). Alexandria, VA: HumRRO International, Inc.

Mengelkoch, R. F., Adams, J. A. and Gainer, C. A. (1971). The forgetting of instrument flying skills, *Human Factors*, **13**, 397–405.

Morrison, J. E. (1985). *Guidebook for Analysis and Design Phases of Course Revision* (ARI Research Product 85–15). Alexandria, VA: U.S. Army Research Institute for the Behavioral and Social Sciences.

Neisser, U. (1967). *Cognitive Psychology*. New York: Appleton-Century-Crofts.

Pipe, P. (1975). *Objectives—Tool for Change*. Belmont, CA: Fearon Publishers.

Quinkert, K.A. (1987). *Preliminary Training Requirements Analysis for the Commanders Independent Thermal Viewer (CITV)* (ARI Reserarch Product 87–19). Alexandria, VA: US Army Research Institute for the Behavioral and Social Sciences.

Smith, R. G. (1971). *The Engineering of Educational and Training Systems*. Lexington, MA: Heath Lexington Books.

Spence, K. W. (1956). *Behavior Theory and Conditioning*. New Haven, CN: Yale University Press.
Vineberg, R. and Joyner, J. N. (1980). *Instructional system development (ISD) in the armed services: Methodology and application* (HumRRO Technical Report 80–1). Alexandria, VA: Human Resources Research Organization.
Watson, J. B. (1913). Psychology as the behaviorist views it, *Psychological Review*, **20**, 158–177.
Wells, R. and Hagman, J. D. (1989). *Training Procedures for Enhancing Reserve Component Learning, Retention, and Transfer* (ARI Technical Report 860). Alexandria, VA: US Army Research Institute for the Behavioral and Social Sciences.
Wickens, C. D. (1989). Attention and skilled performance. In D. H. Holding (ed.). *Human Skills*, 2nd edn. London: John Wiley and Sons.

# Chapter 2

# Skill acquisition

**John Annett**
*University of Warwick*

The defining characteristics of skill (or a skill) are that it is behaviour which is (a) goal-directed, (b) well organised and economical of effort, and (c) acquired through training and practice rather than being innate or instinctive. While the term skill has traditionally been used to refer to motor rather than verbal or intellectual performance, the use was broadened by Bartlett (1958) to encompass cognitive skills such as thinking and problem solving and by social psychologists (e.g. Argyle, 1969) who refer to social skills, particularly to those of the manipulative sort such as persuasion.

This extended usage, while perhaps illuminating some aspects of cognitive and social psychology, widens the concept of skill to the extent that a single theory of acquisition is unlikely to be able to account for all cases. For example, should a theory of skill acquisition apply equally to the learning of football and a foreign language? Probably not. If truly comprehensive concepts of skill and skill acquisition are required, then they would be that *a skill is a behavioural solution to a particular class of problems,* and *skill acquisition is the process of discovering the solution.*

## ANALYSIS OF PROBLEMS

The idea that a skill is a solution to a problem illuminates some of the most important features of skill acquisition. At first, the novice may have a goal with no appropriate behaviour in the repertoire which leads directly to the goal. This is true of both physical and intellectual skills. Riding a bicycle without falling off is a problem if you have never done it before just as much as is solving a differential equation or selling an icebox to an eskimo. Calling a skill 'a solution to a problem' then directs our attention to the analysis of the problem—that is, how to model successful performance. Instead of simply thinking of learning as a matter of honing existing behaviour to a higher level of efficiency, we ask questions about the nature of the processes underlying

*Training for Performance: Principles of Applied Human Learning.* Edited by J. E. Morrison
© 1991 John Wiley & Sons Ltd

performance and what might happen to them in the course of learning. The following examples illustrate the point.

**Modelling skills**

The first example is a theoretical model of bicycle riding by Doyle (1988) which describes the physical dymanics of the rider–machine–terrain system as shown in Figure 2.1. The model describes the sensory information available to the rider and a description of the outputs necessary to keep the system within certain goal tolerances, for example upright, moving forward, avoiding obstacles, and so on. The control system is represented as three nested feedback loops which control lateral displacement, heading change, and roll rate respectively. The 'problem' for the novice cyclist is that the physical dynamics of the machine lead to instability (a high roll rate) when the handlebars are turned to change direction and this is also strongly affected by the forward velocity. Novices typically travel slowly when instability is higher than at faster speeds, and are anxious about avoiding obstacles. However, applying the wrong correction to the handlebar can introduce instability, especially at low speeds, and so the initial stages of learning can be difficult.

The skilled cyclist has learned just how much pressure to apply and how long to apply it to the handlebar to produce an appropriate turn without falling. This can be best learned by practising in an area free of obstacles and by inducing a sufficiently high forward velocity to increase the natural stability of the machine. When this basic skill of controlling the roll rate has been acquired, the learner can devote more attention to the skills of controlling direction, some of which are probably already in the repertoire having been

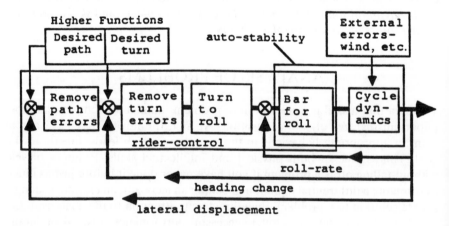

**Figure 2.1.** The essential control functions in bicycle riding. After Doyle, (1988). Reproduced by permission of Elsevier Science Publishers.

learned at least in part through the normal processes of navigating through foot traffic.

A very different kind of skill, typing, has been modelled by Rumelhart and Norman (1982). Learning to copy type means learning to make fast accurate finger movements in response to a series of visual stimuli (i.e. the text). The problem for the learner is that whereas normal visual reaction time is of the order of 190 milliseconds, the average interval between keystrokes of a moderately skilled typist is about 60 milliseconds. The model, which was actualised as a computer simulation, describes how information about the text and about the current positions of the hands in relation to the keyboard might be processed.

As shown in Figure 2.2, text input is first 'read' by a perceptual system which identifies words. The mechanism for instructing individual finger movements comprises two parts, individual 'keypress schemata' and a servo system which relates finger position to locations on the keyboard. The keypress schemata are activated by rules which specify their order, such that in typing 't-h-e' the schema for 'h' is inhibited until 't' has fired. The levels of activation of the schemata are subject to small random variations so that sometimes this sequencing mechanism fails, producing errors such as 'hte' instead of 'the'. The perceptual interpretive mechanism can operate in parallel with a low

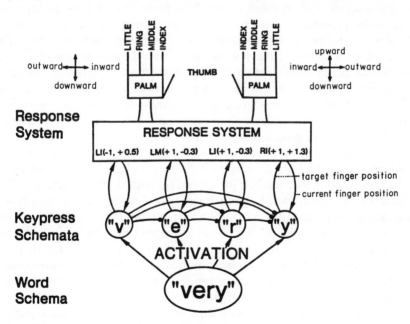

**Figure 2.2.**   Rumelhart and Norman's (1982) schema model of typing. Lines ending in arrows indicate activation while those ending in solid circles indicate inhibition. Reproduced by permission of the authors.

level servo-mechanism which simply indicates the proximity of each finger to its appropriate key and adds its input to the activation of that schema when the finger is sufficiently near. The simulation, although on the author's admission still far from comprehensive, gives a plausible account both of typing speeds and of the kinds of errors made by typists. By indicating how the speed problem might be 'solved', the model also provides an interesting commentary on the role of practice. Just as in the cycling example, a low level semi-autonomous feedback loop is critical to the performance of a skill which also includes other elements (e.g. reading and spelling) that have been acquired independently. Practice with the keyboard is presumably necessary to keep an accurate internal representation of the layout required by the position servo.

**Analysing tasks**

In both of these examples, the theoretical model of the skill is expressed in information-processing terms: that is, the model specifies what sensory or input information is necessary for performance and how it is used or translated into action. This information can be selected (i.e. attended to or ignored), it can be stored in long- or short-term memory, and it can be translated into action by production rules of the form 'if input = x then execute action y'. This is not to say these processes are introspective or that the skilled performer is able to explain which inputs are being attended to or to state the precise rules by which input is turned into action. Nevertheless a psychological theory of the skill in such terms can lead to hypotheses about what sources of information the learner must attend to, what must be retained in memory, and what transformation (or production rules) must be acquired. With a well-articulated model expressed in these terms, it then becomes possible to specify what it is the trainee must learn to do in acquiring a given skill and to set up an appropriate training programme.

The process of modelling a task in this way is known by the generic term *task analysis* and a number of specific techniques have been developed in the past few decades. The method developed by Annett and Duncan (1967), and Annett *et al.* (1971) called Hierarchical Task Analysis (HTA) was based on the work of R.B. Miller (1953) and draws on the structural analysis of behaviour due to Miller, Galanter and Pribram (1960). The central idea is that the performance of a skill can be analysed into a nested hierarchy of operations and sub-operations. An operation is a statement of (a) the conditions under which an action (b) is appropriate and (c) the condition indicating successful completion of the action.

The top level of the hierarchy is represented by a very general statement of goals, for example 'drive a car safely from A to B'. At an intermediate level of description we have subtasks such as steering, gear changing, and procedures such as starting and stopping. Each of these can in turn be analysed into more detailed components. If necessary the analysis can be continued down to the level of describing precisely what cues the operator should use and exactly which actions will be adequate in a specific manoeuvre such as reversing around a corner. John Patrick gives an example of HTA and further discussion of the technique in Chapter 5.

This kind of analysis enables the trainer to specify effectively what aspects of the skill problem the trainee still has to solve and to provide various kinds of assistance. The kinds of problems faced by a learner may be quite varied. In some cases, the learner who is having difficulty in performing a task simply needs information, such as where to find a component, or knowledge of a rule, such as what to do when a particular symptom appears. In other cases it may be helpful to draw attention to particular sensory cues whose significance is not obvious to the novice. In still other cases, when speed or precision is needed, the training solution may be more practice of one particular task component. It is inherent in task analysis that the identification of learning problems is, in practice, the shortest route to identifying the type of training required. HTA is effective because it directly addresses the basic question of what exactly is learned when skill is acquired. We now go on to consider the kinds of experimental evidence of skill learning found in the research literature.

# EVIDENCE OF LEARNING

Early studies of skill acquisition, such as those by Bryan and Harter (1897, 1899) in morse telegraphy, Book (1908) on typewriting, and Swift (1910) on ball tossing, all followed the methods pioneered by Ebbinghaus (1885) for the study of verbal learning and memory in which the number of trials of repetitive practice was the principal independent variable. In motor skills, speed and accuracy of performance were the common dependent variables: just as Ebbinghaus used simplified stimulus materials, so also relatively simple motor responses formed the basis of studies of skill acquisition.

**Quantitative changes**

Changes in individual variables, for example time to complete a task or execute a movement, probability or magnitude of error, the amount of 'work' accomplished per attempt or per unit time, and other numerically specifiable variables, can all be taken as indicators of skill acquisition and plotted on a learning curve. Learning curves are typically negatively accelerated, suggesting a progressive process, such as trial and error, in which each trial provides an opportunity to strengthen some aspect of the response or stimulus–response connection, or to eliminate some less than ideal feature.

These early researchers attached considerable significance to learning curves and relatively flat sections known as *learning plateaux*. Bryan and Harter interpreted plateaux discovered in morse code learning as evidence for the development of a habit hierarchy in which the trainee learns first to deal with single letters and later with letter strings, a process which only yielded practical benefits when mastered to some point signalled by the end of the plateau. In the 1940s and 1950s the widespread interest in the learning theories of Thorndike and Hull focused attention firmly on repetition and practice and the mathematical properties of the learning curve. Actual performance was, according to Hull's (1943) theory, a joint function of *habit strength* and a number of other factors, principally the current level of motivation or *drive*, and the amount of *inhibition* which builds up as a function of the repetition of an action. Habit strength, or pure learning, was thought to be a function of the number and value of *reinforcements* or rewards following a response to a given stimulus. The shape of the observed learning curve was thus determined by schedule of reinforcement, for example reinforcement on every trial or less frequently, and the distribution of practice, since rest between trials theoretically allowed inhibition to dissipate. Practice variables, such as the frequency of reinforcements, distribution of practice trials, practice on part of the whole task, and the regulation of task difficulty, were important features of skill acquisition research until the 1960s when information-processing concepts began to displace those of behaviourist 'learning theory' associated with Thorndike and Hull.

Snoddy (1926) showed in studies of mirror tracing that learning curves for relatively simple tasks which are practised many hundreds or thousands of times produce a linear function when the logarithm of a performance score is plotted against the logarithm of number of practice trials. This finding has been repeated in a number of instances of skills which comprise short routines repeated many times, such as cigar rolling (Crossman, 1959) and a choice of reaction tasks (Seibel, 1963) and many others (Newell and Rosenbloom, 1981). Newell and Rosenbloom have argued that this log–log linear law of learning can be accounted for by a single basic learning process which they refer to as *chunking*. Chunking basically means that initially separate processes are grouped together and dealt with as simple wholes. The grouping of letters into words observed by Bryan and Harter is an example of chunking, but others could include any well-learned routine that can be recalled or produced as a unit, not having to be assembled from separate parts.

It is probably unwise to draw firm conclusions about the nature of basic learning processes from the shape of the learning curve. Such curves are simply plots of actual performance, and as Hull suspected, may derive from a number of different underlying or intervening variables including motivation and fatigue as well as physical features of the task, such as the minimum cycle time of a machine, which may limit performance.

Other researchers (Woodrow, 1939; Adams, 1957; Fleishman, 1960; Jones, 1970) have used the methodology of individual differences to seek evidence of underlying processes in the interrelationships between many different variables and how they change as a function of practice. Fleishman and Hempel (1954) related performance on a Discrimination Reaction Time Task to performance on other psychomotor and intellectual tests and found that the proportion of variance accounted for by a factor specific to the task and to some other 'motor' factors tended to increase as a function of practice while 'intellectual' factors measured by verbal and spatial tests tended to account for progressively less of the total variance as a function of practice. The conclusion, attractive to some theorists but heavily criticised by others (e.g. Adams, 1987), was that cognitive processes become less important and motor processes specific to the task become more important as learning progresses.

## Qualitative changes

Evidence of skill acquisition can also be derived from qualitative changes in performance, including changes in technique, the adoption of less effortful and more effective working methods, simplification of movement patterns and the grouping together of actions and stimulus inputs, changes in error patterns, changes in attention, and the ability to cope with additional simultaneous tasks and to resist the deleterious effects of fatigue and stress. Some of these changes may occur slowly but some, for example a change of method, can be abrupt. Touch typing provides an example of a qualitative change in technique, which incidentally leads to quantitative improvements. Touch typists can achieve fast speeds because they do not have to look at the keyboard between keystrokes. According to Long (1975, 1976) they carry out a visual check on the keyboard only about three times per 1000 keystrokes, although the number goes up with difficult text material. Resistance to the detrimental effects of environmental stressors such as heat or noise was shown by Mackworth (1950) to be related to level of skill already achieved by practice. Errors tend to occur in a variety of tasks, including morse telegraphy and vigilance (monitoring) tasks, which are carried out under adverse conditions such as high temperature or being a long time on watch. Mackworth found 'the better the operator the smaller the decrement in his accuracy of work. . .'. However, we cannot be sure whether these effects are due to greater skill *per se* or to becoming adapted to the stress itself since Mackworth's high ability subjects were experienced in both respects. Nevertheless, changes in skill due to practice remains an attractive hypothesis in view of other evidence such as the effects of extended practice on increasing the ability to do two things at the same time (cf. McLeod, 1977; Spelke, Hirst and Neisser, 1976).

# THEORIES OF SKILL ACQUISITION

Research into the processes of skill acquisition recognises two fundamental paradigms, *practice* and *instruction*. In practice experiments the learner is active and makes repeated attempts to perform the task. Under instruction, by contrast, the experimenter (or trainer) provides verbal instruction, text illustrations, models and simulations, advice and correction, while the learner remains essentially passive, at least during instruction. Practice is readily quantified in terms of number of discrete trials or amount of time spent, at least if the central features of the task remain constant. Tracking tasks (in which the learner attempts to align a cursor with a moving target or keep a moving indicator at a constant reading) and linear positioning tasks (in which the subject learns to make a discrete movement of a specific extent) have been the most popular experimental situations for studying the effects of practice. However, almost any task in which uniform responses are required can serve to show how a single feature of performance, such as speed or accuracy, changes as a function of number of trials. Instruction, on the other hand, does not provide such a simple experimental paradigm. Information presented in text material, verbal instruction, or a demonstration is not easily quantified and is at best treated as a binary (all-or-none) variable. For example, in an early experiment, Judd (1908) investigated the effect of instruction in the principles of refraction on the transfer of a dart-throwing task between targets seen through different depths of water. One group of subjects receiving instruction did not learn the initial adjustment any faster than those who received no instruction; however, these subjects were better able subsequently to learn to hit a target at a different depth. The problem with this sort of experiment is that we do not have any independent measure of the quality of the instruction and hence it is not easy to generalise from a single set of results. Maybe some other instructor could explain the principles of refraction more simply or perhaps another might not do it so well. Thus we clearly cannot conclude simply from Judd's experiment that instruction will always improve transfer but not acquisition.

The distinction between practice and instruction also reflects the assumption that quite different processes may be responsible for learning. Practice provides the opportunity for a uniform, slow, incremental, and essentially automatic learning process, while instruction achieves its effects through cognitive processes which may include rapid changes in knowledge of relevant information, in perceptual organisation, or in response strategy. One of the fundamental research issues is whether separate theories of acquisition are needed to account for the culturally transmitted, vicariously acquired aspects of skill on the one hand and the personal effects of individual practice on the other. Fitts (1964) characterised skill acquisition as a progressive shift of the control of performance from cognitive to non-cognitive processes. In his three-phase theory of skill acquisition the initial cognitive phase is dominated by learning rules and procedures and other items of factual knowledge by means of instruction or trial and error. The second and third stages are dominated by practice during which stimuli become connected with responses (the associative phase) and performance becomes increasingly independent of cognitive control (the autonomous phase). The Fitts sequence, which has been echoed by many writers (Rumelhart and Norman, 1978; Annett, 1986; Anderson, 1982, 1987), implies that not only are different training techniques appropriate at different stages in learning but also different processes underlie the learning that does occur. Fitts did not claim that sharp distinctions could always be made between these three phases, but for the purpose of this review, the main topics will be discussed in the order suggested by the Fitts sequence.

**Cognitive processes**

The first or 'cognitive' phase which is dominated by verbal instruction and demonstration is seen 'as a first step in the development of an executive program' (Fitts and Posner, 1967, p. 12). Behavioural elements which are already in the learner's repertoire are selected and rearranged, and other changes may occur, for example changes in attention, particularly focusing on relevant cues. Items of factual information relevant to the task may also be learned. The two principal classes of cognitive methods are *verbal instruction* and *demonstration*. The central theoretical problem is how information received 'passively' by these two methods gets translated into the capability for action. It is primarily this issue which divides 'cognitive' from 'behaviourist' theories of learning: however, as Adams (1987) pointed out, theory in this aspect of motor learning is somewhat underdeveloped. Figure 2.3 represents my own attempt to formulate the problem of the relationships between cognitive and non-cognitive processes in a way that suggests lines of empirical research. The top of the diagram represents two classes of inputs—words and actions. (Other classes of input such as stimuli arising from non-human sources are not shown.) The central part of the diagram represents internal processes and the bottom represents the output, either words or actions. The left-hand side of the diagram represents the non-verbal domain of actions while the right-hand side represents words, or the verbal domain.

The central part of Figure 2.3 is divided into four areas, the top pair representing receptive and interpretive processes and the bottom pair representing productive processes. They are represented separately in recognition of the fact that production can be inhibited; however, as we shall see, a fairly intimate relationship between receptive and productive processes can be assumed.

A number of different experimental paradigms, represented as routes

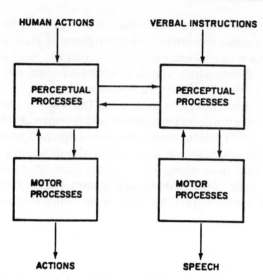

**Figure 2.3.** The 'action-language bridge'. Hypothetical relationships between verbal and non-verbal systems involved in imitating and describing actions and in following verbal instructions.

through the system, are indicated by arrows. Most, but not all of these, are from the top down, in the conventional direction of perception → action. Some routes proceed from the top straight down, with the output mode matching the input mode (i.e. actions are imitated and words are repeated), while some cross over between the action and verbal systems. In particular, verbal instructions can be translated into actions, a familiar instructional paradigm; but perceived actions can also be translated into words. The latter route corresponds to the less familiar task (at least as far as experimental research is concerned) of giving a verbal account of actions. The most obvious case is the radio sports commentator, but generally we are talking of the production of eyewitness accounts.

*Verbal instruction*

Before going on to discuss what can be gained from the model, I must defend the two important assumptions: (a) that action and language systems can be regarded as separate; and (b) that representational and productive systems are separable. The first assumption is justified in terms of neurological evidence that the ability to learn and perform skilled actions is to a large extent independent of verbal learning and memory. I have reviewed the evidence in detail elsewhere (Annett, 1982, 1985, 1990), but the most striking examples are found in cases of ideo-motor apraxia such as the patient described by Geschwind and Kaplan (1962). This patient was able to follow verbal instructions, such as 'show me how you use a hammer', with the right hand but not with the left, although the latter was not paralysed. Furthermore, when a hammer was placed in his left hand the subject was able to demonstrate its use. This patient was found on post-mortem examination to have extensive damage to the corpus collosum such that verbal instructions, which are processed in the left hemisphere, could not be passed to the right hemisphere, which controls the left hand. Translation between verbal and non-verbal codes is undoubtedly more complex than making a simple anatomical connection; but as this example shows, traffic between the two systems across what I have called the *action–language bridge* deserves more attention than it has received. A number of studies (Annett, 1985, 1986, 1990; Bainbridge, 1979; Berry and Broadbent, 1984, 1987, 1988) have confirmed that it is often difficult to explain in words how a skilled action is performed. In the case of a familiar skill, such as tying a bow, it is clear that the translation from actions to words is normally mediated by a process of self-observation. Subjects typically rely on 'going through the motions' either overtly by making gestures or by generating images which they are then able to describe. There are also clear limitations on what the subjects are able to describe. Bow tying, for example, is typically described in terms of actions or outcomes, such as making a loop, rather than as the pattern of finger and hand movements which are actually employed. In other words, the representations stored in memory generally do not provide kinematic detail but are expressed in terms of objectives to be achieved, for instance the knot is pulled tight. Looking at the action–language bridge from the opposite view, namely that of turning verbal instructions into actions, it appears that again kinematic detail is not the most successful form of communication about actions. Coaches typically use metaphor and imagery to convey complex movement information. For example a squash coach of my acquaintance describes the stance to be adopted to receive service as 'like a Red Indian on the warpath'. This produces a comprehensive image of an alert stance with feet apart and knees bent, and the right hand raised holding the racket at about shoulder height.

In learning a complex skill, such as flying, a great deal of factual information is also acquired. Sometimes factual information may have direct relevance to actual performance. For example, skill in detecting and correcting infrequently occurring errors in process control tasks typically requires an extensive store of factual information as well as the use of efficient search strategies (Bainbridge 1979, 1988). Even sport skills require knowledge of the rules. Skilled games players typically exhibit a rich factual database of 'declarative' information (Starkes, 1987), also French and Thomas (1987) have demonstrated that as children gain proficiency in a sport skill so their factual knowledge of the game increases. Of course it does not necessarily follow that simply because theoretical instruction often precedes practice that learning *is* the conversion of declarative knowledge into procedural knowledge (as proposed by Anderson, 1987). The ability to perform a skill and the verbal knowledge relating to it may develop in parallel. It may even be the case that some kinds of verbally accessible knowledge only emerge after the skilled performer has the leisure to reflect on his own or other people's performance. As noted earlier, some aspects of motor skill may never have been, and may never be, translated into declarative knowledge.

The model in Figure 2.3 also distinguishes between not only verbal and non-verbal processes but also representational and production processes in both modalities. The representational processes are involved in perceiving and imagining; in other words, what is proposed is a pair of mechanisms (one verbal and one non-verbal) that are involved in the interpretation of incoming data, speech and actions, respectively. The production processes are involved in the execution of speech and motor acts, but they can be inhibited when engaged in inner speech or imaginary action. This close association between representation and production is a feature of some recent theories of speech perception and production (e.g. MacKay, 1982) but has not previously been suggested in relation to action perception and production. The unique aspect of my proposal (Annett, 1982) is that there is a specialised action perception system which serves the purpose of interpreting the actions of others and also of organising our own. The work of Johansson (1973) and others such as Cutting (1978) illustrates the way in which movement and intention can be efficiently extracted from minimal visual data. A few point light sources attached to various parts of the body are sufficient to allow an observer with no other cues to identify human movement and even to deduce unseen features, such as the nature of the load carried and the sex of the actor. These findings are consistent with the existence of a finely tuned system such as one might expect of a social species where the behaviour of others is one of the crucial sets of environmental information needed for survival. This is precisely the kind of mechanism which is needed as a basis for understanding imitation and observational learning.

*Demonstration and observational learning*

The dominance of behaviourists theories of learning has inhibited the development of theories of the cognitive processes underlying imitation. Bandura's theory (Bandura, 1977, 1986) covers the broad span of observational learning, including circumstances in which the learner will adopt another individual as a model. (Social learning theory is discussed in detail by Latham and Crandall in Chapter 9 of this volume.) A complete theory of observational learning must, however, account for the mechanism by which perceived action is coded in such a way as to be capable of generating action. The model outlined in the previous section suggests that encoding of action information is a specialised process closely linked to action production. An action is 'perceived' when a 'description' has been achieved. A 'description' not only identifies an action but also at the same time is a recipe for producing that action. Since the work of Bernstein (1967) has become more widely known through 'ecological' writers such as Turvey (1977) and Turvey and Kugler (1984), it has become increasingly apparent that the central representation of actions rarely if ever involves detailed patterns of instruction to individual muscles. The 'description' of an action is more like a programme which, when given appropriate data concerning current conditions, can produce a particular result, such as moving an object from one place to another.

If successful imitation of an action requires the learner to acquire a description of the action, then it is worth looking at factors which might prevent or distort this process. Conjurers who practise sleight of hand operate largely by misleading the audience into misinterpreting what they see. Even without the intention to deceive, however, the demonstration of a skill may fail to provide the observer with an adequate description. Sheffield (1961), in a systematic review of teaching by demonstration, drew attention to the importance of breaking down the demonstration of complex skills into 'natural' units. Most individuals seem to be able to do this intuitively. For example, video recordings of subjects first tying a bow and later *demonstrating* how to tie a bow actually make characteristically different kinds of movement (Annett, 1990). In demonstrating the task, the 'natural units' (picking up the loose ends, twisting them together, etc.) tend to be separated out into discrete sections with pauses between them, and the movements are not simply slowed but are often amplified in scale. For instance, in demonstrating the final step in which the knot is pulled tight, the pulling action is made in an exaggerated form which can be two or three times the amplitude of the normal action.

There is a growing body of evidence that action perception typically involves identifying and encoding specific features. Newtson (1980) suggested that skilled observers monitor movement features, particularly encoding 'break points' where a particular feature undergoes a significant transformation. In these experiments, subjects were shown filmed movement sequences and were required to detect whether or not short sections of the record lasting up to 0.5 seconds had been deleted. Over half the deletions that occurred at break points were detected as against less than one-third of those occurring between break points. Whiting, Bijlard and den Brinker (1987) studied the use made by subjects of a model in the acquisition of a complex dynamic skill resembling slalom skiing. The subjects stood on a 'ski simulator', consisting of a platform mounted on a pair of bowed rails. The platform was attached to springs which tended to hold it in a central position and the subjects' task was to move the platform rhythmically to the left and right against the springs using the legs and trunk with an action pattern similar to skiing. Two groups of subjects practised over five daily sessions: while one group was allowed to discover an efficient technique for performing the task, an experimental group was shown a 1.5 minute video recording of an expert working on the apparatus during training. The opportunity to observe the skilled model enabled subjects in the experimental group to achieve a more fluent performance than control subjects, although they did not differ in either the amplitude or frequency of movement. Whiting *et al.* argued that fluency is the best measure of skill since it represents efficient use of effort. They also pointed out that this result was obtained without subjects necessarily imitating all aspects of the model's performance. It appears they had been able to extract some higher order feature of the movement pattern and apply it to their own productions.

Many skills, for instance sport skills, are not easily broken down into distinct elements or performed at significantly slower speed, so it is difficult for the unskilled observer to produce an adequate description. It is here that video recordings or even diagrams accompanied by verbal explanation may enable the observer to 'see' how the skill works and to form an adequate description. There is some evidence that skilled performers do have more detailed perceptions of actions. Imwold and Hoffman (1983) found that experienced instructors recognised more components in recordings of handsprings than novices. Vickers (1988) showed that when visual fixations were recorded, expert gymnasts were more likely to attend to the relevant body parts as well as being able to make more accurate judgements about filmed performances. These findings in motor learning compare with those of de Groot (1965) and Chase and Simon (1973) in relation to chess indicating that skilled players perceive and retain more information about the distribution of pieces on a chessboard than do novices and non-players.

Detailed differences between the performances of the model and the imitator can also show how the action has been 'described'. A demonstration which contains enough elementary descriptions to exceed short-term memory will result in an unsuccessful attempt, typically because one or more units are omitted. Depending on the nature of the task this may well result in overall failure. Smyth and Pendelton (1989) have recently shown that short-term memory for discrete meaningless movements is only about four items. A typical error made by young children is to produce a mirror reversal of the demonstrated movement and this too may be interpreted as a failure in producing the appropriate description. Imitation of tongue protrusion and hand gestures has been recorded in neonates (Meltzoff and Moore, 1977) and imitation is well documented in other species (van Lawick-Goodall, 1971, in chimpanzees and Kawai, 1965, in Japanese macaques). Despite this early onset of ability to imitate, children do improve in their ability to perceive and reproduce action patterns. Thomas, French and Humphries (1977) testing girls aged 7 and 9 on a stabilometer skill found that the younger children gained less benefit from seeing a model than older children, who also were better able than the younger ones to use the model as a source for correcting the partially established skill.

Video recordings have been used both to provide demonstrations by skilled models and also to provide feedback to learners from their own performances. Burwitz (1981), reviewing the use of demonstrations and video tape recordings in teaching gymnastic skills, found the results were sometimes disappointing and offered a number of possible reasons. Sometimes the time delay between performance and viewing the recording may be too long and critical features of the model's performance may not be easy to see. Scully and Newell (1985) confirmed that video demonstration was more effective with the Bachman ladder task in which the successful technique was clearly discernible than with a ball rolling task in which the difference between successful and unsuccessful trials was not apparent from the gross kinematic pattern visible in the recording.

To summarise, observational learning of skills has been a somewhat neglected research field, no doubt because it did not fit any of the popular models of skill acquisition. However, a theoretical framework is beginning to emerge to which the encoding of motor information is the key. The perception of action appears to be selective in a way which makes sense. As social organisms, we are naturally interested in interpreting the actions of others and so have developed a sensitivity to a variety of features of body movement. The attractive hypothesis is that the ability to perceive an action pattern is closely coupled with the ability to reproduce it, but before this hypothesis can be adequately tested we need to learn more about the perception and encoding of movement information and how it varies with age and experience.

**Practice**

Practice is the *sine qua non* of skill acquisition, but the mechanism by which repetition is effective is still a matter of speculation. The negatively accelerated learning curves noted by the earliest workers or the log–log linear function relating performance to the amount of practice identified by later workers (Crossman, 1959; Seibel, 1963; Newell and Rosenbloom, 1981; Welford, 1987) suggest an underlying process which is both homogeneous and slow, such as laying down a memory trace or engram. Theories are traditionally divided into two camps, namely those that suggest that exercise or repetition *per se* is effective and those that emphasise the selective possibilities offered by repeated trials. Exercise theorists propose that each learning trail offers an opportunity to acquire some new information or to strengthen associations between stimuli or between stimuli and responses, while selection theorists propose that trials offer the opportunity to strengthen some aspect of behaviour and/or weaken others. It is of course possible to propose both kinds of process. For instance, Rumelhart and Norman (1978) suggested that new knowledge could be accumulated ('accreted' was their term), and that processes dealing with new information might also be 'tuned', that is selectively adjusted to take account of new information, or even 're-structured' (see also Cheng, 1985), which is a more drastic kind of reorganisation than tuning.

One of the early attempts at an information-processing account of skill acquisition by Annett and Kay (1956, 1957) began with the proposition that there is a fixed capacity to process stimulus information. Since information is proportional to stimulus uncertainty, the apparent improvement in the rate of processing information, which comes with increasing skill, might be accounted for by a progressive reduction in stimulus uncertainty. This comes about as the learner builds up an internal model of the environment and particularly of the non-random relationships between events. These also include events brought about as a consequence of previous actions. For example, after practice the flight of a dart becomes progressively more predictable from feedback received during the course of preparing for and executing a throw. Two specific predictions follow from the theory, one concerning part-task training and one concerning the withdrawal of knowledge of results. The first prediction is paradoxical in that it suggests that tasks which have high sequential interdependency are best learned initially in parts. The reason for this is simply that when a novice practises such a task, his own error will feed forward to generate a more unpredictable environment than would otherwise be the case. The second prediction is that knowledge of results can only be safely withdrawn without performance loss when it has become effectively redundant. When performing a task the operator receives a stream of feedback signals and, as a result of repeated trials, will build up a probabalistic model of sequential dependencies between them. On the basis of the model, events relating to the final outcome are predictable from events occurring earlier in the sequence. Hence, an experienced golfer knows before the swing is complete if the shot it likely to be good.

Among other 'elementary' learning principles which have been proposed to account for the log–log linear relationship are 'chunking' (Newell and Rosenbloom, 1981) and discrimination (Welford, 1987). The idea of grouping emerged from Bryan and Harter's studies of morse telegraphy in which trainees progressed from transcribing each letter as a separate item to identifying whole words as units. The modern term 'chunking', originating from Miller's (1956) notion of chunks of information, suggests that processing resources, such as memory, are limited in the number of separate chunks which can be held in store or actively processed at any one time. A chunk is any set of mental entities (or 'expressions'), perceptual or motor, which can be dealt with (e.g. stored in memory) as a single unit. Chunking is an automatic process, and learning progresses as elementary chunks become grouped together as larger chunks. Newell and Rosenbloom (1981) argue that such a process offers a good fit to the empirical power law of learning in a variety of perceptual–motor and cognitive tasks.

Starting with data from reaction time studies, Welford (1987) has challenged the goodness of fit to a log–log linear plot and proposed an alternative mechanism based on signal detection theory. He suggests that in choice reaction time tasks, which in the Cambridge tradition of Craik and Hick have been taken as a paradigm of skill, practice has the effect of making the connections between stimuli and responses more distinctive. The parameter $d'$ (*dee prime*), which is taken as a measure of perceptual discrimination independent of *beta* (the subject's response criterion), increases linearly with the square root of the number of times the stimulus has been presented. Practice, therefore, increases the signal-to-noise ratio of stimuli. Since making one response rather than another is seen as depending on stimulus discriminability, reaction time is progressively reduced by repeated practice.

Theoretical claims for particular fundamental processes made on the basis of goodness of fit should be treated with caution, particularly when, as in this case, it is quite hard to find data which do not, at least approximately, fit a log plot. As I have previously pointed out (Annett, 1985), however attractive a quantitative model at first appears, the experimental data themselves often present problems by the absence of good estimates of origin and asymptote. A truly satisfactory theory would have to account for not only the fit of the learning curve but also changes in response time distributions (Long, Nimmo-Smith and Whitfield, 1983). Welford (1987) in fact claimed a better fit of choice reaction time data to a linear/square root plot provided that a discontinuity is recognised between the first eight or nine trials and later trials. He explained that there may be an initial 'restructuring' cognitive process followed by a slower motor learning process based on improved discrimination resulting from repeated experience.

A different kind of theory based on the effects of pure 'exercise' was proposed by MacKay (1982). His theory is particularly relevant to serial skills of which speech production is an example. The production of a coherent speech string is seen as being controlled in a hierarchical fashion. At the top of the hierarchy, a sequence of ideas is generated taking account of both semantic and syntactic rules. This feeds down into a phonological system that organises the ideas into sound patterns. Finally, activation feeds down into a muscle movement system which directly controls the vocal apparatus. This hierarchy is activated from the top down through a network of connections that determine which items are activated and in what order. The learning principle is that when a node is activated by receiving stimulation from other nodes it is 'primed', that is to say, its potential for firing is raised. A particular node will fire when its priming exceeds that of all the other nodes in its domain. The theory predicts a number of phenomena found in serial production skills. For instance, sequence errors are seldom random but, like Spoonerisms, appear to result from failures in the sequencing mechanism. Most substitution errors occur within the same category, that is noun for noun, verb for verb, and so on. The model also makes some interesting predictions relating to improvements in performance resulting from rehearsing a skill in imagination rather than overtly.

*Mental practice*

Mental practice deserves a brief digression since learning effects cannot be attributed to any external consequences, such as rewards and punishments, nor can they be attributed to the effects of repeated external stimulation. Change can only take place through the medium of some internal trace or representation of the skill. Mental practice has a long history, William James (1890) having observed that we learn to skate in the summer and swim in the winter. A substantial number of studies (see reviews by Corbin, 1972; and Richardson, 1967) have shown that rehearsing a skill in imagination can result in improvements in performance which, although usually less marked than those achieved by physical practice, are nonetheless greater than those found after no practice or rest.

A number of theories advanced to account for mental practice effects were compared by means of a meta-analysis by Feltz and Landers (1983). A classic theory, illustrated by the electromyogram (EMG) studies of Jacobson (1932), is that mental practice evokes activity in the motor output system and, although this is largely suppressed, it is detectable in EMG records. According to the theory, this activity is enough to generate minimal kinaesthetic feedback through which some learning is mediated. While EMG activity has been reported in mental practice, for example Suinn (1972) with the mental rehearsal of skiing, there is no firm evidence that this activity is related to the specific response pattern being learned as opposed to generalised activation. A more plausible theory, supported by Feltz and Landers's (1983) meta-analysis, is that mental practice permits the rehearsal of cognitive processes associated with task performance. Tasks which involved learning mazes and other sequential skills were found to be much more likely to produce significant improvements with mental practice than others, such as balancing tasks, which were more purely motoric in character. However, a revised analysis (Feltz, Landers and Becker, 1988) failed to confirm this conclusion.

Some results by Johnson (1982) (see also Annett, 1985) illustrate the specifically cognitive nature of mental rehearsal in one kind of motor task. Johnson used a linear positioning task to demonstrate the well-established phenomenon of interference in short-term motor memory. If, between learning to make a linear movement of a particular extent and having to recall it, the subject is required to make a movement of a very different extent (say twice as long), then the recalled movement is overestimated. Johnson first showed that instructions to imagine making a movement twice as long produced the same bias in recall as an interpolated overt movement. Then, by adding a

variety of secondary tasks to the instruction to imagine making the movement, he showed that only tasks which involved spatial imagery disrupted the
effect. Most interestingly, subjects required to tap on the table with the hand
they were simultaneously imagining moving laterally retained the imagery-
induced bias. Thus the effect of imaginary movement was shown to be completely isolated from any muscular activity.

MacKay's theory, as well as accounting for features of skill acquisition
referred to above, also offers an account of mental practice. MacKay (1981)
showed that the sub-vocal repetition of novel sentences gave practice effects
which were, if anything, larger than those obtained by overt practice. The
argument is that uttering a novel sentence will involve the activation of an
unfamiliar pattern of nodes representing the semantic and syntactic structure
of the sentence. Since activation leads to priming, these nodes will be rendered more likely to fire in this new pattern and even relatively few trials will
have an effect on the speed with which the whole sequence is run off. The
lower level nodes controlling the muscles to produce familiar morphemes are
not much affected even by overt practice since they are already well rehearsed
and hence optimally primed. MacKay's results certainly fit the predictions and
may be taken as supporting the 'cognitive' explanation of mental practice, but
attempts by Beladaci (see Annett, 1988) to extend these predictions to typing
have met with less success. According to the theory, skilled typists who, by
definition, have had a great deal of practice at the perceptual–motor level
should show relatively greater benefit from mentally practising unfamiliar
sequences of words. This prediction was not confirmed nor was the prediction
that mental practice would bring about more improvement with nonsense
material that meaningful sentences, and so this ingenious theory must be
considered as still 'not proven'.

*Feedback and knowledge of results*

The paradigms of instruction and practice come together in one of the central
research issues in skill acquisition. Practising with knowledge of results (KR)
provided by an instructor, either directly or through some automatic scoring
device, is one of the most effective ways of acquiring a skill (see reviews by
Bilodeau, 1969; Annett, 1969; Salmoni, Schmidt and Walter, 1984). The central theoretical question about KR is what is the nature of the underlying
learning process? Is it, as Thorndike (1933) and other behaviourists such as
Skinner (1953) would claim, an automatic process (reinforcement) by which
stimuli are linked to responses; or is it, as most later theorists (Annett, 1969;
Adams, 1971; and Schmidt, 1975) maintain, a cognitive process in which feedback information is used to modify responses or to store up useful
information?

Before attempting to answer this question let us briefly review the basic experimental paradigm and typical results. Thorndike (1932) developed the most widely used experimental technique. The subject is required to attempt to draw a line, or make a simple linear movement of some specified extent, usually without the aid of vision or other intrinsic cue. After each attempt, the subject is given KR, which may simply be 'right' or 'wrong' or may be more detailed such as '$N$ units of distance too long—or too short'. Sometimes more complex tasks, such as tracking, are used. KR may be in the form of some continuous signal, such as a light or sound indicating 'on target', or in the form of a time-on-target or an error score provided at intervals between trials. In even more complex tasks, KR might come in the form of scores relating to more than one aspect of performance such as the kinematic pattern of the response.

Thorndike's theory specified that the reinforcing effects of KR in strengthening the stimulus–response bond were best served when KR was provided immediately after the relevant response and on as many occasions as possible. While results generally fit this pattern, there are complications. Strict temporal contiguity can be violated without detrimental effects on learning provided the interval between response and feedback is not filled with other activities (Lorge and Thorndike, 1935). Some experiments have confounded delay of KR with intertrial interval but Bilodeau and Bilodeau (1958a), in a comprehensive study independently varying the interval between response and KR and post-KR delay, demonstrated decisively that delay of KR as such was of no consequence.

According to reinforcement theory the strength of an S–R bond is directly proportional to the number of reinforcements but in animal studies (e.g. Ferster and Skinner, 1957) partial reinforcement schedules (i.e. giving a reward on some trials but not on others) make for slower acquisition but also promote greater resistance to extinction. The principle was applied by analogy to tracking training by Houston (1947) and by Morin and Gagné (1951). These experimenters used a gunnery simulator in which the trainee tracks a target projected on to a screen and receives artificial feedback in the form of a filter that makes the target change to red whenever a hit is scored. The results confirmed the prediction that on removal of KR, by analogy with experimental extinction, the hit score declined less rapidly for those subjects on a 50% schedule as compared with those receiving the red filter with every hit. However, the filter treatment seems to have acted as a 'crutch' to performance rather than as an aid to learning since performance tended to decline rapidly once it was remmoved. Hence, its value as a training aid was seriously in question. Again Bilodeau and Bilodeau (1958b) carried out the definitive study using a version of the line drawing or linear positioning task with KR given after every trial or every 2, 3, 4, 5, or 10 trials. They found that the rate of learning was directly proportional to the absolute number of trials on which KR was provided but unfortunately did not report on performance after withdrawal of KR. Annett (1959) in a similar task found that error on with-drawal of KR was less, but not significantly so, if subjects had received KR on alternate trials only.

Salmoni *et al.* (1984) rightly complained that many investigators have paid more attention to acquisition than retention following the withdrawal of KR or transfer to the non-KR condition. Annett and Kay (1957) pointed out that what really counts is what happens when the learner transfers from practising on the training device, or from under the watchful eye of an instructor, to the actual task. The provision of temporary KR is only of value if the trainee can subsequently get all the information needed from cues which are intrinsic to the task. Figure 2.4 shows some of the principal feedback loops involved in performing a task such as tracking or discrete linear positioning. The upper level represents the human operator, in this context the learner, and the second level down represents the machine or experimental apparatus. The arrows represent feedback loops which are active during or following a response. At the top level, numbers 1, 2 and 3 are internal feedback loops concerned with the central control of attention (1), proprioceptive control (3) and exteroceptive control (2). In a positioning task, for example, loop 2 would represent the situation in which the learner can see whether his response is correct as he makes it. All these feedback loops are *intrinsic* to the task, hence the term *intrinsic feedback.*

If the learner is operating a machine then feedback typically comes via loop 4, that is through a display such as a moving pointer or some other artificial indicator. Loop 2 may not be available. For example, in driving a car there are two sources of feedback concerning speed: the changing visual field through the windscreen (loop 2) and the speedometer (loop 4). Both normally provide intrinsic feedback but we tend to rely on the speedometer when precise control of speed is important; it is not required that we learn to judge speed

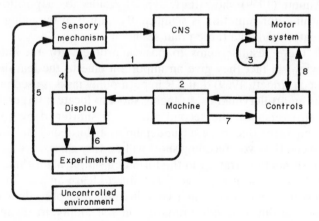

**Figure 2.4.**   The principal feedback loops involved in the control of a machine.

without the help of the instrument. At the bottom of the diagram, the experimenter (or instructor) can form an additional feedback loop, either substituting for the display by giving verbal feedback or embellishing it with additional comments on standards, hints on corrective strategies, and so on. This feedback loop (5) is *extrinsic* if it is only used as a temporary measure during training, and so it is important that the trainee not only learns *from* it but also learns *to do without* it. Dependence on extrinsic feedback may be reduced by having to do without it on some trials, by being 'weaned' from it, or by the instructor drawing attention to feedback which is intrinsic to the task—whether it be proprioceptive or some exteroceptive source of feedback. Further experimental confirmation that these techniques give better retention than providing extrinsic feedback on every trial comes from studies by Ho and Shea (1978) and by Schmidt *et al.* (1989).

The rejection of the reinforcement interpretation of KR depends not just on the failure of a number of predictions to do with the frequency and timing of KR (see Annett, 1969, for a detailed review), but on how well an information-processing account fits the data. The main evidence comes from findings that acquisition is enhanced by the information content of KR where the amount of information is a function of the precision or amount of detail in KR. Trowbridge and Cason (1932) showed that telling subjects not only if their responses were right or wrong but also the direction and extent of error enhanced both acquisition and retention of a discrete line-drawing task. Although this result supports the information-processing viewpoint, a number of subsequent studies (Annett, 1959; Bilodeau, 1953; Bilodeau and Rosenbach, 1953; Green, Zimilies and Spragg, 1955) failed to confirm that learning and retention bore any simple relationship to the degree of precision in KR. In linear positioning tasks, giving directional KR is beneficial to a point but further increases in precision typically fail to yield benefits. The data in Figure 2.5 from Annett (1959) show fairly typical results for a positioning task. Neither learning nor retention is significantly improved by giving KR to an accuracy greater than on a three-point scale.

Although these results seems to pose a problem for the information-processing view, in fact they give an important clue to the learning mechanism. I argued (Annett, 1969) that KR in positioning tasks is used in much the same way as an artilleryman uses ranging shots to locate a target. If the first attempt is an overshoot, the second attempt is shortened by an arbitrary amount; if this turns out to be an undershoot, a third shot halving the difference between the two preceding shots will be very close.

Figure 2.6 shows this strategy in the form of a simple algorithm. The interesting point here is that it is perfectly possible to learn an accurate response using a short-term memory which contains only the preceding item. The efficiency of learning depends primarily on the ability to distinguish differences in intrinsic feedback between the current response and the

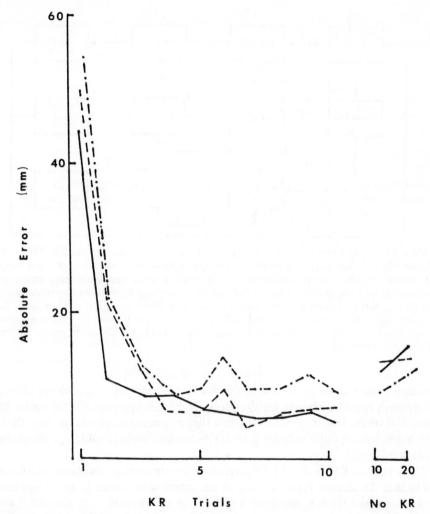

**Figure 2.5.** Acquiring a positioning skill under three levels of precision of KR: (—) accuracy to the nearest 2 millimetres; (---) accuracy to the nearest 17 millimetres; (-·-·) accuracy to the nearest 40 millimetres. The three groups do not differ significantly over the 10 learning trials, but during 20 retention trials with no KR the least accurate KR gives slightly better retention.

immediately preceding response. In tasks of this kind three or four trials provide enough feedback information to enable the subject to produce responses which are as accurate as this discrimination permits. The data from Annett (1959) in Figure 2.5 suggest there is no further improvement in accuracy after four trials. Although subjects given the least accurate results (to the nearest 40 mm for a target of 60 mm) managed to achieve an accuracy of

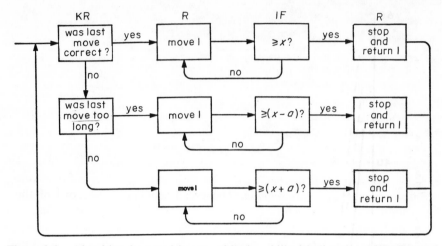

**Figure 2.6.** Algorithm for acquiring a positioning skill with directional KR. Depending on whether KR for the immediately preceding movement was 'correct', 'too long' or 'too short', the learner attempts to match the internal feedback from the next movement with the memory trace of the preceding movement, or to a value discernibly smaller (if KR was 'too long') or greater (if KR was 'too short'). KR = Knowledge of results; R = response; IF = internal feedback; x = memory trace of feedback from preceding movement; a = an arbitrary value of feedback stimulation in excess of the difference threshold.

around 10 mm, those given KR to the nearest 17 mm and 2 mm did not differ. Retention is slightly better for the group given least precise KR for up to 70 post-KR trials. This may reflect the fact that providing more information than the learner can handle induces 'hunting' behaviour which could itself interfere with long-term storage.

This view of KR as providing corrective information, or guidance, requires only that the learner retain a trace of the intrinsic feedback from a response for as long as it takes to compare it with feedback from the next attempt. Two later, and better known, theories give KR a role in establishing long-term memories.

Adams's *closed loop* theory (Adams, 1971) proposed two long-term 'traces', one a *perceptual trace* which is a store of response-produced intrinsic feedback which is laid down and added to on every trial, and a second called (rather confusingly) the *memory trace* which is a brief motor programme required to initiate a response. Responses later come under the control of the perceptual trace as concurrent feedback is compared with the stored information from previous responses. In a pair of studies, Adams and his colleagues demonstrated that: (a) learning was primarily due to the strengthening of the perceptual trace since providing enhanced feedback cues leads to better learning (Adams, Goetz and Marshall, 1972); and (b) the greater the number of practice trials, the better subjects were able to estimate the correctness of their responses (Adams, Gopher and Lintern, 1977).

Schmidt (1975) produced a variant of the information-processing account of KR as *schema theory*. A schema, as understood by Schmidt, is a kind of generalised memory used in the generation of new responses of a given class. The schema notion has the advantage that it allows for the fact that skilled responses are by no means uniform, but instead are often matched to the varying needs of the occasion. The schema notion reflects the flexibility of many motor skills that enables the performer to meet new environmental demands by producing novel responses. Like Adams's theory two kinds of memory are hypothesised, one motor—the *recall schema*—and one perceptual—the *recognition schema*. The recall schema is a record of the relationships between previously executed response instructions (or motor output) under different initial conditions and their outcomes. The recognition schema stores relationships between past sensory consequences and actual outcomes or results. Both kinds of schema are built up by experience and the greater the variety of experience (within a given class of responses such as linear displacements or the hand), the easier it will be to abstract a general rule from specific cases. Schema theory therefore makes the specific prediction that variability of instances in learning will enhance transfer to new responses of the same class, and this turns out to be generally the case (Shapiro and Schmidt, 1982).

It is important to place these theories and experiments dealing with very simple responses in perspective. The provision of KR for multidimensional tasks, such as gymnastic or flying skills, is rarely a matter of giving precise quantitative information concerning a single response parameter. While overall achievement may be reduced to a single score, this may not be useful if it does not enable the learner to identify specific aspects of performance which should be modified. For example, studies of feedback, which gives information about spatial and temporal aspects of performance, do not always give better learning than simpler forms of KR (Newell and Walter, 1981). Moreover the use of video recordings, which provide detailed feedback on complex performance, has had rather mixed success as an aid to training (Rothstein and Arnold, 1976). KR is useful as an aid to learning only to the extent that the learner can identify the relationship between response output, intrinsic sensory feedback, and the outcome.

## Automatisation

The development of skill is also characterised in the Fitts sequence as a progressive change in the way in which task information is processed, or more precisely in the nature of the control processes involved, such that early in skill acquisition responses are produced under direct conscious control while after a great deal of practice performance becomes automatic, being run off with little conscious attention or mental effort. Again it is tempting to adopt as a general hypothesis that most, if not all, of what we mean by skill acquisition is the process by which controlled processing becomes automatised. Logan (1985) has, however, drawn attention to a number of important differences between skilled performance and automatic behaviour. Highly skilled performance can still be very flexible; thus, skilled typists may make errors but typically correct them very quickly (Rabbitt, 1978). While a skill may include automatic procedures it often also includes a high level of cognitive activity and even metacognitive processes. Much has been made of the difficulty some skilled performers find in explaining just how they achieve their results (Annett, 1985, 1986; Berry and Broadbent, 1984) but it would be wrong to assume that this ability was present at some earlier stage of practice and then has somehow been lost along the way towards high levels of skill. Neither novices nor skilled swimmers are very good at answering certain kinds of factual questions about swimming technique (Annett, 1985), nor is it true that early attempts at a skill are dominated by conscious, controlled processes, with every move being thought out in detail. On the contrary novice swimmers and cyclists may have problems learning to control their automatic, but inappropriate, responses to the novel situation in which they find themselves.

*Controlled versus automatic processing*

The supposed process of automatisation has had to carry a heavy theoretical burden, but the nature of the process is still poorly understood. In the first place, the criteria for automatisation are debatable but are often said to include speed (i.e. being faster than controlled processes), relative uniformity of kinematic pattern, being involuntary, being relatively unavailable to introspective analysis, being free from interference by other concurrent tasks, and being independent of load as measured by stimulus or response information. Debates such as that between Neisser, Hirst and Spelke (1981) and Lucas and Bub (1981), or between Cheng (1985) and Schneider and Shiffrin (1985) have typically hinged on which criteria are taken as indicating true automaticity.

The nature of automatisation has been formulated in a number of different ways. Schneider and Shiffrin (1977) propose flatly that there are two kinds of process, controlled and automatic, and have sought to distinguish them in a series of studies using visual search tasks in which subjects are required to distinguish target items, for example digits, from distractors, say letters. Consistent mapping of members of the target set to a particular response produces automaticity, as measured by several of the criteria mentioned above, with quite modest amounts of practice. Automaticity in this context simply implies that there is a simple computational link between input and output, a kind of private line which is always open and not subject to crosstalk. A different and more traditional account of automaticity distinguishes between *closed-loop* and *open-loop* control. In a closed-loop task, such as compensatory tracking, the motor output is linked to and driven by an error feedback signal while in an open-loop task, such as striking a ball with a bat, the motor output is driven by a once-for-all pattern of signals, or *motor program*, which determines the form and magnitude of the response. Closed-loop tasks usually take longer to perform than open-loop tasks because feedback information is typically subject to a temporal lag and also requires processing capacity. Speed can be traded for accuracy by paying more attention to feedback information and vice versa. The effect of practice may be to make feedback information redundant (Annett and Kay 1957) or to create an accurate motor program (Keele, 1968) capable of generating responses without the need for feedback.

*Motor programs*

One of the major theoretical issues in motor control during the 1970s concerned the nature of motor programs. The concept of a motor program as a precise set of output instructions is not credible in the light of the considerable flexibility shown by skilled performers in adapting responses to detailed variations in task requirements. Yet there is evidence for various degrees of motor preparation in well-practised tasks of short duration. Keele and Posner (1968), for example, found probe reaction times predictably slower when probe signals are in competition with program preparation, and Rosenbaum (1985) similarly found time to initiate a response increases proportionately to the complexity of the program required to generate the response. The motor program concept became something of a straw man for those who, like Turvey (1977) argued that motor control is a highly distributed rather than a centralised process and hence requires less 'central' storage of information than the motor program theory seems to demand. This leads to an alternative conceptualisation of automaticity in terms of levels of control. Complex tasks, like driving, cannot be adequately described as either a collection of motor programs or simple feedback loops, but are better characterised as hierarchically organised control structures. At the highest level of control, strategic decisions are made about which route to follow and whether to minimise journey time or the risk of accident. At a lower level of control, specific decisions are made about whether to turn off at the next junction, whether to overtake, and so on. At a still lower level, decisions (largely unconscious) are made about how far and when to turn the steering wheel, and how hard and when to step on the brake pedal. The development of automaticity in this view refers to the gradual changes in the focus of attention and control away from the lower functions towards higher level goals.

Fuchs (1962) demonstrated this principle in the context of a second-order tracking task. In zero order, the subject responds to the current size of the

40

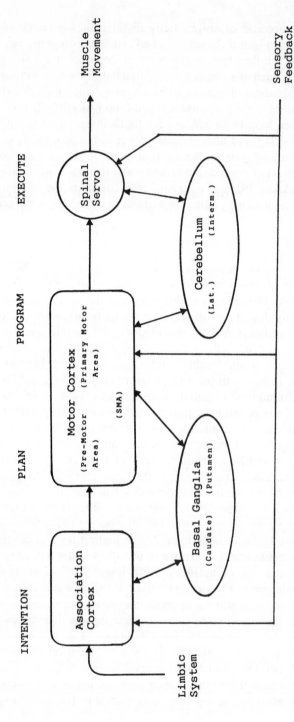

**Figure 2.7.** A simplified diagram of the principal structures involved in the production of a voluntary action.

error signal; in first-order control, the subject responds to the rate at which the error signal is changing; and in second-order control, to the acceleration of the error. The performance of a human tracker can be described approximately by a differential equation with the coefficients in the successive terms of the equation taken as estimates of the weights given by the subject to position, velocity, and acceleration information. With nine two-minute trials daily for 20 days, the weight given by subjects to the momentary position error decreased while the weighting given to acceleration error steadily increased. After 20 days, when subjects were required to carry out a second tracking task simultaneously, this change was reversed and performance tended to regress back from acceleration control to position control. Some clear examples of changes in level of control can be found in keyboard skills. Shaffer (1981), in an elegant analysis of the performances of highly skilled pianists using a specially equipped piano, has shown how the relative timing of notes is subject to high level control. Variations in timing, or rubato, are important to the emotional expression of music. A detailed analysis over different performances showed that the relative timing of individual keystrokes was consistent with varying the rate of an internal 'clock' rather than piecemeal adjustments to individual inter-keystroke intervals. The motor programs representing sequences of movements were themselves subject to a timebase that the virtuoso varies to express his or her musical intentions. The simulation of typing skill by Rumelhart and Norman (1982) described near the beginning of this chapter also illustrates this principle of different levels of control. The model envisages at least two distinct levels: a higher level concerned with interpreting the 'copy' to be typed and getting the words (word schemata) and letters (keypress schemata) in the right sequence; and a lower level which is concerned with moving the fingers around to locate particular keys. The common error of doubling the wrong letter for instance typing 'bokk' instead of 'book', can be interpreted as implying an intermediate level of control representing double striking—a doubling schema—which, from time to time, is applied to the wrong letter. The theory that automatisation refers to the lowest levels of control is consistent with current theories of motor control that strongly suggest, on both behavioural and neurological grounds, that voluntary action involves the integration of a number of semi-autonomous systems, rather like an army in which subordinates have quite a lot of freedom to interpret, sometimes even reject, orders from above on the basis of their special knowledge of local conditions.

# NEURAL BASES OF MOTOR LEARNING

The viewpoint adopted in this chapter is that skill acquisition is likely to involve more than one learning process. Recent evidence on the neural bases of motor learning supports this general position and adds an important dimension to the purely behavioural studies reviewed in preceding sections. Figure 2.7 summarises current views on the principal neural structures involved in the production of voluntary movement and their interconnections. At least three different 'levels' of the nervous system are distinguishable: the top level which is concerned with strategy or *what* to do; the middle level is concerned with tactics or *how* to do it; and the third level which controls the actual execution. The effects of training and practice may operate at any or all of these levels and the specific nature of the learning mechanism will depend in part on which structures are involved.

At the lowest level, the motor servo controls the coactivation of muscles which is necessary for smooth changes in the angles made by the joints to take place. There are two principal feedback circuits, one via the spinal cord and one at a high level via the cerebellum. The latter is particularly important in relating muscular output to concurrent data from internal and external senses. It is this circuit which is modified when adapting to new perceptual–motor relationships, for example when adjusting to spectacles which invert the visual field or to tracing a pattern seen in a mirror. 'Getting your sea-legs' is another example of the adaptation of the motor output to match the unusual relationships between the vestibular sensations of movement and the normal visual cues. This kind of motor learning is a temporary readjustment: the sailor ashore quickly loses his sea-legs. Marr (1969) has suggested a specific mechanism for this kind of adaptation involving an interaction between the *inferior olive* and the *cerebellar cortex*. Motor output signals are copied to the inferior olive which then receives feedback from the receptors; a comparison between the intended and the actual output is then signalled back to the cerebellar cortex and a mismatch results in a modification of the response of specific groups of cells to incoming information. Marr's theory has been confirmed by Ito (1984) who also showed that the effect was produced by a temporary change in the responsiveness of Purkinje cells to a specific neurotransmitter. This kind of learning, or adaptation as Brooks (1986) prefers to call it, can proceed independently of the higher centres of motor control and is unaffected by lesions which affect other kinds of memory, while damage to the inferior olive prevents learning at this level and destroys the effects of previous adaptation.

Another part of the cerebellum, the lateral cerebellum, is concerned with a different kind of learning at the middle level of the motor control hierarchy. In a series of experiments in which monkeys were trained to make simple positioning responses, Brooks (Brooks, 1986; Brooks, Kennedy and Ross, 1983) noted that learning occurred in two distinct phases. In the first the monkeys did not know which was the correct response, a right or left movement, and their 'uncertainty' was demonstrated in long reaction times and slow controlled movements of the lever. However, once the animals had discovered in which direction to move the lever, and began to do so on a better than chance basis, the pattern of their motor responses also began to change. Slow, somewhat irregular, controlled adjustment began to give way to fast and accurate biphasic movements characterised by an initial acceleration matched to the required movement amplitude, followed by a precisely timed deceleration—in short a typical motor program. This type of motor learning involves interaction between the cerebellum and two frontal areas of the brain, the *pre-motor area* (PMA) and the *supplementary motor area* (SMA). A comparator system in which the actual motor output is matched to an intended output is required. Brooks (1988) noted that both the PMA and SMA are connected with the *cingulate gyrus*, part of the *limbic system* which mediates needs and wants. Once the organism has decided *what* it wants to achieve it then becomes possible to match intentions with achievements, that is to learn *how*.

While interactions between association cortex and the limbic system represent the highest level of control, what the organism wants or intends, the SMA and the PMA are involved in anticipatory planning of action. Using a brain scanning technique to measure the flow of blood in different parts of the brain as an indication of local neural activity, Roland *et al.* (1980) investigated SMA activity during successive stages of learning a sequential manual skill. Subjects were required to learn a series of simple movements, touching the tip of the thumb with the fingertips of the same hand in a prescribed sequence. In this task, localised blood flow indicated neural activity in both the *primary motor cortex* and the SMA. When subjects were asked to carry out the task in imagination only, the bloodflow to the primary motor cortex was reduced but remained high in the SMA. By contrast when subjects were required to squeeze rhythmically a small spring-loaded cylinder between finger and thumb, an overlearned and rather boring task, SMA activity was reduced while primary motor cortex activity remained high. These results are consistent with the hypothesis that these areas of the frontal cortex are brought into play during the learning of a motor task but are not needed for the routine execution of a well-learned activity. Passingham (1987) showed that removal of the SMA abolishes the ability to learn movements cued by preceding actions in sequential tasks. Sasaki and Gemba (1986) were able temporarily to abolish a learned wrist movement in monkeys by cooling the surface of the PMA, but in this case the skill returned after restoration of normal temperature showing that this area is mediating a longer term motor memory. Brooks (1988) concludes that these cortical areas are modulated by the limbic system during motor learning and help to establish both short- and long-term motor memories relating motor actions to the demands of external and internal stimuli.

One of the striking features of motor learning is its persistence. Skills such as bicycle riding and swimming are not forgotten even after years without practice. Even the relatively 'cognitive' skill of typing is resistant to lack of practice as shown in a study by Hill (1934, 1957) who learned to type first in 1907 and, with no intervening practice, relearned after 25 years and again 50 years after the original learning. In the first relearning trial, it took only one day's practice to regain the typing speed it had originally taken 27 days to achieve. On the second relearning trial, he regained the original end of training performance level after only 8 days' practice, clear evidence of long-term retention of the skill. Milner's famous amnesic patient H. M. was able to learn and retain motor skills, such as tracking and mirror drawing while having no memory of the tester or previous training sessions (Corkin, 1968). H. M. had suffered lesions to the *hippocampus* and *amygdala*, two areas which have been shown in animal studies (Mishkin, Malamut and Bachevalier, 1984) to be responsible for learning to recognise objects and their locations; however, these animals can learn, albeit somewhat slowly, to connect visual stimuli with particular responses. The *striatum*, an evolutionary ancient part of the forebrain, has connections with both sensory and motor systems. Animals with lesions in this area fail to learn simple perceptual–motor habits. While the neurological evidence is still far from complete, it seems that there are a number of different neural mechanisms underlying the acquisition of skill, some serving the cognitive aspects of skill and others operating at more primitive levels in the formation of perceptual–motor links and the selection of efficient motor patterns.

# SUMMARY AND CONCLUSIONS

A skill is a solution to a problem and the view is taken that skill acquisition is best understood if the nature of the problem to be solved is first understood. Information-processing concepts provide the best available framework within which to analyse specific skills. Two contrasting examples, bicycle riding and typing, illustrate how proficiency is acquired. Analysis is particularly important in designing training since it enables the instructor/trainer to design procedures to help the learner solve the specific skill problem.

The acquisition of skill is marked by qualitative and quantitative changes in performance, both of which may provide clues to underlying learning processes. The log–log linear law of learning, which describes the typical relationship between performance time and number of practice trials, has often been interpreted as indicating a single underlying learning process. However, qualitative changes in performance may suggest a number of different sources of improvement, including a changed understanding of the task, selection of different responses, variations in technique, and the redistribution of attention.

Skill is acquired both through the automatic effects of repetitive practice, and also through various methods of instruction which involve high level cognitive processes. The relationship between cognitive and non-cognitive processes in skill is still not fully understood but must depend on links between stored representations of actions (procedural knowledge), and linguistic units (declarative knowledge). Observational learning is mediated by action–perception processes, and hence effective demonstrations must take into account the way the trainee perceives and interprets complex action patterns. Verbal communication about actions is often effective only if it can make use of established action imagery. Trainees find it easier to follow instructions which summon up clear movement images.

Practice offers the opportunity to acquire information relevant to the performance of a skill. This may include information about patterns of stimuli presented by the task, and about the consequences of different responses. Some theorists have emphasised the perceptual aspects of skill learning while classical learning theory has emphasised the selective effects of consequences, especially in the form of knowledge of results. KR has to be placed in the context of all the information available to the skilled performer, especially other forms of feedback information which are intrinsic to the task. The principal role of KR seems to be informative rather than reinforcing in the sense used by behaviourists. In the early stages of learning, KR may be used to identify the essential parameters of a response pattern, especially if they are difficult to ascertain by other means. The fact that mental practice has been shown to have some effect on skill acquisition does, however, suggest that not all the effects of practice can be attributed to information feedback, and there is clearly a role for sheer repetition as such in acquiring skill.

Repetition generally leads to automatisation, but this does not always mean that performance is inaccessible to cognitive influence. A better description is that attention is directed to more abstract features of performance, such as the sequence of actions, or their timing and rhythm. Neurological evidence tends to confirm the existence of several different motor learning processes, some controlled by parts of the brain responsible for organisation and planning, and others by mechanisms which relate actions to intentions.

# REFERENCES

Adams, J. A. (1957). The relationship between certain measures of ability and the acquisition of a psychomotor criterion response, *Journal of General Psychology*, **56** 121–134.

Adams, J. A. (1971). A closed loop theory of motor learning, *Journal of Motor Behaviour*, **3**, 111–150.

Adams, J. A. (1987). Historical review and appraisal of research on the learning, retention and transfer of human motor skills. *Psychological Bulletin*, **101**, 41–74.

Adams J. A. Goetz, E. T. and Marshall, P. H. (1972). Response feedback and motor learning, *Journal of Experimental Psychology*, **92**, 391–397.

Adams, J. A., Gopher, D. and Lintern, G. (1977). Effects of visual and proprioceptive feedback on motor learning, *Journal of Motor Behaviour*, **9**, 11–22.

Anderson, J. R. (1982). The acquisition of cognitive skill, *Psychological Review*, **89**, 369–406.

Anderson, J. R. (1987). Skill acquisition: Compilation of weak-method problem solutions, *Psychological Review*, **94**, 192–210.

Annett, J. (1959). *Aspects of the Acquisition of Skill.* Unpublished D Phil thesis, University of Oxford.

Annett, J. (1969). *Feedback and Human Behaviour.* Harmondsworth: Penguin.

Annett, J. (1982). Action, language and imagination. In L. Wankel and R. B. Wilberg (eds). *Psychology of Sport and Motor Behavior: Research and Practice*, pp. 271–282. Edmonton: University of Alberta.

Annett, J. (1985). Motor learning: A review. In H. Heuer, U. Kleinbeck and K-H. Schmidt (eds). *Motor Behavior: Programming, Control and Acquisition*, pp. 189–212. Berllin: Springer.

Annett, J. (1986). On knowing how to do things. In H. Heuer and C. Fromm (eds). *Generation and Modulation of Action Patterns*, pp. 187–200. Berliln: Springer.

Annett, J. (1988). Motor learning and retention. In M. M. Gruneberg, P. E. Morris and R. N. Sykes (eds). *Practical Aspects of Memory: Current Research and Issues*, Vol. 2, pp. 434–440. London: Academic Press.

Annett, J. (1990). Relations between verbal and gestural explanations. In G. R. Hammond (ed). *Cerebral Control of Speech and Limb Movements*, pp. 295–314. Amsterdam: North Holland.

Annett, J. and Duncan, K. D. (1967). Task analysis and training design, *Occupational Psychology*, **41**, 211–221.

Annett, J. and Kay, H. (1956). Skilled performance, *Occupational Psychology*, **30**, 112–117.

Annett, J. and Kay, H. (1957). Knowledge of results and skilled performance, *Occupational Psychology*, **31** 69–79.

Annett, J., Duncan, K. D., Stammers, R. B. and Gray, M. J. (1971). *Task Analysis.* London: HMSO.

Argyle, M. (1969). *Social Interaction.* London: Methuen.

Bainbridge, L. (1979). Verbal reports as evidence of the process operator's knowledge, *International Journal of Man–Machine Studies*, **11**, 311–436.

Bainbridge, L. (1988). Types of representation. In L. P. Goodstein, H. B. Andersen and S. E. Olsen (eds). *Tasks, Errors and Mental Models*, pp. 55–91. London: Taylor and Francis.

Bandura, A. (1977). *Social Learning Theory.* Englewood Cliffs, NJ: Prentice-Hall.

Bandura, A. (1986). *Social Foundations of Thought and Action: A social cognitive theory.* Englewood Cliffs NJ: Prentice-Hall.

Bartlett, F. C. (1958). *Thinking: An experimental and social study.* London: Allen and Unwin.

Bernstein, N. (1967). *The Co-ordination and Regulation of Movements.* London: Pergamon Press.

Berry, D. C. and Broadbent, D. E. (1984). On the relationship between task performance and associated verbal knowledge, *Quarterly Journal of Experimental Psychology*, **36A**, 209–231.

Berry, D. C. and Broadbent, D. E. (1984). On the relationship between task performance and associated verbal knowledge *Quarterly Journal of Experimental Psychology*, **36A**, 209–231.

Berry, D. C. and Broadbent, D. E. (1987). Explanation and verbalisation in a computer-assisted search task, *Quarterly Journal of Experimental Psychology*, **39A**, 585–609.

Berry, D. C. and Broadbent, D. E. (1988). Interactive tasks and the implicit-explicit distinction, *British Journal of Psychology*, **79**, 251–272.

Bilodeau, E. A. (1953). Speed of acquiring a simple motor response as a function of the systematic transformation of KR, *American Journal of Psychology*, **60**, 409–420.

Bilodeau, E. A. and Bilodeau, I. McD. (1958a). Variation in temporal intervals among critical events in five studies of knowledge of results, *Journal of Experimental Psychology*, **55**, 603–612.

Bilodeau, E. A. and Bilodeau, I. McD. (1958b). Variable frequency of knowledge of results and the learning of a simple skill, *Journal of Experimental Psychology*, **55**, 379–383.

Bilodeau, E. A. and Rosenbach, J. H. (1953). Acquisition of response proficiency as a function of rounding error in informative feedback, *USAF Human Resource Research Center Research Bulletin*, No. 53–21.

Bilodeau, I. McD. (1969). Information feedback. In E. A. Bilodeau and I. McD. Bilodeau (eds). *Principles of Skill Acquisition*. New York: Academic Press.

Book, W. F. (1908). The psychology of skill: With special reference to its acquisition in typewriting, *University of Montana Publications in Psychology, Bulletin No. 53*.

Brooks, V. B. (1986). *The Neural Basis of Motor Control*. Oxford: Oxford University Press.

Brooks, V. B. (1988). Limbic assistance in task-related use of motor skill. *Paper presented to the Study Week on the Principles of Design and Operation of the Brain. Pontificia Academia Scientarium, the Vatican.*

Brooks, V. B., Kennedy, P. R. and Ross, H. G. (1983). Movement programming depends on understanding of behavioural requirements, *Physiology and Behavior*, **31**, 561–563.

Bryan, W. L. and Harter, N. (1897). Studies in the physiology and psychology of the telegraphic language, *Psychological Review*, **4**, 27–53.

Bryan, W. L. and Harter, N. (1899). Studies on the telegraphic language: The acquisition of a hierarchy of habits, *Psychological Review*, **6**, 345–375.

Burwitz, L. (1981). The use of demonstrations and video-tape recorders in sport and physical education. In I. M. Cockerill and W. W. MacGillivary (eds). *Vision and Sport*. Cheltenham: Stanley Thornes.

Chase, W. G. and Simon, H. A. (1973). Perception in chess, *Cognitive Psychology*, **4**, 55–81.

Cheng, P. W. (1985). Restructuring vs automaticity: Alternative accounts of skill acquisition, *Psychological Review*, **92**, 414–423.

Corbin, C. B. (1972). Mental practice. In W. D. Morgan (ed.). *Ergogenic Aid and Muscular Performance*. New York: Academic Press.

Corkin, S. (1968). Acquisition of motor skill after bilateral medial temporal lobe excision, *Neuropsychologia*, **6**, 255–265.

Crossman, E. R. F. (1959). A theory of the acquisition of speed skill, *Ergonomics*, **2**, 153–166.

Cutting, J. E. (1978). Generation of male and female synthetic walkers, *Perception*, **1**, 395–405.

de Groot, A. D. (1965). *Thought and Choice in Chess*. The Hague: Mouton.

Doyle, A. J. R. (1988). The essential human contribution to bicycle riding. In J. Patrick and K. D. Duncan (eds). *Training, Human Decision Making and Control.* Amsterdam: North Holland.

Ebbinghaus, H. (1885). *Uber das Gedachtnis.* Leipzig: Duncker. (Published [1964] in translation as *Memory: A contribution to experimental psychology.* New York: Dover.)

Feltz, D. L. and Landers, D. M. (1983). The effects of mental practice on motor skill learning and performance: A meta-analysis, *Journal of Sport Psychology,* **5**, 25–57.

Feltz, D. L., Landers, D. M. and Becker, B. J. (1988). A revised meta-analysis of the mental practice literature on motor skill learning. *Background paper prepared for the Committee on Techniques for the Enhancement of Human Performance, National Academy of Sciences.* (Available through the publication on request program.)

Ferster, C. B. and Skinner, B. F. (1957). *Schedules of Reinforcement.* New York: Appleton-Century-Crofts.

Fitts, P. M. (1964). Perceptual-motor skill learning. In A. W. Melton (ed.) *Categories of Human Learning.* New York: Academic Press.

Fitts, P. M. and Posner, M. I. (1967) *Human Performance* Belmont, C. A. Brookes/ Cole Publishing Company.

Fleishman, E. A. (1960). Abilities at different stages of practice in rotary pursuit, *Journal of Experimental Psychology,* **60**, 162–171.

Fleishman, E. A. and Hempel, W. E. (1954). Changes in factor structure of a complex psychomotor task as a function of practice, *Psychometrika,* **19**, 239–252.

French, K. E. and Thomas, J. R. (1987). The relation of knowledge development to children's basketball performance, *Journal of Sport Psychology,* **9**, 15–32.

Fuchs, A. H. (1962). The progression–regression hypothesis in perceptual–motor skill learning. *Journal of Experimental Psychology,* **63** 177–183.

Geschwind, N. and Kaplan, E. (1962). A human disconnection syndrome, *Neurology,* **12**, 675–685.

Green, R. F., Zimilies, H. L. and Spragg, S. D. S. (1955). The effects of varying degrees of knowledge of results on knob-setting performance, *SPECDEVCEN Technical Report 241-76-20.*

Hill, L. B. (1934). A quarter century of delayed recall, *Journal of General Psychology,* **44**, 231–238.

Hill, L. B. (1957). A second quarter century of delayed recall, or relearning at eighty, *Journal of Educational Psychology,* **48**, 65–69.

Ho, L. and Shea, J. B. (1978). Effects of relative frequency of knowledge of results on retention of a motor skill, *Perceptual and Motor Skills,* **46**, 859–866.

Houston, R. C. (1947). *The Function of Knowledge of Results in Learning a Complex Motor Skill.* Unpublished MA thesis, Northwestern University, Evanston, Illinois.

Hull, C. L. (1943). *Principles of Behavior.* New York: Appleton-Century-Crofts.

Imwold, C. H. and Hoffman, S. J. (1983). Visual recognition of a gymnastic skill by experienced and inexperienced inexperienced instructors. *Research Quarterly for Exercise and Sport Sciences,* **54**, 149–155.

Ito, M. (1984). *The Cerebellum and Neural Control.* New York: Raven Press.

Jacobson, E. (1932). Electrophysiology of mental activities, *American Journal of Psychology,* **44**, 677–694.

James, W. (1890). *Principles of Psychology.* New York: Henry Holt.

Johansson, G. (1973), Visual perception of biological motion and a model for its analysis, *Perception and Psychophysics,* **14** 201–211.

Johnson, P. (1982). The functional equivalence of imagery and movement, *Quarterly Journal of Experimental Psychology,* **34A**, 349–365.

Jones, M. B. (1970). A two process theory of inidividual differences in motor learning, *Psychological Review,* **77**, 353–360.

Judd, C. H. (1908). The relation of special training and intelligence, *Educational Review,* **36**, 28–42.

Kawai, M. (1965). Newly acquired precultural behavior in the natural troupe of Japanese monkeys on Koshima islet, *Primates,* **6**, 1–30.

Keele, S. W. (1968). Movement control in skilled motor performance, *Psychological Bulletin,* **70**, 387–403.

Keele, S. W. and Posner, M. I. (1968). Processing of visual feedback in rapid movements, *Journal of Experimental Psychology,* **77** 155–158.

Logan, G. D. (1985). Skill and automaticity: Relations, implications and future directions. *Canadian Journal of Psychology,* **39**, 367–386.

Long, J. B. (1975). Effects of randomly delayed visual and auditory feedback on keying performance, *Ergonomics,* **18**, 337–347.

Long, J. B. (1976). Visual feedback and skilled keying: Differential effects of masking the print copy and the keyboard, *Ergonomics,* **19** 93–110.

Long, J. B., Nimmo-Smith, I. and Whitfield, A. (1983). In W. E. Cooper (ed.). *Cognitive Aspects of Skilled Typewriting,* pp. 145–195. New York: Springer.

Large, I. and Thorndike, E. L. (1935). The influence of delay in the after-effect of a connection, *Journal of Experimental Psychology,* **18**, 186–194.

Lucas, M. and Bub, D. (1981). Can practice result in the ability to divide attention between two complex language tasks? Comment on Hirst *et al. Journal of Experimental Psychology: General,* **110**, 495–498.

Mackworth, N. (1950). Researches in the measurement of human performance. *Medical Research Council Special Report Series No. 268.* London: HMSO. (Reprinted in W. H. Sinaiko, (ed.) (1961) *Selected Papers on Human Factors in the Design and Use of Control Systems.* New York: Dover.

MacKay, D. G. (1981). The problem of rehearsal or mental practice. *Journal of Motor Behavior,* **13**, 274–285.

MacKay, D. G. (1982). The problems of flexibility, fluency and speed-accuracy trade-off in skilled behavior, *Psychological Review,* **89**, 483–506.

Marr, D. (1969). A theory of cerebellar cortex, *Journal of Physiology,* **141**, 437–470.

cLeod, P. (1977). A dual task response modality effect: Support for multi-process models of attention, *Quarterly Journal of Experimental Psychology,* **29**, 651–667.

Meltzoff, A. N. and Moore, M. K. (1977). Imitation of facial and manual gestures, *Science,* **198**, 75–80.

Miller, G. A. (1956). The magical number seven, plus or minus two: Some limits on our capacity for processing information, *Psychological Review,* **63**, 81–97.

Miller, G. A., Galanter, E. and Pribram, K. (1960). *Plans and the Structure of Behavior:* New York: Holt, Reinhart & Winston.

Miller, R. B. (1953). Handbook of training and equipment design, *USAF WADC Technical Report 53–136.*

Mishkin, M., Malamut, B. and Bachevalier, J. (1984). Memories and habits: Two neural systems. In G. Lynch, J. L. McGough and N. M. Weinberger (eds). *Neurobiology of Learning and Memory.* New York: Guilford Press.

Morin, R. E. and Gagné, R. M. (1951). Pedestal sight manipulation test performance as influenced by variations in type and amount of psychological feedback, *USAF HRRC Research Note P & MS 51–7.* Brooks AFB, TX: US Air Force Human Resources Research Command.

Neisser, U., Hirst, W. and Spelke, E. S. (1981). Limited capacity theories and the notion of automaticity: Reply to Lucas and Bub, *Journal of Experimental Psychology: General,* **110**, 499–500.

Newell, A. and Rosenbloom, P. S. (1981). Mechanisms of skill acquisition and the law of practice. In J. R. Anderson (ed). *Cognitive Skills and their Acquisition.* Hillsdale, NJ: Lawrence Erlbaum.

Newell, K. M. and Walter, C. B. (1981). Kinematic and kinetic parameters as information feedback in motor skill acquisition, *Journal of Human Movement Studies,* **7,** 235–254.

Newtson, D. (1980). Foundations of attribution: The perception of ongoing behavior. In J. Harvey, W. Ickes and R. Kidd (eds). *New Directions in Attribution Research.* Hillsdale NJ: Lawrence Erlbaum.

Passingham, R. E. (1987). Two cortical systems for directing movements. In *Motor Areas of the Cerebral Cortex: Ciba Foundation Symposium 132,* pp. 151–164. Chichester: Wiley.

Rabbitt, P. M. A. (1978). Detection of errors by skilled typists, *Ergonomics,* **21,** 945–958.

Richardson, A. (1967). Mental practice: A review and discussion. *Research Quarterly for Exercise and Sport Sciences,* **38,** 95–107 and 263–273.

Roland, P. E., Larsen, B., Lassen, N. A. and Skinhoj, E. (1980). Supplementary motor area and other cortical areas in organisation of voluntary movements in man, *Journal of Neurophysiology,* **43,** 118–136.

Rosenbaum, D. A. (1985). Motor programming: A review and scheduling theory. In H. Heuer, U. Kleinbeck and K-H. Schmidt (eds). *Motor Behavior: Programming control and acquisition,* pp. 1–33. Berlin: Springer.

Rothstein, A. L. and Arnold, R. K. (1976). Bridging the gap: Application of research on videotape feedback and bowling, *Motor Skills: Theory into Practice,* **1,** 35–62.

Rumelhart, D. E. and Norman, D. A. (1978). Accretion, tuning and restructuring: three modes of learning. In J. W. Cotton and Roberta L. Klatzky (eds). *Semantic Factors in Cognition,* pp. 37–53.

Rumelhart, D. E. and Norman, D. A. (1982). Simulating a skilled typist: A study of skilled cognitive motor performance, *Cognitive Science,* **6,** 1–36.

Salmoni, A. W., Schmidt, R. A. and Walter, C. B. (1984). Knowledge of results and motor learning: a review and critical appraisal, *Psychological Bulletin,* **95,** 355–386.

Sasaki, K. and Gemba, H. (1986). Effects of premotor cortex cooling upon visually initiated hand movements in the monkey, *Brain Research,* **374,** 278–286.

Schmidt, R. A. (1975). A schema theory of discrete motor skill learning, *Psychological Review,* **82,** 225–260.

Schmidt, R. A., Young, D. E., Swinnen, S. and Shapiro, D. C. (1989). Summary knowledge of results for skill acquisition: Support for the guidance hypothesis, *Journal of Experimental Psychology: Learning Memory and Cognition,* **15,** 352–359.

Schneider, W. and Shiffrin, R. M. (1977). Controlled and automatic human information processing 1: Detection, search and attention, *Psychological Review,* **84** 1–66.

Schneider, W. and Shiffrin, R. (1985). Categorisation (restructuring) and automatisation: Two separable factors, *Psychological Review,* **92,** 424–428.

Scully, D. M. and Newell, K. M. N. (1985). Observational learning and the acquisition of motor skills: Towards a visual perception perspective, *Journal of Human Movement Studies,* **11,** 169–186.

Seibel, R. (1963). Discrimination reaction time for a 1023-alternative task, *Journal of Experimental Psychology,* **66,** 215–226.

Shaffer, L. H. (1981). Performances of Chopin, Bach and Bartok: Studies in motor programming, *Cognitive Psychology*, **13** 326–376.

Shapiro, D. C. and Schmidt, R. A. (1982). The schema theory: recent evidence and developmental implications. In J. A. S. Kelso and J. E. Clark (eds). *The Development of Movement Control and Coordination*, pp. 113–173. New York: Wiley.

Sheffield, F. D. (1961). Theoretical considerations in the learning of complex sequential tasks from demonstration and practice. In A. A. Lumsdaine (ed.). *Student Response in Programmed Instruction*. Washington DC: NAS-NRC.

Skinner, B. F. (1953). *Science and Human Behavior*. New York: Macmillan.

Smyth, M. M. and Pendelton, L. R. (1989). Working memory for movements, *Quarterly Journal of Experimental Psychology*, **41A**, 235–250.

Snoddy, G. S. (1926). Learning and stability, *Journal fo Applied Psychology*, **10**, 1–36.

Spelke, E., Hirst, W. and Neisser, U. (1976). Skills of divided attention, *Cognition*, **4**, 215–230.

Starkes J. L. (1987). Skill in field hockey: The nature of the cognitive advantage, *Journal of Sport Psychology*, **9**.

Suinn, R. (1972). Behavior rehearsal training for ski races, *Behavior Therapy*, **3** 210–212.

Swift, E. J. (1910). Relearning a skillful act: An experimental study of neuromuscular memory, *Psychological Bulletin*, **7** 17–19.

Thomas, J. R., French, K. E. and Humphries, C. A. (1986). Knowledge development and sport skill performance: Directions for motor behavior research, *Journal of Sport Psychology*, **8**, 259–272.

Thorndike, E. L. (1932). *The Fundamentals of Learning*. New York: Teacher's College, Columbia University.

Thorndike, E. L. (1933). A theory of the effects of the action or the after effects of a connection upon it, *Psychological Review*, **40**, 434–489.

Trowbridge, M. H. and Cason, H. (1932). An experimental study of Thorndike's theory of learning, *Journal of General Psychology*, **7**, 245–258.

Turvey, M. T. (1977). Preliminaries to a theory of action with reference to vision. In R. Shaw and J. Bransford (eds). *Perceiving Acting and Knowing: Towards an ecological psychology*. Hillsdale NJ: Lawrence Erlbaum.

Turvey, M. T. and Kugler, P. N. (1984). An ecological approach to perception and action. In H. T. A. Whiting (ed.). *Human Motor Actions: Bernstein reassessed*, pp. 373–412. Amsterdam: North Holland.

van Lawick-Goodall, J. (1971). *In the Shadow of Man*. London: Collins.

Vickers, J. N. (1988). Knowledge structures of expert–novice gymnasts, *Journal of Human Movement Science*, **7**, 47–72.

Welford, A. T. (1987). On rates of improvement with practice, *Journal of Motor Behavior*, **19**, 401–415.

Whiting, H. T. A., Bijlard, M. J. and den Brinker, B. P. L. M. (1987). The effect of the availability of a dynamic model on the acquisition of a complex cyclical action, *Quarterly Journal of Experimental Psychology*, **39A**, 43–59.

Woodrow, H. (1939). Factors in improvement with practice, *Journal of Psychology*, **7**, 55–70.

Sharda, R. et al. (1988). Performance of a Chapter Book and Tutorial studies in multi programming. *Operations Research*, 36(1), pp. 13-22.

Sherman, D. R. and Schmidt, R. A. (1987). The relative contributions and frequency of developmental instructions. In D. A. Kleiber and J. P. Crandall (eds.), *The Developmental Context of childhood Developments*, pp. 31-52. New York: Wiley.

Sheridan, S. E. (1991). *Teaching Human Relations*. The learning of complex social tasks from demonstration and practice. In A. N. Johnstone (ed.), *Student Strategies: A Festschrift for Donald A. Schmidt*. Des Plains, IL: NASPERC.

Skinner, B. F. (1953). *Science and Human Behaviour*. New York: Macmillan.

Smith, P. L. and Ragan, T. J. (1993). Volume learning in the application, other applications, *Contemporary Psychology*, 21, 3, pp. 56-59.

Smith, P. L. (1989). Individual and stability. *Contemporary Review of Psychology*, 18, 1, 38.

Spalek, T., Hill, W., and Stevenson, A. (1993). Skills acquired in the attention. *Cognitive and Learning*, 33, 2.

Staats, A. (1981). Paired to individuals to the classroom of individuals on the hungry of new functions.

Steinberg, M. (1971). Statistical education. *Journal of Studies in Science Education*, 78, pp. 89-112.

Steel, A. L. (1978). Performance skilled and unspecialised kinds of human behaviour. *Journal of Experimental Psychology*, 22.

Stenberg, R. J. (1997). Some functions. *Psychology in Adult Learning and the Development and the first actions*. (ed.) New functions for early learning on early performance. *Behaviour Analysis*, 3, 560-575.

Thorndike, E. L. (1931). *Fundamentals of Learning*. New York: Teachers' College, Columbia University.

Thorndike, E. L. and Woodworth, R. S. (1901). The influence of the improvement of one connection upon the other. *Psychological Review*, 80, pp. 181-197.

Vandenbos, A. H. and Blatt, A. (1992). An experimental study of human memory. *Learning Laboratories*, 44, 2, pp. 5-33.

Vine, R. E. (1972). Similarity to a group of tasks and of reference in relation to speed and visual learning. *Journal of Experimental Psychology*, 64, 2, pp. 206-217.

Wilson, M. J. and Cooper, R. (1987). An experimental approach to developmental processes. In H. F. A. Writing (ed.), *Human Motor Actions*. *Perspectives*, vol. 19, pp. 39-112, Amsterdam: North Holland.

Wright, T. P., Cooper, E. et al. (eds.), *Environmental and Applications, an environment of human behaviour*.

Wright, R. E. (1947). *The value of improvements*. New York: Academic Press.

Young, D. E. and Schmidt, R. A. (1990). In L. M. (1987). The effect of the availability of information model of the suggestion of a complex system. In the *Contemporary View of Psychology and Statistics*, 104, 2, 2, 22.

Young, D. and Schmidt, R. A. In *The Environment and Statistics*. *Journal of Psychology*.

# Chapter 3

# Long-term retention of motor skills

## Joel D. Schendel[1] and Joseph D. Hagman[2]

[1]HAY Systems, Inc. [2]US Army Research Institute for the Behavioral and Social Sciences

There are some areas of psychology that are of sufficient general interest that everyone knows something about them (or at least thinks that they do). The long-term retention of motor skills is one of those areas. The subject has been more or less fashionable at different times and in different circles, but it never has gone completely out of style. Unlike research on short-term motor retention, which peaked in the late 1960s and began to fade by the early 1970s (Stelmach, 1974), research on the long-term retention of motor skills has been conducted at least since the early 1900s (e.g. Bean, 1912; Swift, 1905). Reviews of this research have been prepared periodically over the past 30 years (e.g. Adams, 1987; Naylor and Briggs, 1961; Prophet, 1976a, 1976b; Schendel, Shields and Katz, 1978; Stelmach, 1974). This chapter would extend this tradition into the 1990s.

There is a danger in preparing a chapter on retention that stands apart from one on learning. As suggested by Schmidt and Bjork (1989) and others, it fosters traditional beliefs about the separability of learning and retention and the processes that underlie them. Learning and retention may be regarded as fundamentally different phenomena and can be studied in isolation from one another. Alternatively, learning may be regarded as entailing processes that are best assessed during the actual practice of a task, not necessarily during a transfer test or after a retention interval. These beliefs are counterproductive and stand in direct opposition to a growing body of research demonstrating the interrelated nature of learning and retention and the practical value of using retention or transfer performance as a key criterion for evaluating performance during training. This research has included consideration for both verbal and motor tasks and for variations in the scheduling of practice such as random versus blocked practice (e.g. Shea and Morgan, 1979), spacing of practice (e.g. Landauer and Bjork, 1978; Stelmach, 1969), and variability of practice (e.g. Catalano and Kleiner, 1984). It has included consideration for variations in the presentation of knowledge of results (KR) (e.g. Lavery, 1962; Schmidt et al., 1989), augmented feedback (e.g. Bilodeau, 1952), and the role of testing during training (e.g. Hagman, 1981, 1983). Much of this research is presented in this chapter.

## Definitions

### Skill

The term 'skill' is used here in the same sense as it has been used by Adams (1987) and suggested by others (e.g. Bartlett, 1948a, 1948b; Pear, 1927). The term refers to a wide variety of complex, learned behaviors that depend heavily on motor processes for goal attainment. Cognitive and perceptual processes also may be involved, but skilled performance centers around 'muscular performances' (Pear, 1948, p. 92).

### Retention

The term 'retention' refers to the maintenance or sustainment of skills in the absence of practice. The period between initial training and subsequent performance is called the *retention interval*. The focus of this chapter is on long-term retention, where retention intervals usually are measured in terms of days, weeks, months, or even years.

### Purpose and scope

The purpose of this chapter is to provide a better understanding of how specific variables affect the long-term retention of motor skills. These variables have been organized loosely into three categories: task variables, procedural variables, and learner variables.

### Task variables

Task variables relate to the nature of the task or skill to be acquired and learning environment. They include duration of the retention interval, response class, degree to which the task is inherently amenable to learner organization, display–control compatibility, and display specificity.

### Procedural variables

Procedural variables relate to the manner in which training, testing, or both occur. They include repetition, repetition schedule, mental practice, KR, response-produced feedback, augmented feedback, testing, test expectation, variability of practice, and refresher training. Research related to interference theory and the forgetting of motor movements was intentionally omitted, since it has been treated in a number of previous reviews (e.g. Adams, 1987; Stelmach, 1974).

*Learner variables*

Learner variables refer to the 'natural' or 'initial ability' variables thought to be held before training occurs and to underlie the learning and retention of a task. These variables have been operationally defined in different ways and are so noted in the text.

Following the discussion of task, procedural, and learner variables, two methods for predicting long-term retention performance are presented. One method of prediction depends on an assessment of task characteristics; the other method depends on the use of performer self-assessments. The chapter concludes with a discussion of methods for optimizing retention and directions for future research.

In preparing this chapter, special consideration was given to research performed in applied settings. Much of this research was sponsored by the military (e.g. Hagman and Rose, 1983; Schendel *et al.*, 1978) and involved the use of military tasks. There is nothing peculiar about military tasks. From a learner's perspective, they force the same types of problem solving as tasks found in other applied settings. However, research on long-term retention has been of special interest to the military, since soldiers' skills must be sustained continuously at high levels and since opportunities for refresher training these skills may not be available when they are needed. There are difficulties associated with the study of long-term retention in applied military contexts (e.g. Thompson *et al.*, 1981), but most of these difficulties also are encountered when conducting related research in other contexts.

Research on tasks having few 'real-world' applications was included only if the results were practically indicative or suggestive. Research on verbal tasks was included as needed to fill the 'gaps' in the motor skills literature, to provide an effective or intriguing contrast with research on motor tasks, and to suggest directions for future research.

# TASK VARIABLES

**Duration of the retention interval**

The general course of retention is predictable. Performance typically decreases rapidly soon after training and continues to drop, but at a slower rate, as the retention interval increases. That retention usually decreases with time is a well-established principle that dates back at least to the late 1800s (e.g. Ebbinghaus, 1964). The principle applies to motor responses as well as verbal ones. Of course, the exact shape of any forgetting curve depends on a host of variables, many of which are treated in this chapter.

**Response class**

*Definitions*

Motor responses, typically, are classified as predominantly continuous, discrete, or procedural in nature. Continuous responses involve the repetition of a movement pattern that has no discernible beginning or end (e.g. riding a bicycle). Discrete responses are usually of short duration and have a distinct beginning and end (e.g. moving a gear shift lever) (Schmidt, 1975). Procedural tasks are composed of a series of discrete motor responses. The responses themselves usually are easy to execute. It is deciding what responses to make and in what sequence that pose the main problems for the learner. Familiar examples of procedural tasks include disassembly and assembly tasks (e.g. Schendel and Hagman, 1982) and tasks that involve flipping switches, moving levers, or setting dials in sequence (e.g. Mengelkoch, Adams and Gainer, 1971).

*Continuous responses*

The most commonly employed continuous task in studies of motor memory is tracking (Adams, 1967). There are two types of tracking tasks—pursuit tracking and compensatory tracking. In pursuit tracking, the operator can see both the target to be followed and the tracking device or cursor. His or her job is to keep the cursor aligned with the target so that the discrepancy between the two is nullified. Keeping an M16A1 rifle sight (cursor) on a moving target is an example of a pursuit tracking task (e.g. Schendel and Johnston, 1983).

In compensatory tracking, neither the target nor its position is displayed. The operator knows only the difference between an error indicator and a fixed reference. The task is to nullify this difference. For example, error-nullifying principles are the basis of certain navigational instruments that signal the operator to begin directional (or attitudinal) corrections if he or she strays off the intended course.

Once learned, continuous movements such as those involved in pursuit tracking (Reynolds and Bilodeau, 1952; Ryan, 1962; Smith, Jr., 1971) and compensatory tracking (Adams and Hufford, 1962; Ammons *et al.*, 1958; Battig *et al.*, 1957; Mengelkoch *et al.*, 1971) show little or no forgetting over retention intervals measured in terms of months or even years.

*Discrete responses*

Much research has been conducted on the short-term retention of simple, discrete motor movements (e.g. Stelmach, 1974). However, little research has been performed testing the long-term retention of these movements. That research which is available suggests that discrete responses are not well retained in the absence of practice. In one study, Martin (cited by Schmidt, 1982) had subjects move a hand over two barriers and then return to a starting switch as quickly as possible. Retention performance reportedly dropped 50% over a four-month retention interval.

*Procedural responses*

Perhaps the most notable contributions to the study of the retention characteristics of procedural responses have been made by investigators concerned with the long-term retention of piloting skills. Summary papers and reviews have been prepared by several authors (e.g. Gardlin and Sitterley, 1972; Prophet, 1976a, 1976b; Smith and Matheny, 1976).

Studies dealing with the maintenance of instrument flying skills (Adams and Hufford, 1962; Mengelkoch *et al.*, 1971), manned spacecraft flight operations (Sitterley, 1974; Sitterley and Berge, 1972; Sitterley, Zaitzeff and Berge, 1972), and lunar landing skills (Cotterman and Wood, 1967) have consistently found that the important procedural aspects of flight control deteriorate to unacceptable levels over retention intervals measured in terms of weeks or months. Adams and Hufford (1962), for example, investigating the retention of a complex bomb-toss maneuver, found a 95% loss of procedural response proficiency over a 10-month retention interval, but found no practically important effect on the retention of continuous flight control responses. Likewise, data on the retention of basic combat skills (McDonald, 1967; Vineberg, 1975), the preparation and firing of Nike-Hercules missiles (Grimsley, 1969a, 1969b), and Second World War air combat gunnery procedures (Russel, Valentine and Harris, 1945) support the conclusion that procedural skills cannot be maintained in the absence of regular practice.

*Interpretations*

Several hypotheses have been offered to account for the difference in the retention characteristics of procedural and continuous motor tasks. One hypothesis is that procedural tasks are primarily *verbal* or *cognitive* in nature, and it is for this reason that they are more difficult to remember than primarily *motor*, continuous movements (e.g. Schmidt, 1982; Stelmach, 1974). A related hypothesis is that continuous movements are easier to remember because they are more integrated or coherent than procedural tasks. According to this hypothesis, continuous responses are not fundamentally different from procedural responses, they only promote retention to the extent that they are not 'random' and provide some degree of 'logical sequential patterning' of responses (e.g. Naylor and Briggs, 1961, p. 8). Another hypothesis suggests that differences in the retention characteristics of procedural and continuous motor tasks are at least partially attributable to differences in the way in which trials are indexed and errors are scored. Methods used to score the retention of discrete motor responses may be relatively more sensitive to slight performance deviations than methods used to score the retention of continuous responses (e.g. Adams, 1967; Schmidt, 1982). Yet another hypothesis is that continuous tasks may allow for considerably more repetition of responses than procedural tasks, resulting in overlearning and less forgetting (e.g. Adams, 1967; Schmidt, 1982).

Regardless of which interpretation finds support, regular refresher training is necessary to support the retention of procedural skills. Fortunately, procedural skills are typically less expensive and simpler to train and maintain than continuous tasks. As one example, Braby et al. (1982) had groups of naive subjects learn a complex engine starting procedure. Experimental subjects were pretrained using photographs or detailed line drawings of the equipment to help them locate controls and interpret displays. These subjects also were allowed to practice with low-cost paper mock-ups prior to training in a cockpit procedure trainer. Of those subjects trained in this manner, 12 of 19 performed the engine starting procedure correctly the first time in the trainer. This compares with two of 16 who performed the procedure correctly the first time in the trainer after using the student workbook and flight manual. Additionally, follow-up interviews with instructors in the field indicated that the experimental group required only about one-third as much time to first perform the engine starting procedure as the control group. As another example, Grimsley (1969a, 1969b) found that acquisition and long-term retention of a 92-step procedural task (firing a Nike-Hercules missile), following training on a line drawing of the operational equipment, to equal learning and retention following training on the actual equipment.

**Organization**

Organization may be regarded as inherent in a task, imposed by the learner, or made apparent through various forms of preliminary instruction (e.g. Kieras and Bovair, 1984). Considerable evidence (e.g. Noble et al., 1966; Swink, Trumbo and Noble, 1967; Trumbo et al., 1965; Trumbo, Noble and Swink, 1967) indicates that tasks inherently amenable to learner organization are learned at a faster rate than less structured tasks. Under conditions of moderate learning, highly structured tasks also are retained at a higher level than less structured tasks. Once learning reaches a more advanced stage, however, individuals apparently can retain less structured tasks as well as highly structured ones. As an example, Naylor, Briggs and Reed (1968) trained groups of subjects to perform two tasks simultaneously. The primary task was compensatory tracking. The secondary task involved monitoring a sequence of lights and responding with an appropriate button press. Responses were made either to a highly structured, spatially organized sequence of light activations (i.e. 1, 2, 3, 4, 5, 6, 7, 8, 9) or to a less structured sequence of light activations (i.e. 1, 5, 2, 9, 8, 3, 6, 7, 4). The secondary task was located to the left of the tracking display so that the subject had to look away from the tracking display in order to respond. Training was conducted for either 2 or 3 weeks and was followed by retention testing after either 1 or 4 weeks. As suggested above, retention performance of groups having the highly structured secondary task was better than the performance of groups having the less structured secondary task sequence. However, this effect held only for groups receiving moderate amounts (2 weeks) of training. The structure of the secondary task did not affect the loss of tracking or procedural proficiency in groups receiving greater amounts (3 weeks) of training.

**Display–control compatibility**

Certain display–control relationships appear more 'natural' or 'expected' than others, perhaps because they are more consistent with learners' past experiences with the environment or with principles of human biomechanics than incompatible display–control relationships (e.g. Adams, 1954; Fitts and Seeger, 1953). Examples of display–control relationships normally encountered in the environment include the following: moving a pointer to the right (display) by shifting a lever to the right (control); moving a pointer to the right by rotating a knob in a clockwise direction; or moving a pointer downward by shifting a lever forward (Melton, 1964).

The compatibility of display–control relationships influences the ease of motor learning and transfer (Adams, 1954; Briggs, 1969; Fitts and Seeger, 1953) as well as the quality of performance after a retention interval (Melton, 1964). Individuals training on high-compatibility equipment require less training to achieve and to maintain criterion levels of performance than individuals training on equipment having incompatible display–control relationships. Indeed, Fitts and Seeger (1953) suggested that the performance of individuals afforded a reasonable amount of training on equipment having incompatible display–control relationships may never catch up with the performance of individuals using high-compatibility equipment.

Incompatible display–control relationships may not pose serious performance problems for slow, self-paced tasks that allow a liberal margin for error. However, they have been found to disrupt the performance of time-shared tasks (e.g. Smith, 1959) and can be expected to have similar effects on the performance of externally paced or infrequently performed tasks.

**Specificity of displays**

Most motor tasks, such as tracking, depend heavily on the processing of visual information. At least during the initial stages of learning, the learner is forced to rely on cues he receives from the task display to guide his performance. Later in learning, however, the learner relies more on proprioceptive or other internal sources of information and depends less on the display and other external cues (e.g. Bahrick, Noble and Fitts, 1954; Fleishman and Rich, 1963). This suggests that cues designed to supplement the information provided by the task display may be informative early in learning and facilitate the learning process, but may be relatively uniformative once the learner has 'internalized' the performance.

Trumbo, Ulrich and Noble (1965) tested this hypothesis using a pursuit tracking task and task displays that varied in 'specificity'. Display specificity involved a numerical code and/or several grid systems that, when superimposed on the face of an oscilloscope, permitted several levels of target-location cuing. As suggested, the early acquisition of the tracking task was facilitated under conditions of high-display specificity. However, the specificity of the display did not affect the final levels of skill attained by the learners nor their one-month retention performance. Apparently, later in learning, supplementary cues from a display do not provide information over and above that which already is provided by internal sources and consequently are not important as determinants of retention.

# PROCEDURAL VARIABLES

## Repetition

Given information about the correctness of the response, response repetition improves the performance of both verbal (e.g. Hellyer, 1962) and motor tasks (e.g. Krueger, 1929). As shown in numerous experiments, repetition is a primary determinant of learning, retention, and transfer (e.g. Farr, 1986; Gardlin and Sitterley, 1972; Hagman, 1980; Hurlock and Montague, 1982). Hagman (1980), for example, found that repeating a 52-step procedural task, required to test alternator electrical output, from one to four times during training reduced task performance time and errors during learning and at a retention test conducted 2 weeks later.

Adding repetitions after task proficiency has been achieved also is effective in promoting retention. This procedure is termed *overtraining* (Krueger, 1929). The term 'overtraining' implies something which is excessive and wasteful. However, tests of the effectiveness of overtraining in sustaining skills suggest that just the opposite is the case (e.g. Fleishman and Parker, 1962; Schendel and Hagman, 1982).

Schendel and Hagman's (1982) experimental design depended on the use of three groups of soldiers. One group was trained on the experimental task (assembly/disassembly of the M60 machine gun) to a criterion of one errorless performance. Eight weeks later, soldiers in this group were tested for retention and retrained. The second group was treated in the same manner as the first, except that soldiers in this group received varying amounts of refresher training midway (4 weeks) through the retention interval. The amount of refresher training each soldier received depended on the number of trials that he or she required to achieve one errorless performance during initial training. Thus, for example, if a soldier required four trials to achieve one errorless disassembly and assembly of the weapon, he or she received four additional trials as refresher training. The third group also was treated like the first except that it received 100% initial overtraining. If a soldier in this group required four trials to achieve criterion on the task initially, he or she received four additional trials as overtraining.

Results showed that both groups receiving additional training performed better than the baseline control. In addition, however, the group that received initial overtraining performed as well after 8 weeks of no practice as the group that received refresher training midway through the retention interval.

An illustration of the way in which repetition is believed to support retention is shown in Figure 3.1. The dotted line represents a hypothetical point of minimum task proficiency. Once performance falls below this point, a need for refresher training would be indicated. Subjects in the high-repetition

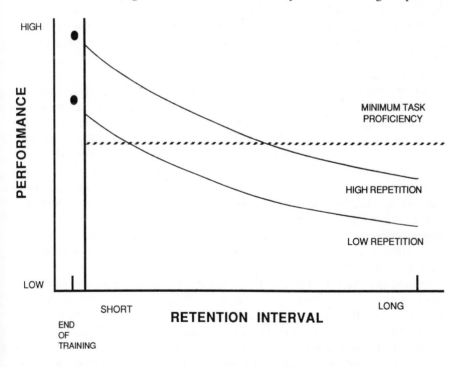

**Figure 3.1.** Learning and retention for low- and high-repetition training groups.

training condition will take longer to decline to this point, and, thus, will require less frequent refresher training than subjects in the low-repetition training condition. Furthermore, high-repetition subjects will outperform low-repetition subjects over the entire duration of the retention interval (Loftus, 1985; Slamecka and McElree, 1983).

## Repetition schedule

### Verbal tasks

For verbal tasks, results of extensive laboratory and field research indicate that acquisition is better when the interval between task repetitions is minimized (i.e. massed training). However, retention is better when the interval between repetitions is increased (i.e. spaced training) (e.g. Crowder, 1976; Glover and Corkill, 1987; Greene, 1989).

In general, the retention benefits of spaced training for verbal tasks increase as the interval between repetitions increases (Crowder, 1976), provided that it is not too long (Glenberg, 1974; Young, 1966). Presumably, when the inter-repetition interval is too long, excessive forgetting occurs between repetitions, and learning suffers (Atkinson and Shiffrin, 1968).

It is not clear how long is too long for an inter-repetition interval. However, some research suggests that spacing benefits with verbal materials sometimes can be found with inter-repetition intervals of up to 2 weeks (Glenberg and Lehman, 1980).

Two interpretations have been offered to account for the retention benefits accompanying spaced training. One suggests that spacing improves recall because to-be-remembered information is stored with a greater variety of retrieval cues (e.g. Crowder, 1976). When a word, for example, is repeated twice in succession (i.e. massed training), each mental representation of the word will have a very similar set of accompanying associations or cues (e.g. adjacent words, casual thoughts, etc.) to aid later retrieval from memory. If the repetitions are spaced, however, each representation will have a set of potentially different retrieval cues. The greater the number and variety of these accompanying cues, the greater the benefit on memory will be.

The other interpretation suggests that learners become bored with successive repetitions of the same material. So when they receive two presentations of a word, one after another, they do not devote as much attention or mental effort to processing the second presentation. To illustrate this point, Johnston and Uhl (1976) had two groups of college students perform two tasks concurrently. The primary task was to listen to several lists of about 100 words presented over headphones to the right ear at a rate of one every 5 seconds. Some of the words were repeated four times in the list, either in succession (massed repetitions), or at four separate times during the list (spaced repetitions). The secondary task was to press a button as quickly as possible whenever a faint tone was heard over the headphones in the left ear.

As predicted, students retained more words after spaced than after massed presentations. In addition, their reaction times to the tones decreased across successive repetitions when they were massed, whereas the times increased with repetitions when they were spaced. These results are depicted in Figure 3.2.

Presumably, under massed repetitions, students paid less attention to the successive word presentations and had more attention to devote to detection of the tone, whereas the opposite occurred when word repetitions were spaced.

*Motor tasks*

For motor tasks, learning and retention appear comparable under massed and spaced repetition schedules (Holding, 1965; Schmidt, 1975). Although performance of continuous tasks appears better under spaced scheduling (Ammons, 1951), massing of repetitions often leads to boredom and fatigue that mask

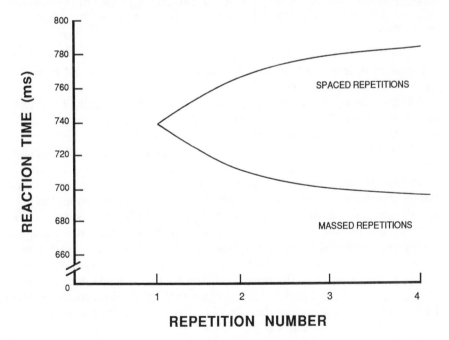

**Figure 3.2.** Time to detect tone presentations during word repetitions. From Johnston and Uhl, 1976, *Journal of Experimental Psychology: Human Learning and Memory*, **2**, 156. Copyright 1976 by the American Psychological Association. Adapted by permission.

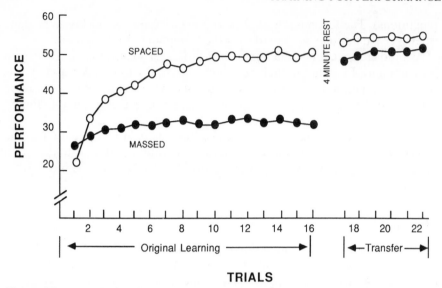

**TRIALS**

**Figure 3.3.** Acquisition (left) and transfer (right) performance on the stabilometer. From Stelmach, 1969, *Research Quarterly*, **40**, 200. Copyright 1969 by the American Alliance for Health, Physical Education, Recreation and Dance. Adapted by permission.

the amount of learning that actually takes place (e.g. Adams and Reynolds, 1954; Lewis and Lowe, 1956).

As an example, Figure 3.3 shows results obtained by Stelmach (1969) using the stabilometer. The task entailed having each subject attempt to remain balanced on a horizontally pivoted board. Scores on the stabilometer represent the total amount of board movement, measured in 12-degree increments, during a 30-second interval. Subjects in the spaced practice group received 16 trials (30 seconds practice/30 seconds rest) before the 4-minute rest period. Subjects in the massed practice group received an equivalent amount of practice (8 minutes) but without inter-trial rest periods. Following the rest period, both groups transferred to a spaced practice condition. Under this condition, both groups received six trials of spaced practice with 30-second rest periods between trials. Before the 4-minute rest period, the performance of the massed practice group was depressed relative to the spaced practice group. However, after the rest period, once subjects in the massed practice group had had a chance to recover from the effect of fatigue, the performance of the two groups was statistically equivalent.

There are some training situations where spaced repetitions are definitely recommended. These include the training of (a) dangerous tasks where fatigue from continuous practice could put performers at risk (Schmidt, 1975); (b) poorly motivated learners who are adversely affected by the rigorous nature of massed scheduling (e.g. Kleinman, 1980); and (c) high ability learners who tend to make more responses during massed scheduling, quickly become fatigued, and accordingly respond at a lower level of proficiency than learners of lower ability (e.g. Eysenck and Frith, 1977). Spaced schedules also appear more effective for mental practice (e.g. Corbin, 1972).

**Mental practice**

Repetition need not be overt or 'hands on' to be effective. This is fairly obvious for verbal tasks for which rehearsal rarely is overt. It is not so obvious for motor tasks where, by definition, physical movements are required for demonstration of successful learning, retention, or transfer.

Undoubtedly, physical practice is important in the acquisition and performance of motor tasks. However, there is evidence that the performance of motor tasks also can be enhanced by mental practice (e.g. Corbin, 1972; Feltz and Landers, 1983; Richardson, 1967a, 1967b).

Mental practice involves imagining the performance of a movement without overt action. The beneficial effects of mental practice do not appear restricted to particular types of tasks; however, they do appear larger for cognitively oriented motor tasks, such as procedural tasks, than for predominantly physical or strength tasks (e.g. Feltz and Landers, 1983).

Different hypotheses have been offered to account for the beneficial effect of mental practice on motor learning and performance. Based on a meta-analysis of 60 studies, Feltz and Landers (1983) advanced two hypotheses as most reasonable. One hypothesis suggests that mental practice serves primarily to promote the cognitive–symbolic, problem-solving aspects of motor learning (e.g. Sackett, 1934). For example, mental practice may give a performer a chance to generate and mentally 'try out' certain hypotheses about the best course of action to take under a given set of conditions. According to this hypothesis, motor tasks that are more cognitive in nature are more likely to show positive effects of mental practice than ones that are relatively difficult to represent symbolically. Another equally compelling hypothesis is that mental practice serves a kind of priming function which allows the performer to prepare for action, adjust his or her arousal level, and generally prepare for good performance (Schmidt, 1982).

Although clear data showing benefits of mental practice are difficult to obtain, the weight of the evidence appears to support the following conclusions: (a) a combination of physical and mental practice is better than mental practice alone (Singer, 1975); (b) mental practice is effective both early in training when verbal–cognitive processes are most involved (e.g. Adams, 1971; Fitts and Posner, 1967; James, 1890; Singer and Witker, 1970), and later in training when movements have been learned and performers are more likely to be able to conceptualize them mentally (Clark, 1960; Singer, 1975); and (c) mental practice sessions probably should not exceed 5 minutes in length if effective concentration is to be maintained (e.g. Gilmore and Stolurow, 1951; Twining, 1949). More on the subject of mental practice is provided in John Annett's discussion of skill acquisition in Chapter 2 of this volume.

## Knowledge of results

Knowledge of results (KR) refers to externally provided information about the discrepancy between a learner's actual response and the criterion response. Announcements such as 'right', 'wrong', and '3 inches too far' are all examples of KR. An account of the role of KR in motor learning is beyond the scope of this chapter; there are several literature reviews available on the subject (Adams, 1968, 1971; Annett, 1969 and Chapter 2 of this volume; Bilodeau, 1969; Newell, 1977; Salmoni, Schmidt and Walter, 1984). Two findings from that literature, however, are especially pertinent:

1. The early acquisition of a skill depends heavily upon KR. Performance generally improves with KR and deteriorates, or shows no further improvement, when it is withdrawn (e.g. Bilodeau, Bilodeau and Schumsky, 1959; Newell, 1974). Rate of improvement during acquisition usually increases (up to a point) with increases in both the absolute frequency (e.g. Bilodeau, 1969) and the precision of KR (e.g. Rogers, 1974).
2. When performance is evaluated by a long-term retention test, individuals who receive more or better KR perform best during acquisition but typically perform *worse* during retention testing than individuals who receive less 'useful' KR (e.g. Schmidt *et al.*, 1989) or have KR gradually withdrawn during practice (e.g. Winstein and Schmidt, 1990).

The first finding is consistent with common understandings of the action of KR. The second finding is not. This finding is easier to understand in the context of the research in which it was generated.

Schmidt *et al.* (1989) had four groups of college students learn to perform a complex arm movement under different conditions of KR. One group received KR (movement–time error) after each trial. The other groups received KR in summary form only after the last trial in a set was complete. Summary KR entailed viewing a graph showing errors across trials within a set. The lengths of the sets (the number of trials summarized on the graph) varied across groups and were either 5, 10, or 15 trials in length. Training continued for 90 trials and was followed by two, 25-trial retention tests without KR. One test occurred after a 10-minute retention interval; the other test occurred after a 2-day retention interval.

As shown in Figure 3.4, students in the one-trial summary condition performed best during acquisition. Students in the other groups showed slower

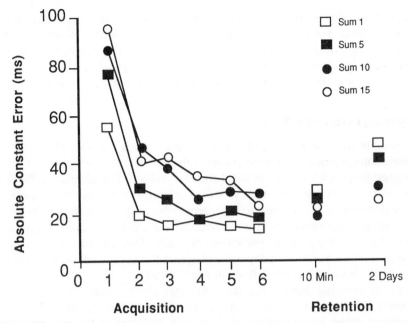

**Figure 3.4.**    Mean errors in a movement-patterning task for four different summary-KR lengths in acquisition and on no-KR retention tests given after 10 minutes or 2 days. From Schmidt *et al.*, 1989, *Journal of Experimental Psychology: Learning, Memory, and Cognition*, **15**, 355. Copyright 1989 by the American Psychological Association. Adapted by permission.

improvement rates and lower end-of-training performance levels. In general, larger movement–time errors were observed as the summary length of KR increased. During retention, however, the 15-trial group performed best. Furthermore, larger errors were observed as the summary length of KR provided during acquisition decreased. Thus, a clear negative relationship was found between performance during acquisition and performance during retention. These results are consistent with those obtained earlier by Lavery (1962), which until recently were regarded as spurious (e.g. Schmidt, 1982).

In the Winstein and Schmidt (1990) experiment, KR was given in acquisition on every training trial (100% condition) or 'faded', such that it was given on every trial early in training and was gradually withdrawn as training progressed (50% condition). Retention performance was tested after 10 minutes and 2 days, either with or without KR (separate experiments). In both experiments, students in the 100% and 50%-faded conditions performed comparably during acquisition. However, retention scores favored the 50%-faded condition with larger differences appearing at the longer retention interval. Again, the data contradict traditional views of learning and retention. In this case, students afforded 50% less KR during learning showed better long-term retention.

As observed by Schmidt and Bjork (1989), these results suggest that, while KR is essential for initial guidance, at some point during learning, it can produce a kind of dependency. The learner comes to rely too heavily on KR for response guidance purposes and, consequently, fails to put forth the effort necessary in learning to sustain effective performance during retention.

## Response-produced feedback

Movements have sights, sounds, and feelings associated with them. These sensory consequences of movement are referred to collectively as 'response-produced feedback'. The theoretical status of response-produced feedback is controversial, but few doubt its practical importance for the acquisition of motor skills. Early in acquisition, the learner appears to use KR, together with the feedback information that is received, to establish a memorial representation of how a correct response should be made. This representation is weak initially, so the learner must depend heavily on KR for information about the correctness of the response (Bilodeau et al., 1959).

Later in learning, however, after a stronger representation of the correct response has been stored in memory, the learner can detect and correct movement errors by comparing the feedback qualities of the response with those of the stored representation. The learner no longer needs to depend on KR for error information. This information is inherent in the feedback that the learner has received from past performances and that is received from the present performance, and it enables the learner to 'know' when a performance is correct in the absence of KR (e.g. Adams, 1971, 1987).

Findings on the importance of response-produced feedback for learning have been consistent. In general, the more response-produced feedback a learner receives, the more accurate and confident his responses will be (Schmidt and Wrisberg, 1971; Stelmach, 1973). In addition, retention is facilitated by increasing the number of feedback channels during training, as shown for a wide variety of tasks and retention intervals (e.g. Mengelkoch et al., 1971; Stelmach and Kelso, 1975), with the most important feedback channel being vision (Adams, Goetz and Marshall, 1972; Adams, Gopher and Lintern, 1977; Henderson, 1977).

## Augmented feedback

Besides response-produced feedback, which is intrinsic to the response(s) to be learned, it is possible to provide augmented feedback during training in the form of extra cues or information that would normally not accompany the task being performed. The presence of augmented feedback during training typically facilitates performance and speeds up training (e.g. Briggs, 1969). Unfortunately, these beneficial effects are transitory and usually do not transfer to situations where augmented feedback is not present. As shown in Figure 3.5, performers typically show no benefit from having been trained with augmented cues once these cues are removed. For example, Bilodeau (1952) showed this to be the case for a target gunnery task. Under the normal sighting procedure, gunners were required to adjust their controls so as to frame or superimpose a number of dots on a moving target airplane. Gunners in Group A received normal feedback in the form of visual error (i.e. the spatial difference between the dots and the target). Those in Group B received normal feedback plus augmented feedback in the form of a target color change from white to red when a response shifted from incorrect to correct. Although subjects in Group B performed better than subjects in Group A when augmented feedback (i.e. target reddening) was present, they failed to show superior performance when the augmented feedback was removed.

The interpretation offered for the lack of positive transfer from augmented to non-augmented feedback conditions is reminiscent of the interpretation offered by Schmidt and Bjork (1989) and others to account for the failure of KR to affect performance in the expected manner following acquisition. Learners come to depend on the augmented cues. When these cues are removed, performance declines because the intrinsic task cues normally present to guide performance have not been attended to (e.g. Boldovici, 1987; Kinkade, 1963).

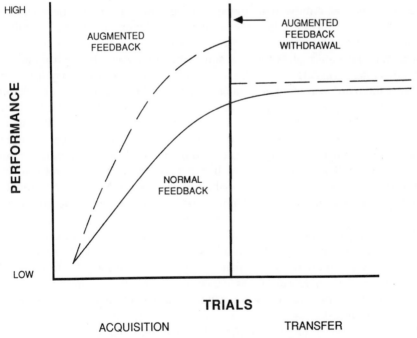

**Figure 3.5.** Effect of withdrawing augmented feedback during training.

A procedure not totally unlike the KR 'fading' procedure employed by Winstein and Schmidt (1990) has been recommended as a means for promoting the rapid training effects of augmented feedback while encouraging discrimination and use of intrinsic task cues necessary for successful performance when augmented cues are withdrawn. The procedure is called 'adaptive withdrawal' (Lintern and Roscoe, 1980). Under this procedure, augmented feedback is provided only when a learner's response exceeds a specific error limit or deviates significantly off course. As training continues and responses improve, augmented feedback is withdrawn because the number of error-free responses gradually increases.

The use of an adaptive withdrawal technique makes good sense on an intuitive level, but research testing its utility has largely been negative. This is not to suggest that some degree of adaptivity in the delivery of augmented feedback cannot be effective under certain conditions (e.g. Boldovici, 1979), only to indicate that adaptive techniques cannot be applied uncritically to the skills arena (e.g. Adams, 1987). Issues surrounding the use of adaptive training are covered in greater depth by Lintern (Chapter 6 in this volume).

## Testing

Training generally consists of study trials, where subjects are presented with the information or movement to be learned, and test trials where subjects attempt to recall or reproduce the response from memory. Testing usually is conducted for two reasons: to motivate learners to study and to assess how much they have learned. A third reason to include testing during training is to enhance long-term retention. Like several other variables treated in this chapter that have differential effects on acquisition and retention, study trials tend to promote acquisition, whereas test trials tend to promote retention (e.g. Hagman, 1981, 1983; Hagman and Brosvic, in preparation; Izawa, 1970).

The retention benefits associated with testing are quite reliable and found with rote verbal material (e.g. Allen, Mahler and Estes, 1969; Hogan and Kintsch, 1971; Roediger and Payne, 1982; Thompson, Wenger and Bartling, 1978, Exp. 4), text passages (e.g. Foos and Fisher, 1988; Nungester and Duchastal, 1982), and motor tasks (Hagman, 1981, 1983; Hagman and Brosvic, in preparation). In studying the long-term retention of verbal paired-associates, Allen *et al.* (1969), for example, found that an immediate test trial, performed after 10 paired stimulus and response study trials, reduced error frequency nearly 50% as compared to 10 paired study trials without the test trial. In addition, long-term retention, as measured by response times and errors, showed further improvement when five test trials were introduced prior to the final retention test.

Hagman (1981; 1983, Exp. 2) first demonstrated the long-term retention benefits of test trials for a motor task. Three groups of subjects either repeated or alternated study and test trials while being trained to reproduce the end location of straight, horizontal arm movements. During study trials, subjects moved a slide along a linear track until contacting a physical stop which was pre-positioned by the experimenter at the criterion end location. During test trials, subjects attempted to reproduce the criterion end location with the stop removed. The sequence of study and test trials for each group is shown in Table 3.1. Recall accuracy associated with each sequence was compared during learning and after retention intervals of 3 minutes and 24 hours.

The left-hand side of Figure 3.6 shows the mean absolute error recall scores for learning test trials; the right-hand side of the figure depicts the mean recall scores for retention test trials. End-location recall was more accurate when study trials were repeated or alternated with test trials during training than when test trials were repeated. This effect was most apparent at end-of-cycle test trials (i.e. Trials 6, 12, and 18). However, study-trial repetition and study- and test-trial alternation methods were not nearly as effective as test-trial repetition in promoting retention.

**Test expectation**

At least for verbal materials, even the expectation that a test will be given will promote retention over and above that found when a test is not expected (Foos and Clark, 1983). Apparently, individuals study differently depending on whether or not they think they will be evaluated. They also study differently depending on *how* they expect to be tested. Schmidt (1983), for example, found that subjects remember prose in greater detail when they expect to be tested via recall as opposed to recognition. Test expectation followed by actual testing, however, still produces the best retention, even though people generally prefer test-free training (Halpin and Halpin, 1982).

**Table 3.1.** Learning and retention trial sequence for each training method group (S = Study; T = Test).

| Group | Cycle 1 | | | | | | Cycle 2 | | | | | | Cycle 3 | | | | | | 3 min | 24 hr |
|---|---|---|---|---|---|---|---|---|---|---|---|---|---|---|---|---|---|---|---|---|
| | 1 | 2 | 3 | 4 | 5 | 6 | 7 | 8 | 9 | 10 | 11 | 12 | 13 | 14 | 15 | 16 | 17 | 18 | T | T |
| S/T | S | T | S | T | S | T | S | T | S | T | S | T | S | T | S | T | S | T | T | T |
| T | S | T | T | T | T | T | S | T | T | T | T | T | S | T | T | T | T | T | T | T |
| S | S | S | S | S | S | T | S | S | S | S | S | T | S | S | S | S | S | T | T | T |

*Note*: From 'Retention of military tasks: A review' by J. D. Hagman and A.M. Rose, 1983, *Human Factors*, **25**(2), 203. Copyright 1983 by the Human Factors Society, Inc. Adapted by permission.

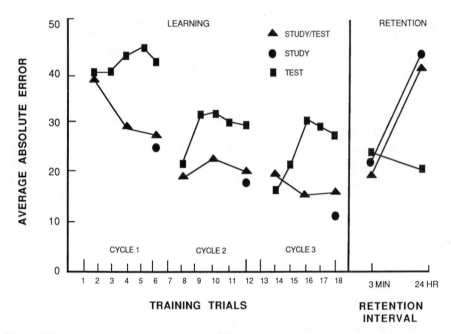

**Figure 3.6.** Average test scores at acquisition and retention trials performed by each training method group. From Hagman, 1983, *Journal of Experimental Psychology: Learning, Memory, and Cognition*, **9**, 339. Copyright 1983 by the American Psychological Association. Adapted by permission.


### Variability of practice

Variability of practice influences the learning, transfer, and long-term retention of both verbal (Battig, 1972, 1979) and motor responses (Lee and Magill, 1983; Shea and Morgan, 1979; Shea and Zimny, 1983; Wulf and Schmidt, 1988). Shea and Morgan (1979), for example, examined the learning of three motor tasks (referred to here as A, B, and C) that required knocking over a series of barriers in a prescribed order as quickly as possible. Each task was defined by a separate barrier knock-down sequence, indicated by a diagram shown to subjects before the start of each movement. Training involved practicing these movements in either a blocked or random presentation order over a total of 54 trials. Blocked practice required subjects to perform 18 trials of Task A, then 18 trials of Task B, followed by 18 trials of Task C. Random practice involved a random ordering of Tasks A, B, and C across the 54 training trials. After training, subjects were tested for retention after no-practice intervals of 10 minutes and 10 days. The major results from this experiment are presented in Figure 3.7.

As shown in the figure, blocked-order training produced better results

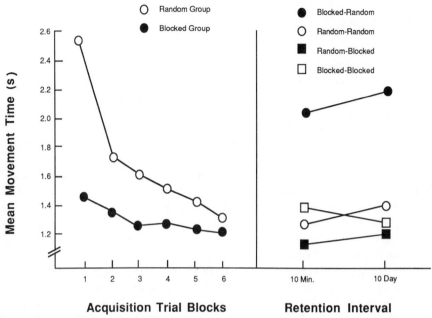

**Figure 3.7.** Acquisition (left) and retention (right) performance on complex movement and speed tasks under random and blocked presentations. From Shea and Morgan, 1979, *Journal of Experimental Psychology: Human Learning and Memory*, **5**, 183. Copyright 1979 by the American Psychological Association. Adapted by permission.

during training trials, but random-order training produced better results at both retention tests.

Drawing on the previous theorizing of Battig (1979) to explain these findings, Shea and Zimny (1983) reasoned that random practice produces inter-task interference (caused by switching from one movement type to another) during training. Learning under such interfering conditions encourages more elaborate processing of movement-related information and increases distinctiveness among the movements to be learned.

An alternative interpretation was offered by Lee and Magill (1983), who argued that random practice during training causes forgetting of the 'solution' to the movement problem. This forgetting forced subjects in the random practice condition repeatedly to regenerate movement solutions. In contrast, subjects in the blocked practice condition were able to use the solution generated on the previous trial(s), leading to fewer separate generations and less learning.

Regardless of the interpretation, these results carry clear implications for the design of training programs that require coverage of multiple tasks over successive training sessions. They also lend further evidence to the view that performance during acquisition is not necessarily indicative of performance at retention and transfer.

**Refresher training**

Refresher training frequently is used to offset the effects of forgetting, to provide opportunities for new learning, or to improve on-the-job safety and performance (e.g. Brown, Briggs and Naylor, 1963; Cotterman and Wood, 1967). For instance, Sitterley and Berge (1972), studying the effects of various practice strategies on the long-term retention of simulated manned spacecraft operations, found that procedural performance deteriorated to unacceptable levels within 1 to 4 months of no practice. After 1 month, subjects took five times longer to complete the procedural sequence than they did at the end of training. Additional performance decrements were not evident after 2 and 3 months of no practice, but after 4 months of no practice, subjects required 17 times more time to complete the procedural sequence than they did following training. In sharp contrast, subjects afforded some form of refresher training showed no signs of losing their end-of-training proficiency levels over retention intervals of up to 6 months.

Time to refresher train individuals to their original levels of task proficiency is consistently less than 50% of initial training time (Ammons *et al.*, 1958; Mengelkoch *et al.*, 1971). However, retraining time will vary depending on such variables as: (a) length of the retention interval (e.g. Neumann and Ammons, 1957); (b) nature of the task (e.g. Ammons *et al.*, 1958; Lersten, 1969); (c) frequency of refresher training sessions (Hagman and Wells, in preparation); and (d) temporal spacing of successive sessions (e.g. Bahrick, 1979). As noted later in this chapter, retraining time also is affected by subjects' ability levels (e.g. Grimsley, 1969b).

*Length of the retention interval*

Neumann and Ammons's (1957) subjects learned a procedural switch-flipping sequence to a criterion of two consecutive correct trials. Initial learning was followed for different groups by one of five retention intervals ranging in duration from 1 minute to 1 year. Results showed that forgetting occurred after only 20 minutes without practice, and it was nearly complete after 1 year. Furthermore, relearning was faster than original learning for all groups, and the number of trials required to regain criterion-level proficiency increased with the length of the retention interval.

*Nature of the task*

Different tasks have different retention characteristics. Having information about the rates at which specific tasks will be forgotten and the factors contributing to this forgetting is critical for effective and efficient management of refresher training resources.

Shields, Goldberg and Dressel (1979) examined the retention characteristics of 20 common soldier tasks over retention intervals ranging from 4 to 12 months following initial basic combat training. The tasks examined were either verbal (e.g. reporting of enemy information) or procedural in nature (e.g. loading and firing the M203 grenade launcher, donning the gas mask, and cardiopulmonary resuscitation). They found that retention, as measured by the percentage of soldiers performing each task correctly (i.e. those receiving a 'Go') declined over time, and that the rate of decline depended on the task.

The number of steps required by a task was the best predictor of forgetting. Shields *et al.* (1979) also found consistencies in the kinds of steps missed across tasks. Soldiers tended to forget steps that were not cued by the equipment or by previous steps, such as those involving safety. In preparing the M72A2 light antitank weapon for firing, for example, soldiers frequently forget the step involving checking to make sure that the backblast area is clear prior to missile launch.

*Frequency of sessions*

Forgetting is rarely, if ever, complete. In practice, some skill almost always is retained or 'saved' and can be applied at a later refresher training session (e.g. Neumann and Ammons, 1957). Perhaps it is because of this saving that relearning during refresher training usually is faster than initial learning. This effect is shown in Figure 3.8 which presents the theoretical course of learning and retention over multiple refresher training sessions.

The observation that savings from prior learning exist suggests that the need for refresher training will decrease as the number of prior refresher training sessions increases. Hagman and Wells (in preparation, Exp. 1) recently confirmed this hypothesis. They varied the interval (i.e. 1, 7, and 21 days) between initial training and each of three successive refresher training sessions for separate groups of college students attempting to learn a paired-associates aircraft identification task. They found that: (a) the amount of required relearning varied inversely with the number of prior refresher training sessions; and (b) the amount of savings incurred from these sessions was an inverse function of the temporal interval separating them.

*Temporal spacing of sessions*

The timing of refresher training sessions is complicated by a number of practical considerations. If time intervals between successive sessions are too long, then performance may fall below acceptable levels and entail considerable risk. Emergencies may arise, requiring correct performance, before an individual has had an opportunity to retrain. If time intervals between successive sessions are too short, then administrative costs will be unnecessarily inflated.

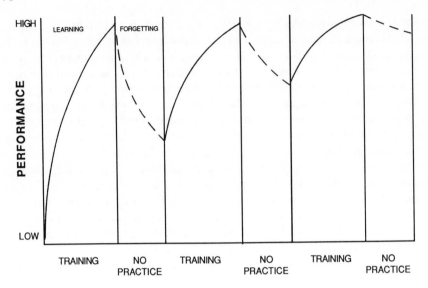

**TRAINING SESSIONS AND NO-PRACTICE INTERVALS**

**Figure 3.8.**   Theoretical course of learning and retention over multiple refresher training sessions.

Training effectiveness considerations also are important. Bahrick's (1979,
Exp. 2) results suggest that, at least for verbal tasks, the length of the interval
between successive refresher training sessions should be tailored to job performance demands. Bahrick's separate groups of college students learned 50
English–Spanish paired associates over six successive refresher training sessions, separated by constant intervals of 0, 1, and 30 days. All groups were
then tested for retention 30 days after the last refresher training session.
Performance improved monotonically over the six refresher training sessions
for all groups and was faster for shorter inter-session intervals. At the 30-day
retention test, however, both the 0-day and 1-day groups showed significant
forgetting, whereas the 30-day group did not.

Bahrick (1979, Exp. 2) argued that students in the 30-day group were able
to determine what learning strategies were most effective for remembering
information over 30-day intervals and change ineffective strategies in anticipation of the 30-day retention test. In contrast, students in the 0-day and 1-day
groups, had no opportunity to try out the effectiveness of their learning strategies for long-term retention prior to taking the 30-day test.

If correct, then refresher training sessions should be scheduled at intervals
similar to usage intervals experienced on the job. For example, if one expects
to recall or use certain information about once every three months or so on
the job, then refresher training should not be scheduled more frequently than

that. Otherwise, to-be-remembered information may not be encoded in a manner that will allow it to endure over a similarly long retention interval.

## LEARNER VARIABLES

For motor tasks, rate of acquisition varies as a positive function of the initial ability level of the learner. For example, research using eight training tasks ranging in complexity from a simple reaction time task to a problem-solving task (Fox, Taylor and Caylor, 1969), research using a 92-step procedural task (Grimsley, 1969b), and research using 13 basic training skills (Vineberg, 1975) all defined ability in terms of subjects' mental aptitude test scores and all indicated faster learning by those who had higher scores. Other studies, defining ability in terms of the learner's early performance on a to-be-retained balancing task (Carron, 1971; Carron and Marteniuk, 1970) or using expert judgments of motor proficiency as an index of ability on five novel gross motor tasks (Purdy and Lockhart, 1962) obtained analogous results.

In addition to being faster learners, individuals of higher ability usually achieve higher end-of-training performance levels and retain their skills at higher levels than individuals of lower ability (e.g. Grimsley, 1969b; Vineberg, 1975). As a result, individuals of higher ability require less refresher training than individuals of lower ability. Furthermore, refresher training can be shorter for persons of higher ability because they relearn more quickly than persons of lower ability (e.g. Grimsley, 1969b).

Forgetting functions may start and end higher over a given retention interval for individuals of higher ability than for those of lower ability, but the weight of the evidence suggests that individuals of different initial ability forget at the same rate (e.g. Carron, 1971; Grimsley, 1969; Purdy and Lockhart, 1962; Vineberg, 1975). If this is the case, it suggests that retention differences found among individuals of varying ability can be reduced by ensuring a common level of original learning during acquisition. Of course, this would mean providing additional training time to individuals of lower ability (Hagman and Rose, 1983).

The observation that individuals of higher and lower ability forget at the same rate is counterintuitive and may stem from difficulties associated with accurately indexing learning levels. Performance during acquisition can be contaminated by variables that have temporary elevating and depressing effects. Additionally, inferences about learning are susceptible to errors induced by scoring artifacts (e.g. ceiling effects).

Another potential source of difficulty is indexing forgetting levels. For example, if the interval is too short, differential forgetting rates may not have time to appear. Also, any attempt to measure forgetting rates must entail the use of at least two retention tests. One of these tests should occur immediately following training; the other should occur at the end of the retention interval. The lack of an immediate retention test is a common failing of retention experiments. Simply because everyone was trained to a common criterion does not mean that everyone is starting at the same point on a retention curve.

# PREDICTING RETENTION

Answers to questions like the following are of significant practical importance to training planners in military, industrial, and other educational contexts:

1. When will a specific task be forgotten?
2. Which tasks are most susceptible to forgetting?
3. What proportion of job incumbents will be able to perform a task correctly after an extended period of no practice?
4. When and how often should refresher training be scheduled for maximum payoff?

Various approaches have been taken toward finding answers to these questions (e.g. Goldberg and O'Rourke, 1989; Hall *et al.*, 1986; Konoske, Wetzel and Montague, 1983; Rigg and Gray, 1981; Rose *et al.*, 1985a; Schendel *et al.*, 1984). Two are highlighted here. One approach uses task characteristics to predict retention; the other approach relies on the process of self-assessment. Both approaches grew out of research sponsored or conducted by the Army during the late 1970s and mid-1980s.

## Task rating approach

Rose *et al.* (1985a) developed a procedure for predicting the retention of both cognitive and motor tasks over retention intervals of up to 1 year. As described in the associated user's manual (Rose *et al.*, 1985b) and elsewhere (Hagman, Hayes and Bierwirth, 1986), the Rose *et al.* procedure depends on performing two steps. The first step involves rating each task in terms of its difficulty to remember. This rating is based on specific task characteristics known to influence retention. One characteristic, for example, is whether or not a task is supported by performance aids (e.g. technical manuals, flow charts, checklists). Performance aids reduce memory load, making tasks easier to perform with them than without them (e.g. Hagman and Schendel, 1981; Shields, Joyce and Van Wert, 1979). Another characteristic is task length, as defined by the number of performance steps required. Retention tends to decrease as task length increases (e.g. Shields, Goldberg and Dressel, 1979), and, thus, longer tasks tend to be more difficult to remember than shorter tasks. In all, tasks are rated on a maximum of 10 characteristics (see

Table 3.2) and receive an empirically derived retention rating score from 1 to 220 based on the presence or absence of each characteristic. The lower the rating score, the faster a task is expected to be forgotten.

The second step involves inserting a task's retention rating score into the retention prediction matrix shown in Table 3.3. The numbers along the left-hand column of the table are the task retention rating scores; the numbers along the top row are the months since last practicing the task. The numbers in the body of the table refer to the percentage of soldiers expected to be able to perform the task correctly.

For instance, suppose that the task 'Identify and employ hand grenades' has a retention rating score of 120 and has not been practiced for 2 months. Reading across the '120' row to the column labeled 2 months, it is predicted that 40% of the soldiers will be able to perform this task correctly. Table 3.4 shows retention rating scores for some additional Army tasks.

To test the validity of task retention rating scores, Rose *et al.* (1985a) trained three groups of soldiers ($n = 140$) on 22 tasks to a criterion of one correct performance. Groups were then tested for retention either 2, 4, or 6 months later. A strong positive relationship was observed between actual and predicted performance at each retention test, with correlations being around 0.9 at the 2-month retention test and 0.7 at the other two retention tests.

## Self-assessment approach

A drawback to categorization schemes, like the one developed by Rose *et al.* (1985a), is that they only provide relatively general guidance. They are less useful in dealing with particulars—predicting how well a particular individual will perform a particular task after a given retention interval. Research performed by Schendel *et al.* (1984) was carried out in a preliminary attempt to find a solution to this problem. The research was based on the assumption that individuals can assess their own memory states with reasonable accuracy (e.g. Flavell and Wellman, 1977; Hart, 1965; Hunt, 1980; Yussen and Levy, 1975). Data collection involved the use of a questionnaire that required soldiers to attempt to predict their own retention of a task immediately in advance of performing it. It also involved asking soldiers to rate the confidence they had in the accuracy of their self assessments.

**Table 3.2.**  Task characteristics related to retention.

| | |
|---|---|
| • Job/memory aided | • Quality of job/memory aids |
| • Length | • Definite step sequence |
| • Built-in logic to steps | • Mental requirements |
| • Number of facts | • Complexity of facts |
| • Movement demands | • Time demands |

**Table 3.3.**   Retention prediction matrix.

| Retention rating score | Retention interval (Months) | | | | | | | | | | | |
|---|---|---|---|---|---|---|---|---|---|---|---|---|
| | 1 | 2 | 3 | 4 | 5 | 6 | 7 | 8 | 9 | 10 | 11 | 12 |
| 180 or more | 100 | 100 | 100 | 100 | 100 | 100 | 100 | 100 | 100 | 100 | 100 | 100 |
| 175 | 97 | 96 | 92 | 90 | 87 | 85 | 83 | 81 | 79 | 77 | 75 | 73 |
| 170 | 94 | 90 | 85 | 81 | 76 | 72 | 69 | 65 | 62 | 59 | 56 | 53 |
| 165 | 92 | 85 | 78 | 72 | 66 | 61 | 56 | 52 | 48 | 44 | 40 | 37 |
| 160 | 89 | 80 | 71 | 64 | 57 | 51 | 45 | 40 | 36 | 32 | 29 | 26 |
| 155 | 86 | 75 | 64 | 56 | 48 | 42 | 36 | 31 | 27 | 23 | 20 | 17 |
| 150 | 83 | 70 | 58 | 49 | 40 | 34 | 28 | 24 | 20 | 16 | 14 | 11 |
| 145 | 80 | 66 | 52 | 42 | 34 | 27 | 22 | 17 | 14 | 11 | 9 | 7 |
| 140 | 77 | 60 | 46 | 36 | 27 | 21 | 16 | 12 | 10 | 7 | 6 | 4 |
| 135 | 74 | 55 | 40 | 30 | 22 | 16 | 12 | 9 | 6 | 5 | 3 | 2 |
| 130 | 70 | 50 | 35 | 25 | 17 | 12 | 8 | 6 | 4 | 3 | 2 | 1 |
| 125 | 67 | 45 | 30 | 20 | 13 | 9 | 6 | 4 | 2 | 1 | 1 | 0 |
| 120 | 63 | 40 | 25 | 16 | 10 | 6 | 4 | 2 | 1 | 0 | 0 | 0 |
| 115 | 59 | 36 | 20 | 12 | 7 | 4 | 2 | 1 | 0 | 0 | 0 | 0 |
| 110 | 54 | 29 | 16 | 8 | 4 | 2 | 1 | 0 | 0 | 0 | 0 | 0 |
| 105 | 50 | 25 | 12 | 6 | 3 | 1 | 0 | 0 | 0 | 0 | 0 | 0 |
| 100 | 44 | 20 | 8 | 4 | 1 | 0 | 0 | 0 | 0 | 0 | 0 | 0 |
| 95 | 38 | 15 | 2 | 0 | 0 | 0 | 0 | 0 | 0 | 0 | 0 | 0 |
| 90 | 31 | 10 | 3 | 1 | 0 | 0 | 0 | 0 | 0 | 0 | 0 | 0 |
| 85 | 22 | 5 | 1 | 0 | 0 | 0 | 0 | 0 | 0 | 0 | 0 | 0 |
| 80 or less | 3 | 0 | 0 | 0 | 0 | 0 | 0 | 0 | 0 | 0 | 0 | 0 |

**Table 3.4.**   Example tasks with ratings.

| Task | Retention rating score |
|---|---|
| Perform operator maintenance on goggles | 220 |
| Determine national stock number for repair part | 195 |
| Move under direct fire | 170 |
| Determine magnetic azimuth using a compass | 155 |
| Administer first aid for an open abdominal wound | 140 |
| Identify and employ hand grenades | 120 |
| Live off the land | 100 |
| Identify armored vehicles | 75 |
| Techniques of movement in urban terrain | 65 |

Self-assessments were collected from 153 soldiers who reported not having qualified with the M16A1 rifle for 1 to 60 months and who were about to undergo qualification testing (hereafter referred to as 'record fire'). After completing the questionnaire, soldiers zeroed their weapons and fired record fire. The course of fire consisted of 40 silhouette targets at ranges between

50m and 300m. Soldiers fired the first half of the course from a foxhole supported position and fired the second half of the course from a prone unsupported position. Targets fell when hit, allowing performance to be scored by observers standing at the firing line.

Overall, correlations between predicted and actual scores were not high. At best, predictions accounted for only about 10% of the variance associated with record fire scores. However, the data were logically consistent. Soldiers who expressed the most confidence in their predictions, in fact, did a better job predicting how well they were going to shoot than other subjects. For example, the predicted scores of those who estimated their chances of accurate prediction at the highest levels accounted for 25% of the variance associated with record fire scores. Also, among those sampled, subjects who reported firing recored fire within the previous 12 months were more accurate in their predictions than subjects who reported not firing record fire as recently.

The vast majority of the soldiers were biased toward predicting success: 75% predicted that they would hit more targets than they actually did. Of the 34 soldiers who failed to qualify, only five predicted that they would fail.

It would be premature to recommend the use of self-assessments for generating retention estimates. They are simple and inexpensive to collect, but are subject to distortion, both intentional and unintentional (e.g. Burnside, 1982). Methods for increasing the accuracy of these estimates are needed before self-assessments of retention performance can be used with any degree of certainty.

## SUMMARY AND CONCLUSIONS

The purpose of this chapter was to identify some of the key variables for the long-term retention of motor skills. In preparing this chapter, evidence was organized loosely into three categories: task variables, procedural variables, and learner variables. Key observations were as follows:

1. In general, retention decreases with time. The exact shape of any forgetting curve depends on a host of variables, a key one of which is level of original learning.
2. Motor responses, typically, are classified as predominantly continuous, discrete, or procedural in nature. Continuous responses, such as those involved in tracking, show little forgetting over time. Discrete and procedural responses, on the other hand, cannot be maintained in the absence of regular practice. Fortunately, procedural skills are usually less expensive and simpler to maintain than continuous skills.
3. Learners apparently can impose organization on psychologically

unstructured tasks through the learning process. As a result, task organization does not appear an important variable for the long-term retention of well-learned responses. However, it is an important variable for the retention of less well-learned responses.

4. Display–control relationships can influence the ease of motor learning and transfer as well as the quality of performance after a retention interval.

5. Display specificity may affect the early learning of a skill. However, later in learning, these cues do not provide information over and above that which already is provided by internal sources. As a result, they may not be important determinants of retention.

6. Repetition is important both to learning and retention. Adding repetitions after task proficiency has been achieved—overtraining—also is effective in promoting retention.

7. Repetition schedule has different effects on verbal and motor tasks. For verbal tasks, acquisition is better when the interval between repetitions is minimized (i.e. massed training), and retention is better when the interval between repetitions is increased (i.e. spaced training). For motor tasks, learning and retention appear comparable under both massed and spaced repetition schedules.

8. Mental practice can enhance the acquisition and performance of motor tasks. However, research is lacking to demonstrate its effectiveness in promoting the long-term retention of motor skills.

9. KR is critical during the early acquisition of motor skills. However, individuals who receive more or better KR and who perform best during acquisition typically perform worse during retention testing than individuals who receive less useful KR or have KR gradually withdrawn during training.

10. Learning and retention are facilitated by increases in the quantity and quality of response-produced feedback during training.

11. Learners may come to depend on augmented cues. Where this is the case, performance during acquisition may improve, but performance during retention frequently suffers when these cues are removed.

12. The use of test trials during training has been found to slow acquisition performance but enhance the long-term retention of both verbal and motor skills.

13. The expectation of a test is likely to enhance the long-term retention of motor skills. Again, however, data are lacking to support this proposition.

14. Variability of practice has been found to slow acquisition while increasing performance at retention.

15. Refresher training can be used to offset the effects of forgetting. Retraining time will vary depending on such variables as length of retention interval, nature of the task, frequency of refresher training sessions, temporal spacing of successive sessions, and learners' initial ability levels.

16. Individual ability levels are important as determinants of retention insofar as they influence a learner's time to achieve a standard level of performance. Individuals of higher initial ability tend to achieve higher levels of proficiency and retain skill at higher levels than individuals of lower initial ability.
17. A number of methods for predicting the retention of specific tasks have been developed. Those highlighted in this chapter depended on the use of task characteristics and learner self-assessments.

## Optimizing retention

In 1962, Fleishman and Parker reported extremely high positive correlations (0.80 to 0.98) between learners' levels of original learning and later retention. Furthermore, they found that the strength of the observed correlations did not dissipate with time. The relationship remained high and stable over retention intervals ranging from 1 month to 2 years. Assuming level of original learning is key to later retention, then establishing conditions of practice which serve to promote learning is fundamental to optimizing retention. How do we establish these conditions of practice?

As suggested by Schmidt and Bjork (1989) and evidenced throughout this chapter, acquisition and retention cannot and should not be arbitrarily separated. In the absence of assessing learning at a transfer or retention test, erroneous conclusions about the best conditions for practice can result. Measures of performance during acquisition can be confounded by temporary performance effects which disappear quickly once the practice session is finished. And, it is performance during retention or transfer which ultimately determines the success of any training program.

Several variables have been 'friendly casualties' of research that has not separated out transitory performance effects from more permanent learning effects. These variables include scheduling of practice, 'usefulness' and frequency of KR, and augmented feedback. Other variables, such as testing during training, which degrade performance during acquisition but promote learning, show equal promise for improving the long-term retention of motor skills.

## Directions for future research

Several directions for future research were suggested during the course of this review. Research on the conditions of practice that optimize retention is perhaps most important. Then, too, several areas were covered in this chapter for which only data on verbal task performance were available. These areas include temporal spacing of refresher training sessions and test expectation. Other areas for which data generally appear to be lacking include the effect of mental practice on skill retention and the use of self-assessments in predicting retention performance. Incorporating a retention test after a period of mental practice appears a logical means for separating out learning and transitory 'priming' effects. However, we are aware of little research dealing with mental practice and long-term retention. Richardson (1967a, 1967b) identified two related studies, but their results did not permit any general conclusions. Similarly, work performed by Schendel et al. (1984), related to the use of self-assessments in predicting M16A1 rifle marksmanship performance, was preliminary in nature and raised as many questions as it answered.

Another potentially high payoff area for retention research lies in team training. There is a growing body of literature on crew, group, team, and unit training and performance (e.g. Baum, Modrick and Hollingsworth, 1982; Morgan et al., 1984; Salas et al., 1985). Much of the initial growth of this literature has come as a result of efforts at the US Army Research Institute (ARI) Fort Benning Field Unit (e.g. Dyer, 1984) and the Naval Training Systems Center (NTSC), Orlando, Florida (e.g. Oser et al., 1989). Yet, while research on the retention of team skills is being considered (Morgan and Salas, 1988), little is being conducted except for that recently started under the sponsorship of ARI's Presidio of Monterey Field Unit (J. H. Banks, personal communication, 10 January 1990). The results of team skill retention research can be expected to be of special interest to many. Both individual and team skills contribute to overall performance in a wide range of applied contexts.

## ACKNOWLEDGEMENTS

The opinions expressed in this chapter are those of the authors and do not necessarily represent those of the US Army.

## REFERENCES

Adams, J. A. (1954). Psychomotor response acquisition and transfer as a function of control–indicator relationships, *Journal of Experimental Psychology*, **48**, 10–18.
Adams, J. A. (1967). *Human Memory*. New York: McGraw-Hill, Inc.
Adams, J. A. (1968). Response feedback and learning, *Psychological Bulletin*, **70**, 486–504.
Adams, J. A. (1971). A closed-loop theory of motor learning, *Journal of Motor Behavior*, **3**, 111–149.
Adams, J. A. (1987). Historical review and appraisal of research on the learning, retention, and transfer of human motor skills, *Psychological Bulletin*, **101**, 41–74.
Adams, J. A., Goetz, E. T. and Marshall, P. H. (1972). Response feedback and motor learning, *Journal of Experimental Psychology*, **92**, 391–397.
Adams, J. A., Gopher, D. and Lintern, G. (1977). Effects of visual and proprioceptive feedback on motor learning, *Journal of Motor Behavior*, **9**, 11–22.

Adams, J. A. and Hufford, L. E. (1962). Contributions of a part-task trainer to the learning and relearning of a time-shared flight maneuver, *Human Factors*, **4**, 159–170.

Adams, J. A. and Reynolds, B. (1954). Effect of shift in distribution of practice conditions following interpolated rest, *Journal of Experimental Psychology*, **47**, 32–36.

Allen, G. A., Mahler, W. A. and Estes, W. K. (1969). Effects of recall tests on long-term retention of paired associates, *Journal of Verbal Learning and Verbal Behavior*, **8**, 463–470.

Ammons, R. B. (1951). Effects of prepractice activities on rotary pursuit performance, *Journal of Experimental Psychology*, **41**, 187–191.

Ammons, R. B., Farr, R. G., Bloch, E., Neumann, E., Dey, M., Marion, R. and Ammons, C. H. (1958). Long-term retention of perceptual–motor skills, *Journal of Experimental Psychology*, **55**, 318–328.

Annett, J. (1969). *Feedback and Human Behavior*. Baltimore, MD: Penguin.

Atkinson, R. C. and Shiffrin, R. M. (1968). Human memory: A proposed system and its control processes. In K. W. Spence and J. T. Spence (eds). *The Psychology of Learning and Motivation*, vol. 2, pp. 89–195. New York: Academic Press.

Bahrick, H. P. (1979). Maintenance of knowledge: Questions about memory we forgot to ask, *Journal of Experimental Psychology: General*, **108**, 296–308.

Bahrick, H. P., Noble, M. E. and Fitts, P. M. (1954). Extra-task performance as a measure of learning a primary task, *Journal of Experimental Psychology*, **48**, 298–302.

Bartlett, F. C. (1948a). The measurement of human skill, *Occupational Psychology*, **22**, 31–38.

Bartlett, F. C. (1948b). The measurement of human skill. *Occupational Psychology*, **22**, 83–91.

Battig, W. F. (1972). Intratask interference as a source of facilitation in transfer and retention. In R. F. Thompson and J. F. Voss (eds). *Topics in Learning and Performance*. New York: Academic Press.

Battig, W. F. (1979). The flexibility of human memory. In L. S. Cermak and F. I. M. Craik (eds). *Levels of Processing and Human Memory*. Hillsdale, NJ: Erlbaum.

Battig, W. F., Nagel, E. H., Voss, J. F. and Brogden, W. J. (1957). Transfer and retention of bidimensional compensatory tracking after extended practice, *American Journal of Psychology*, **70**, 75–80.

Baum, D. R., Modrick, J. A. and Hollingsworth, S. R. (1982). *The Status of Air Force Team Training for Command and Control Systems*, Vol. I. (AFHRL–TP–82–7). Wright-Patterson Air Force Base, OH: Air Force Human Resource Laboratory.

Bean, C. H. (1912). The curve of forgetting, *Archives of Psychology*, **3**, 1–45.

Bilodeau, E. A. (1952). *Some Effects of Various Degrees of Supplemental Information Given at Two Levels of Practice upon the Acquisition of a Complex Skill* (Research Bulletin No. 52–15). US Air Force Human Resources Resource Center.

Bilodeau, E. A., Bilodeau, I. McD. and Schumsky, D. A. (1959). Some effects of introducing and withdrawing knowledge of results early and late in practice, *Journal of Experimental Psychology*, **58**, 142–144.

Bilodeau, I. McD. (1969). Information feedback. In E. A. Bilodeau (ed.). *Principles of Skill Acquisition*. New York: Academic Press.

Boldovici, J. A. (1979). *Toward a Theory of Adaptive Teaching, with Implications for Armor Training Devices*. Unpublished manuscript, Human Resources Research Organization, Fort Knox, KY.

Boldovici, J. A. (1987). Measuring transfer in military settings. In S. M. Cormier and J. D. Hagman (eds). *Transfer of learning*, pp. 239–260. San Diego, CA: Academic Press.

Braby, R., Kincaid, J. P., Scott, P. and McDaniel, W. C. (1982, June). Illustrated formats to teach procedures. *IEEE Transactions on Professional Communication*, PC–25, 61–66.

Briggs, G. E. (1969). Transfer of training. In E. A. Bilodeau (ed.). *Principles of Skill Acquisition*. New York: Academic Press.

Brown, D. R., Briggs, G. E. and Naylor, J. C. (1963, May). *The Retention of Discrete and Continuous Tasks as a Function of Interim Practice with Modified Task Requirements* (AMRL-TDR-63-35). Wright-Patterson Air Force Base, OH.

Burnside, B. L. (1982, May). *Subjective Appraisal as a Feedback Tool* (Tech. Rep. 604). Alexandria, VA: US Army Research Institute for the Behavioral and Social Sciences.

Carron, A. V. (1971). Effect of ability upon retention of a balance skill after two years, *Perceptual and Motor Skills*, 33, 527–529.

Carron, A. V. and Marteniuk, R. C. (1970). Retention of a balance skill as a function of initial ability level, *Research Quarterly*, 41, 478–483.

Catalano, J. R. and Kleiner, B. M. (1984). Distant transfer and practice variability, *Perceptual and Motor Skills*, 58, 851–856.

Clark, L. V. (1960). Effect of mental practice on the development of a certain motor skill, *Research Quarterly*, 31, 560–569.

Corbin, C. B. (1972). Mental practice. In W. P. Morgan (ed.). *Ergogenic Aids and Muscular Performance*, pp. 93–118. New York: Academic Press.

Cotterman, T. E. and Wood, M. E. (1967, April). *Retention of Simulated Lunar Landing Mission Skills: A test of pilot reliability* (AMRL–TR–66–222). Dayton, OH: Wright-Patterson Air Force Base.

Crowder, R. G. (1976). *Principles of Learning and Memory*. Hillsdale, NJ: Lawrence Erlbaum Associates.

Dyer, J. L. (1984). Team research and training: A state-of-the-art review. In F. A. Muckler (ed.). *Human Factors Review: 1984*. Santa Monica, CA: Human Factors Society.

Ebbinghaus, H. (1964). *Memory: A contribution to experimental psychology*. New York: Dover. (Original work published in 1885.)

Eysenck, H. J. and Firth, C. D. (1977). *Reminiscence, Motivation, and Personality: A case study in experimental psychology*. London: Plenum Press.

Farr, M. J. (1986). *The Long-Term Retention of Knowledge and Skills: A cognitive and instructional perspective* (Contract No. MDA 903 84 C 0031). Alexandria, VA: Institute for Defense Analyses.

Feltz, D. L. and Landers, D. M. (1983). The effects of mental practice on motor skill learning and performance: A meta-analysis, *Journal of Sport Psychology*, 5, 25–57.

Fitts, P. M. and Posner, M. I. (1967). *Human Performance*. Belmont, CA: Brooks/Cole Publishing Company.

Fitts, P. M. and Seeger, C. M. (1953). SR compatibility: Spatial characteristics of stimulus and response codes, *Journal of Experimental Psychology*, 46, 199–210.

Flavell, J. H. and Wellman, H. M. (1977). Metamemory. In R. V. Kail, Jr and J. W. Hagen (eds). *Perspectives on the Development of Memory and Cognition*. Hillsdale: Erlbaum.

Fleishman, E. A. and Parker, S. F. (1962). Factors in the retention and relearning of perceptual–motor skill, *Journal of Experimental Psychology*, 64, 215–276.

Fleishman, E. A. and Rich, S. (1963). Role of kinesthetic and spatial–visual abilities in perceptual–motor learning, *Journal of Experimental Psychology*, **66**, 6–12.

Foos, P. W. and Clark, M. C. (1983). Learning from text: Effects of input order and expected test, *Human Learning*, **2**, 177–185.

Foos, P. W. and Fisher, R. P. (1988). Using tests as learning opportunities, *Journal of Educational Psychology*, **80**, 179–183.

Fox, W. L., Taylor, J. E. and Caylor, J. S. (1969, May). *Aptitude Level and the Acquisition of Skills and Knowledges in a Variety of Military Training Tasks* (HumRRO Tech. Rep. 69–6). Alexandria, VA: Human Resources Research Organization.

Gardlin, G. R. and Sitterley, T. E. (1972, June). *Degradation of Learned Skills—A review and annotated bibliography* (D180–15080–1). Seattle, WA: Boeing Company.

Gilmore, R. W. and Stolurow, L. M. (1951). Motor and 'mental' practice of ball and socket task, *American Psychologist*, **6**, 295.

Glenberg, A. M. (1974). *Retrieval Factors and the Lag Effect* (Tech. Rep. No. 49). Ann Arbor, MI: Human Performance Center, The University of Michigan.

Glenberg, A. M. and Lehman, T. S. (1980). Spacing repetitions over 1 week, *Memory and Cognition*, **8**, 528–538.

Glover, J. A. and Corkill, A. J. (1987). Influence of paraphrased repetitions on the spacing effect, *Journal of Educational Psychology*, **79**, 198–199.

Goldberg, J. H. and O'Rourke, S. (1989). Prediction of skill retention and retraining from initial training, *Perceptual and Motor Skills*, **69**, 535–546.

Greene, R. L. (1989). Spacing effects in memory: Evidence for a two-process account, *Journal of Experimental Psychology: Learning, Memory and Cognition*, **15**, 371–377.

Grimsley, D. L. (1969a, February). *Acquisition, Retention, and Retraining: Effects of high and low fidelity in training devices* (HumRRO Tech. Rep. 69–1). Alexandria, VA: Human Resources Research Organization.

Grimsley, D. L. (1969b, June). *Acquisition, Retention, and Retraining: Training category IV personnel with low fidelity devices* (HumRRO Tech. Rep. 69–12). Alexandria, VA: Human Resources Research Organization.

Hagman, J. D. (1980). *Effects of Training Task Repetition on Retention and Transfer of Maintenance Skill* (Res. Rep. No. 1271). Alexandria, VA: US Army Research Institute for the Behavioral and Social Sciences (ADA 101 859).

Hagman, J. D. (1981). *Testing During Training: Why does it enhance motor task retention?* (Tech. Rep. No. 535). Alexandria, VA: US Amry Research Institute for the Behavioral and Social Sciences.

Hagman, J. D. (1983). Presentation- and test-trial effects on acquisition and retention of distance and location, *Journal of Experimental Psychology: Learning, Memory, and Cognition*, **9**, 334–345.

Hagman, J. D. and Brosvic, G. M. (in preparation). *Effects of Repeated Testing on Acquisition and Retention of Motor Skills* (Tech. Rep.). Alexandria, VA: US Army Research Institute for the Behavioral and Social Sciences.

Hagman, J. D., Hayes, J. F. and Bierwirth, W. (1986). A method for estimating task retention: Research pays off, *Army Trainer*, **6**, 54–55.

Hagman, J. D. and Rose, A. M. (1983). Retention of military tasks: A review, *Human Factors*, **25**, 199–213.

Hagman, J. D. and Schendel, J. D. (1981). Effects of refresher training on job-task performance. *JSAS Catalog of Selected Documents in Psychology*, **11**, 91 (Ms. No. 2391).

Hagman, J. D. and Wells, R. (in preparation). *Effects of Refresher Training Session Frequency and Temporal Separation on Retention and Relearning* (Tech. Rep.).

Alexandria, VA: US Army Research Institute for the Behavioral and Social Sciences.

Hall, E. R., Willis, R. P., Thompson, J. R. and Schalow, S. R. (1986). *Skill Deterioration and Retraining Needs of Navy Individual Ready Reserve* (Tech. Rep. 86–007). Orlando, FL: Naval Training Systems Center.

Halpin, G. and Halpin, G. (1982). Experimental investigation of the effects of study and testing on student learning, retention, and ratings of instruction, *Journal of Educational Psychology*, **74**(1), 32–38.

Hart, J. T. (1965). Memory and the feeling of knowing experience, *Journal of Educational Psychology*, **56**, 208–216.

Hellyer, S. (1962). Supplementary report: Frequency of stimulus presentation and the short-term decrement in recall, *Journal of Experimental Psychology*, **64**, 650.

Henderson, S. E. (1977). Role of feedback in the development and maintenance of a complex skill, *Journal of Experimental Psychology*, **3**, 224–233.

Hogan, R. M. and Kintsch, W. (1971). Differential effects of study and test trials on long-term recognition and recall, *Journal of Verbal Learning and Verbal Behavior*, **10**, 562–567.

Holding, D. H. (1965). *Principles of Training*. New York: Pergamon Press.

Hunt, D. P. (August 1980). *Effects of Human Self-Assessment Responding on Learning* (Tech. Rep. 466). Alexandria, VA: US Army Research Institute for the Behavioral and Social Sciences.

Hurlock, R. E. and Montague, W. E. (1982). *Skill retention and its implications for navy tasks: An analytical review* (SR 82–21). San Diego, CA: Navy Personnel Research and Development Center.

Izawa, C. (1970). Optimal potentiation effects and forgetting-prevention effect of tests in paired-associate learning, *Journal of Experimental Psychology*, **83**, 340–344.

James, W. (1890). *Principles of Psychology*, Vol. I. New York: Holt.

Johnston, W. A. and Uhl, C. N. (1976). The contributions of encoding effort and variability to the spacing effect on free recall, *Journal of Experimental Psychology: Human Learning and Memory*, **2**, 153–160.

Kieras, D. E. and Bovair, S. (1984). The role of a mental model in learning to operate a device, *Cognitive Science*, **8**, 255–273.

Kinkade, R. G. A. (1963). *A Differential Influence of Augmented Feedback on Learning and on Performance* (WADC Air Force Systems Command Tech. Rep. AMRL-TDR–63–12). Dayton, OH: US Air Force, Wright Air Development Center.

Kleinman, M. (1980). Distribution of practice and pretask ability in the acquisition of three discrete gross motor skills, *Perceptual and Motor Skills*, **51**, 935–944.

Konoske, P. J., Wetzel, S. K. and Montague, W. E. (1983, April). *Estimating Skill Degradation for Aviation Antisubmarine Warfare Operators (AWs): Assessment of job and training variables* (NPRDC SR 83–28). San Diego, CA: Navy Personnel Research and Development Center.

Krueger, W. C. (1929). The effect of overlearning on retention, *Journal of Experimental Psychology*, **12**, 71–78.

Landauer, T. K. and Bjork, R. A. (1980). Optimum rehearsal patterns and name learning. In M. M. Gruneberg, P. E. Morris and R. N. Sykes (eds). *Practical Aspects of Memory*. London: Academic Press.

Lavery, J. J. (1962). Retention of simple motor skills as a function of type of knowledge of results, *Canadian Journal of Psychology*, **16**, 300–311.

Lee, T. D. and Magill, R. A. (1983). The locus of contextual interference in motor-skill acquisition, *Journal of Experimental Psychology: Learning, Memory, and Cognition*, **9**, 730–746.

Lersten, K. C. (1969). Retention of skill on the Rho apparatus after one year, *Research Quarterly*, **40**, 418–419.

Lewis, D. and Lowe, W. F. (1956). Retention of skill on the SAM complex coordinator, *Proceedings of the Iowa Academy of Science*, **63**, 591–599.

Lintern, G. and Roscoe, S. N. (1980). Adaptive perceptual–motor training. In S. N. Roscoe (ed.). *Aviation Psychology*, pp. 239–250. Ames: Iowa State University Press.

Loftus, G. R. (1985). Evaluating forgetting curves, *Journal of Experimental Psychology: Learning, Memory and Cognition*, **11**, 397–406.

McDonald, R. D. (1967, December). *Retention of Military Skills Acquired in Basic Combat Training* (HumRRO Tech. Rep. 67–13). Alexandria, VA: Human Resources Research Organization.

Melton, A. W. (1964, September). *Retention of Tracking Skills* (DA–49–007–MD–1020). Ann Arbor, MI: University of Michigan.

Mengelkoch, R. F., Adams, J. A. and Gainer, C. A. (1971). The forgetting of instrument flying skills, *Human Factors*, **13**, 397–405.

Morgan, B. B., Jr, Coates, G. D., Kirby, R. H. and Alluisi, E. A. (1984). Individual and team performances as functions of the team-training load, *Human Factors*, **26**, 127–142.

Morgan, B. B., Jr and Salas, E. (1988). A research agenda for team training and performance: Issues, alternatives, and solutions, *Proceedings of the 10th Interservice Industry Training Systems Conference*. Orlando, FL: National Security Industrial Association.

Naylor, J. C. and Briggs, G. E. (1961, August). *Long Term Retention of Learned Skills: A review of the literature* (ASD Tech. Rep. 61–390). Canton, OH: Aerospace Medical Laboratory, Wright-Patterson Air Force Base.

Naylor, J. C., Briggs, G. E. and Reed, W. G. (1968). Task coherence, training time, and retention interval effects on skill retention, *Journal of Applied Psychology*, **52**, 386–393.

Neumann, E. and Ammons, R. B. (1957). Acquisition and long term retention of a simple serial perception motor skill, *Journal of Experimental Psychology*, **53**, 159–161.

Newell, K. M. (1974). Knowledge of results and motor learning, *Journal of Motor Behavior*, **6**, 235–244.

Newell, K. M. (1977). Knowledge of results and motor learning. In J. Keogh and R. S. Hutton (eds). *Exercise and Sport Sciences Reviews*, Vol. 4. Santa Barbara, CA: Journal Publishing Affiliates.

Noble, M., Trumbo, D., Ulrich, L. and Cross, K. (1966). Task predictability and the development of tracking skill under extended practice, *Journal of Experimental Psychology*, **72**, 85–94.

Nungester, R. and Duchastel, P. (1982). Testing versus review: Effects on retention, *Journal of Educational Psychology*, **74**, 18–22.

Oser, R., McCallum, G. A., Salas, E. and Morgan, B. B. Jr., (1989, March). *Toward a Definition of Teamwork: An analysis of critical team behaviors* (Tech. Rep. 89–004). Orlando, FL: Naval Training Systems Center.

Pear, T. H. (1927). Skill, *Journal of Personnel Research*, **5**, 478–489.

Pear, T. H. (1948). Professor Bartlett on skill, *Occupational Psychology*, **22**, 92–93.

Prophet, W. W. (1976a, October). *Long-Term Retention of Flying Skills: A review of the literature* HumRRO Tech. Rep. 76–35). Alexandria, VA: Human Resources Research Organization.

Prophet, W. W. (1976b, October). *Long-Term Retention of Flying Skills: An annotated bibliography* (HumRRO Tech. Rep. 76–36). Alexandria, VA: Human Resources Research Organization.

Purdy, B. J. and Lockhart, A. (1962). Retention and relearning of gross motor skills after long periods of no practice, *Research Quarterly*, **33**, 265–272.

Reynolds, B. and Bilodeau, I. McD. (1952). Acquisition and retention of three psychomotor tests as a function of distribution of practice during acquisition, *Journal of Experimental Psychology*, **44**, 19–26.

Richardson, A. (1967a). Mental practice: A review and discussion, I, *Research Quarterly*, **38**, 95–107.

Richardson, A. (1967b). Mental practice: A review and discussion, II, *Research Quarterly*, **38**, 263–273.

Rigg, K. E. and Gray, B. B. (1981, December). *The Optimization of Skill Retention through Initial Training Analysis and Design* (MGA Final Report MGA–2081–MRO–0047). Monterey, CA: McFann-Gray & Associates, Inc.

Roediger, H. L. and Payne, D. G. (1982). Hyperamnesia: The role of repeated testing, *Journal of Experimental Psychology: Learning, Memory, and Cognition*, **8**, 66–72.

Rogers, C. A. (1974). Feedback precision and postfeedback interval duration, *Journal of Experimental Psychology*, **102**, 604–608.

Rose, A. M., Czarnolewski, M. Y., Gragg, F. E., Austin, S. H., Ford, P., Doyle, J. and Hagman, J. D. (1985a). *Acquisition and Retention of Soldiering Skills* (Tech. Rep. 671). Alexandria, VA: US Army Research Institute for the Behavioral and Social Sciences.

Rose, A. M., Radtke, P. H., Shettel, H. H. and Hagman, J. D. (1985b). *User's Manual for Predicting Military Task Retention* (Res. Prod. 85–26). Alexandria, VA: US Army Research Institute for the Behavioral and Social Sciences.

Russel, R. W., Valentine, J. A. and Harris, F. J. (1945, January). *Maintenance of Gunner Proficiency in Basic Skills in a Combat Air Force*. Randolph Field, TX: 8th Air Force and Research Division, Central School for Flexible Gunnery.

Ryan, E. O. (1962). Retention of stabilometer and pursuit rotor skills, *Research Quarterly*, **33**, 593–598.

Sackett, R. S. (1934). The influences of symbolic rehearsal upon the retention of a maze habit, *Journal of General Psychology*, **10**, 376–395.

Salas, E., Blaiwes, A. R., Reynolds, R. E., Glickman, A. S. and Morgan, B. B., Jr (1985). Teamwork from Team Training: New Directions, *Proceedings of the 7th Interservice/Industry Training Equipment Conference and Exhibition*, American Defense Preparedness Association, Orlando, FL.

Salmoni, A. W., Schmidt, R. A. and Walter, C. B. (1984). Knowledge of results and motor learning: A review and critical appraisal, *Psychological Bulletin*, **95**, 355–386.

Schendel, J. D. and Hagman, J. D. (1982). On sustaining procedural skills over prolonged retention intervals, *Journal of Applied Psychology*, **67**, 605–610.

Schendel, J. D. and Johnston, S. D. (1983). A study of methods for engaging moving targets, *Human Factors*, **25**, 693–700.

Schendel, J. D., Shields, J. L. and Katz, M. S. (1978). *Retention of Motor Skills* (Tech. Rep. 313). Alexandria, VA: US Army Research Institute for the Behavioral and Social Sciences.

Schendel, J. D., Morey, J. C., Granier, M. J. and Hall, S. (1984, April). Use of self-assessments in estimating levels of skill retention, *Proceedings Psychology in the Department of Defense, Ninth Symposium*, US Air Force Academy, Colorado Springs, Colorado.

Schmidt, R. A. (1975). *Motor Skills*. New York: Harper.

Schmidt, R. A. (1982). *Motor Control and Learning: A behavioral emphasis.* Champaign, IL: Human Kinetics.

Schmidt, R. A. and Bjork, R. A. (1989). *New Conceptualizations of Practice: Common principles in three research paradigms suggest important new concepts for practice.* Unpublished manuscript, University of California, Los Angeles, CA.

Schmidt, R. A. and Wrisberg, C. A. (1971). Further tests of the Adams' closed-loop theory: Response-produced feedback and the error detection mechanism, *Journal of Motor Behavior,* **3**, 318–325.

Schmidt, R. A., Young, D. E., Swinnen, S. and Shapiro, D. C. (1989). Summary knowledge of results for skill acquisition: Support for the guidance hypothesis, *Journal of Experimental Psychology: Learning, Memory, and Cognition,* **15**, 352–359.

Schmidt, S. R. (1983). The effects of recall and recognition test expectancies on the retention of prose, *Memory and Cognition,* **11**, 172–180.

Shea, J. B. and Morgan, R. L. (1979). Contextual interference effects on the acquisition, retention, and transfer of a motor skill, *Journal of Experimental Psychology: Human Learning and Memory,* **5**, 179–187.

Shea, J. B. and Zimny, S. T. (1983). Context effects in memory and learning movement information. In R. A. Magill (ed.). *Memory and Control of Action,* pp. 345–366. Amsterdam: North-Holland.

Shields, J. L., Goldberg, S. L. and Dressel, J. D. (1979). *Retention of Basic Soldering Skills* (Res. Rep. 1225). Alexandria, VA: US Army Research Institute for the Behavioral and Social Sciences.

Shields, J. L., Joyce, R. P. and Van Wert, J. R. (1979, March). *Chaparral Skill Retention* (Res. Rep. 1205). Alexandria, VA: US Army Research Institute for the Behavioral and Social Sciences.

Singer, R. N. (1975). *Motor Learning and Human Performance.* New York: Macmillan.

Singer, R. N. and Witker, J. (1970). Mental rehearsal and point of introduction within context of overt practice, *Perceptual and Motor Skills,* **31**, 169–170.

Sitterley, T. E. (1974, May). *Degradation of Learned Skills: Static practice effectiveness for visual approach and landing skill retention* (D180–17876–1). Seattle, VA: Boeing Aerospace Company.

Sitterley, T. E. and Berge, W. A. (1972, July). *Degradation of Learned Skills: Effectiveness of practice methods on simulated space flight skill retention* (D180–15081–1). Seattle, VA: Boeing Aerospace Company.

Sitterley, T. E., Zaitzeff, L. P. and Berge, W. A. (1972, October). *Degradation of Learned Skills: Effectiveness of practice methods on visual approach and landing skill retention* (D180-15082-1). Seattle, VA: Boeing Aerospace Company.

Slamecka, N. J. and McElree, B. (1983). Normal forgetting of verbal lists as a function of their degree of learning, *Journal of Experimental Psychology: Learning, Memory, and Cognition,* **9**, 384–397.

Smith, J. F. and Matheny, W. G. (1976, May). *Continuation Versus Recurrent Pilot Training* (AFHRL Tech. Rep. 76–4). Canton, OH: Wright-Patterson Air Force Base.

Smith, N. C., Jr (1971). Long-term retention of a pursuit motor skill, *Perceptual and Motor Skills,* **32**, 773–774.

Smith, S. (1959). *Performance on a Following Tracking Task and a Simultaneously Operating Dial Pointer Centering Task as a Function of Tracking Control–Display Relationship and Dial Task Difficulty.* Unpublished doctoral dissertation, University of Rochester, Rochester, NY.

Stelmach, G. E. (1969). Efficiency of motor learning as a function of intertrial rest, *Research Quarterly,* **40**, 198–202.

Stelmach, G. E. (1973). Feedback: A determiner of forgetting in short-term motor memory, *Acta Psychologica*, **37**, 333–339.

Stelmach, G. E. (1974). Retention of motor skills. In J. Whilmore (ed.). *Exercise and Sport Sciences Review*. New York: Academic Press.

Stelmach, G. E. and Kelso, J. A. S. (1975). Memory trace strength and response biasing in short-term motor memory, *Memory & Cognition*, **3**, 58–62.

Swift, E. J. (1905). Memory of a complex skillful act, *American Journal of Psychology*, **16**, 131–133.

Swink, J. D., Trumbo, D. and Noble, M. (1967). On the length–difficulty relation in skill performance, *Journal of Experimental Psychology*, **74**, 356–362.

Thompson, C. P., Wenger, S. K. and Bartling, C. A. (1978). How recall facilitates subsequent recall: A reappraisal, *Journal of Experimental Psychology: Human Learning and Memory*, **4**, 210–221.

Thompson, T. J., Morey, J. C., Smith, S. and Osborne, A. D. (1981, October). *Basic Rifle Marksmanship Skill Retention: Implications for retention research* (Res. Rep. 1326). Alexandria, VA: US Army Research Institute for the Behavioral and Social Sciences.

Trumbo, D., Noble, M. and Swink, J. (1967). Secondary task interference in the performance of tracking tasks, *Journal of Experimental Psychology*, **73**, 232–240.

Trumbo, D., Ulrich, L. and Noble, M. (1965). Verbal coding and display coding in the acquisition and retention of tracking skill, *Journal of Applied Psychology*, **49**, 368–375.

Trumbo, D., Noble, M., Cross, K. and Ulrich, L. (1965). Task predictability in the organization, acquisition, and retention of tracking skill, *Journal of Experimental Psychology*, **70**, 252–263.

Twining, W. E. (1949). Mental practice and physical practice in learning a motor skill, *Research Quarterly*, **20**, 432–435.

Vineberg, R. (1975, June). *A Study of the Retention of Skills and Knowledge Acquired in Basic Training* (HumRRO Tech. Rep. 75–10). Alexandria, VA: Human Resources Research Organization.

Winstein, C. J. and Schmidt, R. A. (1990). Reduced frequency of knowledge of results enhances motor skill learning. *Journal of Experimental Psychology: Learning, Memory, and Cognition*, **16**, 677–691.

Wulf, G. and Schmidt, R. A. (1988). Variability in practice: Facilitation in retention and transfer through schema formation or context effects, *Journal of Motor Behavior*, **20**, 133–149.

Young, J. L. (1966). *Effects of Intervals between Reinforcements and Test Trials in Paired-Associate Learning* (Tech. Rep. 101). Institute for Mathematical Studies in the Social Sciences, Stanford University.

Yussen, S. R. and Levy, V. M., Jr (1975). Developmental changes in predicting one's own span of short-term memory, *Journal of Experimental Child Psychology*, **19**, 502–508.

# Chapter 4

# Transfer of training

**Dennis H. Holding**
University of Louisville

Transfer of training occurs whenever the effects of prior learning influence the performance of a later activity. In this very broad sense, transfer is an extremely widespread phenomenon, playing a part in almost every instance of learning. The knowledge and skills acquired throughout life tend to be cumulative, so that an adult will rarely, if ever, be required to learn anything completely new. Viewed in this light, an exercise such as the use of biographical records of past activities for the prediction of job performance may be regarded as an application of the principles of transfer of training. Furthermore, the learning process may itself be viewed as consisting of successive instances of transfer. Thus, McGeoch (1942) already insisted that no learning could occur without transfer from one trial to the next, providing continuity of practice. The phenomenon of within-task transfer has taken on new importance as an issue for cognitive models of learning (Gray and Orasanu, 1987), especially in situations where mental models are required to mediate transfer in the acquisition of complex skills. However, most of the relevant research is concerned with the transfer between distinguishably separable tasks, or task versions, treated as whole units.

How such transfer takes place is clear enough in outline, although obscure in detail. Given similar or apparently similar circumstances, people tend to respond in the same way, thus transferring acquired skills to new tasks. As is well known, Thorndike and Woodworth (1901) laid the groundwork for modern work on transfer. Reacting against the traditional educational view of transfer as formal discipline, which held that exercising mental faculties generally improved the mind, they formulated the theory that transfer occurred only when two tasks contained identical elements. Later work has usually broadened the definition of identical elements to include degrees of similarity. It is difficult to disagree with any broad interpretation of the identical elements theory, which is virtually tautologous, since whenever transfer occurs one tends to assume that the participating tasks must have had some elements in common. The difficulty lies in specifying what the crucial similarity is, or even at what level of generality the mediating elements should be sought, in any given case of transfer.

*Training for Performance: Principles of Applied Human Learning.* Edited by J. E. Morrison
© 1991 John Wiley & Sons Ltd

It is not clear whether the appropriate level of analysis should be defined by the stimulus or response, the motor program, the concept, the neural net, the strategy, the mental model, or perhaps even the faculty. Even though Thorndike and Woodworth insisted that the common elements should be objectively specificable, this condition can be satisfied at various levels. In fact, what limited transfer they obtained in their own experiment on estimating the areas of different shapes already seems to implicate between-task similarities at a level more general than is represented by the simple stimulus and response. The transfer of shape characteristics probably constitutes an instance of the perceptual invariances to which Lintern, *et al.* (1987) ascribe the transfer found across aircraft simulators with differing displays.

The search for transfer at successively higher levels of analysis will continue below. However, before attempting to identify the nature of the most important similarities between tasks, it is first necessary to consider some of the design and measurement issues that bear on transfer research. There are many ways to design transfer studies, depending on the purpose of the research, but the basic principles are essentially simple. Such design principles are normally phrased in terms of the relationships between two separate tasks. Admittedly, it will sometimes be found necessary to evaluate an entire training scheme in terms of its transfer to some criterion activity, where the activity itself consists of a group of tasks or functions. Nevertheless, it can usually be assumed that the principles governing such transfer are identical with those derived from laboratory research. The overwhelming majority of laboratory studies, in turn, have been simply concerned with the effects of learning one task on the later acquisition of another.

## BASIC DESIGNS

The first task to be learned, which might consist of anything from proofreading or learning geometry to juggling balls or practicing on a simulator, is traditionally designated as Task A. The acquisition of skill at Task A provides the learning whose transfer to a second task is to be evaluated. The second task, which again might represent any activity that yields a scorable outcome, is designated as Task B. When the learning on Task A is transferred to performance on Task B, the resulting transfer may be positive, negative, or zero. If learning Task A results in better scores on Task B than would otherwise have been the case, then the transfer is positive. This is far more common than the negative case. When, as will tend to happen if the two tasks are unrelated, learning Task A has no effect on Task B, there is obviously zero transfer. Finally, in the occasional cases where learning Task A makes for worse performance on Task B, the transfer is described as negative.

## Traditional designs

Describing the amount of transfer to Task B by comparing the scores with what would otherwise have been the case implies that such a standard of comparison exists. In other words, any transfer experiment requires a control group. The simplest design calls for a group of control subjects who practice only Task B, to be used for comparison with the experimental subjects who practice first Task A and then Task B. Comparing the Task B scores for the two groups will then yield the amount of transfer from Task A. However, it is often convenient to measure the transfer in both directions simultaneously, from A to B and from B to A. In this case, one group will practice A followed by B, and the other B followed by A. The comparison between the two B scores will still give the transfer from A to B, and the comparison between the two A scores will give the transfer from B to A.

It is sometimes recommended that the control and experimental treatments should be assigned to matched groups to insure that the scores are comparable in all respects other than the transferred learning, but matching can be of dubious benefit. It is obviously reasonable to arrange that the two groups are drawn from the same population with regard to general characteristics, such as age, sex, or educational level, and to take into account any other easily ascertainable performance variables. The difficulty arises if it becomes necessary to perform an explicit matching operation, because this will constitute an additional stage in the experiment—a kind of Task C. The control group will thus practice Tasks C then B, while the experimental group will perform C, then A, then B. If C and B are uncorrelated there are no transfer problems, but the matching will be ineffective. On the other hand, if C is closely enough related to B to predict performance on B then the matching will be successful but Task C will itself contribute transfer effects to B, and possibly differential transfer effects to A, thus clouding the comparison. It is interesting to note that analogous problems with unwanted transfer effects also occur when within-subjects designs are used for other purposes, as Poulton (1973) has demonstrated in human performance studies. The majority of transfer experiments therefore rely only on the random sampling of unmatched control and experimental groups.

A different type of design consideration emerged in much of the early work, which was often concerned with the related topic of 'retroactive' effects rather than with the proactive influence of A on B. The retroaction paradigm is used to investigate whether learning Task B has an interfering or facilitating effect on the retention of Task A. Hence, an experimental group will first learn Task A and will then learn Task B, but will later be retested on Task A. A control group will also begin by learning Task A, but will then either rest or perform some unrelated activity before taking the final retest on A. In this case, if the experimental scores on the final A test are better than the corresponding control scores, learning Task B is said to have produced retro-active facilitation. If the experimental scores are poorer than the controls, then Task B has produced retroactive interference (or retroactive inhibition). As Adams (1987) points out in his review, this type of design is now infre-quently used, although it plays an important part in the history of transfer theories.

**Further complications**

Of course, many other transfer designs are both possible and represented in the literature. No single design is always correct, as the form taken by any transfer design must be dictated by the aims of the research. For example, if one is primarily interested in quantitative rather than qualitative comparisons of training benefits, the design will call for varying the number or duration of Task A, and perhaps Task B, practice trials. A typical case was discussed by Roscoe (1971), whose concern lay in quantifying the effectiveness of transfer of training. The relevant data here consisted of the number of flying hours saved by practicing for different amounts of time on an aircraft simulator. In this situation there is no need to vary the qualitative relationships between Tasks A and B, since it can be assumed that all transfer will be positive. Hence, the appropriate design consists of setting an acceptable criterion for proficiency on Task B (in this case flying the real aircraft), varying the number of hours spent on Task A (the simulator), and then observing the time subse-quently required to reach the Task B criterion.

Varying the time spent on Task A will normally be accomplished by a between-subjects design using several separate groups each of which receives a different amount of training. Such designs will usually call for at least four groups (three training and one control) but more economical designs appear to have other disadvantages. Boldovici (1987) has recommended using a within-subjects procedure instead, implemented by arranging for a single group to alternate between training on Task A and testing on Task B so that transfer measures are available at different points in the training sequence. This is a potentially useful suggestion, although Morrison and Holding (1990) point out that using such a procedure incurs the risk that unknown amounts of transfer might occur in the reverse direction, from the test trials to the training sessions.

Many other kinds of design consideration stem from concerns with the qualitative relationships between the two tasks. As we shall see, it has often been found necessary to distinguish between the stimulus–response (display–control; input–output) components of Tasks A and B, because changes in the similarity relationships between these different components may have varying consequences for the transfer outcome. Observing these distinctions may give rise to more complex transfer designs, which are often seen in the verbal learning literature surveyed by Postman (1972). In this context, it is traditional to use the letters of the alphabet to refer to the word lists used for paired-associate learning.

Retaining the traditional letters at the risk of some confusion, Task B might consist of the list pair A–B, where each item or word in list A has to be associated with each corresponding word in list B. This task might be preceded, in what we have called Task A, by the learning of list pair A–B itself (as a form of control group); by learning C–B (varying the stimulus words); by learning A–D (varying the response words); by learning B–A (reversing the order); or by learning a modified A–B list in which the individual stimulus and response items have been transposed (thus causing confusion). Several comparable designs may be encountered in perceptual–motor learning. In addition, a further group might begin by learning a list pair C–D as Task A, to control for the non-specific transfer brought about by simply practicing list learning. Again, a comparable group is occasionally used to distinguish general from specific effects in the transfer of motor skills.

Another form of design complication arises when it becomes necessary to evaluate the transfer effects of a large number of experimental variables, as may happen in practical circumstances. In Simon and Roscoe's (1984) study, the Task A training for a tracking task B could vary in terms of order of control, display lag, pursuit versus compensatory mode, prediction time, or control gain. These possibilities give rise to a prohibitively large number of training configurations, particularly in combination with different amounts of Task A training. The problem was handled by selecting eight configurations of varying difficulty level, which were transferred to three selected Task B combinations after two levels of training. This procedure gave rise to 48 different Task A–Task B relationships, whose analysis as an incomplete factorial (with subsequent regression analyses) is described in the original article. Among other results, the experiment confirmed that transfer may be asymmetrical between hard and easy versions of a task. However, the main conclusion may be the methodological point that complex designs are capable of providing rapid survey information about the effects of large numbers of transfer variables.

## MEASUREMENT OF TRANSFER

The information one obtains from a transfer study also depends on the measure chosen. However, like the choice of experimental design, the decision concerning the most appropriate form of measurement of transfer will depend on the purpose of the experiment. Despite the suggestion of normativeness sometimes associated with transfer formulas, there is no single correct way to measure transfer from one task to another. Brief reflection will show that the transfer relationship involves too many variables for any single measure to represent all the possible comparisons. At the very least, what is needed for completeness seems to be a mathematical function rather than a single point measurement.

The transfer relationship should derive its properties from three different learning curves: the curve for Task A; the curve for Task B after A; and the control curve for Task B. The amount of transfer observed will depend on the point at which transfer is made from the A curve, on the shape of the B after A curve, and on the points of difference between B after A and the control B curve. Each of these curves can vary in starting point, in ending point, and in the shape of the intervening trend. It is therefore obvious that no single figure of merit can reflect the many possible outcomes. For example, after an intermediate number of trials on Task A, the subsequent scores on B might begin low, but rapidly improve to equal or surpass the control B scores. After many trials on Task A, the later scores might begin high, subsequently sagging to remain below the B asymptote. Hence, any transfer formula will lose information which might be relevant to the research, and should be interpreted with caution.

**First-shot transfer**

Many of the early formulas were what Hammerton (1989) calls 'first-shot' measures. Such formulations make the assumption that primary interest attaches to the point at which people trained on Task A first enter the learning curve for Task B, without addressing the important developments that sometimes occur as learning proceeds. The assumption implies that Task A learning and Task B learning are simply additive, which may be correct in cases where simulator training precedes the simulated task. Where Tasks A and B are qualitatively different, the two forms of learning may interact to yield a Task B-after-A curve that departs from the control Task B curve.

Nevertheless, many experiments terminate at the stage of initial transfer, simply following the practice trial or trials on Task A with a single transfer trial on Task B. In these circumstances, it may be useful to represent the amount of transfer obtained as a proportion of the total possible learning available on Task B. The maximum possible for Task B can sometimes be supplied in advance, for instance if there is a known perfect score. Most often, and especially in motor skills research, a perfect score does not exist, so the amount of possible learning must be obtained by finding the difference between the initial and final (asymptotic) control group scores on Task B. Obviously, the initial score is subtracted from the final score for hits or times on target, while the final score is subtracted from the initial score for error measures. As laid out by Gagné, Foster and Crowley (1948) for error scores, percentage transfer is defined in the following way:

$$\% \text{ Transfer } = \frac{\text{Control B, initial} - \text{Experimental B}}{\text{Control B, initial} - \text{Control B, final}} \times 100 \qquad [4.1]$$

Representing the amount of transfer as a percentage has the advantage that results so expressed can be compared across different tasks within an experiment or across several different experiments. Of course, the comparison of different experiments should also be accompanied by far more sophisticated meta-analyses than are provided by simply assembling the transfer percentages (cf. Green and Hall 1984). However, the percentage measure is particularly appropriate as a first step in cases such as investigating mutual transfer, from A to B and from B to A, where A and B have different learning curves.

Consider the hypothetical example constructed in Figure 4.1, which depicts mutual transfer between artificial versions of (a) baseball and (b) cricket. Samples of talented performers are postulated to improve from scores of 1–5 at baseball or from 2–42 at cricket. After learning to play cricket, people can transfer to baseball by starting with 3 home runs, an improvement of 2. After baseball, people transfer to cricket by scoring 12, for an improvement of 10 runs. In absolute terms, there appears to be more transfer from baseball to cricket than from cricket to baseball, but the percentage scores tell the opposite story. The transfer from cricket to baseball confers an advantage equivalent to 50% (3–1/5–1) of the baseball learning curve whereas transferring from baseball to cricket gives only 25% (12–2/42–2) of the possible learning, which seems a more reasonable account of the data.

A theoretical problem with the Gagné–Foster–Crowley type of formula is that the scales they generate tend to be asymmetrical, with unequal scope for positive and negative transfer. It might also be thought undesirable that the scales should extend to infinity. The exact range depends on the measure chosen, but can vary from +100 to –100 when a perfect score has been defined, or otherwise from +∞ to –∞. These properties have little disadvantage in practice, as it is quite acceptable and meaningful to encounter transfer of greater than 100%. However, Murdock (1957) suggested an alternative scale, based on using the sum of the control and experimental scores as the denominator, which runs symmetrically from +100 to –100. As expressed for hits, or correct responses, the formula states the following relationship:

$$\% \text{ Transfer } = \frac{\text{Experimental(tot)} - \text{Control(tot)}}{\text{Experimental(tot)} - \text{Control(tot)}} \times 100 \qquad [4.2]$$

Using this formula makes the assumption that each term in the equation can be represented by a total score, which is more appropriate to list learning than to performance such as tracking. Furthermore, the inability to represent

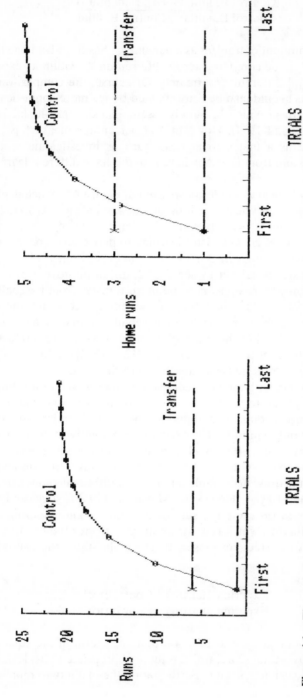

**Figure 4.1.** The use of transfer percentages (hypothetical data). Absolute improvement is greater from baseball to cricket (left), but percentage immprovement is greater from cricket to baseball (right).

transfer of greater than 100% is actually a drawback. For instance, Farrell and Fineberg (1976) found that 15 hours of specialized training produced as much transfer to low-level helicopter navigation as over 2000 hours of general flying experience, which suggests an efficiency considerably in excess of 100%. Consequently, the Murdock formula has not been widely adopted. In any case, both the Gagné–Foster–Crowley and the Murdock formulas have a disadvantage for many purposes because they are not designed to reflect changes in the savings on Task B, in time or trials, produced by differential learning on Task A.

It is important to notice that a first-shot measure, showing the difference between experimental and control groups on the first trial of Task B, will not necessarily predict how many Task B trials will eventually be saved, nor how this figure may change with first-task learning. A case in point was provided by Hammerton and Tickner (1967), who compared different measures for transfer from various approximate simulations to a joystick-controlled railroad trolley task. Training with a television representation of the task, for example, gave both 98% first-shot transfer and 100% savings in later trials, but training with a symbolic CRT display gave disparate scores. Transfer from this task eventually yielded 77% savings, although the initial first-shot advantage was only 24%.

## Continuous measures

Methods for the calculation of savings scores, or what are sometimes known as substitution ratios, have been considered in detail by Roscoe (1971, 1972). As indicated above, the prototypical case occurs when training is given on a device such as an aircraft simulator before transferring to practice on real flight skills. Transfer effectiveness is viewed as a continuous function of first-task learning rather than as a single value. Some criterion for performance must exist to define mastery on the target activity, such as meeting the standards for flying solo, so that the time saved by simulator training can be calculated. It is further assumed that transfer is positive, and that the amount of transfer will be monotonically related to the number of training trials or hours on the simulator.

The *incremental* transfer effectiveness of training on the device will vary systematically from trial to trial. If 10 flying hours are normally needed to attain proficiency, as indicated by a control group, only 8.6 might be needed after the first hour of simulator training, thus giving a 1.4 hours savings score. However, a second hour on the simulator might only save a further 1.2 hours of flying time. If we sum the two savings scores, the two simulator hours have jointly saved 2.6 flying hours, thus averaging 1.3 hours each. This figure is the *cumulative* transfer effectiveness ratio (CTER), which can be expressed as follows:

$$CTER = \frac{Control\ (time\ to\ criterion) - Experimental\ (time\ to\ criterion)}{Experimental\ (simulator\ hours)} \qquad [4.3]$$

The CTER can be drawn as a continuous curve against the amount of first-task training. A typical CTER curve is shown as part of Figure 4.2. Whenever the ratio drops below unity, it indicates that the training on Task A is consuming more time than it saves on the criterion Task B. Training should therefore be discontinued at this point, at least in circumstances where training time is the prime consideration. However, in practice, it will often be the case that training on the simulator costs less than training on the real equipment. This is, after all, one of the reasons for adopting simulator training. In these circumstances, the simplest expedient is to substitute cost figures in place of training hours, using total expenditure to criterion instead of time to criterion in equation [4.3]. Then, whenever the simulator training costs more than it saves, the recommendation is again that training should be discontinued. More complex approaches to cost allocation are briefly considered below.

It can be argued that the CTER measure, although less complicated than some later formulations, is nevertheless more elaborate than is necessary for many purposes. A simpler practical approach, termed the A + B method, was advocated by Holding (1977). The A + B formulation simply requires one to add the time spent in simulator training (A) to the time subsequently spent reaching the criterion (B). Using the numbers adopted in the example above, where receiving 1 hour of training on the simulator later requires only 8.6 flying hours, the value of A + B is obviously 9.6. After 2 training hours which

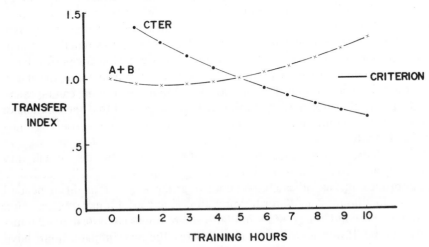

**Figure 4.2.** Comparison of training effectiveness measures. CTER is the cumulative transfer effectiveness ratio, and A + B is the summed training time. After Holding (1987).

save a further 1.2 flying hours for a total of 2.6, the value becomes 9.4 (2 + 7.4). These values can be plotted in a manner similar to the CTER.

Analogously, whenever the combined value of A + B rises above the 10 hours required without special training, it can be inferred that the simulator has ceased to make an effective contribution. Thus, it can be seen in Figure 4.2 that the A + B curve suggests cut-off in the same place as it indicated by the CTER curve. Furthermore the minimum point, which occurs at about 2 hours in Figure 4.2, can be interpreted as the point at which simulator training is at its most effective. The A + B method has the advantage of dispensing with the savings calculation altogether and thus only requires a control group if the time to Task B criterion is not previously known. Again, when costs are important, then expense can be substituted for training time just as before. In either case, the formula is simply the following:

A + B value = Experimental (simulator) + Experimental (criterion task)

[4.4]

Bickley (1980) resolved total training (A + B) cost relationships into a linear curve for device training costs together with an exponential 'iso-performance' curve relating the cost on B to time on A. It appeared that combining these two functions also had the effect of optimizing cost–benefit at the minimum of the A + B curve. Carter and Trollip (1980) had an apparently different aim, starting from the assumption that training costs were fixed and then developing methods for allocating training time that would maximize the performance achieved. In this case, the form adopted for the iso-performance curve was hyperbolic. However, despite the difference in the two approaches, it can be shown (Cronholm, 1985) that either minimizing the costs for achieving fixed performance levels, or maximizing the level of performance for fixed costs, will give rise to the same optimal solution described above.

# TRADITIONAL ISSUES

The current, quantitative preoccupation with the amount and value of transfer was preceded by a long period of qualitative investigations designed to explore what transfers to what. This latter question was the main concern of the early work on transfer, which raised a number of issues that still confront us, albeit transformed by changes in terminology and theoretical perspective. Most of the early work was concentrated in three different areas, which were investigated almost independently of one another. One body of work dealt with bilateral transfer, the almost automatic transfer that takes place between the limbs. A second area was devoted to the study of retroactive effects, briefly described above. The third and largest area was concerned with what might be called transfer proper.

## Bilateral transfer

The phenomenon of bilateral transfer, or 'cross-education', was known to historical figures such as Weber and Fechner (Woodworth and Schlosberg, 1954), who noted that skills learned with the left hand were transferred virtually intact to the right hand. The right-to-left transfer relationship was carefully investigated by Swift (1903), with similar conclusions. Later work explored the limitations of bilateral transfer in such tasks as mirror drawing, or ball-and-cup games, and Cook (1934) used a stylus maze to plot the transfer relationships between hand and foot, as well as hand to hand. Transfer appeared greatest between the two hands, fairly high between the two feet, and appreciable between ipsilateral hands and feet. The least transfer occurred between the contralateral hands and feet.

The work on bilateral transfer was thought to be of theoretical interest mainly for its neurophysiological bearing on the relations between the cerebral hemispheres, and played no part in the early controversy over the broad issues connected with formal discipline. However, the phenomenon is still of potential interest for theories of motor control, and has resurfaced in the investigation of mental practice. (Note that other factors concerning mental practice are discussed by Annett in Chapter 2.) Kohl and Roenker (1983) contrasted the idea that internal feedback should be relatively specific to the practiced limb with the prediction that the outflow from a central motor program should not, testing these hypotheses by giving mental or physical practice with the right or the left hand in a pursuit rotor task. Physical practice conferred more benefit to the same hand than when bilaterally transferred, whereas mental practice was equally good with either hand (and significantly better than no practice), thus favoring a motor outflow explanation for the mental facilitation effect.

Like the bilateral transfer work, the early literature on retroaction pursued an independent course. Most of the work concerned verbal learning, and failed to differentiate between the stimulus and response aspects of the experimental tasks. Probably the most important developments began with work investigating retroactive effects as a function of the degree of similarity between learned materials such as paired associates, chess problems, and digit lists. Rather unexpectedly, Skaggs (1925) confirmed earlier indications that interference increased as the materials became more similar. Obviously, such a trend could not continue indefinitely, since at maximum similarity (in other words, identity), one ought to observe strong facilitation.

As a consequence, Robinson (1927) formulated what has become known as the Skaggs–Robinson hypothesis, or paradox, which states essentially that decreasing similarity leads first to interference and then to neutrality. The Skaggs–Robinson hypothesis was never fully confirmed, in part because of methodological problems such as treating the first and second halves of a list as independent learning episodes. Furthermore, some studies produced reversed effects. Nevertheless, the basic finding has been obtained in a number of different settings. For example, McGeoch and McDonald (1931) found greater interference with increasing similarity both within and across different classes of material varying from synonyms to nonsense syllables. Slamecka (1960) found the same effect in connected discourse, where the similarity of topics in presented sentences seemed to mediate retroactive interference. These types of effects must later be taken into account when considering the problems of negative transfer.

## Similarity

Loss of interest in the Skaggs–Robinson hypothesis was largely due to its failure to separate similarity relationships into separate stimulus and response components. In contrast to the retroaction work, studies in transfer of training had separated these relationships at quite an early stage. The four basic relations between Task A and Task B (which may be modified to accommodate degrees of similarity rather than sameness) are:

1. same stimuli—same responses
2. different stimuli—same responses
3. different stimuli—different responses
4. same stimuli—different responses.

Poffenberger (1915) had investigated cases (1), (3), and (4) in paired-associate learning. Wylie (1919) next supplied data on condition (2), observing transfer between lights, sound or shock as stimuli for maze-running responses by rats, and Bruce (1933) confirmed the differences between (2), (3) and (4) in verbal learning. The consensus was that (1) gave maximum transfer, (2) gave positive transfer, (3) gave no transfer, and (4) tended to give negative transfer.

Osgood (1949) extended these results to include different degrees of similarity, using his own verbal learning results as a guide for compiling a combined transfer and retroaction surface. Although the perspective provided by this three-dimensional graph has been very influential, not all of the predictions that it incorporates have stood the test of time. For example, an extensive contemporary study by Bugelski and Cadwallader (1956) did confirm that transfer and retroaction measures were highly correlated, but failed to observe the predicted negative transfer in case (4) where the responses differ. In general, it seems true that transfer is positive in case (2), the amount tending to decline as the stimuli become less similar, although the degree of similarity is not always easy to specify. Case (3), where both stimuli and responses differ, should certainly give little transfer provided that there is no unsuspected mediation of similarity. The conclusion regarding case (1) is not necessarily true, because training on the task itself does not always produce the maximum transfer. Instances of greater than 100% transfer, such as found by Levine (1953) for tracking tasks with different control delays, are not uncommon.

In any case, similarities between stimuli or tasks are not immutable. Functional similarity depends on the subject's cognitions and experiences, and may vary from time to time. An early example of the liability of functional similarity comes from the work on stimulus generalization, which yields a number of transfer predictions. Gagné and Foster (1949), for example, found that successive practice trials initially had the effect of increasing the breadth of generalization, so that subjects became more inclusive (and thus more likely to transfer) at an intermediate stage of learning. With further practice trials the effect was reversed, giving rise to sharper discrimination instead. It is perhaps for this reason that too much practice on a simulator device such as the Link trainer is said to result in poor transfer. Overlearning becomes specific to the device, thus making it difficult for the trainees to generalize to the real equipment.

The generalization findings also imply that one might expect positive and negative transfer to alternate from time to time, depending on the degree of practice at both Tasks A and B. The greatest chances for negative transfer should occur when both tasks are at an intermediate degree of practice, as observed by Siipola and Israel (1933) and several subsequent investigators, since the increased generalization at this stage provides the maximum potential for confusability. On the other hand, if learning becomes increasingly specific as Task B practice continues further, it is easy to accept that initially negative transfer, as from verbal pretraining to a motor task (McCormack, 1958), might become positive on later trials. These changing relationships are shown in Figure 4.3, which should enjoin caution in interpreting first-shot transfer findings.


**Fidelity**

When transfer to the actual equipment takes place from a simulator or other training device, the similarity issue becomes one of fidelity. It is commonly pointed out that what is required is functional fidelity rather than strict physical fidelity, which is often difficult and expensive to reproduce. Functional fidelity can often be achieved with quite loose simulation of the display characteristics of a task, since practicing the correct responses seems more important than receiving identical stimuli, as in case (2) above. For example, an early success story was reported by Flexman, Matheny and Brown (1950), who obtained good transfer to flying skills after displaying a single line manipulated by the instructor in place of a complete artificial horizon. In a recent

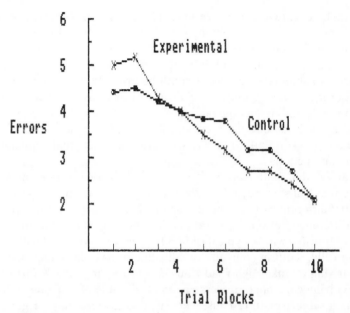

**Figure 4.3.** Negative transfer changing first to positive transfer and eventually to zero difference from the control group as practice proceeds. After McCormack (1958).

review of computer operation, Alessi (1988) even insists that some departure from fidelity tends to favour transfer of training.

Allen, Hays and Buffardi (1986) describe physical fidelity as the property of looking like the real equipment, in contrast to acting like the real equipment, which represents functional fidelity. With similar stimuli for the same response one would predict positive transfer from good functional fidelity, and this proved to be the case when the authors investigated an electromechanical trouble-shooting task. However, variations in physical fidelity also affected some of the scores, depending on the measure chosen, because physical and functional changes interacted. Of course, it is important in such cases for the trainee's attention to be drawn to the critical cues in the task. Admittedly, the consequences of different kinds of display changes are not simple, and differences such as those between landscape depiction and schematic grids can make for appreciable changes in training results (Lintern *et al.*, 1987). However, comparable differences had only non-significant effects in training for a bombing task (Lintern *et al*, 1989), where the differing stimuli supported high positive transfer.

**Rules and principles**

Similarity may be mediated in various ways, such as by word associations in verbal learning, although there appear to be limits to the amounts of transfer conveyed by cognitive generalizations. The transfer of general principles has had a checkered history, beginning with Judd's (1908) well-known reaction to the identical elements theory. Although it was later confirmed (Hendrickson and Schroeder, 1941) that explaining the refraction of light helped children to aim darts at submerged targets, it could be argued that the circumstances of this experiment were unduly specialized. In any case, Colville (1957) later showed that spending an equivalent amount of time on practicing skills gave as good a result as learning mechanical principles. Again, Kresse, Peterson and Grant (1954) found no difference between conceptual explanations and practical instruction.

It may be that both approaches are valid. Salomon and Perkins (1989) propose that transfer may take either the high road or the low road, but with somewhat different consequences. The distinction corresponds approximately to the difference between general and specific transfer. What they regard as low-road transfer will be typical of highly practiced skills and will occur fairly automatically, requiring only minor adjustments as in switching from driving a car to driving a tank. High-road transfer will require some effort of abstraction, involving controlled processing, and is capable of bridging wider gaps in time or in subject matter. Thus, when it works, there may be good transfer from learning a computer language to other computer tasks, but the effect will depend on specifically teaching for transfer and the acquisition of appropriate metacognitive habits. However, there is a history of failures to transfer computer experience and, more generally, a common recognized problem of 'inert' knowledge that fails to connect with new instances or applications.

For the most part, it seems difficult for people to generalize acquired knowledge and methods to new applications and problem solutions. Thus, what Gray and Orasanu (1987) characterize as the 'surprising specificity of transfer' seems to echo Thorndike and Woodworth's (1901) conclusions on specificity. In a representative study, Ross (1984) tried to make use of the analogies between similarly structured probability problems, which were presented under the guise of different cover stories. However, transfer from one problem to another was only good when the cover stories contained the same subject matter. Specificity seemed important because transfer dropped sharply when the subject matter differed from one cover story to another.

More detailed forms of specificity were observed when subjects had to infer arithmetical rules on the basis of right and wrong instances, as in discovering that the answer to the stimulus 43 should be 50, because 50 = 43 + 4 + 3. Sommers, Holding and Fingerman (1978) found that transfer to new rules was affected by the domain from which hypotheses were sampled. Later transfer to the rule that 43 = 36, because 36 = 43 − (4 + 3), was fairly easy and could be accomplished in two or three trials. In this case the new rule was drawn from the same domain, merely requiring subtraction instead of addition, but using the same sum of digits. However, it took three to ten times as many trials (depending on the instructions) to transfer to a problem that required the use of outside constants, such as the otherwise simple rule that 43 = 47 because 47 = 43 + (3 + 1). Problems like the latter are quite easy when presented first, but switching domains has a negative effect on transfer.

In analogical problem solving, it may be useful to distinguish between solution procedures and the representations that mediate solutions. The transfer of solution procedures is ineffective in most cases when the nature of the problems is diverse, unless deliberate hints or instructions are given. However, Novick (1990) has reported successful spontaneous transfer between problems that could all be solved by the use of a matrix representation. Prior experience with geometric and algebraic representations were discarded by subjects in favor of a matrix, earlier required in a probability problem, which could be used to solve a logic problem. Perhaps the use of a matrix might be regarded as a high-level solution procedure, although its method of employment differs between the two kinds of problem.

The practical aspects of problem-solving transfer are found in areas such as industrial trouble-shooting. Most of the early work in this context has concluded that the teaching of theory, as in the form of a 'technical story' concerning the operation of a chemical plant (Shepherd et al., 1977), transfers poorly to the diagnosing of faults in process control. Again, translating general principles into action seems inferior to more specific training. Giving explicit heuristics such as 'high temperature and pressure in column head associated with low level in reflux drum indicates overhead condenser failure . . .' worked better than presenting the technical story, even for transfer to unfamiliar faults.

More recent work by Patrick and Haines (1988) seemed to show some advantage for the technical story approach, which helped trainees to diagnose new faults drawn from the same category as the training examples. This form of training did transfer to diagnoses made in a new plant layout, although not to novel faults from untrained categories. Unfortunately any advantage due to teaching either theory or diagnostic heuristics was no longer apparent in related experiments where transfer was to a process flow that contained a recycle loop (Patrick et al., 1989). Both methods gave quick diagnosis decisions, with few instrument readings, but were equally inaccurate even for faults that remained unchanged by the recycle loop. It is evident that the transfer of both general and specific principles must be regarded as extremely fragile.

## SPECIAL PROBLEMS

Of the many transfer issues that deserve further discussion, three seem particularly important. One type of problem is posed by the existence of asymmetrical transfer, which occurs when the amount of transfer from A to B is different from the amount transferred from B to A. This effect cannot be explained in terms of similarity, because if A is similar to B in some respect then B is equally similar to A. Next, brief mention must be made of a second, related problem which occurs in trying to evaluate the benefits of part–whole transfer. The third special problem concerns the prediction of negative transfer, which has proved somewhat intractable over the years. Admittedly, it does not often happen that training on task A makes people worse on task B. However, it can happen, at least on some measures of performance, and there is an obvious practical advantage in understanding the conditions in which negative transfer might be expected or prevented.

**Asymmetrical transfer**

The work on bilateral transfer already showed some indications of asymmetry, with unequal amounts of transfer depending on the direction of transfer. However, the problem of asymmetry first emerged as a major issue in connection with tasks that differed in difficulty. Although the normal educational progression is from easy to difficult tasks, several experiments demonstrated better transfer in what was interpreted as the difficult-to-easy direction. An early example was provided by Szafran and Welford (1950), who found that practicing the difficult task of throwing chains over a bar while seeing the target through a mirror gave better transfer to the simpler task, of throwing directly at the target, than occurred in the reverse direction. Baker, Wylie and Gagné (1950) found similar effects in transfer between tracking tasks using different gear ratios, and Gibbs (1951) showed better transfer from complex to simple tracking tasks than from simple to complex.

On the other hand, there were a number of counter-examples. Baker and Osgood (1954), for instance, showed better easty-to-difficult transfer in learning pitch discriminations, while Lincoln and Smith (1951) found that pursuit rotor training transferred better from the slower, easier speeds than from the more difficult, faster speeds. It is clear that some explanation is needed to account for these discrepancies, and it also seems clear that such an explanation cannot rely on the concept of task difficulty. As Holding (1965) pointed out, there is no such thing as difficulty, viewed as a separately measurable entity. Tasks are regarded as difficult when they generate high error scores or long learning curves, but these effects derive from the manipulation of specific variables such as target size, number of choices, or size of memory load, each of which will have individual implications for transfer. The problem is to find ways of generalizing across classes of such variables in order to predict the direction of transfer.

An early review by Day (1956) proposed that variations in perceptual demand should produce easy-to-diffficult transfer effects, while variations in motor demand make for difficult-to-easy results. However, this conclusion is already falsified by the examples given above. Changes in target speed are not primarily perceptual, but give easy-to-difficult superiority, and interposing a mirror is not primarily a motor constraint, but gives difficult-to-easy superiority. Other variables that have shown easy–difficult effects include target amplitude, and some forms of task complexity. In the reverse direction, difficult–easy results have arisen from changes in control characteristics or in display–control relationships, and from other forms of complexity. It has also been shown that both directions of effect may be observed in the same experimental task, given relatively minor changes in the task variables.

A plausible way to explain these conflicting results is to examine the trade-off between at least two opposing tendencies in transfer. On the basis of experimental results on pursuit tracking, Holding (1962) suggested that the situation could be described in terms of the balance between learning more, and learning better. Learning more is a consequence of the principle of *inclusion*, and learning better depends on what may loosely be called the acquisition of appropriate *performance standards*. Interpreted broadly, inclusion occurs whenever learning Task A involves also learning Task B, but the learning of B omits elements of A. For example, learning to calculate a statistic may involve learning to obtain square roots, but learning square roots is only a minor component of learning the statistic. As Briggs (1969) noted, the more inclusive task will usually also be the more difficult, so that the inclusion principle would predict superior transfer in the difficult-to-easy direction. However, in many cases the more complex task will be too difficult to master, or may inculcate poor or inappropriate standards of performance. In such cases the learning of better methods of smaller error tolerances, or more accurate anticipations, will tend to favor transfer from the simpler to the more difficult task.

A demonstration of both effects was constructed by measuring transfer between tracking tasks varying in target amplitude, at two different bandwidths of the frequencies that comprised a target course (Holding, 1962). Practicing at the high amplitude obviously included some practice at smaller excursions, but practice at the smaller did not include the higher peaks. Hence, when the frequency demand was low (at the narrower bandwidth), the inclusion principle dominated and transfer was greater from the difficult to the easy version. However, at the broader course bandwidth the high amplitude task was impossible to master, while practice at the smaller amplitude allowed for the learning of better anticipation and smaller margins of error. Consequently, the direction of optimum transfer was reversed, with better results from easy to difficult.

Confirmation of the inclusion effect has been provided by Williges and Baron (1973) who found difficult-to-easy superiority in complex tracking where successive target courses were systematically ordered. The inclusion principle like other transfer relationships, can also be interpreted more broadly in application to such cognitive factors as movement strategies. Fumoto (1981) obtained asymmetrical transfer on a modified pursuit rotor device which required far and near movements at regular or irregular intervals. Detailed analysis of the results suggested that an intermittent movement strategy developed on the difficult irregular task was also viable on the easier, regular version. In contrast, the smooth continuous strategy encouraged by practice on the regular task was inappropriate for the irregular version, so that difficult-to-easy transfer proved superior.

The opposite result, apparently overshadowing strategy inclusion effects, was obtained by Livesey and Laszlo (1979). In this case something like the performance standards effect seems to have given rise to better transfer from the simpler task, which consisted of stabbing at larger rather than smaller moving dots. The easier task apparently allowed for better, instead of broader, learning despite the fact that both tasks were found to encourage accuracy over speed. A recent example of better easy-to-difficult transfer occurred in work on flight simulators by Lintern, Roscoe and Sivier (1989). Easier training, without a crosswind component, transferred better to the criterion task than more difficult training with a crosswind, even though the criterion task included a crosswind. Again, poorer learning on the more difficult version seems to have provided less transfer.

Certain effects are more difficult to classify because both asymmetric mechanisms may work in the same direction. Learning the task that was more inclusive nevertheless led to better learning in an experiment by Kessel and Wickens (1982), where subjects had to detect changes in the system dynamics of a pursuit task. Skill acquired by controlling the system transferred well to the subsidiary task of simply monitoring the system, but there was no transfer in the reverse direction from monitoring to controlling. It appeared that only the controlling task directed the subjects' attention to the critical perceptual cues, which could then be utilized in the monitoring task. Attention was paid to inappropriate cues during practice at monitoring, thus leading to poorer transfer.

Of course, asymmetrical effects are often obtained in cognitive tasks. Inclusion relations occur in text editing, for example where the knowledge acquired by using a line editor may include more rules than using a screen editor. Other cases include attempting to read text in which letters have been distorted. Such examples may lead to the situation where transfer from A to B is not equivalent to the reverse, perhaps because training on A constitutes better preparation for B than practice on B itself (Kolers and Roediger, 1984). It is possible to account for these cases in terms of the inclusion versus performance standards principles, although the interpretation of the concepts requires some extension. Tversky (1977) suggested that asymmetries in knowledge transfer may occur simply because A is a better model for B than B is for A. However, this approach makes no distinction between learning more and learning better, and has little predictive power unless supported by more detailed cognitive theories.

## Part–whole transfer

A special case of inclusion occurs when a whole task is divided into parts which are given separate training according to one of several possible schedules. The object here is almost always to compare part training with whole training as preparations for performing the whole task, and the possible asymmetries in transferring from the whole task to component parts have not been at issue. A variant of this paradigm occurs when the 'whole' task in fact requires dual-task performance. In these circumstances, it appears that practice on the single tasks that form part of the dual-task combination may provide rather poor transfer (Schneider and Detweiler, 1988), because subjects continue to need extensive practice at integrating the concurrent tasks. It should be noted that evaluating such issues by using within-subjects designs does not appear to be appreciably contaminated by asymmetric transfer effects (Vidulich, 1988).

The early literature on part–whole training contained many instances in which whole training was superior, although the necessity for part training obviously increases with the size and complexity of the target activity. The effectiveness of part training may also depend on the manner in which a task is subdivided into parts. An influential paper by Naylor and Briggs (1963) indicated that, in addition to task complexity, the efficiency of part methods also depended on the degree of interdependence of the parts. With independent parts separate training was considered effective, but with interdependent parts the whole method seemed superior. The empirical backing for this conclusion is rather weak, and a recent attempt by Holding and Baker-Noren (1986) to assess interdependence by using performance operating characteristics found only that whole training was superior at each level of resource sharing. It is possible that this result arose because the division of the task into parts took the form of fractionation, which occurs when normally concurrent components are separated for isolated practice.

The review by Wightman and Lintern (1985) suggests that whole task practice is nearly always preferable to the fractionation of parts. However there are many instances in which part practice is preferable to whole practice when the division into parts has been accomplished by segmentation. Using this method, a task is subdivided into several successive stages which are practiced separately. Recent interest has centered on techniques of chaining, in which segmented part practice accumulates successively. It has been shown that backward chaining, in which practice would occur on part 3, then 2 and 3, then 1 and 2 and 3, is preferable to whole training for flying skills. However, Ash and Holding (1990) recently found that forward chaining is superior to backward chaining for a musical keyboard task, and the issue must be regarded as remaining open. The part–whole issue is more fully discussed by Lintern in Chapter 6 of this volume, in connection with methods of practice.

## Negative transfer

A major objective in the design of many training schemes is the avoidance of negative transfer. This may perhaps seem odd, as negative transfer is so rarely reported. In their review of motor skills, Bilodeau and Bilodeau (1961) concluded that negative transfer is difficult to produce, and when produced is obtained only in small amounts, which rapidly convert to positive transfer. More recently, Schmidt and Young (1987) have confirmed that very few instances of negative transfer occur in the research literature. This finding is itself curious, since negative transfer is simply positive transfer in an inappropriate context. The trainee goes on doing what was learned in Task A but the experimental demands, or the real-world consequences, have changed so that the Task B requirements are now different. This sequence of events might have been expected to occur fairly often.

The difficulty is that the change in requirements seldom affects the entire activity, with the result that the overall performance scores rarely show negative effects. Overall negative transfer is found only when there has been a violent change in demand, masked by a general background of similarity. In verbal learning, these conditions are not met in the A–B, A–C paradigm, but do occur in the special case where the pairings of stimulus and response items in the A–B list have been completely reshuffled (Porter and Duncan, 1953). Probably the best instance of negative transfer in sensorimotor learning was provided by Lewis, McAllister and Adams (1951), but this result was obtained by completely reversing the display–control relationships in a complex task controlled by a joystick and rudder bar. One recent instance of negative transfer was found in visual search, where Fisk and Rogers (1988) interchanged the target words with the original distractor items.

In most cases, however, negative transfer will only be evidenced by occasional, intrusive errors. Prolonged practice at typing, for example, will produce high overall transfer to using a word processor, but within this positive transfer there will be a tendency toward sporadic errors due to hitting the carriage return at the end of a line of text. Whether or not this type of result shows up as negative transfer will depend on how performance is scored or, for practical purposes, on the consequences of making an error. Transfer from flying one airplane to another may bring high, potentially positive, transfer, but the effect would be vitiated by the classic error of pulling a lever to raise the undercarriage instead of setting the flaps. The consequences of dropping on to the runway are sufficiently adverse to warrant characterizing the result as negative transfer, despite the overall transfer of skill. Hence, positive and negative transfer can be shown to coexist, provided that multiple measures of performances are available. In fact, there were already indications of concurrent facilitation and interference in the Lewis, McAllister and Adams (1951) studies, and McFann (1953) found overall facilitation occurring at the same time as increased errors in a line-tracing task.

A pertinent example of the conflict between different performance measures was obtained, but not utilized, by Osgood (1949). The 'empirical law' for negative transfer incorporated in his transfer and retroaction surface proposed that, with identical stimuli, negative transfer increases as the required responses become more dissimilar. This statement has repeatedly been shown to be untrue (Holding, 1976), and does not really reflect the trends in the original data. Osgood's (1946) own findings for two different measures, based on varying semantic similarities between word lists in a retroaction paradigm, are plotted in Figure 4.4. The times taken to respond, which might be regarded as a subsidiary measure, do tend to follow the suggested pattern, increasing slightly with word dissimilarity. However, if negative transfer is regarded as prior learning appearing in an inappropriate context, the most direct indication of its occurrence should be given by the presence of intrusive errors. As Figures 4.4 shows, the intrusions from prior lists clearly follow the reverse relationship, decreasing markedly as word similarity diminishes.

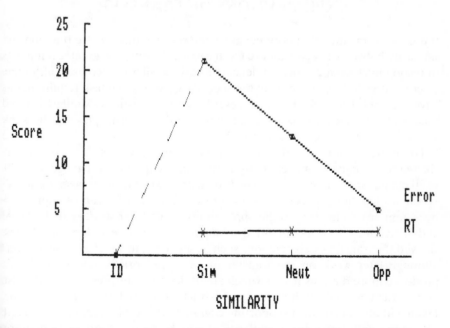

**Figure 4.4.** Transfer as a function of word similarity. Although response times decrease marginally with increasing similarity, the intrusions from other lists follow the Skaggs–Robinson curve, increasing with similarity. Based on data from Osgood (1946).

The situation is therefore quite well described by the Skaggs–Robinson hypothesis. As Tasks A and B become more similar, the practical chances of negative transfer become greater. The reasons for this effect might be basically cognitive, because the subjects simply become confused about which response is appropriate, or might be a consequence of automaticity, with prolonged practice giving rise to habit interference. In any case, when the task stimuli become more similar or the required responses become less discriminable, trainees are more likely to commit intrusive errors. Holding (1976) incorporated these relationships into a revised transfer surface, also depicting the abrupt change from negative to positive transfer that takes place when Tasks A and B approach identity. This reversal underlies the Skaggs–Robinson paradox, and occurs whenever high similarity is scored as identity. At this point the trainee continues to respond in the same way, but is credited with positive instead of negative transfer because the criterion has changed. With slightly reduced similarity, if the experimenter or the real world distinguishes between Tasks A and B while the trainee does not, making the same response would be considered evidence of negative transfer.

# EXPLANATIONS OF TRANSFER

It is easy to conclude that both negative and positive transfer are functions of similarity between Tasks A and B. Both cases arise from the greater tendency to respond in the same way that occurs as task similarity increases, although negative transfer appears only in the special case where the task requirements have changed. The difficulty lies in describing what constitutes similarity or, as was expressed above, to what extent the transfer of principles can be substituted for the transfer of identical elements.

There are obvious transfer implications to be drawn as the task stimuli change from mauve to magenta, as the response requirements change from 20 to 30 cm per second, or even as words on a list change from 'repose' to quasi-synonyms like 'low arousal'. It is less obvious that transfer can be supported by as tenuous a similarity as the applicability of a similar strategy to Tasks A and B. Even early work intended to support the identical elements theory showed the transfer of abstractions such as speed habits in letter cancellation, although later work on the transfer of strategies, briefly reviewed above, produced more dubious results which are difficult to interpret. In fact, it must be regarded as doubtful how far the abstraction of similarity can usefully be taken without specifying a supporting cognitive or neural mechanism. Instead of attempting to investigate similarity, it may be more important to enquire what it is that transfers, and what structures or processes underlie the observed transfer.

## Motor control theories

One variant of the above approach is to postulate a mechanism so general that the need for transfer is eliminated, because both Tasks A and B are served by the same mechanism. Gibbs (1951), for example, put forward a detailed analysis of the human operator regarded as a servo-mechanism that incorporates many internal control loops with self-regulating properties. Such a system will respond automatically and correctly over a wide range of related activities, such as tracking tasks with different input and output characteristics. Transferring between tracks at different amplitudes will require the adjustment of only one or two parameters, using the existing potential of the system. Much of this is very plausible, although supplementary assumptions are required to handle asymmetric transfer effects.

An alternative conception with analogous consequences is the schema theory propounded by Schmidt (1975). A schema, in this context, is a representation of an entire class of cognate actions. Perhaps it should be characterized as constituting the *prototype* for a range of motor programs and their feedback consequences. Once again the theory suggests that new responses will be generated automatically (in this case by a schema that incorporates closed-loop processes), so that transfer is rendered unnecessary. Similarly, the theory of motor control proposed by Turvey, Shaw and Mace (1978) defines the sets of muscles used for functionally equivalent responses as coordinative structures with wide applicability. Any pattern of activity will be controlled by a structural prescription that specifies which muscle groups are required, and by a metrical prescription that determines the amount of activity to be carried out. Since the metrical prescription is easily modified, positive transfer will again be expected over a wide range of skills.

One test of the generalized motor programme concept was conducted by Heuer and Schmidt (1988), with ambiguous results. Although motor programs tend to preserve the relative timing between successive phases of an activity, transfer from one motor pattern to another, which differed only in duration, was no better than transfer to a pattern generated by a non-linear transformation of the timing relationships. This finding seems to imply that timing characteristics are not determined by invariant properties of motor programs, but are the outcomes of preferred strategies. However, the experiment does not directly disconfirm the schema theory, which is inherently difficult to submit to experimental test.

One line of relevant evidence concerns the effects of variety of practice, which should lead to the development of richer schemata and thus to positive transfer over a wide range of activity. Hence evidence like that of Newell and Shapiro (1976), showing that variable practice gives rise to some transfer outside the original range of responses, has been taken to support the schema notion. However, variety of practice has previously been identified as beneficial for other reasons. Wolfe (1951) devoted a section of his training chapter to variety of practice materials, on the grounds that use of the technique prevented the learning of irrelevant habits, and Duncan (1958) showed that varied practice on a lights-and-lever task even improved performance when the stimulus lights were replaced by nonsense syllables. Macrae and Holding (1965) argued that providing guidance at a variety of movement extents helped to define the required range of activity, finding varied practice better than simply practicing the transfer task. In a more recent example, Shea and Morgan (1979) found better transfer after giving random rather than blocked practice trials, but ascribed the results to the processing strategies induced by contextual interference. However, formulations of the type indicated by schema theory undoubtedly capture important explanatory concepts.

Most theories of cognitive motor skills, such as Shaffer's (1975) account of expertise at typing, postulate hierarchical systems exerting control at two or more levels. For example, Mackay's (1982) model for speech production employs a conceptual system (propositional, conceptual, lexical), a phonological system (syllabic, phonological, phonemic, phonetic), and a muscle movement system. Presumably some transfer will be mediated at each of these levels, in a manner reminiscent of Salomon and Perkins's (1989) high and low roads. However, more practice will usually have occurred at the lower levels of the hierarchy; for instance, one makes the movements for the sound 't' more often than one plans a paragraph on transfer. Hence, the linkages to the lower nodes will be differentially strengthened so that more transfer should be predicted, with some empirical justification, toward the base of the hierarchy.

**Cognitive theories**

Building mental models can assist both learning and transfer. Such models may take the explicit form of network representations of the external environment, mapping the angular relations between experienced locations (Holding and Holding, 1989). Alternatively, mental models may map the abstract paths between initial problem states and desired subgoals, which may be generated by applying different operators within the problem spaces used to represent cognitive tasks. Eberts and Schneider (1985) found that giving augmentation cues to assist the development of mental models for a complex tracking task led to better transfer, even though the technique did not produce better original learning. In Kieras and Bovair's (1984) experiment, teaching the subjects a model for an imaginary science fiction device led to better learning.

Such models can include both procedural knowledge, relating to methods, and declarative knowledge, relating to facts. This distinction alone can be used to generate predictions for transfer, as Anderson (1987) suggests. Applying the same procedures to the same declarative knowledge should give good transfer across different tasks, but the same declarative knowledge may be useless if different procedures are required. Most interest attaches to the transfer of procedures, which are often represented in terms of production rules (sets of if–then statements). When these are associated with specific variables, such rules can mediate transfer directly through their application to a broad range of different cognitive operations or behavior patterns.

The ACT* theory outlined by Anderson (1983) regards the acquisition of skill as a form of knowledge compilation in which general production rules come to govern specific segments of declarative knowledge. As learning proceeds, a core of relatively specific procedures is formulated and the requisite declarative knowledge becomes directly incorporated into production rules. The accomplishment of these processes requires that production rules and subgoal information should be jointly present in working memory, a condition normally satisfied during practice at a task. Hence, actual practice will be more important than instruction in producing learning. However, because practice tends to make procedures increasingly specific, the range over which transfer takes place will become confined to the tasks that share those procedures.

Some instances of these effects have been drawn from analyses of text editing (Singley and Anderson, 1985). Expert typists either transferred between two line editors, or simply practiced typing at the terminal, before final transfer to a screen editor. As expected, transfer was high between the closely related line editors, intermediate from the line editors to the screen editor, and minimal from typing practice alone. Subsequent analyses of the keystroke data found detailed differences in transfer of the line-locating and text-modifying components of the task, which could be attributed to differences in the inclusiveness of the underlying goal structure. Some anomalies occurred, due to specific problems such as transferring the habit of using the carriage return to locate lines. Nevertheless, the experiment illustrates the advantages to be gained by making detailed analyses of transfer.

Although existing cognitive theories have made progress in explaining the mechanisms of transfer, one final complication must be considered. Transfer is not always spontaneous and, at least in some instances, its effectiveness may depend on metacognition (Flavell, 1979). For example, one may better avoid negative transfer when driving on the left, or right, by reminding oneself of the pitfalls. Metacognitive processes, which may be taken to include the awareness of knowledge, the self-assessment of skills, and perhaps the allocation of attention, apparently vary in effectiveness at different stages of the transfer process. As Gick and Holyoak (1987) point out, the learner may have to strive actively to remember and apply appropriate knowledge at the time of retrieval. However, unless the need for such effort is signaled by metacognitive deficiencies in feelings of knowing, the attempt may not be made. Given such considerations, it should not be surprising that training in metacognitive skills can facilitate transfer.

## SUMMARY AND CONCLUSIONS

The topics addressed in the chapter have ranged over a wide selection of transfer issues. After describing the basic requirements for experimental design, we considered the problems of measurement that affect conclusions drawn from transfer experiments. Traditional first-shot measures can give useful information in cases where interest attaches to the initial level of performance on a task, or where the experiment does not continue beyond that stage. Savings scores give a different type of information which is valuable when examining protracted second-task performance, as is often required in evaluating training schemes.

The issues of historical importance, from bilateral transfer work to the main body of research on retroaction and transfer, tend to revolve around interpretations of the similarity relationship. Separating the similarities between tasks into stimulus and response aspects can provide some clarification, although early claims to predict the details of transfer on this basis seem unjustified. When similarity is considered in terms of device fidelity, the stimulus aspects of physical fidelity appear less important than the response aspects of functional fidelity. At the more general level of rules and principles, some transfer seems to occur, but with more specificity than might be expected. The teaching of theory also seems to fare badly in applied, industrial training.

The special problem of asymmetrical transfer raises issues extraneous to similarity. Although early examples of asymmetry were provided by changes in task difficulty, other factors seem more important. The principle of inclusion, offset where necessary by differences in the quality of learning, explain many of the findings. Part–whole transfer was briefly reviewed, prompting the conclusion that the segmentation technique, perhaps accompanied by chaining, gives useful results. Negative transfer can be viewed as raising questions of measurement, but is sometimes of practical importance where intrusive errors must be avoided. In line with the Skaggs–Robinson hypothesis, such errors are more likely to occur as tasks become more similar, particularly where differences between the required responses are obscure.

Recent theories suggest that the basis for similarity in transfer is best sought by identifying the mechanisms that underlie performance. For motor skills, explanations may rely on servo loops, schema constructs, or coordinative structures. The beneficial effects of variety of practice tend to support the idea that some form of flexible, inclusive structure is required. Cognitive motor theories postulate hierarchical control systems, with more transfer occurring at the lower levels. Transfer between cognitive tasks may be mediated by mental models, which are often represented as production systems. Finally, the outcome of transfer may be influenced by metacognitive processes.

# REFERENCES

Adams, J. A. (1987). Historical review and appraisal of research on the learning, retention, and transfer of human motor skills, *Psychological Bulletin*, **101**, 141–174.

Alessi, S. M. (1988). Fidelity in the design of instructional simulations, *Journal of Computer-Based Instruction*, **15**, 40–47.

Allen, J. A., Hays, R. T. and Buffardi, L. C. (1986). Maintenance training simulator fidelity and individual differences in transfer of training, *Human Factors*, **28**, 497–509.

Anderson, J. R. (1983). *The Architecture of Cognition*. Cambridge, MA: Harvard University Press.

Anderson, J. R. (1987). Skill acquisition: Compilation of weak-method problem-solutions, *Psychological Review*, **94**, 192–210.

Ash, D. W. and Holding, D. H. (1990). Backward versus forward chaining in the acquisition of a keyboard skill, *Human Factors*, **32** 139–146.

Baker, K. E., Wylie, R. C. and Gagné, R. M. (1950). Transfer of training to a motor skill as a function of variation in rate of response, *Journal of Experimental Psychology*, **40**, 721–732.

Baker, R. A. and Osgood, S. W. (1954). Discrimination transfer along a pitch continuum, *Journal of Experimental Psychology*, **48**, 241–246.

Bickley, W. R. (1980). *Training Device Effectiveness: Formulation and Evaluation of a Methodology* (ARI Research Report 1291). Alexandria, VA: US Army Institute for the Behavioral and Social Sciences.

Bilodeau, E. A. and Bilodeau, I. McD. (1961). Motor-skills learning, *Annual Review of Psychology*, **12**, 243–280.

Boldovici, J. A. (1987). Measuring transfer in military settings. In S. M. Cormier and J. D. Hagman (eds). *Transfer of Learning*, pp. 239–260. New York: Academic Press.

Briggs, G. E. (1969). Transfer of training. In E. A. and I. McD. Bilodeau (eds). *Principles of Skill Acquisition*, pp. 205–234. New York: Academic Press.

Bruce, R. W. (1933). Conditions of transfer of training, *Journal of Experimental Psychology*, **16**, 343–361.

Bugelski, B. R. and Cadwellader, T. C. (1956). A reappraisal of the transfer and retroaction surface, *Journal of Experimental Psychology*, **52**, 360–366.

Carter, G. and Trollip, S. (1980). A constrained maximization extension to incremental training effectiveness, or, how to mix your training technologies, *Human Factors*, **22**, 141–152.

Colville, F. M. (1957). The learning of motor skills as influenced by knowledge of mechanical principles, *Journal of Educational Psychology*, **48** 321–327.

Cook, T. W. (1934). Studies in cross-education. III. Kinesthetic learning of an irregular pattern, *Journal of Experimental Psychology*, **17**, 749–762.

Cronholm, J. N. (1985). The optimization of training systems, *Proceedings of the Symposiums on the Transfer of Training to Military Operational Systems*, pp. 237–259. Brussels, Belgium: NATO.

Day, R. H. (1956). Relative task difficulty and transfer of training in skilled performance, *Psychological Bulletin*, **53**, 160–168.

Duncan, C. P. (1958). Transfer after training with single versus multiple tasks, *Journal of Experimental Psychology*, **55**, 63–72.

Eberts, R. and Schneider, W. (1985). Internalizing the system dynamics for a second-order system, *Human Factors*, **27**, 371–393.

Farrell, J. P. and Fineberg, M. L. (1976) Specialized training versus experience in helicopter navigation at extremely low altitudes, *Human Factors*, **18**, 305–308.

Fisk, A. D. and Rogers, W. A. (1988). The role of situational context in the development of high-performance skills. *Human Factors*, **30**, 703–712.

Flavell, J. H. (1979). Metacognition and cognitive monitoring, *American Psychologist*, **34**, 906–911.

Flexman, R. E., Matheny, W. G. and Brown, E. L. (1950). *Evaluation of the Link and Special Methods of Instruction* (Aeronautics Bulletin No. 8). Champaign, IL: University of Illinois.

Fumoto, N. (1981). Asymmetric transfer in a pursuit tracking task related to change of strategy, *Journal of Motor Behavior*, **13**, 197–206.

Gagné, R. M. and Foster, H. (1949). Transfer to a motor skill from a pictured representation, *Journal of Experimental Psychology*, **39**, 342–355.

Gagné, R. M., Foster, H. and Crowley, M. E. (1948). The measurement of transfer of training, *Psychological Bulletin*, **45**, 97–130.

Gibbs, C. B. (1951). Transfer of training and skill assumptions in tracking, *Quarterly Journal of Experimental Psychology*, **3**, 99–110.

Gick, M. L. and Holyoak, K. J. (1987). The cognitive basis of knowledge transfer. In S. M. Cormier and J. D. Hagman (eds). *Transfer of Learning*, pp. 9–46. New York: Academic Press.

Gray, W. D. and Orasanu, J. M. (1987). Transfer of cognitive skills. In S. M. Cormier and J. D. Hagman (eds). *Transfer of Learning*, pp. 183–215. New York: Academic Press.

Green, B. and Hall, J. (1984) Quantitative methods for literature review, *Annual Review of Psychology*, **35**, 37–53.

Hammerton, M. (1989). Tracking. In D. H. Holding (ed.). *Human Skills*, pp. 171–196. Chichester: John Wiley.

Hammerton, M. and Tickner, A. H. (1967). Visual factors affecting transfer of training from a simulated to a real control situation, *Journal of Applied Psychology*, **51**, 46–49.

Hendrickson, G. and Schroeder, W. H. (1941). Transfer of training in learning to hit a submerged target, *Journal of Educational Psychology*, **32**, 205–213.

Heuer, H. and Schmidt, R. A. (1988). Transfer of learning among motor patterns with different relative timing, *Journal of Experimental Psychology: Human Perception and Performance*, **14**, 241–252.

Holding, C. S. and Holding, D. H. (1989). Acquisition of route network knowledge by males and females, *Journal of General Psychology*, **116**, 29–41.

Holding, D. H. (1962). Transfer between difficult and easy tasks, *British Journal of Psychology*, **53**, 397–407.

Holding, D. H. (1965). *Principles of Training*. Oxford: Pergamon Press.

Holding, D. H. (1976). An approximate transfer surface, *Journal of Motor Behavior*, **8** 1–9.

Holding, D. H. (1977). Transfer of training. In B. B. Wolman (ed.). *International Encyclopedia of Psychiatry, Psychology, Psychoanalysis and Neurology*, pp. 268–272. New York: Van Nostrand.

Holding, D. H. (1987). Concepts of training. In G. Salvendy (ed.). *Handbook of Human Factors*, p. 958. New York: Wiley.

Holding, D. H. and Baker-Noren, J. A. (1986). *Component Independence in Part-Task Training* (HumRRO Report FR–PRD–86–22). Alexandria, VA: Human Resources Research Organization.

Judd, C. H. (1908). The relation of special training to general intelligence, *Educational Review*, **36**, 28–42.

Kessel, C. J. and Wickens, C. D. (1982). The transfer of failure-detection skills between monitoring and controlling dynamic systems, *Human Factors*, **24**, 49–60.

Kieras, D. E. and Bovair, S. (1984). The role of a mental model in learning to operate a device, *Cognitive Science*, **8**, 255–273.

Kohl, R. M. and Roenker, D. L. (1983). Mechanism involvement during skill imagery, *Journal of Motor Behavior*, **15**, 179–190.

Kolers, P. A. and Roediger, H. L. (1984). Procedures of mind, *Journal of Verbal Learning and Verbal Behavior*, **23**, 425–449.

Kresse, F. H., Peterson, R. N. and Grant, D. A. (1954). Multiple response transfer as a function of supplementary training with verbal schematic aids. *Journal of Experimental Psychology*, **48**, 381–390.

Levine, M. (1953). *Transfer of Tracking Performance as a Function of Delay between the Control and the Display* (WADC Technical Report 52–237). Dayton, Ohio: Wright Air Development Center.

Lewis, D., McAllister, D. E. and Adams, J. A. (1951). Facilitation and interference in performance on the modified Mashburn apparatus: I. The effects of varying the amount of original learning, *Journal of Experimental Psychology*, **41**, 247–260.

Lincoln, R. S. and Smith, K. U. (1951). Transfer of training in tracking performance at different target speeds, *Journal of Applied Psychology*, **35**, 358–362.

Lintern, G., Roscoe, S. N. and Sivier, J. E. (1989). Display principles, control dynamics, and environmental factors in pilot performance and transfer of training, *Proceedings of the Fifth International Symposium on Aviation Psychology*, pp. 134–148. Columbus, OH.

Lintern, G., Sheppard, D. J., Parker, D. L., Yates, K. E. and Nolan, M. D. (1989). Simulator design and instructional features for air-to-ground attack: A transfer study, *Human Factors*, **31**, 87–99.

Lintern, G., Thomley-Yates, K. E., Nelson, B. E. and Roscoe, S. N. (1987). Content, variety, and augmentation of simulated visual scenes for teaching air-to-ground attack, *Human Factors*, **29**, 45–59.

Livesey, J. P. and Laszlo, J. I. (1979). Effect of task similarity on transfer performance, *Journal of Motor Behavior*, **11**, 11–21.

Mackay, D. G. (1982). The problems of flexibility, fluency, and speed-accuracy tradeoff in skilled behavior, *Psychological Review*, **89**, 483–506.

Macrae, A. W. and Holding, D. H. (1965). Method and task in motor guidance, *Ergonomics*, **8**, 315–320.

McCormack, P. D. (1958). Negative transfer in motor performance following a critical amount of verbal pretraining, *Perceptual and Motor Skills*, **8**, 27–31.

McFann, H. H. (1953). Effect of response alteration and different instructions on practice and retroactive facilitation and interference, *Journal of Educational Psychology*, **46**, 405–410.

McGeoch, J. A. (1942). *The Psychology of Human Learning*. New York: Longmans, Green.

McGeoch, J. A. and McDonald, W. T. (1931). Meaningful relation and retroactive inhibition, *American Journal of Psychology*, **43**, 579–588.

Morrison, J. E. and Holding, D. H. (1990). *Designing a Gunnery Training Strategy* (HumRRO Report FR–PRD–90–12). Alexandria, VA: Human Resources Research Organization.

Murdock, B. B. (1957). Transfer designs and formulas, *Psychological Bulletin*, **54**, 313–326.

Naylor, J. C. and Briggs, G. E. (1963). Effects of task complexity and task organization on the relative efficiency of part and whole methods, *Journal of Experimental Psychology*, **65**, 217–224.

Newell, K. M. and Shapiro, D. C. (1976). Variability of practice and transfer of training: Some evidence towards a schema view of learning, *Journal of Motor Behavior*, **8**, 233–243.

Novick, L. R. (1990). Representational transfer in problem solving, *Psychological Sciences*, **1**, 128–132.

Osgood, C. E. (1946). Meaningful similarity and interference in learning, *Journal of Experimental Psychology*, **36**, 277–301.

Osgood, C. E. (1949). The similarity paradox in human learning: A resolution, *Psychological Review*, **56**, 132–143.

Patrick, J. and Haines, B. (1988). Training and transfer of fault-finding skill, *Ergonomics*, **31**, 193–210.

Patrick, J., Haines, B., Munley, G. and Wallace, A. (1989). Transfer of fault-finding between simulated chemical plants, *Human Factors*, **31**, 503–518.

Poffenberger, A. T. (1915). The influence of improvement in one single mental process upon other related processes, *Journal of Educational Psychology*, **6**, 459–474.

Porter, L. W. and Duncan, C. P. (1953). Negative transfer in verbal learning, *Journal of Experimental Psychology*, **46**, 61–64.

Postman, L. (1972). Transfer, interference and forgetting. In J. W. Kling and L. A. Riggs (eds). *Woodworth and Schlosberg's Experimental Psychology*, pp. 1019–1132. New York: Holt, Rinehart and Winston.

Poulton, E. C. (1973). Unwanted range effects from using within-subject experimental designs, *Psychological Bulletin*, **80**, 113–121.

Robinson, E. J. (1927). The 'similarity' factor in retroaction, *American Journal of Psychology*, **30**, 297–312.

Roscoe, S. N. (1971). Incremental transfer effectiveness, *Human Factors*, **13**, 561–567.

Roscoe, S. N. (1972). A little more on incremental transfer effectiveness, *Human Factors*, **14**, 363–364.

Ross, B. H. (1984). Remindings and their effects in learning a cognitive skill, *Cognitive Psychology*, **16**, 371–416.

Salomon, G. and Perkins, D. N. (1989). Rocky roads to transfer: Rethinking mechanisms of a neglected phenomenon, *Educational Psychologist*, **24**, 113–142.

Schmidt, R. A. (1975). A schema theory of discrete motor skill learning. *Psychological Review*, **82**, 225–260.

Schmidt, R. A. and Young, D. E. (1987). Transfer of movement control in motor skill learning. In S. M. Cormier and J. D. Hagman (eds). *Transfer of Learning*, pp. 48–79. New York: Academic Press.

Schneider, W. and Detweiler, M. (1988). The role of practice in dual-task performance: Toward workload modelling in a connectionist/control architecture, *Human Factors*, **30**, 539–566.

Shaffer, L. H. (1975). Control processes in typing, *Quarterly Journal of Experimental Psychology*, **27**, 419–432.

Shea, J. B. and Morgan, R. L. (1979). Contextual interference effects on the acquisition, retention, and transfer of a motor skill, *Journal of Experimental Psychology: Human Learning and Memory*, **5**, 179–187.

Shepherd, A., Marshall, E. C., Turner, A. and Duncan, K. D. (1977). Diagnosis of plant failures from a control panel: A comparison of three training methods, *Ergonomics*, **20**, 347–361.

Siipola, E. M. and Israel, H. E. (1933). Habit-interference as dependent upon stage of training, *American Journal of Psychology,* **45**, 205–227.
Simon, C. W. and Roscoe, S. N. (1984). Application of a multifactor approach to transfer of training research, *Human Factors,* **26**, 591–612.
Singley, M. K. and Anderson, J. R. (1985). The transfer of text-editing skill, *Journal of Man-Machine Studies,* **22**, 403–423.
Skaggs, E. B. (1925). Further studies in retroactive inhibition, *Psychological Monographs,* **34** (161).
Slamecka, N. J. (1960). Retroactive inhibition of connected discourse as a function of similarity of topic, *Journal of Experimental Psychology,* **60**, 245–249.
Sommers, T. G., Holding, D. H. and Fingerman, P. (1978). Rule shift, repeated confirmation, and hypothesis subset sampling, *Bulletin of the Psychonomic Society,* **11**, 227–230.
Swift, E. J. (1903). Studies in the psychology and physiology of learning, *American Journal of Psychology,* **14**, 201–251.
Szafran, J. and Welford, A. T. (1950). On the relation between transfer and difficulty of initial task, *Quarterly Journal of Experimental Psychology,* **2**, 88–94.
Thorndike, E. L. and Woodworth, R. S. (1901). The influence of improvement in one mental function upon the efficiency of other functions, *Psychological Review,* **8**, 247–262.
Turvey, M. T., Shaw, R. E. and Mace, W. (1978). Issues in the theory of action. In J. Requin (ed.). *Attention and Performance VII,* pp. 557–598. Hillsdale, NJ: Erlbaum Associates.
Tversky, A. (1977). Features of similarity, *Psychological Review,* **84**, 327–352.
Vidulich, M. A. (1988). Speech responses and dual-task performance, *Human Factors,* **30**, 517–529.
Wightman, D. C. and Lintern, G. (1985). Part-task training for tracking and manual control, *Human Factors,* **27**, 267–283.
Williges, R. C. and Baron, M. L. (1973). Transfer assessment using a between-subjects central-composite design, *Human Factors,* **15**, 311–319.
Wolfe, D. (1951). Training. In S. S. Stevens (ed.). *Handbook of Experimental Psychology,* pp. 1267–1286. New York: John Wiley.
Woodworth, R. S. and Schlosberg, H. (1954). *Experimental Psychology.* New York: Holt.
Wylie, H. H. (1919). An experimental study of transfer of response in the white rat, *Behavior Monographs,* **3** (16).

# Chapter 5

# Types of analysis for training

## J. Patrick
### University of Wales College of Cardiff

The development of an effective training programme depends upon a systematic analysis of the job or task to be trained. This statement would receive unanimous endorsement by those involved in training. However, despite agreement on *what* has to be achieved, there is little consensus of *how* to accomplish this goal. From an academic perspective there are many ways of carrying out some form of analysis of the job or task (e.g. Bainbridge, 1989; Fleishman and Quaintance, 1984; Gael, 1988; McCormick, 1979; Meister, 1985; Wilson *et al.* 1988). Not surprisingly practitioners are confused with the many labels and techniques which proliferate. In addition any systematic analysis is difficult and time consuming and yet in a real sense you 'get what you pay for'. It is partly for these reasons that analyses of jobs or tasks are not always performed during the development of a training programme. For example, a national survey in the United Kingdom of employers of computer personnel found that fewer than one in five had carried out any formal analysis of the jobs of programmer, systems analyst, and analyst programmer before developing training provision (Spurgeon, Michael and Patrick, 1984).

This chapter examines the role of analysis in different aspects of training and the different types of analysis available. This is a shorter account of this topic than that given by Patrick (in press).

## THE ROLE OF ANALYSIS

Identification of the nature of the job or tasks to be trained provides information that is necessary for a variety of activities in the development of training. In order to appreciate the role of job or task analysis, it is useful to consider the development of training from a systems perspective. Such an approach views the development of training as a system which is defined in terms of its goals. This system can, in turn, be broken down into its subsystems and associated subgoals and the interrelationships between them. This approach

*Training for Performance: Principles of Applied Human Learning.* Edited by J. E. Morrison
© 1991 John Wiley & Sons Ltd

has resulted in what are known as Instructional Systems Development (ISD) models. Many ISD models exist, some of which are detailed by Andrews and Goodson (1980). The best known of these is the IPISD model (Interservices Procedures for Instructional Systems Development—Branson *et al.*, 1975) which was developed for use in the US military. The IPISD model divides the development of training into five stages: analysis, design, development, implementation and control. These stages are divided into a total of 19 substages. Such stages represent a rational approach to instructional development, which should occur more or less irrespective of any specific training content or context. A feature of IPISD and other ISD models is that analysis is the first stage in the development of training which provides important information for subsequent stages.

The main stages in the development of training and their interaction with the selection of trainees can be illustrated with another more global ISD model. Figure 5.1 represents an adaptation of Eckstrand's (1964) training system (Patrick, 1980), which identifies the major functions in the development of training. Each function (represented by a rectangular box in Figure 5.1) requires some form of analysis of the characteristics of the tasks to be trained. Different types of information are needed for the majority of these functions and therefore different analysis techniques are required.

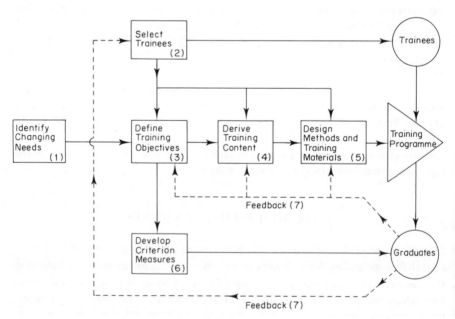

**Figure 5.1.**   Tasks or functions in the development of training. Reproduced by permission from Patrick (1980), adapted from Eckstrand (1964).

Training development functions 1, 3, 4 and 6 (Figure 5.1) can be grouped together since they require information about activities, equipment, and objectives relating to performance in the real job situation. This information is context dependent and has been labelled 'task oriented' (Patrick, 1980) in order to distinguish it from information of a psychological nature. Let us assume that some actual or potential training need exists in an organisation (1) perhaps as a consequence of the introduction of new technology, staff changes, or unacceptable levels of production in terms of quality or quantity. This need might be stated in general terms or may arise as a consequence of some job analysis technique, such as a checklist or task inventory. This need has to be translated into clear behavioural or performance objectives (3) which form the focus of the training programme. In turn these performance objectives indicate the criterion measures needed (6) in order to evaluate whether trainees have attained these objectives after undergoing the training programme. Finally, the knowledge/skill requirements to attain these objectives in the task domain have to be unravelled into the content of a training course (4). All of these functions within the development of training require an analysis which is task oriented or non-psychological in nature. Such an analysis makes categorical statements about the nature of the activities, objectives, and so forth associated with performance of the actual task in its context (e.g. industrial, educational or sports). Some task-oriented techniques are discussed in the third section of this chapter.

The remaining functions in Figure 5.1 concern the possibility of having to select from a pool of potential trainees (2) and designing training (5) in the widest sense of the term. Design involves not only the superficial characteristics of how training material is going to be delivered and presented but also the more fundamental issues of how an optimal learning environment is designed in terms of both the structure and sequence of training material.

Both selection of trainees and design of training functions require some information about the psychological characteristics of the task. So too does the development of training content which involves an analysis of the skill and knowledge required. Given the current high levels of unemployment and rapidly changing job demands, often requiring a higher intellectual component, it is frequently necessary to select *for* retraining. Naturally a trade-off exists between selection and training and the selection decision interacts with both the objectives, content and design of training (3, 4 and 5). Ideally one should estimate 'transferability' of potential trainees to the new job or task. This entails considering trainees' existing knowledge, skill, motivation, and interests besides the availability of training resources which includes the time required to learn, training equipment, and so forth (Patrick, 1980). The psychological demands of the task are then matched against some estimate of how trainees will be able to meet them via a training programme. Various psychological approaches to analysis are discussed in the last two sections of this chapter.

Identification of training content may involve eliciting expert knowledge which can then be passed on to others via the training programme. There has been much interest in the analysis of so-called 'mental models' (or knowledge representation) although techniques are mostly *ad hoc* at the present state of the art. Such analyses do not use formal taxonomies of performance (e.g. abilities or information-processing categories) and are generally more micro-scopic in their level of detail. Some examples of this more cognitive analysis are given towards the end of this chapter.

The transition from training content to training design is acknowledged to be notoriously difficult by many writers in this area (e.g. Wheaton *et al.*, 1976). A comprehensive and integrated set of prescriptive principles for training design does not exist despite the many publications on this topic (e.g. Reigeluth, 1983; Romizowski, 1981, 1984). This is not to deny that many principles of learning and instruction do exist which can be usefully integrated into the development of training. Of course any training programme should be designed to accommodate the individual differences of trainees such as aptitudes, age, and learning styles. This consideration gave rise, in the 1960s, to a large literature whose purpose was to identify individual difference vari-ables which interacted with aspects of training and instruction. This was la-belled 'Aptitude-Treatment Interaction' (ATI) research (e.g. Cronbach, 1967). Arguably this search for important and pervasive individual difference variables in training has not been as successful as might be expected from the volume of work in this area. There are notable exceptions such as the research on individual differences related to anxiety (e.g. reviewed in Sieber, O'Neil and Tobias, 1977). Also Belbin's (1964) study of letter sorters in the London postal areas remains a classic example of how to design training to accom-modate difficulties of the older worker (e.g. short-term memory, interference between activities, and pacing). Glaser (1980) argued that one of the reasons for the lack of progress in finding interactions between instruction and indi-vidual differences is that cognitive processes have not generally been analysed in sufficient detail and many individual difference measures are gross descriptors.

In summary, some analysis of the job or task to be mastered is required to provide information for different stages in training development. This infor-mation is of two types: (a) 'task oriented', which is primarily used to specify training needs, objectives, and some aspects of content; and (b) 'psychologi-cal', which contributes to the selection of trainees, to the design of training, and also to the development of training content particularly for complex tasks. Since these different types of information have to be related to one another in carrying out some training decisions, it is understandable why there has been much debate on how to link them (e.g. Dunnette, 1976). Unfortunately this epistemological issue can only be resolved by empirical methods, which make questionable statistical assumptions, or by subjective judgement. Neither is satisfactory.

# TYPES OF ANALYSIS

The term analysis is used in a broad sense in this chapter. It not only refers to readily recognised techniques or methods of job or task analysis but also to descriptions of cognitive phenomena which involve less explicit analysis. Some analysis techniques have well-defined procedures and have a similar status to psychometric instruments. For example GOMS, which is a technique developed by Card, Moran and Newell (1983) for analysing and predicting performance for routine cognitive skills in the area of human–computer interaction. GOMS analyses cognitive processes into 'goals', 'operators' for achieving these goals, 'methods' for sequencing these operators and 'selection rules' for choosing between alternative methods. In occupation/industrial psychology, McCormick and colleagues have developed the Position Analysis Questionnaire (PAQ) which is a formal job analysis technique with Form B using 194 job elements or items in a structured questionnaire format (McCormick, Jeanneret and Mecham, 1972). At the other extreme are more microscopic analyses of complex tasks which do not involve formal instruments. They are no less valuable because they involve improvisation and need to be judged by the care and rigour by which they were developed. One well-known and successful example is provided in the study by Pew, Miller and Feeher (1981) which analysed the decisions of operators during various nuclear power plant incidents.

In 1968, Wheaton published an important paper which discussed how taxonomies or classifications of human performance differ in terms of purpose, descriptors, and methodological procedures. Wheaton's ideas have profound implications for the construction and comparison of any taxonomic schemes, including formal and informal job/task analysis techniques. These notions have been taken up by Fleishman and Quaintance (1984) in their review of taxonomies of performance, by Pearlman (1980) in a review of job classification with respect to personnel selection, and by Patrick (1980) in a review of types of analysis required for training purposes. The thrust of Wheaton's thesis is similar to that argued by Stevens (1946) concerning the nature of measurement. Analysis or description of a phenomenon involves an abstraction and construction process. Therefore it is necessary to make explicit the procedures involved. In the context of job/task analysis, different descriptors and methodologies are used by different techniques which result in different products. Therefore, one means of differentiating types of analysis is to identify the different procedures employed. Two further implications can be drawn from Wheaton's thesis. Firstly, it is difficult if not impossible to find a function for translating satisfactorily the products of one type of analysis into those of another. Secondly, questions asking which type of analysis is correct in a given situation are trivial. More important, particularly in our discussion of training, is how relevant and useful is the information provided by different analyses to stages in the development of training.

Patrick (in press) has adapted Wheaton's distinctions and elaborated various dimensions along which analyses may differ. For our present discussion it is helpful to compare analyses in terms of (a) nomenclature, (b) purpose, (c) descriptive base, (d) structuring procedures, and (e) data collection methods.

**Nomenclature**

The terms 'job' and 'task' are typically used within industrial and occupational training contexts although it is difficult to define these terms. Generally 'job' refers to a person's contractual duties of employment and includes all the 'tasks' performed. The IPISD model (Branson *et al.*, 1975), discussed previously, defines a task as 'the lowest level of behavior in a job that describes the performance of a meaningful function in the job under consideration' (p. 16). In addition one important aspect of a task is that it is goal directed. Wheaton (1968) identifies two dimensions along which even task definitions vary. The first of these involves the breadth or scope of the definition with respect to the general work environment; while the second is whether a task has some objective reality of its own, or whether it is intrinsically linked to the perceptions and values of the performer who therefore subjectively defines it.

The term 'skills analysis' can be added to the terms 'job analysis' and 'task analysis' which have already been used in this chapter. Within industrial or occupational psychology these terms are frequently used interchangeably. 'Job analysis' is the more general and widely used term which refers to any techniques or methods for analysing a work situation. In contrast the term 'task analysis' usually refers to techniques used within the context of training. This is exemplified by the definition of task analysis by Annett *et al.* (1971) as 'the process of collecting information necessary to reach decisions about what to train, how to train, even how well to train and perhaps how much to spend on training' (p. 1). More recently, with the increased interest in cognitive activities, it has become fashionable to use the terms 'cognitive task analysis' (e.g. Means and Gott, 1988) or (knowledge) 'representation' (e.g. Bainbridge, 1988; Ringland and Duce, 1988). Many other terms exist which also imply some form of analysis or description such as 'mental model'. Irrespective of which term is preferred, all analyses abstract information from a subject-matter by applying various descriptors and methodological procedures for a particular purpose.

## Purpose

Job and task analysis techniques are used for a variety of purposes and therefore should be judged by how well they accomplish these goals. Zerga (1943) distinguished 20 uses of job analysis. Some job analyses are multi-purpose and can be used for various occupational problems other than training including job evaluation, personnel selection, and performance appraisal. Examples include Functional Job Analysis (Fine and Heinz, 1958) part of which forms the basis for the *Dictionary of Occupational Titles* (DOT) which is a classification of jobs in the US economy; McCormick's Position Analysis Questionnaire (PAQ) which is used for various occupational issues; and Smith's (1973) work on generic skills which divides work into major categories such as mathematics, communication, reasoning, interpersonal, and manipulative skills. All of these multi-purpose techniques provide information which is arguably too global for the training functions discussed in the previous section. For example, ratings from PAQ for each job element represent an average or overall judgement about the extent to which a job element applies to *all* the tasks involved in that job. For training purposes such information needs to be refined with respect to *each* task within a job. In other words, in the process of analysis using such wide-ranging techniques, a great deal of information is inevitably lost which cannot be retrieved without a re-examination of the job. Not surprisingly, analysis techniques which are directed towards training or some of the functions in the development of training are more effective than such multi-purpose techniques.

## Descriptive base

An important dichotomy can be drawn between analyses that involve psychological distinctions and those that do not. It has previously been argued that both types of analysis are required for training purposes. In order to derive the objectives and content of training, detailed task-oriented descriptions are necessary. On the other hand, selecting trainees with the most appropriate qualities and designing training in a psychologically expedient manner require an analysis of the task/job in psychological terms. Various writers have emphasised the difference between these two types of analysis. Miller (1962) is well known for his distinction between task description and task analysis, the latter being concerned with the cognitive processes involved in performing the task. In various publications, Leplat (e.g. 1987) has contrasted the 'prescribed' task which is defined by the organisation with the 'real task' which is often quite different and refers to how the person actually carries out the task. Similarly, there are many examples in cognitive psychology where actual problem solving or reasoning behaviour deviates from some supposed rational or ideal method (e.g. Johnson-Laird, 1985).

As Morgan (1972) pointed out, there are many variables which can be used to describe or analyse jobs. These include the job's content, context, or the requirements of the job holder. Therefore analyses can be divided into the approaches or descriptive terms employed. Task-oriented analyses use descriptors related to the equipment, objectives of performance, or the observable activities involved. In contrast, psychological analyses may describe the cognitive processes required by the task in information-processing terms; the abilities or aptitudes required by the job incumbent; the different types of learning and their associated training conditions; and the knowledge structure or mental model to be acquired in terms of rules, heuristics, semantic networks, and so on. These different psychological approaches to analysis are discussed in this chapter.

## Structuring procedures

Many analyses go further than just using descriptors of the subject matter in a qualitative manner. These descriptors can be structured or classified on the basis of theoretical or practical distinctions or some statistical methodology.

The most common theoretical distinctions used to organise descriptions of a job or task are from the information-processing approach. The Position Analysis Questionnaire, Form B (McCormick, Jeanneret and Mecham, 1969), is made up of 194 job items from six divisions, three of which cover information input (35 items), mental processes (14 items), and work output (49 items). Similarly the Occupational Analysis Inventory (OAI) developed by Cunningham and colleagues (Cunningham et al., 1983) adopts an information-processing approach. In the educational context both Sternberg (e.g. 1985) and Feuerstein (1980) have developed ambitious programmes aimed at improving basic intellectual or cognitive processes which have been influenced and organised by the information-processing approach.

Alternatively the elements of an analysis can be grouped into categories which have some practical significance for that domain. Thus, Wirstad (1988) divided nuclear power plant operators' knowledge into 13 areas such as knowledge of safety regulations, reactor core knowledge, and knowledge of displays and controls in the control room.

Various statistical procedures can be used to structure the analysis particularly if the elements are quantified along some scale. It is often desirable to quantify, for example, the use, frequency, importance, or criticality of job or task elements by the use of rating scales. Thus Christal (e.g. 1974) developed a task inventory for monitoring the content of a range of jobs in the US Air Force partly to determine training requirements. Christal and colleagues developed a suite of computer-based statistical programs (e.g. cluster and regression analyses) for manipulating and structuring the task statements from the inventory which were quantified in terms of relative time spent. Factor analysis is another technique frequently used in job analysis. While such statistical techniques are useful for organising and reducing the data, they make various statistical assumptions and, of course, do not guarantee any psychological validity for the resulting analysis.

**Data collection methods**

There is a variety of well-established methods by which information concerning a job or task can be collected. Recently, the analysis of an expert's knowledge or skills has been labelled 'knowledge elicitation'. Traditional data collection methods include the use of existing documentation (such as operating manuals) observation, interviews, questionnaires, simulation, and discussion (with job incumbents, supervisors or experts in the domain). Each of these methods has various well-documented advantages and disadvantages. It is therefore sensible to use as many methods as possible to corroborate information collected during one analysis. In situations that involve a trained job analyst synthesising the information, the use of more than one analyst and the calculation of reliability measures are necessary safeguards against biased or unreliable data.

**Conclusions**

We have discussed five dimensions along which analyses may differ: nomenclature, purpose, descriptive base, structuring procedures, and data collection methods. All of these dimensions are important in determining the nature of any *one* analysis. Therefore we have to be careful not to oversimplify when distinguishing 'types' or 'methods' of analysis. When some speak of different job analysis methods they refer to only one of these dimensions. For example Morsch (1964) differentiated job analysis methods in terms of the data collection methods employed. It is not surprising that genuine confusion exists concerning the differences among the many analysis techniques. Arguably the most significant dimension of any analysis is the nature of its subject matter (psychological or not) and the constructs and descriptors used to describe it. For this reason the next two sections are concerned with different task-oriented and psychological analyses which may be used in the context of training with their associated advantages and disadvantages.

# TASK-ORIENTED APPROACHES

We have discussed how the development of training requires the identification of training needs, the specification of training objectives, and the identification of training content. All of these functions within training require some task-oriented approaches to analysis. Firstly, we will discuss the importance and nature of training objectives. Next, two traditional methods of analysis will be described which enable training needs, objectives, and content to be identified.

## Specification of training objectives

One essential element of training is the use of correctly stated behavioural or performance objectives. Undoubtedly more has been written about the importance of training objectives than any other area of training. The specification and use of different types of objective have been discussed widely (e.g. Davies, 1976) while serious criticisms have been made of the importance assigned to behavioural objectives in the development of instruction by MacDonald-Ross (1973).

Mager (1962) argued in his classic account that the main purpose of training objectives was to communicate instructional intent and therefore they should have three components:

> *First*, identify the terminal behaviour by name; you can specify the kind of behaviour that will be accepted as evidence that the learner has achieved the objective.
> *Second*, try to define the desired behaviour further by describing the important conditions under which the behaviour will be expected to occur.
> *Third*, specify the criteria of acceptable performance by describing how well the learner must perform to be considered acceptable.
>
> (Mager, 1962, p. 12)

An example provided by Mager of an objective is:

> Given a DC motor of ten horsepower or less that contains a single malfunction, and given a standard kit of tools and references, the learner must be able to repair the motor within a period of 45 minutes. (p. 39)

Gagné and Briggs (1974) proposed five components for writing such objectives which overlap with those proposed by Mager and include specification of the situation, the object, the action, the tools and other constraints, and the capability to be learned. Gagné and Briggs provided the following example of how a typist's task of copying a letter can be specified by these five components.

| | |
|---|---|
| Given a written longhand letter | (Situation) |
| executes | (The learned capability, a motor skill) |
| a copy | (Object) |
| by typing | (Action) |
| using an electric typewriter making one carbon of a one page letter | (Tools and other constriants) |
| | (Gagné and Briggs, 1974, p. 81) |

It is interesting to notice that while such rules for writing adequate objectives are useful, a great deal depends upon the use of verbs to describe performance which are concrete (Duncan, 1972) and action-oriented (Gagné and Briggs, 1974). This will reduce the ambiguity inherent in such verbs as 'know' or 'understand'. It could be recommended therefore that when developing performance objectives a set of action verbs should be initially defined. Such an approach is adopted in a study by Frederickson and Freer (1978) of the basic electronic skills of maintenance personnel. These authors provided a list of 12 action verbs which make distinctions in maintenance functions (e.g. to inspect, adjust, test) with associated definitions. This is one means of reducing the ambiguity of training objectives.

In our discussion of the ISD approach, it was evident that training objectives affect both the content of training and the criterion measures developed for evaluation purposes. Inaccurate specification of objectives will therefore result in an inappropriate training programme which is also evaluated incorrectly. Training objectives should be consistent with other training development activities as given in any ISD model. To this end, Merrill and colleagues (e.g. Merrill, Reigeluth and Faust, 1979) in collaboration with the Navy Personnel Research and Development Center (NPRDC), San Diego developed procedures which attempted to ensure that objectives, test items, and training materials were both adequate and consistent with each other. This instructional technique and variants of it have been labelled the Instructional Strategies Diagnostic Profile (Merrill et al., 1977), the Instructional Quality Inventory (Ellis et al., 1978), and the Instructional Quality Profile (Merrill, Reigeluth, and Faust, 1979). Figure 5.2 provides an overview of this instructional technique which can be divided into six areas: purpose–objective consistency, objective adequacy, objective–test consistency, test adequacy, test–presentation consistency, and presentation adequacy. (Presentation refers to training materials.) Such principles have been elaborated in considerable detail by NPRDC and provide useful prompts for the specification of training objectives in the context of the development of training.

Discussion of training objectives has been taken forward by Merrill (1983) in his Component Display Theory in which Mager's prescriptions for

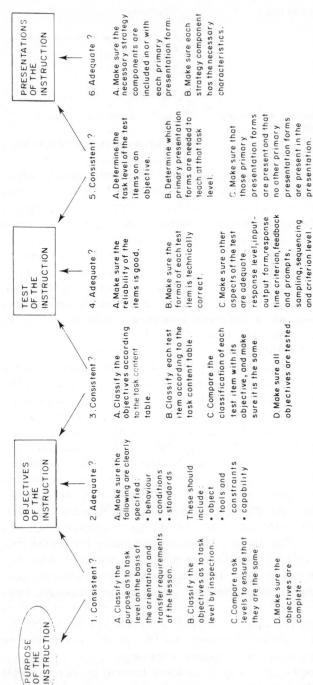

**Figure 5.2.** A summary of aspects of instructional quality analysed by the Instructional Quality Profile. From Merrill, Reigeluth and Faust (1979). Reproduced by permission of Academic Press.

objectives are used in the context of different types of learning. These ideas are discussed in the fourth section of this chapter.

## Critical Incident Technique

Flanagan and colleagues devised this famous technique during the Second World War. It is not a formal technique but rather a collection of procedures and principles. The best source is Flanagan's original description (Flanagan, 1954). Flanagan argued that extreme behaviours in a job are particularly informative and also can be more accurately identified. Thus he suggested that analysis of a job should be directed towards collecting 'critical incidents'. These critical incidents were defined as 'extreme behavior, either outstandingly effective or ineffective with respect to attaining the general aim of the activity' (Flanagan, 1954, p. 338). Five stages are involved in the Critical Incident Technique.

1. Determination of the general aim and objectives of the activity, that is job or task to be investigated.
2. Preparation of plans and specifications for collecting factual incidents about the activity including instructions to observers.
3. Collection of the incidents from interview, observation, and so on.
4. Analysis of the incidents from interviews, observation, and so on.
5. Interpreting and reporting.

During the data collection stage, anything from a few hundred to a few thousand critical incidents may be identified depending upon the complexity of the job. Flanagan proposed that one criterion for stopping collecting such incidents was when only two or three out of 100 new incidents provided additional information.

An example of the use of the Critical Incident Technique is given by Kirchner and Dunnette (1957) in a study of salespersons. A total of 135 incidents were collected from forms sent to 85 sales managers in one company. An example of an effective incident was:

A salesperson driving down the street saw a truck containing equipment for which company products might be used. He followed the truck to find the delivery point, made a call on this account which was a new one and obtained an order. (p. 56)

An example of an ineffective incident was:

A salesman received a complaint from a customer, about the quality of a particular type of tape. He failed to look into the matter or write up a formal complaint. The defective tape was returned to the jobber and no credit was issued to the

jobber or to the retailer involved. While the account was not lost, the customer
was dissatisfied for a long time. (p. 55)

The next stage typically involves organising incidents into categories although this is left to the skill and ingenuity of the analyst. In the Dunnette
and Kirchner study, 15 areas of competence were identified which were as
follows:

1. Following up complaints, requests, orders, and leads.
2. Planning ahead.
3. Communicating all necessary information to sales managers.
4. Communicating truthful information to managers and customers.
5. Carrying out promises.
6. Persisting on tough accounts.
7. Pointing out uses for other company products besides the salesman's own
   line.
8. Using new sales techniques and methods.
9. Preventing price-cutting by dealers and customers.
10. Initiating new selling ideas.
11. Knowing customer requirements.
12. Defending company policies.
13. Calling on all accounts.
14. Helping customers with equipment and displays.
15. Showing non-passive attitude.

It is interesting to note that the authors of this study expected these categories
to generalise to other salespersons' jobs in different contexts. Frequently such
categories are used to devise a checklist for appraisal of existing staff. Dunnette (1976) suggested that a combination of the Critical Incident Technique
with Behaviour Observation Scaling (BOS) is useful in determining the behavioural requirements of jobs.

The Critical Incident Technique identifies important task components
which are either effectively or ineffectively performed. All of these may be
used in the development of a training programme although those performed
ineffectively automatically identify the training needs of some persons. The
disadvantage of using the Critical Incident Technique is that any analysis is
necessarily incomplete. There will be other less extreme task components
which require training. Also the technique is not as straightforward as might
at first appear, because it depends heavily upon the expertise of the analyst in
all of Flanagan's five stages. For example, data collection techniques such as
observation require satisfactory reliability and validity. Flanagan was acutely
aware of these issues and all of his guidelines were intended to maximise
objectivity.

## Hierarchical Task Analysis

Hierarchical Task Analysis is one of a number of techniques which breaks down a task into a series of subtasks. (It is not to be confused with Gagné's hierarchy of skills in the intellectual domain which is discussed later.) It was developed by Annett and Duncan (1967) and has been described by Annett *et al.* (1971), Duncan (1972), and more recently by Shepherd (1985). Patrick, Spurgeon and Shepherd (1986) have provided a guide for practitioners. This type of analysis is particularly suited to identifying training needs, training objectives, and providing a framework for the development of training content.

Hierarchical Task Analysis as the term implies utilises task-oriented descriptions to decompose a task into a hierarchical array of subtasks. It is a logical rather than a psychological technique. The analysis begins by considering a general task and then progressively breaks it down into a series of subtasks which logically comprise and exhaust the higher level task. There are essentially four features of this technique: the process of hierarchical breakdown, the use of 'operations' and their complementary 'plans' to characterise subtasks, and a stopping rule which specifies when further breakdown of the task(s) is not necessary. The two main advantages of such a task analysis from a training perspective are that the logical decomposition process should ensure that *all* of the subtasks are analysed. Secondly, rather than depending upon a fixed number of levels of analysis, it is possible to tailor the level of description to the target population of trainees (through its stopping rule).

Formally Annett *et al.* (1971) described these tasks and subtasks as 'operations' which are 'any unit of behaviour, no matter how long or short its duration and no matter how simple or complex its structure which can be defined in terms of its objective' (p. 3). The process of subdividing these operations is guided by the application of the $p \times c$ stopping rule. This requires an estimate to be made of the probability of inadequate performance without training ($p$) and the costs (in the widest sense) of such inadequate performance ($c$). If either of these estimates is unacceptable and a training solution cannot be identified, then the operation is further redescribed. For example, one of the tasks involved in a production technician's duties in plastics injection moulding is to 'prepare machine for tool removal'. If novice setters are to be trained to perform this task because both the probability of inadequate performance and its associated cost are unacceptable, the task is broken down into six subtasks some of which are further redescribed as detailed in Figure 5.3.

In Hierarchical Task Analysis the concept of a 'plan' is a necessary complement to that of an 'operation'. A plan specifies when and in which sequence the operations (or subtasks) should be performed. Plans, as operations, are

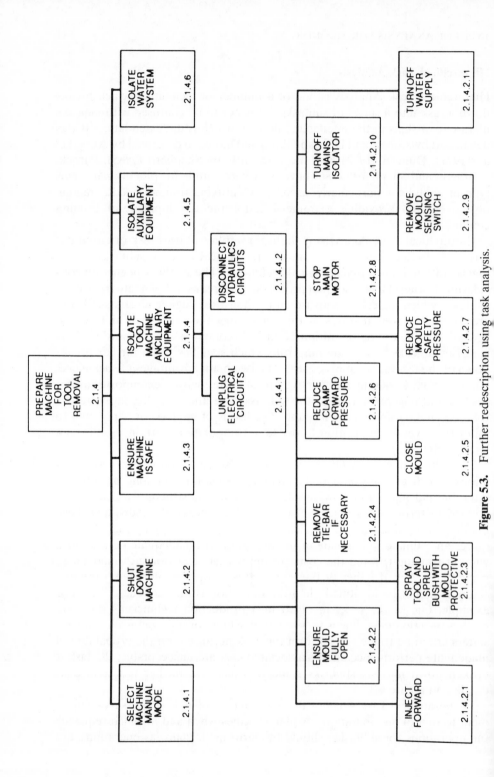

**Figure 5.3.** Further redescription using task analysis.

divided hierarchically into subplans. Some plans are relatively straightforward and involve fixed procedures as are often found in the start-up and shut-down procedures of machines or plant. If such procedures are not automated, trainees can easily be trained to master such simple plans. On the other hand, some plans may be exceedingly complex and may involve various decisions which will dictate the sequence of operations to be followed. Different types of plan may be involved in one Hierarchical Task Analysis. This is illustrated in part of an analysis of an industrial task concerned with warming up a furnace, adapted from Shepherd (1985), which is represented in Figure 5.4. The overall task 1 which is 'warm up furnace' is broken down into four subordinate tasks 1.1–1.4. Plan 1 governs how these four tasks are to be executed which is by a simple procedure of doing subtask 1.1, then 1.2, then 1.3 and then 1.4. Subtask 1.1 is divided into three sub-subtasks 1.1.1–1.1.3 although the plan 1.1 for their execution specifies no sequence. In contrast subtask 1.4 is split into four

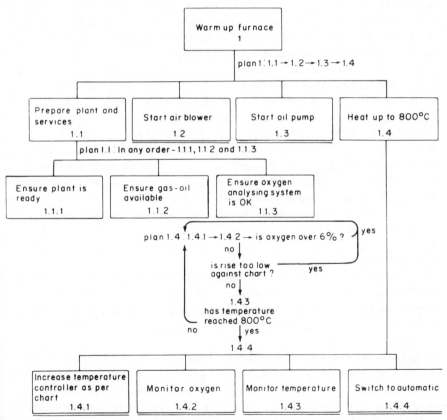

**Figure 5.4.** Part of a Hierarchical Task Analysis of an industrial task, adapted from Shepherd (1985). Operations which are underlined indicate that $p \times c$ is acceptable and therefore do not require further rediscription.

sub-subtasks 1.4.1–1.4.4 and plan 1.4 is an algorithm or decision chart. In this algorithm the manner in which the trainee should move between the sub-subtasks 1.4.1–1.4.4 is controlled by various decisions which ensure that the temperature of the furnace has reached 800°C before the furnace is switched to automatic mode.

In many complex industrial tasks the specification of plans or strategies is important to effective training. Shepherd and Duncan (1980) described such a complex task in which a 'controller' of a chlorine plant has to 'balance' production of gas from various units with its consumption. The primary problem in the task analysis was to identify and specify the plans and subplans involved which could not be easily inferred by the analyst or verbalised by the skilled controllers.

During an analysis it is sometimes necessary to attempt to make explicit the psychological demands which these tasks are likely to make upon the trainee. For this reason Annett et al. (1971) recommended that the input ($I$), action ($A$), and feedback ($F$) characteristics are identified for each subtask or operation, and the associated difficulties for the trainee and their possible training solutions. Shepherd (1985) pointed out that this $IAF$ taxonomy is most useful for perceptual–motor tasks as opposed to cognitive ones. During Hierarchical Task Analysis one might consider using the taxonomies described in the next section which provide frameworks for classifying the nature of the psychological demands that different tasks impose.

In order to improve the reliability of any task analysis, it is worthwhile not only using more than one analyst but also including as many different methods of data collection as possible. It is likely that the analysis will proceed iteratively through three stages: data collection, assimilation of information into a coherent structure, and finally verification that the task analysis faithfully represents activities in the job. Collaboration with technical experts and job incumbents will be necessary not only for the initial data collection but also for the final phase in which the tasks and plans are agreed as correct and comprehensive.

Hierarchical Task Analysis has advantages in the development of training. It is flexible in its level of analysis; it is applicable to any task or work area; its output can be easily translated into training needs, objectives and a framework for training content; finally, it should be logically exhaustive in its elaboration of tasks although this obviously depends upon the skill of the analyst. Its disadvantages are that it is a difficult technique which relies heavily on the skill and ingenuity of the analyst. Values of $p$ and $c$ in the stopping rule are not easily quantified and typically reduce to gross subjective judgements (i.e. satisfactory or not). Reliability studies have not been carried out although the technique has demonstrated its utility, which R. B. Miller (1967) argued to be the most significant criterion, through its many applications in industrial training.

## PSYCHOLOGICAL TAXONOMIES

There are various approaches to the analysis of tasks which involve distinctions of a psychological nature. Many of these involve the use of taxonomies of performance. Three types of psychological taxonomy will be discussed which cover: (a) information-processing requirements; (b) ability/aptitude requirements; and (c) types of learning. All three of these taxonomies are potentially useful for training. The information-processing approach analyses the cognitive processes required in performance of the task and uses terms developed from experimental/cognitive psychology. The ability requirements approach is founded on the belief that individuals possess relatively enduring traits or abilities which can be measured. Therefore, the demands of a task can be described in terms of the abilities required by the performer. Finally a rather different psychological approach is to identify the types of learning involved in the task to be mastered. Some of the most useful taxonomies of learning have been proposed by Gagné in many publications (e.g. Gagné, 1985) and Merrill (1983). These have implications not only for the analysis of a task but also for the subsequent design of training.

### Information-processing requirements

The information-processing paradigm in psychology makes various distinctions between cognitive processes occurring during the input, processing, and output of information. These distinctions can be used to identify potential difficulties in performance of a task which therefore require particular attention during training. Some conventional job analysis methods use job elements of an information-processing nature, e.g. the Position Analysis Questionnaire developed by McCormick and colleagues (e.g. McCormick, Jeanneret and Mecham, 1969, 1972) and the Occupation Analysis Inventory developed by Cunningham and colleagues (e.g. Cunningham *et al.*, 1983). Levine and Teichner (1973) conceptualised task performance as a transfer of information between an input and an output either of which is subject to constraints. It is necessary to identify the nature of these constraints, their location (i.e. input and/or output) and the informational relationships between input and output.

R. B. Miller was one of the better known advocates of the importance of an information-processing analysis in the development of training. His publications began in the 1950s and were concerned with task analysis in the context of training. A useful summary of his work can be found in Fleishman and Quaintance (1984). In his early work (e.g. Miller, 1967), a taxonomy of eight task functions was identified: a concept of purpose; a scanning function; identification of relevant cues; interpretation of cues; short-term memory; long-term memory; decision making and problem solving; and other effector responses. Later, Miller (1974) expanded his taxonomy to 25 categories. The assignment of such categories to a task will depend upon the skill of the analyst. As acknowledged by Miller, inevitably some ambiguity will remain. Even though Miller argued that different task functions have different training implications, the linkage between the description of these categories and training design was not made explicit.

The attraction of using such a scheme proposed by Miller is that information-processing terms are context independent and comprehensive (although changes in categories may be required with refinements in psychology). On the negative side, a simple list of information-processing categories does not illustrate how these categories interact dynamically during performance of task. Decomposition into cognitive processes often ignores higher level cognitive processes or strategies that are the hallmark of skilled performance by experts.

More recent developments in cognitive psychology and learning have emphasised that the traditional information-processing approach has over-emphasised structure and ignored the powerful influence of different cognitive strategies which can be brought to bear on performance (e.g. Broadbent, 1987; Underwood, 1978). The information-processing model of skill suggested that information inevitably passed through stages such as perception, memory, and decision making, each of which imposes various capacity limitations. This preoccupation with structure ignored the influence of cognitive strategies which might be used during both training and performance of the task. Such ideas can be traced back to the influential work of Bruner, Goodnow and Austin (1956) on concept learning.

An illuminating theoretical account of how instruction might be better designed to ensure that appropriate cognitive strategies are used by the trainee to master different types of subject matter is provided by Rigney (1978). Rigney provided the following definition of cognitive strategy:

> Cognitive strategy will be used to signify operations and procedures that the student may use to acquire, retain and retrieve different kinds of knowledge and performance. . . . Cognitive strategies involve representational capabilities of the student (reading, imagery, speech, writing and drawing), selectional capabilities (attention and intention) and self-directional capabilities (self-programming and self-monitoring). (p. 165)

Rigney observed that the traditional approach to training has been to provide specific content and hope that the appropriate cognitive strategies will be generated by the trainee. An alternative and potentially more incisive approach is to train these strategies either directly or indirectly through the use of what Rigney termed 'orienting tasks'. As the term suggests 'orienting tasks' induce the trainee to adopt and develop the necessary cognitive strategies. The role of the applied psychologist is therefore to develop efficient orienting tasks.

The work of Dansereau (1978) and Dansereau *et al.* (1979) exemplified the attempt to develop a 'learning strategy training programme'. This programme comprised instruction intended to improve what were termed 'primary' and 'support' learning strategies. Primary strategies included comprehension techniques (such as paraphrasing using visual imagery and analysis of key ideas) and retention techniques (such as mean–ends analysis). Three support strategies were identified: cultivating a positive learning attitude; concentration (coping with internal and external distractions); and self-monitoring of the learning process. A more indirect learning strategy approach is that in which the 'orienting task' is embedded in the subject-matter to be learned (Rigney, 1978). A good example of this is when questions are interspersed in text which are intended to provoke the learner into actively processing information in the required manner. A review of the literature concerning the effect of the different types, positions, and frequency of such questions in reading text is provided by Rickards and Denner (1978).

Taxonomies of cognitive processes have been developed by Sternberg (1980) and Feurerstein (1980) which adopt an information-processing approach and include higher order or metacognitive processes. These have been used in developing training programmes which aim to improve generic intellectual processes. Sternberg (1985) identified three types of components in intellectual functioning: performance components (e.g. basic processes in task performance which might be classified into input–processing–output categories); metacomponents used in complex tasks (e.g. recognising the nature of the problem and selecting appropriate performance components); and knowledge acquisition, transfer, and retention components. Feuerstein (1980) adopted an information-processing approach in his instrumental enrichment programme which was designed to compensate for deficiencies in cognitive functions. These were divided into impairments at the input, elaborational, and output phases which Feuerstein believed were due to lack of 'mediated learning experiences' during cognitive development. Even though Feuerstein and Sternberg's studies are rarely quoted as exemplifying good training practice, they both involve sophisticated psychological analyses of task performance for the purpose of developing training materials. Their aims are somewhat grander than those of typical training programmes since they are concerned with the transfer of basic cognitive processes underlying intellectual activities.

**Ability requirements**

An alternative psychological approach to analysis involves asking what abilities are required by the person performing the task. If prerequisite abilities can be identified, then it is possible to evaluate the extent to which potential trainees possess them. Selection can therefore be improved and a training programme is likely to need fewer resources.

One major difficulty is *how* to identify the ability requirements of job/tasks. Two possibilities exist. On the one hand, the analyst (preferably a psychologist) infers the abilities from a job or task analysis of the type discussed in the preceding section. This is subjective, potentially unreliable, and lacking demonstrable validity. On the other hand, an empirical study can be carried out to link measures of ability with task performance using statistical methods. Such an approach has been used by Fleishman and colleagues (e.g. Fleishman, 1978). Such a study is difficult and requires considerable resources because a battery of ability measures have to be administered to job incumbents and then correlated with task performance. Subsequently factor analytic methods identify the contribution of different abilities to task performance. Other reasons which make this second option difficult are the findings that the relative contribution of abilities varies with training (e.g. Dunham, Guilford and Hoepfner, 1968) and the importance of a task-specific factor increases with the amount of training (Fleishman and Hempel, 1955). General ability measures will therefore be less useful at explaining or predicting performance at the end of training. This is consistent with the finding that the predictive validity of abilities in selection for jobs is unsatisfactorily low (e.g. Ghiselli, 1966).

The relationship between ability requirements and jobs has been discussed by many writers (e.g. Dunnette 1976; Fleishman and Quaintance 1984). There are many taxonomies of cognitive abilities (e.g. Ekstrom, 1973; Guilford, 1982; Sternberg, 1985) and motor abilities (particularly significant is the work by Fleishman and colleagues, reviewed in Fleishman and Quaintance, 1984). All of these taxonomies are candidates for use during an analysis of a job or series of tasks. The difficulty of identifying these abilities systematically has been noted previously. In addition many argue that it is unnecessary to invoke the notion of abilities, which raise problems of definition, factor analytic methods, and so forth, when making training decisions. It might be argued that it is sensible to ensure in a fairly gross fashion that a potential trainee can cope with the main ability requirements of a job. However, it is not possible to tune aspects of training, such as training design, to accommodate small differences in the abilities of trainees.

### Types of learning

The search for different categories of learning has a long history in psychology. This literature is particularly significant for training if different types of learning can be associated with different training outcomes. Thus the analysis of a job or task into different learning categories can be directly linked to the design of training.

The best known advocate of this approach is Gagné who has published widely on this subject from the 1960s to the present day. He has argued persuasively that varieties of learning can be distinguished in terms of the *conditions* necessary to promote them. His work is therefore explicitly concerned with the design of training unlike the other psychological approaches to analysis which have been discussed. Gagné has revised his ideas which can probably best be traced through the four editions of his book *The Conditions of Learning* published in 1965, 1970, 1977, and 1985, respectively. In his early work, a learning hierarchy of eight types was developed which became absorbed into an analysis of intellectual skills in his later work. Also Gagné became even more concerned with instructional implications in the mid-1970s onwards (e.g. Gagné and Briggs, 1974; Gagné and Dick, 1983) which is also reflected in the title of the fourth edition of Gagné's book (1985)—*The Conditions of Learning and the Theory of Instruction.*

Five varieties of learning outcome exist, according to Gagné: intellectual skills, verbal information, cognitive strategies, motor skills, and attitudes (Table 5.1). These distinctions have been influenced by the work of Bloom and colleagues (Bloom, 1956). The distinction between attitudes and motor skills is straightforward although the relationship between higher order intellectual skills and cognitive strategies is more contentious. The dichotomy drawn between declarative and procedural knowledge (e.g. Anderson, 1980) corresponds broadly to Gagné's categories of verbal information (i.e.

**Table 5.1.** Five varieties of learned capabilities (reproduced by permission from Gagné and Briggs, 1974).

| Kind of capability | Example | Function | Performance category |
|---|---|---|---|
| Intellectual skill | Using a metaphor to describe an object | Component of further learning and thinking | Showing how an intellectual operation is carried out in specific application |
| Cognitive strategy | Induction of the concept 'magnetic field' | Controls learner's behavior in learning and thinking | Solving a variety of practical problems by efficient means |
| Verbal information | 'Boiling point of water is 100°C' | (1) Provides directions for learning; (2) aids transfer of learning | Stating or otherwise communicating information |
| Motor skill | Printing letters | Mediates motor performance | Carrying out the motor activity in a variety of contexts |
| Attitude | Preference for listening to music as a leisure activity | Modifies individual's choices of action | Choosing a course of action towards a class of objects, persons, or events |

knowing that) and intellectual skills (i.e. knowing how). Undoubtedly Gagné's exposition of a learning hierarchy of intellectual skill has been of particular significance to those interested in training. In his 1970 version eight different types of learning were identified: signal learning, stimulus–response connections, chains, verbal associations, discriminations, concepts, rules and problem solving. Each type of learning required different internal conditions (literally those in the learner) and external conditions (concerned with the nature and organisation of training). Gagné argued that competence in types of learning higher in his hierarchy depended upon mastery of lower types of learning. Thus higher types required lower types as prerequisites. For example problem solving required as a prerequisite the rules used for problems to be learned which in turn require as prerequisites that the concepts involved are mastered, and so on. Hence psychological distinctions concerning learning types, which are made during the analysis of a task, are used not only for specifying training conditions but also for training sequence.

Gagné's ideas have received considerable attention and some criticism. In particular, the notion of prerequisite subskills has generated much debate concerning how this notion should be tested and the associated empirical evidence (Bergan, 1980; Resnick, 1973; White, 1973). Of course evidence of positive transfer from one subskill to the next higher one in a hierarchy does not necessarily indicate a prerequisite relationship. Also evidence that competence at a higher level skill is associated with competence at its lower level components does not conclusively indicate how that skill was developed. As indicated in the reviews by Cotton, Gallagher and Marshall (1977) and White (1973) there is little evidence which is methodologically sound in support of Gagné's position. What is needed are further guidelines on how to analyse a task in order to identify a learning hierarchy which corresponds to different learning categories. It is unlikely that a unique solution exists in the analysis of one task. Further comparisons of training sequences which are consistent and inconsistent with Gagné's ideas are needed to test these ideas more rigorously than has occurred in the past.

Merrill (1983, 1988) has described Component Display Theory (CDT) which also relates types of learning to principles of training. CDT is strongly influenced by Gagné's ideas but significantly also relates types of learning to the specification of training objectives using the suggestions put forward by Mager. The foundation of CDT is a performance–content matrix which identifies ten types of learning (see Figure 5.5). This matrix is composed of two dimensions: one concerned with the type of content and the other with the level of performance. This results in ten permissible combinations according to Merrill, examples of which are as follows:

Remember-fact
    e.g. What is the value of Pi?

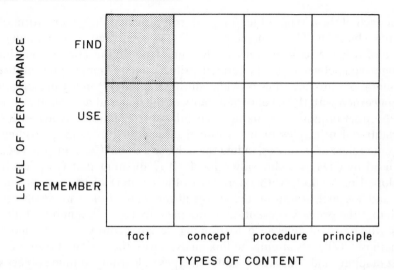

**Figure 5.5.** Performance–content matrix. From Merrill (1983). Reproduced by permission of Lawrence Erlbaum Associates, Inc.

Remember-concept
e.g. What are the characteristics of a conifer?

Use-concept
e.g. Is the mountain in this photograph an example of a folded mountain?

Find-concept
e.g. Sort the rocks on this table into several different piles. Indicate the characteristics by which one of your classmates could sort them into the same piles.

Remember-procedure
e.g. What are the steps in balancing a chequebook?

Use-procedure
e.g. Demonstrate how to clean a clarinet.

Find-procedure
e.g. Write a computer program that will index and retrieve recipes.

Remember-principle
e.g. What happens when water evaporates? Explain in terms of molecule movement and heat.

Use-principle
e.g. Below are pictures of two ocean vessels. One is floating very high in the water and the other is floating very low. Explain at least three different reasons that could account for this difference.

Find-principle
e.g. Set up an experiment to assess the effect of tobacco smoke on plant growth. Report your findings.

(Merrill, 1983, pp. 288, 289)

For each of these types of learning, Merrill provided the generic form of its training objective. The remainder of CDT is concerned with detailing the nature of training required for each learning type. In this connection Merrill distinguished between what he termed 'primary and secondary presentations'. (Presentations are materials provided during training.) Primary presentations are concerned with the level of generality of the material and whether it is of an expository or inquisitory nature. Secondary presentations involve inclusion of traditional principles of instructional design such as help, providing an adequate range of instances, fading the help, and so on. Certainly the vocabulary used by CDT is technically difficult. It is apparent that CDT has been developed particularly with reference to the learning of conceptual knowledge and it is unclear how far the ideas will generalise. For example one might argue that the primary presentations sample only two of a number of dimensions which are of relevance to training design. However, a considerable strength of CDT is its attempt to link analysis with the design of training by a direct mapping and consistency between types of learning, training objectives, test items, and training materials.

# KNOWLEDGE REPRESENTATION

Analysis of complex skills and their associated knowledge requirements is a major problem for training. While the taxonomies discussed in the preceding section are useful, they use relatively global categories and do not indicate how to analyse the detailed psychological components of skill. Cognitive psychology has been concerned with the nature and description of such skill for some time although few generalisations have emerged about how to proceed with such an analysis. Many cognitive analyses are either incomplete or have not been tested by the subsequent development of interventions in the domain (e.g. training, design, or the development of automated devices). Two areas in which progress has been made in analysing complex skill in the context of solving applied problems are human–computer interaction (e.g. Norman and Draper, 1986; Wilson et al., 1988) and process control (e.g. Bainbridge, 1988, 1989; Rasmussen, 1986). The conclusion from many diverse studies in these and other fields is that considerable improvisation, skill, and good fortune is needed to analyse complex skill. This section will attempt to provide a flavour of this work by discussing some examples concerning control and diagnostic skills in the process control industry. However, beforehand some of the main methodological problems associated with such analyses will be discussed briefly.

There are many types of knowledge which underpin performance of complex tasks. Identifying, describing and assembling these into a coherent analysis pose major difficulties. For example, declarative knowledge may take many forms. Reigeluth, Merrill and Bunderson (1978) were concerned with the instructional design implications of different subject-matter. They differentiated between different subject-matter structures including procedural hierarchy (including procedural prerequisite relations and another form similar to a production rule), taxonomy (parts of versus kinds of), theoretical models, and lists. In describing different types of content, they differentiated five types of operations: (i) identity (i.e. factual – '. . . is represented by . . .'); (ii) inclusion (e.g. '. . . are four kinds of . . .'); (iii) intersection ('. . . if both are present . . .'); (iv) order ('. . . do one before two . . .'); and (v) causal ('. . . causes . . .'). These operations represent different types of predicate type knowledge. Bainbridge (1988) distinguished five types of predicate representation which are necessary to describe a process control operator's knowledge of the structure and function of a process: (i) parts-of links, into wholes; (ii) is-a links into categories; (iii) attribute-with-value links; (iv) token-type links, from the name of an attribute to the node defining it and its attribution; (v) cause–effect links. Figures 5.6 and 5.7 from Bainbridge (1988) illustrate how this can be used to describe knowledge about a particular pump.

Even though mapping knowledge in this manner is exceedingly complex, it does not encompass adequately the nature of procedural knowledge underlying complex skill. First, for an analysis of complex skill to be complete, many types of knowledge have to be integrated into a dynamic account which includes the nature of the control, memory processes, and so forth. Second, a hallmark of skilled or expert performance is the ability to switch between different knowledge structures (or mental models) and levels within them during one task activity (e.g. Rasmussen, 1986; Leplat, 1989). This switching takes place quickly and sometimes without conscious awareness. The implication is that various alternative knowledge structures require identification in order to support the development to expert performance. Third, alternative representations of the *same* knowledge are often necessary particularly in the development of intelligent training systems (Ohlsson, 1986). For example Bainbridge (1988) discussed the use of predicate-type and pattern-type representations of the same knowledge for process control operators.

One further methodological problem in the analysis of complex skill which cannot escape mention is the intense debate concerning the validity of verbal report. Verbal reports are used to provide insights into performance of cognitively complex tasks such as reasoning and problem solving. They may be collected from an expert or novice problem solver, in the real or simulated situation, during or after performance. There are two potential shortcomings. First, some procedural knowledge or expertise may not be in verbal form or may not be translated into such a form not least because it is serial in nature. Such knowledge is implicit rather than explicit (Berry and Broadbent, 1984; Hayes and Broadbent, 1988; Karnas and Cleeremans, 1987). Ericsson and Simon (1980) distinguished situations in which verbalisation is of information

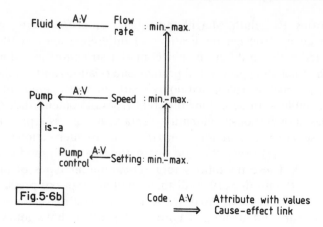

(a) General knowledge about the category 'pumps'.

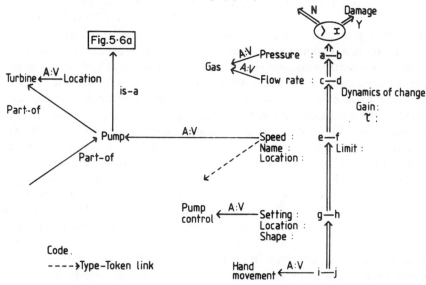

(b) Specific knowledge about a particular pump.

**Figure 5.6.** Knowledge of pumps. From Bainbridge (1988). Reproduced by permission of Taylor and Francis Ltd, London.

already verbally encoded from those which may require the subject to perform various intermediate processing activities in order to produce a verbal response. Second, verbal reports of cognitive behaviour may be unreliable since they involve *post-hoc* rationalisation (Nisbett and Wilson, 1977). Nevertheless Ericsson and Simon (1984) argued that verbalisation *during* problem

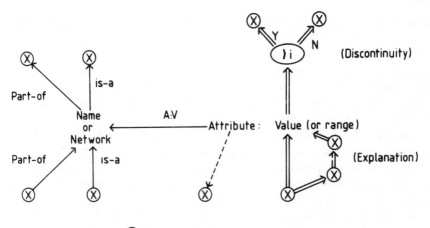

Code. Ⓧ another node, or network of nodes.

**Figure 5.7.** The general structure of a complex node representing structure and function. Bainbridge (1988). Reproduced by permission of Taylor and Francis Ltd, London.

solving can provide useful data concerning cognitive processes. This debate is still continuing.

For all of these reasons, the systematic analysis of complex skill is problematic. It is beyond the scope of psychology to specify satisfactorily the various complex knowledge structures underlying expert performance, except for simple tasks. A similar conclusion was reached by Anderson (1988) in discussing how to develop the expert model in intelligent tutoring systems.

**Top-down, bottom-up, and mixed approaches**

Despite these methodological difficulties, analyses have been performed in complex domains, although they have required considerable improvisation by the analysts. Inevitably, analyses have been incomplete since all the types of knowledge, associated control processes, and alternative representations cannot be specified in a comprehensive and coherent manner. Therefore compromises have to be made.

A distinction can be drawn between top-down, bottom-up, and mixed approaches to analysis. Proceeding in a purely bottom-up manner in a complex psychological domain presents insurmountable problems of how a variety of microscopic analyses are assembled into a whole. On the other hand with a top-down approach, a domain can be divided into broader chunks which can then be subjected to detailed examination. It is likely that a mixed approach, which utilises both top-down and bottom-up approaches, is the most sensible one.

From a training perspective, specification of the goals of task performance is important since it enables the knowledge which is needed to accomplish these goals to be identified. Goals can be used in a top-down type of analysis. Major goals and their interrelationships which have to be acquired by the trainee can become a framework for the analysis. Goals can be divided into subgoals, and so on. It is then possible to have a further analysis which unravels the strategies and associated knowledge requirements for achieving these goals, subgoals, and so on.

The best known descriptive model, which adopts this top-down goal-oriented approach, has been proposed by Rasmussen (e.g. 1986) for the analysis of decision-making tasks (Figure 5.8). This model was developed from an analysis of verbal protocols of process control operators. The subgoals which partition the cognitive activities from initiation to execution of a response are: to detect a need for intervention; to observe some information; to identify the present state of the system; to evaluate possible consequences; to select a desired target state; to select a means of achieving it; to plan a sequence of actions; and then to execute these actions. At this level of description, specification of subgoals generalises to many decision-making tasks. From such an approach, at least two levels of subsequent psychological analysis are feasible. First, the performer's high-level knowledge and use of these subgoals and their interrelationships can be assessed. A novice might be trained to follow the rational sequence whereas with increasing expertise, as Rasmussen noted, various short-cuts may enable certain subgoals to be by-passed. Also at this level different patterns of error, for example by novices and experts, can be identified. Second, a lower level analysis can unravel the methods or cognitive strategies by which subgoals are achieved. As these are analysed, the processing demands and lower level knowledge requirements of the performer can be inferred. Samurcay and Rogalski (1988) used Rasmussen's model to analyse the cognitive activities in a tactical reasoning task and to structure a training solution.

Pew, Miller and Feeher (1981), using a mixed approach, provided an impressive analysis of the decision making of nuclear power plant operators during four critical incidents. The objectives of the analysis were not only to produce training recommendations but also to evaluate potential changes in control room layout and computer-based decision support for operator's activities. The first part of the analysis was top-down and capitalised upon Rasmussen's decision-making model and the eight subgoals were extended to include possible sources of error. The second part of the analysis proceeded in a bottom-up manner. Time lines were developed for each incident using various data collection methods such as retrospective interviews and documentation in order to describe the operator's decisions. For this purpose, nine types of information were collected concerning each decision/action including knowledge and/or belief state, intention, and expectation. From these time lines, 17 decisions were judged as critical (method not specified) and were

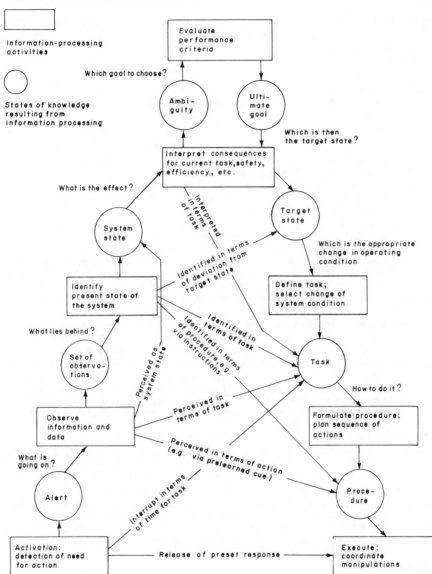

**Figure 5.8.** Decision-making model of information-processing activities and sequences. From Rasmussen (1986), adapted from Rasmussen (1976). Reproduced by permission of Elsevier Science Publishing Company. Copyright © 1986 by Elsevier Science Publishing Co., Inc.

analysed in greater detail using what were termed decision/action analyses. These involved 14 new categories covering, for example, purpose, action, preceding activities, input and output information, knowledge required, and

**Table 5.2.** Decision/action analysis worksheet for the second critical decision in the Oyster Creek nuclear power plant incident (reproduced by permission from Pew, Miller and Feeher, 1981).

---

*Murphy Code*: OY2                          *Location/Date*: Oyster Creek – 5/2/79
*Decision*: Evaluate triple-               *Case*: Loss of feedwater transient
        low-level alarm              *Time*: 1352:52 – 1410:12
                                           *Personnel*: Shift Super. (SS)
                                                      Reactor Operator (RO) (3)
                                                      Engineering Super. (ES)

*Purpose*: Attempt to rationalize apparent differences between triple-low-level instrumentation and standard control room instrumentation.

*Activity*: Send operator to reactor building to read Barton instrument. Compare with indications on Yarway instrument in control room. Decide to use Yarway indication as best estimate of true level of water in system.

*Actions performed*: Receive triple-low-level alarm, indicating water level 4ft 8in over top of active fuel elements. Compare with Yarway and G/MAC indications showing level in annulus to be greater than 11ft 5in. Dispatch operator to read indication on Barton instrument in reactor building. On learning that Barton indicated less than 10in, dispatch operator to verify reading. Decide to trust Yarway indication but to continue monitoring Barton with the expectation that the reason for the discrepancy will become clear.

*Preceding activities*: Open condensate return valve; close A, B, C, E recirculation loop discharge valves; trip recirculation pumps.

*Input information*: Barton instrument indication in reactor building, Yarway and G/MAC instrument indications in control room, and triple-low-level alarm on annunciator panel.

*Output information*: Decision to use Yarway indication as best estimate of water level.

*Knowledge required*: Knowledge that Barton instrument measures level within the shroud, that Yarway and G/MAC instruments measure level in annulus, and that, given natural circulation through open recirculation loop discharge valves B and C, readings from the shroud and annulus should coincide. It was not recognized during the making of this decision that natural circulation was, in fact, not occurring because of earlier inadvertent closure of B and C valves.

*Feedback to operator*: Barton, Yarway and G/MAC readings.

*Accessibility of control (instruments)*: Yarway and G/MAC indications prominently displayed on panel. Triple-low-level alarm attached to Barton instrument prominently displayed on annunciator panel. Barton instrument with analog indicator located in reactor building.

*Visibility of feedback from control position*: Adequate for Yarway and G/MAC.

*Alternative actions*: Instead of assuming that natural circulation was occurring, operators could have checked recirculation loop valve positions and determined that it was not. This check would have disclosed very quickly, as it later did, the reason for the discrepancy in indicated water levels. A second alternative would have been to trust the Barton reading rather than the Yarway. However, see comments below.

*Competing activities*: None.

*Safety criticality*: Continued reliance on control room instrumentation alone, without understanding the source of the discrepancy in water level indications, might eventually have presented a safety concern. However, the input to the core provided by the open bypass valves and injection through the rod bundle provided sufficient water for some period of time.

*Comments*: The training curriculum at Oyster Creek did not include a demonstration of the disparity in water level indications that could arise when the elements of the recirculation loop valve closure procedure had been violated. As a result, operators had no basis, *a priori*, on which to base an inference that the observed disparity was due to failure of natural circulation to occur between the annular region and the interior of the shroud.

---

accessibility of control. In order to provide a flavour of the detail of this material, one of the decision/action analyses for the incident at Oyster Creek on 2 May 1979 is given in Table 5.2. In this incident the reactor tripped on a spurious high pressure signal and an operator subsequently shut down some discharge valves by mistake resulting in a loss of cooling water to the reactor core. The second critical decision in this incident was evaluation of a triple-low-level alarm, the analysis of which is represented in Table 5.2. Components of these 17 critical decisions from the four incidents were then mapped on to the goals and associated sources of error previously identified from the initial top-down analysis. Finally the link between the 17 critical decisions and the potential impact of changes in training, decision support, and so forth was made via the rating of a panel of experts. Their ratings, not surprisingly, varied considerably.

Pew et al's (1981) study therefore used both top-down and bottom-up approaches to the analysis of decision making. Considerable methodological adaptation and innovation was required. Inevitably criticisms can be levelled at parts of the analysis (e.g. retrospective interviews and expert ratings). Nevertheless the great strength of the study is that, at each stage, both the process and products of the analysis are made explicit. Furthermore the analyses integrate the context-specific decision-making components with the more generalisable decision-making model.

In our research work concerning fault-finding, we have adopted this top-down, goal-oriented approach to analyse the cognitive components of fault-finding in a hot strip mill (Patrick 1989). A model was developed which specified three major stages (or goals) of the fault-finding process: initial symptom identification; global fault set reduction; and searching within a programmable logic controller. Each of these goals was further analysed into a set of context-specific subgoals and their interrelationships. Fault-finding strategies were identified in two ways. First, at the global level, strategies were defined in terms of knowledge of these subgoals and relationships or short-cuts between them. Second, different fault-finding strategies were defined with respect to how a subgoal is achieved concerning the evaluation of symptoms. Building upon the distinctions put foward by Rasmussen (e.g. 1984), it is possible to differentiate such lower level fault-finding strategies along two dimensions: the nature of the information used and the nature of the psychological process involved. A fault-finding strategy may use structural, system variable, functional, temporal, or probabilistic information from the domain or a mixture of these. Evaluation of symptoms may involve either some pattern matching of expected to observed symptoms, use of rules or heuristics, or some type of reasoning in which expected symptoms are generated from one or more types of information. Mixed strategies exist. Fault-finding strategies can therefore be defined by their location in a two-dimensional matrix. Hence fault-finding might involve pattern matching of functional information or reasoning using some qualitative model which links system variables. Not all strategies fit neatly into one of the cells of such a matrix. However, as a consequence of this broad top-down analysis of the domain, it is then feasible to engage in a more microscopic analysis which might specify, for example, the nature of the qualitative causal chains of reasoning similar to those noted by Allengry (1987) in the control of nuclear power plants.

## SUMMARY AND CONCLUSIONS

This chapter has reviewed the types of analysis of a job or task which are of use in the development of training. Despite universal agreement that training depends on analysis of the job or task, there is genuine confusion concerning both differences between analysis techniques and how information derived from analysis maps on to the development of training. For this reason we initially discussed the main functions in the development of training from an ISD perspective and the type of information each function required. Broadly, it is possible to distinguish task-oriented information (concerning activities, objectives, equipment, etc.) from that of a psychological nature. Task-oriented information contributes to the specification of training needs, training objectives, and training content; while psychological information is needed to select trainees, design training, and elaborate the content of cognitively complex tasks.

Before reviewing task-oriented and psychological approaches to analysis, we identified some of the major dimensions along which analysis techniques differ. These dimensions were nomenclature, purpose, descriptive base, structuring procedures, and data collection methods. These dimensions can be used to differentiate not only formal job analysis methods but also less formal analyses or descriptions of cognitive tasks.

Our discussion of task-oriented approaches covered some traditional issues and techniques, namely, the specification of training objectives, the Critical Incident Technique (Flanagan, 1954), and Hierarchical Task Analysis (Annett et al., 1971). Most psychological approaches to analysis involve the use of some taxonomy. Three different types of taxonomy were reviewed in the context of training: information processing taxonomies, which provide categories or distinctions which can be used to identify the nature of the cognitive processes required to perform a task; taxonomies of motor or intellectual abilities, which analyse the task in terms of the abilities required by the person performing it; and taxonomies concerned with types of learning which specify their different training conditions. It was concluded that the ability requirements approach was less useful than the other two approaches in the area of training.

A major problem for training both now and in the future is how to analyse complex cognitive tasks. Such analyses are subject to various methodological difficulties including how to build up a complete and coherent analysis which covers the many different types of knowledge used during expert performance. Such analyses can adopt top-down, bottom-up, or mixed approaches. Some examples of analyses of complex tasks in process control were discussed which adopted a top-down goal-oriented approach to analysis. This had some advantages. However, at the present state of the art, no strong generalisations emerge concerning how to analyse complex tasks and much improvisation and ingenuity is required by the analyst.

## ACKNOWLEDGEMENTS

This chapter is partly based on a final report of an ESRC/CNRS research exchange concerned with the analysis and description of complex skills. This research exchange was hosted by Dr J. Leplat at the Laboratoire de Psychologie du Travail, Ecole Pratique des Hautes Etudes, Paris to whom I am grateful for various discussions. The example of fault-finding in a hot strip mill cited in this chapter comes from a collaborative research project, Alvey, MMI 106, between the University of Wales College of Cardiff and British Steel, Port Talbot funded by SERC and the DTI. The author is grateful to John Morrison for comments on an earlier draft of this chapter.

## REFERENCES

Allengry, P. (1987). The analysis of knowledge representation of nuclear power plant control room operators. In H. J. Bullinger and B. Shackel (eds). *Human–Computer Interaction—'INTERACT' 87*. Amsterdam: North Holland. Elsevier.

Anderson, J. R. (1980). *Cognitive Psychology and its Implications*. San Francisco: Freeman.

Anderson, J. R. (1988). The expert module. In Polson, M. C. and Richardson, J. J. (eds). *Foundations of Intelligent Tutoring Systems*. Hillsdale, New Jersey: Lawrence Erlbaum.

Andrews, D. H. and Goodson, L. A. (1980). A comparative analysis of models of instructional design, *Journal of Instructional Development*, **3**(4), 2–16.

Annett, J. and Duncan, K. D. (1967). Task analysis and training design, *Occupational Psychology*, **41**, 211–221.

Annett, J., Duncan, K. D., Stammers, R. B. and Gray, M. J. (1971). *Task Analysis*. (Training Information No. 6.) London: HMSO.

Bainbridge, L. (1988). Types of representation. In L. P. Goodstein, H. B. Anderson, and S. E. Olsen (eds). *Tasks, Errors and Mental Models*. London: Taylor and Francis.

Bainbridge, L. (1989). Cognitive processes and training methods: A summary. In L. Bainbridge and S. A. R. Quintanilla (eds) *Developing Skills with Information Technology*. Chichester: Wiley.

Belbin, E. (1964). *Training the Adult Worker.* (Problems of progress in industry No. 15.) London: HMSO.

Bergan, J. R. (1980). The structural analysis of behaviour. An alternative to the learning-hierarchy model, *Review of Educational Research,* **50**(4), 625–646.

Berry, A. C. and Broadbent, D. E. (1984). On the relationship between task performance and associated verbalizable knowledge, *Quarterly Journal of Experimental Psychology,* **36A**, 209–231.

Bloom, B. S. (ed.) (1956). *A Taxonomy of Educational Objectives. Book 1: Cognitive domain.* New York: McKay.

Branson, R. K., Rayner, G. T., Cox, L., Furman, J. P., King, F. J. and Hannum, W. H. (1975). Interservice procedures for instructional systems development. Executive summary. Centre for Educational Technology, Tallahassee, Florida State University.

Broadbent, D. (1987). Structures and strategies: Where are we now? *Psychological Research,* **49**, 73–79.

Bruner, J. S., Goodnow, J. and Austin, G. (1956). *A Study of Thinking.* New York: Wiley.

Card, S. K., Moran, T. P. and Newell, A. (1983). *The Psychology of Human–Computer Interaction.* Hillsdale, New Jersey: Lawrence Erlbaum.

Christal, R. E. (1974). The United States Air Force Occupational Research Project. Technical Report AFHRL–TR–73–75. Occupational Research Division, Airforce Human Resources Laboratory, Texas.

Cotton, J. W., Gallagher, J. P. and Marshall, S. P. (1977). The identification and decomposition of hierarchical tasks, *American Educational Research Journal,* **14**(3), 189–212.

Cronbach, L. J. (1967). How can instruction be adapted to individual differences? In R. M. Gagné (ed.). *Learning and Individual Differences.* Columbus, Ohio: Merrill Books.

Cunningham, J. W., Boese, R. R., Neeb, R. W. and Pass, J. J. (1983). Systematically derived work dimensions. Factor analyses of the Occupational Analysis Inventory, *Journal of Applied Psychology,* **68**, 232–252.

Dansereau, D. F. (1978). The development of a learning strategies curriculum. In: H. F. O'Neil (ed.). *Learning Strategies.* New York: Academic Press.

Dansereau, D. F., Collins, K. W., McDonald, B. A., Holley, C. D., Garland, J., Diekhoff, G. and Evans, S. H. (1979). Development and evaluation of a learning strategy training programme, *Journal of Educational Psychology,* **71**(1), 64–73.

Davies, I. K. (1976). *Objectives in Curriculum Design.* London: McGraw-Hill.

Duncan, K. D. (1972). Strategies for analysis of the task. In J. Hartley (ed.). *Strategies for Programmed Instruction: An educational technology.* London: Butterworth.

Dunham, J., Guilford, J. and Hoepfner, R. (1968). Multivariate approaches to discovering the intellectual components of concept learning, *Psychological Review,* **75**, 206–221.

Dunnette, M. D. (1976). Aptitudes, abilities and skills. In M. D. Dunnette (ed.). *Handbook of Industrial and Organizational Psychology.* Chicago: Rand McNally.

Eckstrand, G. A. (1964). *Current Status of the Technology of Training.* Report AMRL–TDR–64–86. Aerospace Medical Laboratories, Wright Patterson Air Force Base.

Ekstrom, R. B. (1973). *Cognitive Factors: Some recent literature.* Technical Report No. 2. ONR Contract N00024–71–C–0227, NR150, 329, Princetown: Educational Testing Service.

Ellis, J. A., Wulfeck II, W. H., Merrill, M. D., Richards, R. E., Schmidt, R. V. and Wood, N. D. (1978). *Interim Training Manual for the Instructional Quality Inventory.*

NPRDC Technical Note 87–5. Navy Personnel Research and Development Center, San Diego.

Ericsson, K. A. and Simon, H. A. (1980). Verbal reports as data, *Psychological Review*, **87**(3), 215–251.

Ericsson, K. A. and Simon, H. A. (1984). *Protocol Analysis: Verbal reports as data*. Cambridge, Mass: MIT Press.

Feuerstein, R. (1980). *Instrumental Enrichment: An intervention program for cognitive modifiability*. Baltimore: University Park Press.

Fine, S. A. and Heinz, C. A. (1958). The functional occupational classification structure, *Personnel and Guidance Journal*, **37**, 180–192.

Flanagan, J. C. (1954). The Critical Incident Technique, *Psychological Bulletin*, **51**, 327–358.

Fleishman, E. A. (1978). Relating individual differences to the dimensions of human tasks, *Ergonomics*, **21**(12), 1007–1019.

Fleishman, E. A. and Hempel, W. E., Jr. (1955). The relationship between abilities and improvement with practice in a visual discrimination reaction task, *Journal of Experimental Psychology*, **49**, 301–312.

Fleishman, E. and Quaintance, M. F. (1984). *Taxonomies of Human Performance*. Orlando: Academic Press.

Frederickson, E. W. and Freer, D. R. (1978). *Basic Electronics Skills and Knowledge*. Research Note 79–5. US Army Research Institute, Alexandria.

Gael, S. (ed.) (1988). *The Job Analysis Handbook for Business, Industry, and Government*, Vols 1 and 2. New York: Wiley.

Gagné, R. M. (1985). *The Conditions of Learning and the Theory of Instruction*. New York: CBS College Publishing.

Gagné, R. M. and Briggs, L. J. (1974). *Principles of Instructional Design*. New York: Holt, Rinehart and Winston.

Gagné, R. M. and Dick, W. (1983). Instructional psychology, *Annual Review of Psychology*, **34**, 261–295.

Ghiselli, E. E. (1966). *The Validity of Occupational Aptitude Tests*. New York: Wiley.

Glaser, R. (1980). General discussion: Relationships between aptitude, learning and instruction. In R. E. Snow, P.-A. Federico and W. E. Montague (eds). *Aptitude, Learning and Instruction. Volume 2. Cognitive process analyses of learning and problem solving*. Hillsdale, New Jersey: Lawrence Erlbaum Associates.

Guilford, J. P. (1982). Cognitive psychology's ambiguities: Some suggested remedies, *Psychological Review*, **89**, 48–59.

Hayes, N. and Broadbent, D. E. (1988). Two modes of learning for interactive tasks, *Cognition*, **28** 249–277.

Johnson-Laird, P. N. (1985). Logical thinking: Does it occur in daily life? Can it be taught? In S. F. Chipman, J. W. Segal and R. Glaser (eds). *Thinking and Learning Skills, Volume 2. Research and open questions*. Hillsdale, New Jersey: Lawrence Erlbaum.

Karnas, G. and Cleeremans, A. (1987). Implicit processing in control tasks; some simulation results. In *Proceedings of the First European Meeting on Cognitive Science Approaches to Process Control*, Marcoussis, October.

Kirchner, W. K. and Dunnette, M. D. (1957). Identifying the critical factors in successful salesmanship, *Personnel*, **34**, 54–59.

Leplat, J. (1987). *Methodology of Task Analysis and Design*. Paper presented to European Methodologies in Work and Organisational Psychology Symposium, Hungary, May.

Leplat, J. (1989). Cognitive skills at work. In L. Bainbridge and S. A. R. Quintanilla (eds). *Developing Skills with Information Technology.* Chichester: Wiley.

Levine, J. M. and Teichner, W. H. (1973). Development of a taxonomy of human performance: An information-theoretic approach, *JSAS Catalogue of Selected Documents in Psychology,* **3,** 28 (Ms No. 325).

McCormick, E. J. (1979). *Job Analysis: Methods and Applications.* New York: Amacom.

McCormick, E. J., Jeanneret, P. R. and Mecham, R. C. (1969). A study of job characteristics and job dimensions as based on the Position Analysis Questionnaire. Report No. 6, Occupational Research Center, Purdue University.

McCormick, E. J., Jeanneret, P. R. and Mecham, R. C. (1972). A study of job characteristics and job dimensions as based on the Position Analysis Questionnaire (PAQ). *Journal of Applied Psychology,* **56** 347–368.

MacDonald-Ross, M. (1973). Behavioural objectives—a critical review. *Instructional Science,* **2,** 1–52.

Mager, R. F. (1962). *Preparing Instructional Objectives.* Palo Alto: Fearon Publishers.

Means, B. and Gott, S. P. (1988). Cognitive task analysis as a basis for tutor development: Articulating abstract knowledge representations. In J. Psotka, L. D. Massey and S. A. Mutter (eds). *Intelligent Tutoring Systems: Lessons Learned.* Hillsdale, NJ: Lawrence Erlbaum.

Meister, D. (1985). *Behavioural Analysis and Measurement Methods.* New York: Wiley.

Merrill, M. D. (1983). Component display theory. In C. M. Reigeluth (ed.). *Instructional Design Models: An overview of their current status.* Hillsdale, NJ: Lawrence Erlbaum.

Merrill, M. D. (1988). Applying component display theory to the design of courseware. In D. H. Jonassen (ed.). *Instructional Designs for Microcomputer Courseware.* Hillsdale, New Jersey: Lawrence Erlbaum.

Merrill, M. D., Reigeluth, C. M. and Faust, G. W. (1979). The instructional quality profile: A curriculum evaluation and design tool. In H. F. O'Neil, Jr (ed.). *Procedures for Instructional Systems Development.* New York: Academic Press.

Merrill, M. D., Richards, R. E., Schmidt, R. V. and Wood, N. D. (1977). *Interim Training Manual for the Instructional Strategy Diagnostic Profile.* NPRDC Report 77–14. Navy Personnel Research and Development Center, San Diego.

Miller, R. B. (1962). Task description and analysis. In R. M. Gagné (ed.). *Psychological Principles in Systems Development.* New York: Holt, Rinehart and Winston.

Miller, R. B. (1967). Task taxonomy: Science or technology, *Ergonomics,* **10,** 167–176.

Miller, R. B. (1974). A method for determining task strategies. Technical Report AFHRL–TR–74–26. American Institute for Research, Washington DC.

Morgan, T. (1972). Occupational description and classification. Air Transport and Travel Industry Training Board. Report RE–D–19.

Morsch, J. E. (1964). Job analysis in the United States Air Force, *Personnel Psychology,* **17,** 1–17.

Nisbett, R. E. and Wilson, T. D. (1977). Telling more than we know; verbal reports on mental processes, *Psychological Review,* **84,** 232–259.

Norman, D. A. and Draper, S. W. (eds) (1986). *User Centered Design.* Hillsdale, New Jersey: Lawrence Erlbaum.

Ohlsson, S. (1986). Some principles of intelligent tutoring, *Instructional Science,* **14,** 293–326.

Patrick, J. (1980). Job analysis, training and transferability: Some theoretical and practical issues. In K. D. Duncan, M. M. Gruneberg and D. Wallis (eds). *Changes in Working Life*. Chichester: Wiley.

Patrick, J. (1989). Representation of fault-finding in complex industrial contexts. In *Proceedings of the Second European Meeting on Cognitive Science Applications in Process Control*, p. 269–281. Siena, Italy: University of Siena.

Patrick, J. (in press). *Training*. London: Academic Press.

Patrick, J., Spurgeon, P. and Shepherd, A. (1986). *A Guide to Task Analysis: Applications of hierarchical methods*. Birmingham: Occupational Services Ltd.

Pearlman, K. (1980). Job families: A review and discussion of their implications for personnel selection, *Psychological Bulletin*, **87**(1), 1–28.

Pew, R. W., Miller, D. C. and Feeher, C. E. (1981). *Evaluation of Proposed Control Room Improvements through Analysis of Critical Operator Decisions*. Final Report of Research Project 891. Bolt, Beranek and Newman, Massachusetts.

Rasmussen, J. (1984). Strategies for state identification and diagnosis in supervisory control tasks and design of computer-based support systems. In W. B. Rouse (ed.). *Advances in Man–Machine Systems Research*, Vol. 1, 139–193. JAI Press.

Rasmussen, J. (1986). *Information Processing and Human–Machine Interaction: An approach to cognitive engineering*. New York: North Holland.

Reigeluth, C. M. (ed.) (1983). *Instructional-Design Theories and Models. An overview of their current status*. Hillsdale, New Jersey: Lawrence Erlbaum Associates.

Reigeluth, C. M., Merrill, M. D. and Bunderson, C. V. (1978). The structure of subject matter content and its instructional design implications, *Instructional Science*, **7**, 107–126.

Resnick, L. B. (1973). Hierarchies in children's learning. A symposium. *Instructional Science*, **2**, 311–362.

Rickards, J. P. and Denner, P. R. (1978). Inserted questions as aids to reading text, *Instructional Science*, **7**, 313–346.

Rigney, J. W. (1978). Learning strategies: A theoretical perspective. In H. F. O'Neil (ed.). *Learning Strategies*. New York: Academic Press.

Ringland, G. A. and Duce, D. A. (eds) (1988). *Approaches to Knowledge Representation: An Introduction*. Chichester: Wiley.

Romizowski, A. J. (1981). *Designing Instructional Systems: Decision making in course planning and curriculum design*. London: Kogan Page.

Romizowski, A. J. (1984). *Producing Instructional Systems: Lesson planning for individualised and group learning activities*. London: Kogan Page.

Samurcay, R. and Rogalski, J. (1988). Analyses of operator's cognitive activities in learning and using a method for decision making in public safety. In J. Patrick and K. D. Duncan (eds). *Training, Human Decision Making and Control*. North Holland.

Shepherd, A. (1985). Hierarchical task analysis and training decisions, *Programmed Learning and Educational Technology*, **22**(3), 162–176.

Shepherd, A. and Duncan, K. D. (1980). Analysing a complex planning task. In K. D. Duncan, M. M. Gruneberg and D. Wallis (eds). *Changes in Working Life*. Chichester: Wiley.

Sieber, J. E., O'Neil, H. F., Jr and Tobias, S. (1977). *Anxiety and Instruction*. Hillsdale, New Jersey: Lawrence Erlbaum Associates.

Smith, A. D. W. (1973). General skills in the reasoning and interpersonal domain. Prince Albert, Saskatchewan, Training Research and Development Station.

Spurgeon, P., Michael, I. and Patrick, J. (1984). *Training and Selection of Computer Personnel*. Research and Development No. 18, Sheffield: Manpower Services Commission.

Sternberg, R. J. (1980). Sketch of a componential subtheory of human intelligence, *Behavioural and Brain Sciences*, **3**, 573–614.

Sternberg, R. J. (1985). Instrumental and componential approaches to the nature and training of intelligence. In S. F. Chipman, J. W. Segal and R. Glaser (eds). *Thinking and Learning Skills, Volume 2: Research and Open Questions*. Hillsdale, NJ: Lawrence Erlbaum Associates.

Stevens, S. S. (1946). On the theory of scales of measurement, *Science*, **103**.

Underwood, G. (1978). Concepts in information processing theory. In Underwood, G. (ed.). *Strategies of Information Processing*. London: Academic Press.

Wheaton, G. (1968). *Development of a Taxonomy of Human Performance: A review of classificatory systems relating to tasks and performance*. Technical Report 1, American Institute for Research, Washington.

Wheaton, G., Rose, A. M., Fingerman, P. W., Karotkin, A. L. and Holding, D. H. (1976). *Evaluation of the Effectiveness of Training Devices: Literature review and preliminary model*. Research Memo 76-6. US Army Research Institute for the Behavioural and Social Sciences, Washington.

White, R. T. (1973). Research into learning hierarchies, *Review of Educational Research*, **43** 361–375.

Wilson, M. D., Barnard, P. J., Green, T. R. G. and Maclean, A. (1988). Knowledge-based task analysis for human-computer systems. In G. C. Van der Veer, T. R. G. Green. J.-M. Hoc and D. M. Murray (eds). *Working with Computers: Theory versus outcome*. London: Academic Press.

Wirstad, J. (1988). On knowledge structures for process operators. In L. P. Goodstein, H. B. Anderson and S. E. Olsen (eds). *Tasks, Errors and Mental Models*. London: Taylor and Francis.

Zerga, J. E. (1943). Job analysis: A resumé and bibliography, *Journal of Applied Psychology*, **27**, 249–267.

# Chapter 6

# Instructional strategies

**Gavan Lintern**
*University of Illinois at Urbana-Champaign*

An instructional strategy may generally be viewed as a systematic procedure for restructuring a learning environment with the goal of enhancing learning relative to that achievable with a standard mode of instruction. For the purposes of this review, an instructional strategy is defined as a manipulation or variation on a standard method of practice where the standard condition is an approximation of a self-teaching procedure or of one that might be imposed by a conscientious but not particularly innovative instructor. While standard procedures may have evolved under the guidance of skilled and experienced instructors, there is no clear evidence that those procedures are the best or that they are not seriously deficient in some respects. Research in the area of instructional strategies is directed at identifying an optimum configuration of practice events for instruction.

## THEORETICAL PERSPECTIVE

In general usage, the notion of instructional strategy is unconstrained. For example, there are solidly held beliefs that instruction can be enhanced by making a task easier or by making it more difficult. The arguments in favor of the competing positions sound plausible enough but it is clear that both cannot be true without further qualification. Ideally it would be possible to outline a theory with specific and precise hypotheses about instruction. Failure to find empirical support for these hypotheses, or inconsistent trends would reflect poorly on the theory.

The information-processing model, which is the standard theoretical perspective provided by contemporary cognitive psychology, does not serve well in this regard. Only minor adjustments of theoretical assumptions are required to accommodate competing hypotheses. For example, a standard interpretation of the information-processing model can accommodate the assumption that skill acquisition is enhanced by information feedback that is detailed and immediate (Adams, 1971). A slight adjustment can

*Training for Performance: Principles of Applied Human Learning.* Edited by J. E. Morrison
© 1991 John Wiley & Sons Ltd

accommodate the more recent findings of Schmidt *et al.* (1989) that delayed or summary feedback is desirable. In fact almost any finding could be accommodated with little strain. On this basis alone it is fair to say that *instructional technology* has no viable conceptual foundation beyond the approach of testing intuitions or subjective beliefs, and it is a fact that most hypotheses about instruction have been derived intuitively rather than through deduction from theory.

# EMPIRICAL PERSPECTIVE

One response to the failure of theory is to appeal to data for support of hypotheses about instruction. It is apparent however that a plethora of ideas about instruction are supported by a disappointingly meager database. Often enough, the power of an idea can even overcome non-supportive data so that the mere fact that an experiment has been conducted, no matter what the result, is used as evidence in favor of a theory while negative evidence is ignored (Lintern and Gopher, 1978). On the positive side, there has been some solid empirical work which can offer a useful guide to the types of instructional strategies that could be useful. In particular, research within part training, adaptive training, and flight simulation has produced results in the last decade that have advanced some distance towards the goal of establishing a sound empirical base for the application of instructional strategies.

# ISSUES

Of the many issues that have been raised in relation to the research on *instructional strategies,* in this review I take the position that three are crucial. The first is that effectiveness of instruction ultimately resides in transfer of skill from a training to an operational environment and that an evaluation of transfer is essential. The second is how an emphasis on instructional strategies fits with the traditional view that transfer is based on the similarity between tasks or contexts. The third is the issue of task complexity and experimental methodology; is it desirable for purposes of experimental evaluation and understanding of instructional strategies to strip a complex task to its bare essentials?

### Transfer

An empirical test of an instructional hypothesis must have, as a minimum, an experimental condition that incorporates the essentials of the hypothesis and a comparison or control condition that represents a standard or control procedure for instruction. In that the distinction between performance and learning is a critical issue (Salmoni, Schmidt and Walter, 1984), tests of instructional strategies must employ a transfer or retention design where transfer (or retention) will normally be to the standard or control condition. Transfer testing is sometimes undertaken on a variant of the control training condition that is more difficult or more like an operational task. All of the research reviewed here employs some form of the basic transfer paradigm.

**Fidelity and similarity**

Possibly the most prevalent belief about the design of instruction is that the instructional environment should be like the operational environment to the maximum possible extent. This is a high-fidelity, identity, or similarity approach which is in distinct contrast to the instructional strategy approach. The design of an instructional strategy is based on the assumption that a planned departure from identity can enhance learning and transfer, or at least can make instruction more cost effective. In some cases, instruction might be accomplished with less expensive devices and, even if learning is not as fast, the training program can be more cost effective. However, a specific focus for this chapter is on the empirical data which show that learning and transfer is actually more efficient with a low-fidelity or modified version of a task. It is these data that most clearly demonstrate the limitations of a high-fidelity approach to instruction.

**Complexity**

The emphasis in this review is on research that has employed tasks of at least a moderate level of complexity (i.e. multidimensional with interactions between different task dimensions) and that can be seen to represent important dimensions of some operational tasks. The contrasting approach, more common in basic research, is to fabricate a simple task by abstracting some element of normal human activity or by stripping an operational task of its complexity. The usual approach is problematic in that it is difficult to assess whether the trends found from contrasting an experimental with a control strategy are relevant to complex, operational tasks.

For psychological research in general, the argument in favor of simple laboratory tasks is that they are methodologically more convenient and more valid scientifically because they remove the ambiguities and complexities associated with complex tasks (Banji and Crowder, 1989). Nevertheless, complexity is a fact of life and one that must be dealt with by those interested in applied training issues. Methodological convenience is not a valid reason for simplicity because any research program must accept the challenges posed by the domain of interest whether they be modest or substantive. Nor is it more scientifically valid to experiment with a simple task. Interactions between multiple dimensions of performance are generally to be found in normal human activity and, while these may be difficult to unravel in experimentation with a complex task, they will be ignored entirely with a simple task. In fact, the use of simple tasks will eliminate the possibility of studying dimensions that are crucial in normal human activity and will provide results that are either irrelevant or unrepresentative. This amounts to a claim that the study of complex scenarios will reveal emergent principles that simply are not present within an abstract laboratory task (cf. Banaji and Crowder, 1989). From that perspective, complexity in human behavior poses a challenge that must be confronted.

## PART TRAINING

One approach to instruction is to adjust the task structure so that learning will be enhanced. This is a skills approach in the sense that the adjustment is designed to enhance the acquisition of the criterion task by emphasis on special skills or procedures. The implicit assumption is that enhanced skill on special dimensions of a task will enhance performance of the whole task. Nevertheless, all forms of restructuring are not equal. Task manipulation strategies have not been universally effective. One observation to be made in anticipation of the data is that restructuring could impede learning if it emphasizes non-critical task dimensions or if it forces subjects to practice irrelevant skills. Thus, there is a need for careful analysis prior to the testing of any instructional strategy of a task manipulation type.

Despite the wide acceptance of part training and its almost universal use in some form or another in training programs of any complexity, experimental results have been disappointing. From a review of part training for manual control tasks, Wightman and Lintern (1985) concluded that there is very little evidence to support the use of part-training procedures. A re-evaluation of that gloomy conclusion is now warranted primarily because of results from a series of experiments referred to as the Learning Strategies program (Donchin, 1989). Several experiments were conducted under the umbrella of that program, all of which have some useful implications, and several of which provide strong support for the principle of part training (Lintern, 1989).

### Task analysis for part training research

Training within the Learning Strategies program was conducted on a computer-controlled task which was similar in many respects to a popular arcade video game. The task, which is known as Space Fortress, requires subjects to maneuver a cursor (the ship) in a simulated frictionless environment around a target—the fortress (Figure 6.1, see Appendix to this chapter for detailed description). The task goal is to destroy the fortress by shooting missiles at it while evading missiles from the fortress and evading or destroying other projectiles (mines) that pursue the ship. Subjects are advised of a total score which is calculated as shown in Table 6.1. This is a complex and difficult task which taxes perceptual, cognitive, and motor coordination skills and which typically demands hours of practice to achieve even a moderate level of competency.

One feature of the Learning Strategies program that distinguishes it from most other investigations of training strategies is the considerable effort that was devoted to understanding the task environment as a prelude to conduct of the training research. In a preliminary experiment, 40 subjects practiced the

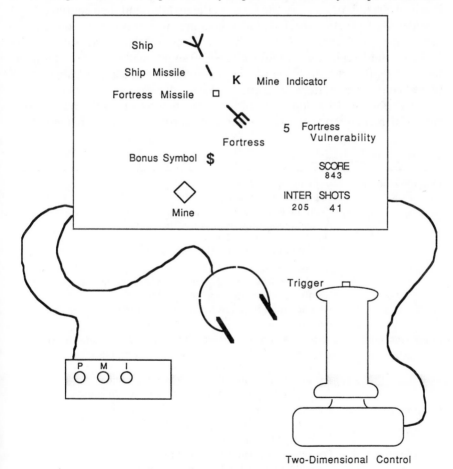

**Figure 6.1.** The Space Fortress task. Adapted from Mane and Donchin (1989). See Appendix to this chapter for a detailed description of this task.

**Table 6.1.** Computation of a total score for the Space Fortress task.

| Points added when: | Points subtracted when: |
| --- | --- |
| Fortress hit (4) | Ship damaged (50) |
| Fortress destroyed (100) | Ship destroyed (100) |
| Bonus points earned (100) | Missiles fired from the ship when initial and bonus allocations are exhausted (3 per shot) |
| Foe mine destroyed (30) | |
| Friend mine energized (20) | |

task for 380 minutes distributed over 10 sessions (Foss *et al.*, 1989). Subjects received a standard set of instructions on the first day and then continued with unsupervised practice through the remaining nine sessions. A three-mode principal components analysis applied to 21 performance measures (Table 6.2) over the 10 training sessions for these 40 subjects allowed the experimenters to identify clusters of strategies preferred by groups of subjects and typical changes in strategy and skill on specific dimensions of performance.

It was possible to group many of the subjects in terms of the pattern they chose for maneuvering the ship around the fortress. A slow circling pattern

**Table 6.2.** Dependent measures of Space Fortress performance.

| | |
| --- | --- |
| Ship movement | Velocity in the $X$-axis.<br>Velocity in the $Y$-axis.<br>Accumulated time of thrust in the $X$-axis.<br>Accumulated time of thrust in the $Y$-axis.<br>Number of screen edge crossings.<br>Number of entries into the fortress line of fire. |
| Tactics | Number of times the ship was damaged by a mine.<br>Number of times the ship was damaged by the fortress.<br>Number of times the fortress was hit.<br>Average time required to destroy the fortress.<br>Percentage of ship missiles that hit the target. |
| Mine handling | Mean reaction time to identification of a foe mine (from the appearance of the mine to the first IFF press).<br>Standard deviation of identification reaction time.<br>Average time required to destroy a foe mine.<br>Average time required to energize a friendly mine. |
| IFF timing | Average IFF (Identify Friend or Foe) interval.<br>Standard deviation of the IFF interval.<br>Number of incorrect IFF intervals. |
| Resource use | Per cent of occasions that the bonus was used.<br>Advantageous use of the bonus option.<br>Total number of missiles fired from the ship. |

could be distinguished from a rapid circling pattern or from straight-line flight. The slow circling strategy appeared to be more effective than other strategies of ship control. It was also possible to identify skill components that improved throughout training. Components that appeared to result in an improved overall game score were efficiency of missile firing, use of the bonus option, and foe mine identification (including the accuracy of the double press required for identification).

Different types of task analyses were undertaken independently by others working with this task. Early empirical work employed an additive factors methodology in which a task-loading manipulation is used to isolate critical task elements (Mane et al., 1984). Gopher, Weil and Siegel (1989) and Frederiksen and White (1989) examined the performances and strategies of expert players. Post-experiment interviews revealed that higher scoring players used specific strategies in the control of the ship and in their interactions with mines. All of these task analyses are mutually supportive in respect of the conclusions that were drawn about the make-up of the Space Fortress task and the learning challenges it posed. A variety of part-training schedules were subsequently tested with the Space Fortress task but all were designed with at least some reliance on one or more of these analyses.

## Component drills

In the first training experiment, 14 minutes of additional part practice was provided prior to 100 minutes of practice (over three sessions) on the whole task (Mane, Adams and Donchin, 1989). This additional practice might best be characterized as component drills. Two minutes of drill was provided for timing practice of the double press required for identification of foe mines, two minutes for recognition practice of mine letter identifiers, and 10 minutes for practice of ship control. Control subjects were given 100 minutes of practice on the whole task. The part-trained group performed better throughout the 100 minutes of whole task practice as measured by total score and also as measured by indices of mine handling and ship control performance. An analysis that equated total training time by compensating for the extra component practice of the part-trained group showed no significant differences although the trends favored the part-trained group.

Newell et al. (1989) argued that the components used by Mane et al. (1989) were not natural or integrated in terms of retaining the coordinative aspect of relative subskills. They proposed that part-training procedures should employ component tasks that allow practice of interactions between subskills. In addition to the ship control task used by Mane et al., Newell et al.'s subjects practiced the component tasks of circling the fortress, firing on the fortress while it fired at the ship, and interacting with mines. They gave some part trained subjects 25 minutes of additional practice on their component task prior to 380 minutes of practice on the whole task. A second group of part-trained subjects had the 25 minutes of additional part practice but were also given some further part practice in their early sessions of training in place of some of the whole practice normally given in those sessions. Control subjects were given 380 minutes of whole-task practice over 10 sessions. The two part-trained groups outperformed the control group on whole-task testing. The group that had additional component practice within their early training sessions showed the best performance. No statistical analysis was performed to test differences among groups with total training time equalized but the trends were clearly in favor of the part-trained groups.

In a second experiment, Newell et al. (1989) contrasted the effects of prior drills with the components they had used in their first experiment to those used by Mane et al. (1989). Twenty-five minutes of component drills were given prior to 180 minutes of whole-task practice (over 5 sessions). The differences between the whole-task performances of the two groups were not significant, but the trends in the data follow an intriguing pattern. Early whole-task performance (session 1) favored the group pretrained on the non-coordinated parts (those that did not allow practice on coordinative aspects of related subskills) whereas later whole-task performances (sessions 3, 4, and 5) favored the group pretrained with the coordinated parts. This suggests that the more complex coordinated parts led to an early disadvantage that was reversed in later training.

This is the type of result that would be missed in typical laboratory training experiments where subjects are trained for only one or two sessions (cf. Schneider, 1985). The typical paradigm may thus lead to an erroneous conclusion regarding the types of components that are best for part training. Of course the lack of statistical evidence regarding this observation is a matter for concern, but it should be noted that this was a less powerful experiment than most undertaken in the Learning Strategies program in that there were only 20 subjects in the experiment (versus 40 or more in most other experiments) and whole-task training was limited to 180 minutes (versus 380 minutes in most other experiments). It is possible that statistical significance for this trend could be demonstrated in a more powerful experiment.

Frederiksen and White (1989) developed an extensive set of component drills following an analysis of 'think aloud' protocols from expert players of the Space Fortress task. They identified three important subgoals of the task: to hit the fortress without being hit by it; to detect, identify, and destroy mines; and to use the bonus option effectively. They then identified a set of subskills that were required to achieve each of these subgoals without compromising success on other elements of the game, and they developed component tasks that could be used to teach these skills. In essence, this resulted in a set of basic subtasks that had much of the character of those used by Mane et al. (1989), but that also combined many of those components into higher level units. The more complex of these higher level training tasks were similar to those used by Newell *et al.* (1989).

In their first experiment, Frederiksen and White (1989) trained a control group for 200 minutes (over six sessions) on a simplified version of the task in which there were no resource options or mines. Through sessions 2 to 5, a part-training group practiced elements for the subgoal of hitting the fortress without being hit and also practiced on some whole-task trials. Total training time was equalized across groups. The experimental group outperformed the control group on the whole-task trials of the sixth session. It should be noted that the part-trained group had no more than 65 minutes' practice on the whole task (versus 200 minutes for the control group) so that the superiority on the whole task must be attributed to their practice on the game components.

From a qualitative analysis it became clear that part-trained subjects had adopted a ship control strategy in which they circled the fortress slowly in a counterclockwise direction while firing at it. In this strategy, the application of thrust to change direction is minimized so that the ship travels in a series of straight lines while maintaining an approximately constant distance from the fortress. Analyses of this task (Foss *et al.*, 1989; Frederiksen and White, 1989; Mane *et al.*, 1984) had shown this to be an optimum strategy because the ship was kept out of the fortress line of fire, but ship control remained sufficiently stable for periodic threats from mines to be dealt with effectively.

A clockwise direction of circling was desirable because a counterclockwise direction brought the ship across the fortress line of fire at the start of a game or at the start of a new cycle after destruction of the fortress or the ship. This happened because the starting configuration, which was identical for the start of every cycle, placed the ship slightly off the fortress line of fire in the clockwise direction. Thus, the initial thrust for a clockwise circle took the ship away from the fortress line of fire. This clockwise circling strategy had been explicitly taught within the subgames used by Frederiksen and White (1989). A small number of their control subjects who spontaneously developed this strategy performed well, in contrast to the remainder of the control subjects. Thus, there is a possibility that it was the explicit instruction of this optimum strategy that contributed substantially to the superior performance of the part-trained subjects.

In their second experiment, Frederiksen and White (1989) compared whole training on the full game (with mines and resources) to part training in which subjects practiced component skills for the three important subgoals: hitting the fortress without being hit, mine handling, and resource management. Whole-task training was extended to 380 minutes (10 sessions), and component training was conducted through sessions 2 to 9. Whole-task performance in session 10 was better for part-trained subjects. It was again apparent that control subjects who spontaneously adopted the slow, counterclockwise circling strategy performed better than other control subjects although they did not do as well as the part-trained subjects. Part-trained subjects also demonstrated more stable ship control (fewer ship rotations) and more efficient use of resources.

**Component emphasis**

The general issue for part-training research would seem to be one of whether the components that can be isolated pose enough of a learning challenge, whether isolated practice on them can speed their learning to any substantial degree, and whether the integration of those components also requires any substantial learning. The work of Frederiksen and White (1989) appears to provide an affirmative answer to the first two questions (although it remains uncertain which of the many component skills contributed to the demonstrated advantage for part training), and the results of Newell et al. (1989, Exp. 2), appear to provide an affirmative answer to the third question. The hierarchical task decomposition approach taken by Frederiksen and White (1989) may be contrasted to an integrated, component emphasis strategy that has also been tested with the Space Fortress task. Gopher et al. (1989) argued that it may be disadvantageous to decompose the whole task if that procedure interferes with the practice of important component integration skills (a similar argument to the one made by Newell et al., 1989).

Gopher et al. (1989) explored these issues with an emphasis manipulation in which subjects continued to practice the whole task but were directed to specific task elements by prior instruction and by performance feedback tailored to direct attention to those task elements. Ship control and mine handling were the emphasized dimensions. During training with ship-control emphasis, an additional feedback counter incremented as a function of the amount of time during which the subject prevented the ship colliding with the fortress or from traveling over the screen edge. This emphasis was designed to encourage development of the slow circling strategy for ship control although no distinction was made between the clockwise or counterclockwise direction. During training with the mine-handling emphasis, one additional feedback counter displayed points accumulated for shooting mines and points lost for being hit by mines. Another counter accumulated points as a function of the speed with which mines were shot.

In addition to a control group trained for 380 minutes (over 10 sessions), one experimental group practiced with ship control emphasis, another with mine-handling emphasis, and a third with frequent switches between both types of emphasis. The emphasis manipulations were used through sessions 1 to 6 with sessions 7 to 10 being devoted to practice on the whole task without any component emphasis. Strict equivalence of training time was maintained across the three groups. The emphasis manipulations led to better whole-task performance in the tenth (final) session, with the double-emphasis manipulation proving superior to either of the two single-emphasis manipulations.

In their qualitative analysis of performance on the whole task, Gopher *et al.* (1989) noted that subjects tended to develop a characteristic strategy and to stabilize it. They further noted that many of the spontaneously developed strategies were not efficient but that subjects did not generally experiment with different strategies once they had developed one. The ship control emphasis served the intended purpose in that all subjects who were trained with this condition developed the desired circling strategy while few subjects in other conditions developed it spontaneously. Nevertheless the equivalence in session 10 of the two single manipulation groups suggests that mine handling is an equally important dimension of this task.

## Component drills versus component emphasis

The two distinct approaches of Frederiksen and White (1989) and Gopher *et al.* (1989) were tested directly by Fabiani *et al.* (1989). Only slight modifications were made to the double-emphasis integrated manipulation of Gopher *et al.* and the hierarchical task decomposition procedure from Experiment 2 of Frederiksen and White. A control group was trained for 380 minutes (10 sessions) on the whole task and strict equivalence of training time was maintained for the two experimental groups. The different training manipulations were implemented in sessions 1 to 7 with sessions 8 to 10 being devoted to whole-task practice.

The integrated manipulation led to poorer performance on the whole task for the first 140 minutes of practice but to better performance thereafter, including through the three sessions of criterion testing. The hierarchical group started whole-task practice at 260 minutes and initially performed more poorly than the control group but surpassed them within 20 minutes. By the end of the tenth session, they had also surpassed the performance of the integrated group. Thus, the data indicate that both forms of part training were more efficient than whole-task training, that integrated training led to better initial transfer to the whole task, and that hierarchical training eventually led to better whole-task performance. It should also be noted that hierarchical practice fared very poorly on a whole-task test after approximately 100 minutes of practice. Thus, hierarchical training may be most efficient only for extended training where there is some opportunity for practice on the whole task before criterion testing. Nevertheless this is an operationally relevant and important situation so that hierarchical training would appear to be the more useful procedure for many normal training requirements.

Fabiani *et al.* (1989) included an additional 95 minutes of testing in which subjects had to perform the whole task concurrently with a variety of working-memory secondary tasks. In general, the two special training groups maintained their superiority during testing with the secondary tasks but the superiority of the hierarchical group over the integrated group was no longer so evident. In particular, with those secondary tasks that were most disruptive, the performance of the hierarchical group was no better than that of the control group, and the integrated group emerged with the best performance. There is an indication here that an integrated task-emphasis training strategy is desirable when performance under task-loaded conditions is anticipated.

**Strategy emphasis**

An observation that is repeated in the reports of research with the Space Fortress task is that the ship control strategy has a substantial influence on game score. It is possible that many of the gains found with the carefully designed instructional strategies that have been tested could be matched with relatively simple instructions about the optimum strategy. Newell *et al.* (1989, Exp. 3) tested this notion in an experiment in which control subjects were given 380 minutes of practice (10 sessions) on the whole task. Three experimental groups were given 25 minutes of practice on integrated subcomponents (see Newell *et al.*, 1989, Exp. 1) prior to their 380 minutes of practice on the whole task. One of the experimental groups was additionally instructed on the strategy of circling the fortress slowly in a counterclockwise direction, another on the strategy of circling in a clockwise direction (with no reference to the speed of circling), and the third was given no advice on strategy. A fifth group of subjects was tested as a no-instruction control group. The normal controls were given a standard set of instructions about the game and the methods of accumulating points. The no-instruction control group were given no instructions at all.

Prior instruction on the slow counterclockwise strategy combined with practice on integrated subcomponents resulted in the best performance which became evident after about 60 minutes of whole-task practice. Instruction on the clockwise strategy was somewhat less effective but still resulted in better performance than found with the control condition or with no instruction on strategy. This experimental condition led to some advantage over the control group for approximately 180 minutes of practice. The no-instruction control subjects performed very poorly and appeared to improve only marginally over their starting scores. These data support the hypothesis about the potency of instructions and advice on strategies for the Space Fortress task.

**Summary**

It is encouraging that after so much mediocre work in part training a program has emerged which has produced strong and useful results. The learning strategies research program used a unique and complex task but it would be disappointing to think that it is the task and not some generalizable advantage for part-training procedures that is important. In an earlier review, Wightman and Lintern (1985) noted that part-training research had devoted almost no effort towards principled task decomposition. Intuitions had dominated in the development of experimental instructional strategies. With the Learning Strategies program a deliberate effort was directed at understanding the task and at identifying important components and dimensions. All experimenters who tested part procedures leaned heavily on this development or preparatory work. There may be a lesson here that good training research relies on the experimenter knowing the task and that task decomposition procedures must be based on more than an intuitive or causal appraisal of the task. Some form of principled or empirical task analysis is evidently essential for the design of part-training procedures.

## ADAPTIVE TRAINING

Adaptive training is a procedure in which a task is initially simplified for training purposes and is then progressively brought back to the criterion level of difficulty. It has some similarity to the simplification procedure of part training (Wightman and Lintern, 1985) but is an individualized form of instruction in that the task difficulty is adjusted on the basis of individual changes in skill. The usual procedure is to adjust the difficulty parameter automatically to maintain near constant error scores. Most of this work has been undertaken with basic laboratory tracking tasks. Task characteristics such as amplitude or frequency of a forcing function have often been manipulated to adjust task difficulty.

Despite the fact that there has been considerable enthusiasm for the application of this technique (see McGrath and Harris, 1971), very few of the several early studies showed any advantage for adaptive versus non-adaptive training (Lintern and Gopher, 1978). As has too often been the case with training research, an almost religious fervor masked the need for careful analysis and solid empirical support. Adaptive training became a slogan and from this perspective any method of adjusting difficulty was expected to benefit instruction. The hard fact is that many manipulations of difficulty change the nature of the task in ways that actually interfere with the acquisition of skills required for performance of the criterion task. A research thrust based on such uncritical acceptance of the basic hypothesis had little chance of success.

### Augmented feedback

Nevertheless there is some plausibility in the assumption that a trainee will be assisted in acquiring skill if those task elements that are particularly difficult are made easier during initial training. Some tasks may be so difficult that a trainee cannot maintain sufficient control to engage in any meaningful prac- tice. Lintern (1980), following a review of augmented feedback training (Lintern and Roscoe, 1980), hypothesized that an adaptive form of feedback augmentation could simplify a task without distorting its fundamental structure. Subjects were trained on a simulated landing task with augmented glideslope indicators (Figure 6.2) that were programmed to switch on only when the student departed from an optimum flight envelope. The augmented feedback was viewed as adaptive because the envelope for switching the cues on or off was broken less frequently and thereby provided less support as the trainee became more skilled at the task. This adaptive technique might also be viewed as an automatic fading or withdrawal procedure. Transfer to the non- augmented simulated landing task was better following instruction with adap- tive cuing than following training with non-adaptive augmented cuing (i.e augmented feedback presented throughout training) or with no augmented cuing.

**Competing processes**

There is an indication here of two competing processes; simplification or enhancement can aid skill acquisition but may also distort the task or develop some unwanted dependencies. This view has been developed recently in rela- tion to the instructional value of post-response feedback (Schmidt *et al.* 1989). Within the adaptive training paradigm, Mane *et al.* (1989) drew a similar conclusion from their work with the Space Fortress task. They manip- ulated the speed of hostile elements as an adaptive variable. Two levels of adaptation were used. The more extreme manipulation reduced the speed of hostile elements for low-skilled subjects to one-quarter of criterion speed. A more moderate manipulation reduced it to only half criterion speed. The less

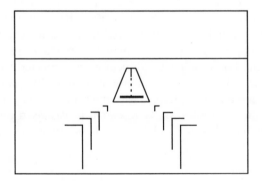

**Figure 6.2.**    Simulated landing display with visual augmented feedback. From Lintern (1980).

extreme form of adaptive training proved superior to both the more extreme form and also to control training. Evidently, a reduction in the speed of hostile elements permitted subjects to learn some aspects of the task more effectively but acquisition of other aspects was disrupted. Thus, the design of an adaptive training manipulation must strike a sensitive balance that exploits the benefits of simplification while minimizing its disadvantages. As with many things in life, more of a good thing is not necessarily desirable.

# FLIGHT SIMULATION

The design of flight training simulators is most often guided by the desire for high fidelity under the assumption that the more a training device is like the criterion device the better it will be. Claims about the need for high fidelity ignore the fact that transfer between situations and systems is pervasive in everyday life and has been well accepted in aviation throughout its history. For example, pilots transition between aircraft types that are different in many respects, and also transfer well from contact (visually referenced) to instrument flight. Although transfer is not assumed to be complete in these cases, it is widely accepted that some skills are carried from one aircraft to the next or from contact to instrument flight.

In contrast to the high-fidelity emphasis is the approach of designing a simulator that is as 'phony as it can be' without compromising training effectiveness (Roscoe, 1980). The low-fidelity approach requires that we provide only the features that are useful in teaching the desired skills. It remains possible that expensive, high-fidelity features for flight simulators add nothing to (and possibly even detract from) training effectiveness (Lintern, 1987). For instance, the provision of real-time interactive visual displays in training simulators is a relatively recent development. Because these systems can be expensive it is reasonable to enquire about their usefulness or about the level of fidelity needed for them to be useful. It remains possible, for example, that even skills which appear to be visually supported might be learned well enough without an elaborate visual display or possibly without any visual representation of a contact world.

**Transfer from instrument to contact flight**

Two transfer studies by Ritchie and his associates (Ritchie and Hanes, 1964; Ritchie and Michael, 1955) provide data which suggest the value of a low-fidelity approach to the instruction of contact flight skills. Acquisition and transfer of flight skills under instrument and contact conditions were examined in both experiments. Flight-naive subjects learned to fly straight and level to a criterion of three errorless trials and then learned to make level

180-degree turns to a criterion of three errorless trials. Some subjects first practiced under instrument conditions and then transferred to visual contact conditions while other subjects first practiced under visual contact conditions and then transferred to instrument conditions.

Data from these expériments are shown in Figure 6.3. Given their similarity it was possible, for the purposes of this review, to enhance the stability of the results by collapsing the data across the two experiments. The performance measure is total trials required to achieve criterion in both tasks. There was evidently an asymmetric transfer effect from instrument to contact and contact to instrument flight. Those trained on instruments in the airplane performed better in contact flight than those given no pretraining at that point. On the other hand, those who were trained first on contact flight showed no better performance on instruments in the airplane than shown in the first session by the group first trained on airplane instruments. These data suggest that instrument training can develop skills useful for contact flight.

**Pictorial versus symbolic representation**

Evidence of transfer from instrument to contact flight raises an important issue for flight training; that is whether a visual system for simulation of contact flight adds anything to the development of contact skills that cannot be gained from a good instrument trainer. Lintern, Roscoe and Sivier (1990) examined this issue in the context of a light-aircraft landing task. The question

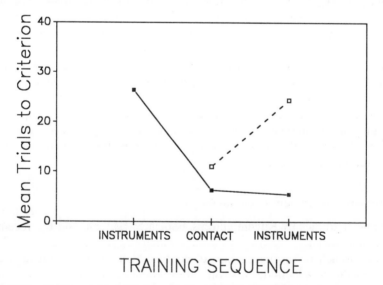

**Figure 6.3.**   Trials to criterion in transfer between instrument and contact conditions. Adapted from Ritchie and Hanes (1964) and Ritchie and Michael (1955).

examined here was whether acquisition of landing skill requires the development of any new visual skills, with the alternate possibility being that acquisition of aircraft control skills poses the major learning challenge. Flight-naive subjects were given the opportunity to learn this task in a flight simulator either with reference to a pictorial representation of an airport scene or with reference to a symbolic display that guided subjects through the desired control behavior but that provided no representation of features found in a normal airport scene.

Transfer to a pictorial representation of the normal airport scene was much poorer (in fact almost non-existent) following training with the symbolic display versus training with the pictorial scene. These data verify the intuition that, for the landing task at least, some pictorial representation of the normal visual environment is essential. It does not necessarily invalidate the implication of the data from Ritchie and his associates that skills useful for contact flight can be acquired from practice in the absence of any pictorial representation of a normal scene, because the two control tasks examined in that experiment may not pose the same level of challenge to visual learning. Nevertheless, the results of Lintern et al. establish that visual learning (and most likely, learning in other perceptual modalities) can be important for the acquisition of some manual control skills.

**Visual fidelity**

In an earlier study, Lintern et al. (1987) examined acquisition of a military bombing skill in a flight simulator under two levels of scene detail. Training with an abstract grid pattern was contrasted to training with a more natural-appearing scene which had representations of fields, roads, and buildings. Transfer to both types of scene was better following training with the more natural scene. As well as supporting the belief that realistic visual representations are useful, these data also indicate that training for an impoverished visual environment is better accomplished with a richer visual environment. This is an important observation for situations in which it is necessary to prepare pilots for flight over naturally impoverished visual environments such as deserts, oceans, and snow fields.

While the data from this experiment might seem to support the push for high-fidelity visual systems, it should be noted that even the higher fidelity level of visual representation was modest in relation to what is possible with the best of the currently available visual systems. More recent research indicates that, at least for the landing task, a schematic scene without ground clutter or texture is as effective as a more highly detailed scene (Lintern and Garrison, in press). In addition there is evidence from the experiment of Lintern et al. (1987; see Lintern, Thomley and Nelson, 1983) that limitations of impoverished visual scenes can be overcome in other ways. In this case subjects trained on the impoverished scene with adaptive visual augmented feedback were at no transfer disadvantage relative to those trained with the more detailed scene (see also Koonce and Lintern, 1991).

### Control manipulation in flight simulation

The early adaptive training literature carried the implication that any means of simplifying a task could provide a useful adaptive dimension. However, the available evidence suggests that while some manipulations can enhance transfer, others can disrupt it (Lintern and Gopher, 1978). A general conclusion is that designers of training systems must select their manipulations with care. This is clearly the message from research by Lintern *et al.* (1990) in which flight-naive subjects were taught a light-aircraft landing task under different crosswind and control-order configurations. Transfer was to normal control order and a constant five-knot crosswind from the left or the right. Subjects were trained with normal (first-order) or simplified (zero-order) roll control and with or without the five-knot crosswind.

Transfer from reduced to normal order was poorer, which is consistent with data from basic tracking studies (Dooley and Newton, 1965; Holland and Henson, 1956) and which also provides further evidence that adaptive manipulation of system order is unlikely to be useful. There was also an interaction between control order and crosswind (Figure 6.4). Subjects trained on normal order with no crosswind performed best in transfer to the criterion condition (which included crosswind). The other three groups performed relatively poorly. This latter result demonstrates the inadequacy of a high-fidelity or similarity approach to training system design in that it shows that simulation of crosswinds during training can actually impede learning for transfer to crosswind landings.

### Summary

The body of evidence emerging from flight training research is generally supportive of the conclusions to be drawn from recent part training and adaptive training research. Careful analysis of the task and the design of a training strategy focused on the learning challenges in the task will often be rewarded with enhanced transfer. Emphasis on stimulating a particular flight scenario in all possible detail is wasteful and may even inhibit the acquisition of important skills. Nevertheless, the data reviewed here are not yet comprehensive enough to establish universal principles for instruction. A strong theoretical formulation is yet to be developed and, in the absence of that formulation, it remains uncertain whether these results can be generalized to a wider range of complex tasks.

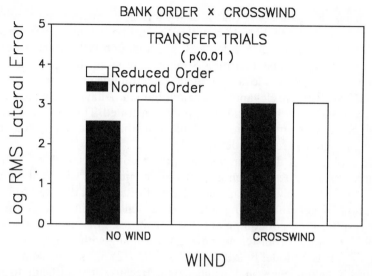

**Figure 6.4.**    Performance in transfer to a simulated landing task with normal roll order and a constant five-knot crosswind from the left or the right. Training was conducted with normal or reduced roll order and with or without the crosswind. From Lintern, Roscoe and Sivier (1990).

## DISCUSSION

**Task complexity**

Task complexity and relevance are issues for instructional design, but they are also issues for behavioral research, and they are issues that have been neglected by mainstream cognitive psychology. Demonstrations that basic psychological research has any widespread implications for normal human functioning in complex systems are difficult to find. From this perspective, the relevance or value of decades of careful and rigorous behavioral research is essentially unknown. Even where solid data are available they have most often been gathered in special laboratory environments and with simple laboratory tasks. Their relevance to operational environments remains uncertain. This is a disturbing trend that needs to be corrected if training research is to be more than an exercise in laboratory science.

One possible approach is to develop a special form of a complex task, as has been done in the Learning Strategies program at the University of Illinois (Mane and Donchin, 1989). In that work a complex video game was programmed with promising features drawn from experimental research on simpler tasks (e.g. the Sternberg information-processing task). This approach exploits the insights gained from previous behavioral research while it approaches the complexity that is characteristic of operational systems. Experimentation with real-world complexity must be planned carefully and the development of a complex video task as a research task offers a useful step towards that goal. The Learning Strategies program has provided several insights that might be relevant in operational training environments (Lintern, 1989). Nevertheless relevance to normal human behavior remains as an unfulfilled promise until that relevance is demonstrated. Thus research with real-world tasks is essential if instructional principles that can benefit applied training programs are to be developed.

The evolution of flight simulation as a laboratory research tool offers the potential for good experimental control in conjunction with real-world relevance. Unfortunately, this capability has not often been directed towards the resolution of general training issues. Research into simulator design most often results in tests of equipment design features. For example, Browning *et al* (1977) showed a transfer advantage for training with computer-generated imagery versus a model board, and Westra (1982) has shown some transient effects for field-of-view and scene detail. Because it is difficult to identify psychological processes that were differentially affected by these manipulations, these results cannot easily be related to behavioral issues. Nevertheless, investigation of general behavioral issues is possible within a complex simulation laboratory (Lintern *et al.*, 1990; Lintern *et al.*, 1987). A systematic and extended program of research with a complex simulation could do much to advance our understanding of strategies that are effective for instruction of operational skills.

**Implications for transfer theory**

The most prevalent idea to be found in conceptual formulation of skill transfer is that of fidelity or similarity. The basic notion is that the training environment should be as much like the transfer environment as possible. The problem with this approach is that some features of similarity are clearly irrelevant; for example the color of a flight simulator need not match that of the airplane. The concepts of functional equivalence (Baudhuin, 1987) or psychological fidelity (Goldstein, 1986) are of little help because they are merely restatements of the fact that some similarities are important while others are not.

Thorndike (1903) forwarded the notion of identical elements and proposed that some specific elements are critical to transfer. It is unclear whether Thorndike regarded these elements as features of the task (e.g. control-display lag) or as skills (e.g. ability to anticipate). He did recognize that the elements had to be identified but offered the view that this would be relatively easy. He was, however, overly optimistic. Several decades later identification of those elements remains a problem.

Contemporary theorists have attempted to resolve this issue. Singley and Anderson (1989) have argued that Thorndike's identical elements can be viewed as production rules. Logan (1988) has argued that instance memories form the basis of what is learned and transferred. Unfortunately neither of these statements offers principles that could be used to identify the specific productions or instance memories that might support transfer. Lintern (in press) has dealt with this issue by proposing an informational theory of transfer. Identities that support transfer are informational and can be isolated through some form of task analysis (Lintern and Liu, submitted). By this view, only the relevant informational properties that support transfer need to be duplicated accurately in both the training and transfer environments.

Theoretical discussions have rarely dealt with the notion that it is possible to get better transfer with a manipulation that results in the training task being less similar to the transfer task. The notion of part training is based on the assumption that this is possible but theorists in general have failed to consider this type of data trend (e.g. Logan, 1988; Singley and Anderson, 1989). The research reviewed in this chapter shows that these types of transfer effects must be taken seriously. An information theory can deal with them through an appeal to the perceptual learning effects discussed by E. Gibson (1969). Perceptual learning is part of the foundation for the information theory of transfer outlined by Lintern (in press). Whether or not one is inclined to accept an informational theory, the transfer effects that have recently been demonstrated in part training and flight simulation research must remove any possibility that a simplistic notion of similarity as espoused in Thorndike's (1903) theory of identical elements or Logan's (1988) theory of instance memory is adequate.

## SUMMARY AND CONCLUSIONS

An instructional strategy was defined as a systematic procedure for restructuring a learning environment with the goal of enhancing learning relative to that achievable with a standard mode of instruction. Despite considerable enthusiasm for instructional strategies, early research generally failed to show that it was possible to improve on standard modes of instruction. However, research in part training, adaptive training, and flight simulation over the past decade has offered considerable encouragement, and has indicated some of the reasons for the earlier failures. An important lesson to be drawn from this review is that careful task analysis is an important part of the preparation for experimentation with instructional strategies. On the other hand, uncritical application of ideas developed from intuition will generally produce disappointing results.

It may also be significant that the research reviewed here has been oriented around tasks of a much higher degree of complexity than usually found in behavioral research laboratories. The success of this research weighs against the belief that behavioral knowledge about instruction is best advanced by experimentation with simple tasks. In addition, these new results weigh heavily against the belief that skill transfer is dependent on high fidelity or task similarity, and they point to the need for a new theoretical framework for understanding skill acquisition and transfer. In fact the success of any special instructional strategy poses considerable difficulty for the general fidelity/similarity view. What is needed is a systematic perspective that can account for diverse transfer effects.

The observation that transfer can be better to 'less' similar conditions offers a particularly significant challenge to theoretical development. It is these data, more than any others, that call for a reappraisal of transfer theory. It would seem nonsensical to suggest that transfer is enhanced by less similar training conditions. It is more likely that these data show the need for a new assessment of what 'similar' means within the context of skill transfer. It remains as a critical issue for training research that there is not yet a widely accepted theoretical perspective that can guide research and integrate the research findings. Development of a useful theory must remain a high priority for research in this area.

## ACKNOWLEDGEMENTS

This work was supported by the Basic Research Office of the Army Research Institute under contract MDA 903–86–C–0169. Dr Michael Drillings is the technical monitor. Gregory A. Morrison assisted with preparation of the figures.

## REFERENCES

Adams, J. A. (1971). A closed-loop theory of motor learning, *Journal of Motor Behavior*, **3**, 111–149.

Banaji, M. R. and Crowder, R.G. (1989). The bankruptcy of everyday memory, *American Psychologist*, **44**, 1185–1193.

Baudhuin, E. S. (1987) The design of industrial and flight simulators. In S. M. Cormier and J. D. Hagman (eds). *Transfer of Learning*. pp. 217–237, Orlando, FL: Academic Press.

Browning, R. F., Ryan, L. E., Scott, P. G. and Smode, A. F. (1977). *Training Effectiveness Evaluation of Device 2F87E, P–3 Operational Flight Trainer*, TAEG Report No. 42, Training Analysis and Evaluation Group, Orlando, FL.

Donchin, E. (1989). The learning strategies project: Introductory remarks, *Acta Psychologica*, **71**, 1–15.

Dooley, R. P. and Newton, J. M. (1965). Transfer of training between quickened and unquickened displays, *Perceptual and Motor Skills*, **21**, 11–15.

Fabiani, M., Buckley, J., Gratton, G., Coles, M. G. H., Donchin, E. and Logie, R. (1989). The training of complex task performance, *Acta Psychologica*, **71**, 259–299.

Foss, M. A., Fabiani, M., Mane, A. M. and Donchin, E. (1989). Unsupervised practice: The performance of the control group, *Acta Psychologica*, **71**, 23–51.

Frederiksen, J. R. and White, B. Y. (1989). An approach to training based upon principled task decomposition, *Acta Psychologica*, **71**, 89–146.

Gibson, E. J. (1969). *Principles of Perceptual Learning and Development.* Englewood Cliffs, NJ: Prentice-Hall.

Goldstein, I. L. (1986). *Training in Organizations: Needs Assessment, Development, and Evaluation*, 2nd edn. Monterey, CA: Brooks/Cole.

Gopher, D., Weil, M. and Siegel, D. (1989). Practice under changing priorities: An approach to training of complex skills, *Acta Psychologica*, **71**, 147–177.

Holland, J. G. and Henson, J. B. (1956). Transfer of training between quickened and unquickened tracking systems, *Journal of Applied Psychology*, **40**, 362–366.

Koonce, J. and Lintern, G. (1991). Visual augmentation and scene content effects in flight training. In *Proceedings of the Sixth International Symposium on Aviation Psychology*, Department of Aviation, Ohio State University, Columbus, Ohio.

Lintern, G. (1980). Transfer of landing skill after training with supplementary visual cues, *Human Factors*, **22**, 81–88.

Lintern, G. (1987). Flight simulation motion systems revisited, *Human Factors Society Bulletin*, **30**(12), 1–3.

Lintern, G. (1989). The learning strategies program: concluding remarks, *Acta Psychologica*, **71**, 301–309.

Lintern, G. (in press). An informational perspective on skill transfer for human–machine systems. *Human Factors*.

Lintern, G. and Garrison, W. (in press). Transfer effects of scene content and crosswind in landing instruction.

Lintern, G. and Gopher, D. (1978). Adaptive training of perceptual–motor skills: Issues, results, and future directions, *International Journal of Man–Machine Studies*, **10**, 521–551.

Lintern, G. and Liu, Y. (in press). Explicit and implicit horizons for simulated landing approaches. *Human Factors*.

Lintern, G. and Roscoe, S. N. (1980). Visual cue augmentation in contact flight simulation. In S. N. Roscoe (ed.). *Aviation Psychology*. Ames, IA: The Iowa State University Press.

Lintern, G., Roscoe, S. N. and Sivier, J. E. (1990). Display principles, control dynamics, and environmental factors in pilot training and transfer, *Human Factors*, **32**, 299–317.

Lintern, G., Thomley, K. and Nelson, B. (1983). Visual display manipulations for simulation training of air-to-ground attack. In *Simulators*, p. 312–316, Institution of Electrical Engineers, London.

Lintern, G., Thomley, K. E., Nelson, B. E. and Roscoe, S. N. (1987). Content, variety, and augmentation of visual scenes for teaching air-to-ground attack, *Human Factors*, **29**, 45–59.

Logan, G. D. (1988). Toward an instance theory of automatization, *Psychological Review*, **95**, 492–527.

Mane, A. M., Adams, J. A. and Donchin, E. (1989). Adaptive and part-whole training in the acquisition of a complex perceptual–motor skill, *Acta Psychologica*, **71**, 179–196.

Mane, A. and Donchin, E. (1989). The Space Fortress Game, *Acta Psychologica*, **71**, 17–22.

Mane, A. M., Coles, M. G. H., Karis, D., Strayer, D. and Donchin, E. D. (1984). The design and use of subtasks in part training and their relationship to the whole task. In *Proceedings of the 20th Annual Conference on Manual Control*, NASA Ames Research Center, Moffett Field, CA.

McGrath, J. J. and Harris, D. H. (eds) (1971). Adaptive training, *Aviation Research Monographs*, **1**(2), Savoy, IL: University of Illinois, Aviation Research Laboratory.

Newell, K. M., Carlton, M. J., Fisher, A. T. and Rutter, B. G. (1989). Whole–part training strategies for learning the response dynamics of microprocessor driven simulators, *Acta Psychologica*, **71**, 197–216.

Ritchie, M. L. and Hanes, L. F. (1964). *An Experimental Analysis of Transfer Effects between Contact and Instrument Flight Training*. Washington, DC: Federal Aviation Agency.

Ritchie, M. L. and Michael, A. L. (1955). Transfer between instrument and contact flight training, *Journal of Applied Psychology*, **39**, 145–149.

Roscoe, S. N. (1980). *Aviation Psychology*, Ames, IA: The Iowa State University Press.

Salmoni, A. W., Schmidt, R. A. and Walter, C. B. (1984). Knowledge of results and motor learning: a review and critical reappraisal, *Psychological Bulletin*, **45**, 355–386.

Schmidt, R. A., Young, D. E., Swinnen, S. and Shapiro, D. C. (1989). Summary knowledge of results for skill acquisition: Support for the guidance hypothesis, *Journal of Experimental Psychology: Learning, Memory, and Cognition*, **15**, 352–359.

Schneider, W. (1985). Training high-performance skills: Fallacies and guidelines, *Human Factors*, **27**, 285–300.

Singley, M. K. and Anderson, J. R. (1989). *The Transfer of Cognitive Skill*. Cambridge, MA: Harvard University Press.

Thorndike, E. L. (1903). *Educational Psychology*, New York: Lemcke and Buechner.

Westra, D. P. (1982). *Simulator Design Features for Carrier Landing: II. In-Simulator Transfer of Training* (NAVTRAEQUIPCEN 81–C–0105–1). Naval Training Equipment Center, Orlando, FL.

Wightman, D. C. and Lintern, G. (1985). Part-task training for tracking and manual control, *Human Factors*, **27**, 267–283.

# APPENDIX: THE SPACE FORTRESS TASK

The ship (controlled cursor) moves in a simulated frictionless environment. A two-dimensional control stick (right hand) is used to apply thrust by forward movement which initiates motion in the direction of heading. Ship rotation is controlled by right and left side movements of the stick. Velocity changes are affected by rotating the ship to a specified heading and by then applying thrust.

Missiles are fired from the ship by a trigger on the control stick. Ten hits separated by at least 250 milliseconds (ms) followed by two hits (of less than 250 ms separation) will destroy the fortress. The 'Fortress Vulnerability' label indicates how many single shots have hit the fortress. The number '10' indicates the fortress can now be destroyed with a double shot (overly rapid firing by the subject before the vulnerability counter reaches 10 will return the counter to zero). The fortress remains at screen center and rotates slowly in the direction of the ship while firing at it. Four hits on the ship will destroy it. If the fortress or the ship is destroyed the fortress vulnerability indicator is reset to zero and a new cycle commences.

Mines (projectiles appearing from the screen edge) must be distinguished as friend or foe by means of the letter indicator. A three-letter set, changed each trial and given to the subject prior to each trial, identifies foe mines, which must be made vulnerable to a shot from the ship by double activation of a press switch (labeled I) controlled by the left hand. The separation interval between the two switch activations must lie between 250 ms and 400 ms (actual interval shown on the screen under the label INTER). Once vulnerable, a foe mine may be destroyed by a missile fired from the ship. Friend mines need not be treated in any special manner prior to being fired on by the ship. If friend mines are hit by a shot from the ship they will crash into the fortress for the same result as a missile fired from the ship. If friend or foe mines are not evaded or shot they crash into the ship to score a hit. They disappear from the screen after 10 s if they are not shot and if evaded successfully. A new mine appears 4 s after the destruction or disappearance of an old one. Shots fired at the fortress have no effect while a mine is on the screen.

At the start of each game, the ship is allocated a supply of 100 missiles. The number of missiles left is indicated under the label 'SHOTS'. After the supply has been exhausted, further missiles cost 3 points each. A sequence of symbols is continuously presented beneath the fortress. A designated symbol ($), referred to as the 'BONUS' symbol, appears twice in succession on each occasion it appears, and on the second appearance (and while it remains on the screen) the subject may use a left-hand push switch to select either 50 more missiles (switch M) or to obtain 100 extra points (switch P).

A game score is indicated under the label 'SCORE'. Points are added as indicated in Table 6.1. Total scores for a 5-minute game for a typical subject range from –2000 to +4000. Subjects are advised of the total score at the end of the trial.

Within the reports of research from the Learning Strategies program total game score was the common dependent measure of performance. Data were collected on approximately 150 other dimensions of task performance (see Table 6.2 for a list of the 21 variables analyzed by Foss *et al*) and several of these have also been used for analyses by some of the research groups. Additionally, some insights have been gained by qualitative analysis of strategies used by subjects, which was facilitated by the capability of recording the task and then of replaying that record.

# Chapter 7

# Trainee characteristics

## Phillip L. Ackerman[1] and Patrick C. Kyllonen[2]

[1]University of Minnesota, [2]US Air Force Human Resources Laboratory

In delineating the scope of individual differences concerns, historical treatments occasionally include classical views of individual differences. For example, Plato (*The Republic*) outlined three basic classes of individual differences, denoted *cognitive* (the faculty of knowing), *affective* (the faculty of feeling), and *conative* (the faculty of volition) (Warner, 1958). In modern terminology, these 'faculties' respectively correspond to *mental abilities* (e.g. intelligence, spatial ability), *temperament, personality* (e.g. emotionality, introversion, masculinity–femininity), and *motivation* (e.g. need for achievement, competitiveness). All three classes are well represented in the theory and practice of psychology. In fact, assessment instruments purporting to measure aspects of each of these faculties are in common use throughout the industrial and educational domains.

The focus of our discussion in this chapter is mainly limited to trainee characheristics within the cognitive or intellectual domain. Although we briefly discuss motivation and personality issues in the context of aptitude–treatment interactions, reviews of trainee characteristics along the lines of motivation and temperament can be found elsewhere (e.g. see Kanfer, 1990, for a review of the motivation area; see Gough, 1976, for a review of the temperament domain).

We start this chapter with a review of the importance of individual differences for the training domain and describe the methods and tactics of research/applications from the individual differences perspective. However, jobs are inherently multifaceted amalgamations of many task components. Even within a single occupation, there is heterogeneity between the amount of time an employee spends in highly demanding cognitive tasks (such as planning and decision making) and the amount of time spent in performing generally consistent perceptual–motor activities (such as word processing, or operating other office or production machinery). In order to summarize theory and empirical research applications, we decided that it would be most parsimonious to consider trainee characteristics with respect to two broad task types: perceptual–motor skills and cognitive skills. Although there are

*Training for Performance: Principles of Applied Human Learning.* Edited by J. E. Morrison
© 1991 John Wiley & Sons Ltd

similarities in the overall approaches taken to investigating these two types of skills, it is clear that there is a fundamental distinction between the determinants of individual differences in acquisition and performance of such skills.

In addition to treatment of the two types of skills, we discuss some major trends in the literature relating individual differences in abilities to training and educational situations. One portion of our discussion focuses on building and applying a taxonomy of learning skills; the other portion focuses on interactions between aptitudes and treatments. We close with a few conclusions concerning the future of individual differences research and applications to training technology.

# BASIC CONCEPTS

Any discussion of the training environment would be pointless without consideration of two types of individual differences, those representing differences *between* individuals (inter-individual differences), and those representing differences *within* particular individuals (intra-individual differences). Both types of individual differences drive the training system. For example, at the simplest level, inter-individual differences in the form of abilities (such as intelligence, spatial or verbal abilities, perceptual or psychomotor abilities) assessed by selection instruments determine the range of talent with which the training program must cope. Other inter-individual differences attributes, including background variables such as previous job or educational experience, may also enter into the selection process. At the very extreme of application of an inter-individual differences perspective, when *only* those applicants who already possess the skills necessary to the job are hired, the training program becomes unnecessary (since the newly hired employees can be put directly on the job with no training). As such, training is only necessary when a suitable pool of applicants already possessing the job skills is unavailable to the organization. Under such circumstances, inter-individual approaches to *selection* focus on potential for job success; that is, they attempt to predict those applicants who will most likely succeed in the training program, or later in on-the-job performance. The key goal of the individual differences approach is to identify aspects of the applicant pool that will, in a cost-effective manner, significantly and importantly determine failure or success in the training or job situations.

In contrast to the perspective on differences across individuals, the focus on intra-individual differences is upon the changes that take place as the individual proceeds from a novice level of task performance, to a skilled, expert level. Intra-individual differences approaches typically concern things like 'ability to learn' or profit from instruction, and the relationship between inter-individual differences measures and the degree of learning that takes place in a single training environment.

Finally, an integrated approach can be taken to both types of individual differences, those occurring between individuals and those within individuals. This approach is identified as focusing on the interactions between inter-individual differences (i.e. aptitudes) and the structure and type of treatments (e.g. different training methods). This aptitude–treatment interaction (ATI) perspective involves the assessment of the degree to which identical training methods are non-optimal for individuals who are at different levels of some inter-individual attribute.

In a sense, training theorists and practitioners can be seen in a sort of competition with the individual differences approach. The more effective a general training procedure can be made (so that a larger proportion of applicants can be trained to criterion levels of skilled performance), the less important an individual differences perspective will be. To be somewhat fanciful, this could be illustrated by the idea that if a mathematics course could be designed so that persons with IQs below 60 could be taught the fundamentals of integral calculus, the IQ will have pretty much lost its usefulness as a selection device—that is, selection can be based on factors other than inter-individual differences in ability. Conversely, the more effective the individual differences approach can be implemented (such as identifying those applicants who will learn in the most facile fashion, and benefit most from any instructional/training environment), the less importance will be accorded to devising training programs that are more effective or allow for the development of skills in the widest possible range of talent.

It is best to keep in mind, then, as the discussion of trainee characteristics unfolds in this chapter, that it is the aim of training research both to raise the level of performance of individuals (an intra-individual differences issue) and to *reduce* the range of individual differences in performance (an inter-individual differences issue). This chapter is devoted to identifying the attributes of individuals that pertain to both of these individual differences issues. The concern is predominantly with ability determinants of learning and skill acquisition, but other related variables will be included as they impinge on the relationship between these attributes and learning and performance. The next section reviews the theoretical approaches and the empirical tactics of individual differences research.

## Individual differences methods

*Aptitude* can most generally be defined as any characteristic of trainees that determines their ability to profit from instruction (Cronbach and Snow, 1977). As such, characteristics such as general intelligence, specific background knowledge, spatial ability, quantitative skill, and psychomotor ability have been treated as aptitudes in numerous theoretical and applied investigations. The scientific question is how do we decide what constitutes an aptitude? How are these aptitudes related to one another? What are the relationships between aptitudes and success in training and school situations?

Historically, investigations into these questions can be divided into four phases. In the nineteenth century, Francis Galton (1869, 1883) was perhaps the first to document systematically the extent to which individuals vary in 'intellectual capacity' as demonstrated in mathematics courses, painting, music, and other fields of endeavor. He, along with James McKeen Cattell (1890) and Clark Wissler (1901), sought to determine the more fundamental sensory discrimination abilities that might underlie differences in global intellectual capacity. This line of research was largely abandoned when it was found that sensory capabilities were relatively uncorrelated with success in school.

An alternative approach to measuring aptitude was taken by Alfred Binet (Binet and Henri, 1895), who found that complex intellectual tasks, or what Cronbach (1970, p. 199) has called 'worksamples of life performance', were correlated with success in school. Spearman (1904, 1927) formalized this approach by suggesting that performance on any mental test represented the contribution of two factors: a general ability ($g$) factor, and a factor(s) specific to the test. The tests developed or at least inspired by Spearman and Binet, are still with us today, largely unmodified, and appear in numerous general aptitude batteries. Furthermore, Spearman's two-factor theory has proven remarkably powerful in predicting success not only in school but also in the workplace (Hunter, 1986). Some have argued that for most training courses, general ability is the most, if not the only, important predictor of success (Ree, 1989).

The next phase of aptitude research was launched by Thurstone's (1935) invention of common factor analysis, a technique for identifying multiple sources of variance underlying a matrix of aptitude-test correlations. In a series of studies (Thurstone, 1938; Thurstone and Thurstone, 1941), Thurstone identified multiple, independent aptitude factors (e.g. Verbal ability, Spatial ability, Number ability, etc.), resulting in a new perspective on individual differences. These experimental findings had a dramatic effect on conceptions of intelligence, leading to an emphasis on classification research and a search for differential validities. As an indication of its impact, during the Second World War, the US military adopted the differential abilities perspective as the basis for its personnel assignment system. The Aviation Psychology Research Program, headed by J. P. Guilford, was established in the US Army Air Forces to assign candidates into pilot, navigator, and other aircrew jobs. According to Humphreys (1986), who worked in the research unit at that time, 'Our tests were described in Thurstonian terms and were given stable differential weights for purposes of classification' (p. 421).

Still, textbook histories of the development of conceptions of intelligence probably overplay the distinction between the Spearman/Binet versus Thurstone schools of thought. Modern factor analytic researchers (Carroll, 1989; Gustafsson, 1988; Horn, 1968; Humphreys, 1986) point out that a hierarchical model of aptitude, which includes a broad general factor along with a set of Thurstonian primary abilities, is the proper characterization of the organization of human abilities. And the book that should turn out to be the summary statement of this line of investigation, a review and re-analysis of the factor analytic literature by J. B. Carroll, embraces the hierarchical perspective.

A criticism continually haunting factor analysts is that they do not have a thorough understanding of the factors they have identified. A related issue is that factor analysis and differential psychology have developed independently of modern cognitive psychology. Thus, the fourth phase of aptitude research can be viewed as an attempt to explain the factors of differential psychology in terms of processes of cognitive psychology. In this research, methods that have been associated more commonly with experimental psychology are used to identify and interpret the psychological underpinnings of broad aptitude factors (Hunt, Frost and Lunneborg, 1973; Sternberg, 1977). We now turn to a discussion of the various methodologies that have been used in these investigations.

*The cognitive correlates method*

Probably the most common methodology for determining the nature of aptitudes is what Pellegrino and Glaser have called 'the cognitive correlates method'. The idea is simple. To determine what underlies some global aptitude construct (such as verbal ability, or general ability), administer a test of that aptitude along with a set of tests that represent more fundamental abilities. The goal is to determine which of the fundamental measures correlate most highly with the global aptitude measure. The pioneering efforts of Galton, Cattell, and Wissler, which tried to determine whether fundamental sensory abilities were related to intellectual capacity, used the logic of the cognitive correlates approach. Surprisingly, this simple, yet powerful method of 'decomposing' complex aptitude constructs was not again employed until its revival by Hunt, Frost and Lunneborg (1973), in their paper with the provocative, if not slightly overstated title, 'Individual differences in cognition: A *new* approach to intelligence' (italics ours).

Cognitive correlates approaches have proven particularly productive in the analysis of general verbal abilities, such as reading comprehension skill. For example, researchers have shown that reading can be largely understood as a combination of visual decoding ability along with retrieval speed from semantic long-term memory (Jackson and McClelland, 1979). Similarly, general verbal learning ability has been shown to be largely accounted for by two independent factors, breadth of general knowledge and speed of searching long-term memory (Kyllonen, Tirre and Christal, in press).

A key ingredient to the successful application of the cognitive correlates method is that the more fundamental measures are clearly understood, or at least are simpler than the complex aptitude construct that is the target of the analysis. Indeed, some have criticized cognitive correlates methodology on the grounds that it is of limited utility if the correlates themselves are not understood, for the investigator ends up merely explaining one unknown construct in terms of several other unknown constructs. However, given the current status of cognitive psychology, where at times it seems that practically no construct is *fully* understood, this is probably an overly harsh assessment of the benefits of the method. Progress is made by identifying correlates that are merely *simpler* than the target construct. For example, a number of investigators have attempted to explain Spearman's *g* by correlating it with simpler tasks such as pitch discrimination (Deary, Head and Egan, 1989), line length discrimination (Kranzler and Jensen, 1989; Young and Chaiken, 1990), and choice-reaction time (Jensen, 1982). The idea, hearkening back to Galton, is that *g* (as measured by complex intelligence tests) to a large part reflects speed of mental functioning, a genuinely fundamental parameter of cognition. One can argue about whether the correlates employed in these studies can be accepted as unambiguous indicators of speed of mental functioning, uncontaminated by putatively higher order cognitive and psychomotor functions. But one would be hard pressed to argue that the replicability of the speed–intelligence correlation is not at least a potential advance in our understanding of the nature of intelligence.

The correlates approach has also been used extensively to explore physiological underpinnings of intelligence. Among the newest and perhaps most promising research of this type is the work of Richard Haier and his colleagues. Using the relatively new technology of positron emission tomography (PET), they have found that adept performers of intelligence test items metabolize less glucose than do others while solving problems (expend less mental energy?) (e.g. Haier *et al*, 1988). This work, only in its infancy, is beginning to be applied to attempt to localize cognitive deficiencies to particular cortical regions of the brain. PET brain imaging technology is capable of greater accuracy of anatomic localization than older technologies such as electro-encephalogram (EEG) and evoked potential (EP) (Haier, in press).

The cognitive correlates approach is typically applied to analyze conventional aptitude constructs, such as verbal ability and general ability, but the method is potentially useful for analyzing a much broader set of constructs. Gitomer (1984) employed a cognitive correlates design to determine the knowledge or skills that underlie proficiency in electronics troubleshooting. He identified a single factor, proficiency in solving logic gate problems, as the only factor that differentiated good from poor troubleshooters. This work has been followed up with further cognitive correlates investigations. It has been shown, for example, that working memory capacity underlies proficiency in learning to solve logic gate problems (Christal, 1990); Kyllonen and Stephens, in press).

*The cognitive components approach*

An approach sometimes employed either as an alternative to, or in conjunction with, cognitive correlates investigations is what Pellegrino and Glaser have called the 'cognitive components' approach, exemplified in Sternberg's (1977) research on analogical reasoning. The approach actually is a set of methods. The investigator begins by developing a detailed information-processing analysis of performance on the target task of interest, such as a complex aptitude test. The information-processing analysis often suggests various processing stages involved in task performance. The investigator then develops techniques for obtaining estimates of an individual's success (usually speed or accuracy) at each stage of performance. Finally, the investigator correlates measures of stage performance with measures of overall task success, to determine the relative importance of the various stages to overall performance. At the end of this process the investigator hopes to be in a position to make statements such as 'the essence of reasoning ability (as indicated by performance on such-and-such a test) is (success at the) encoding (stage)'.

There are two key requirements to using the cognitive components approach successfully. First, the investigator must have (or develop) a good information-processing model of the task analyzed. Fortunately, much of cognitive psychology over the past 20 years has been devoted to developing such models, so there are good task models available in the literature. Second, the investigator must be resourceful in employing (or developing) a method for estimating stage performance or isolating processing success on a single stage of overall task performance. Sternberg (1977) relied extensively on the method of *precueing* to isolate stage performance. Precueing involves presenting a portion of the to-be-solved problem to the subject, followed by presenting the entire problem. If the entire problem involves two stages of processing, and the precued portion only the first stage, then administering some problems with the precue and some problems without allows the investigator to determine the duration of the second stage.

A more common method for isolating processing stages involves simply varying features of the target task directly, casting the aptitude test into a standard experimental design, a process sometimes referred to as constructing a 'faceted task'. Consider a componential analysis of the standard mental rotation task. Subjects try to determine whether two objects that appear in varying spatial orientations can be mentally rotated into congruence with one another (Shepard and Metzler, 1971). Researchers have studied the importance of the encoding and mental rotation stages by varying the complexity of the encoding process (e.g. simple versus complex figures), and the complexity of the rotation process (0, 30, 60, versus 90 degree angularity disparity between the two figures). Comparing a subject's reaction time to different items as a function of such task manipulations provides estimates of interesting psychological parameters, such as encoding thoroughness or speed of mental rotation (Salthouse, *et al.* in press; Pellegrino, Mumaw and Shute, 1984).

Correlates and components approaches are fruitfully employed in combination. For example, Kyllonen *et al.* (in press) created a faceted word meaning comparison task, to isolate the information-processing stages of encoding, decision, long-term memory access, long-term memory search, and motor response. Durations of these stages for individual subjects were estimated through standard componential modeling techniques. Stage duration estimates then were correlated with the criterion task, a test of associated learning. Thus a component approach was used to estimate processing stage durations for individual subjects, but these estimates then served as correlates in an attempt to determine the 'abilities' underlying associative learning proficiency.

*The cognitive training method*

If training on a hypothesized component of an aptitude test increases performance on the aptitude test, there is evidence for the 'reality' of the hypothesized component. This is the logic behind what Sternberg (1984) called the 'cognitive training' method. For example, Kyllonen *et al.* (in press) trained one group of subjects on an elaboration strategy, resulting in about a 20% increase in performance over a no-training control group. This suggests that knowledge of effective mnemonic strategies is an important component of associative learning. Presumably, some subjects come to the task with such knowledge already available, which effectively gives them more of the aptitude that is then tested for.

The training method can serve nicely as a component-validation follow-up to an initial component-identification study. Perhaps the nicest example of this approach in the literature was a series of studies by Fredericksen and colleagues (Frederiksen, Warren and Rosebery, 1985a, 1985b). The initial component-identification phase used componential analysis and correlates methods to identify a set of quite specific information-processing components presumed to underlie reading ability (Frederiksen, 1982). Examples of components were grapheme encoding, parsing sentence constituents, retrieving and integrating word meanings. In the follow-up component-validation phase, Frederiksen *et al.* extensively trained a group of young readers on these specific components, and found a resulting increase in their reading ability.

What is the researcher to conclude if no change on the target aptitude task occurs after even extensive training on a hypothesized component? There are reasons to be cautious about interpreting such a finding as evidence against the reality of the component. First, there may be problems in transfer, or metacognition, that prevent the subject from being able to use this improved skill in the context of the target performance. For example, learners can receive extensive training on problem-solving methods and still not be able to effectively use such knowledge to increase their problem-solving *abilities* (Hayes, 1985). Second, it is important to consider the difference between components-as-determinants and components-as-indicators models. These vary in the causal flow between components and aptitudes. Components-as-determinants models assume that changes in the components cause changes in the aptitude. Components-as-indicators models assume that changes in the aptitude cause changes in the components. Changes in the components will not affect the aptitude in this kind of model. Correlations between components and aptitude tasks, as found for example in a cognitive correlates study, could reflect either an indicator- or determinant-type relationship between the constructs.

### Cognitive task analysis

A precursor to testing hypotheses about components of a complex aptitude construct is generating a list of possible components in the first place. Often, such lists originate from rational analyses of what a person has to know or has to do while solving an aptitude-test problem, or by borrowing from the work of someone who has done such an analysis. In addition, researchers have subjects talk through their problem-solving attempts, and have them retrospectively report on what they did (Ericsson and Simon, 1980). Recording the eye movements of a subject engaged in problem solving has also been a useful stimulus for generating hypotheses about the processes of problem solving (Carpenter and Just, 1988). Such analyses are sometimes accompanied by task manipulations in an attempt to verify whether a reported strategy is actually used. For example, Chase and Ericsson (1982) hypothesized that a subject used a sophisticated encoding strategy on a digit span test, based on the subject's retrospective reports. They then change the digits on the task to ones that would not be amenable to such a strategy, and found a concomitant decline in performance, corroborating the subject's report. The ultimate success of correlates, components, and training methods obviously depends on the quality of hypotheses generated from these kinds of cognitive task analyses. (The same general type of analysis is used as a foundation for developing part-task training methods—see Lintern in Chapter 6 of this volume.)

Although most jobs are multifaceted, the current state of the science and practice of psychology has yielded few, if any, acceptable universal theories about performance and learning. For our present discussion, it is useful to separately consider two broad classes of tasks, namely, those that importantly depend on motor behavior for performance, typically in the form of proceduralized knowledge (such as operation of various types of equipment), and those that are less dependent on motor behavior and more dependent on depth of declarative knowledge and breadth of cognitive skills. First, we will discuss the nature of abilities and skills in the perceptual–motor domain, and then we will discuss abilities and skills in the non-motor domain.

# ACQUISITION OF PERCEPTUAL–MOTOR SKILLS

### Fundamentals of skill acquisition

The best place to start a discussion of perceptual–motor skills is with a delineation of the domain of skill under consideration. An excellent definition has been offered by Adams (1987), and will be adopted here:

(1) Skill is a wide behavioral domain.
(2) Skill is learned.
(3) Goal attainment is importantly dependent upon motor behavior. (p. 42)

Within this class of tasks are numerous job skills, including those that are associated with the practice of clinical medicine or dentistry, computer operator, clerk-typist, heavy machinery operator, truck driver, and so on. In each of these examples, and in innumerable others that the reader could choose to consider, the speed and accuracy, and sometimes even the success or failure, of performance is limited by the incumbent's skills at job components that (a) must be learned, and (b) can only be effected via a substantial involvement of motor behaviors. Note, though, the various examples given here involve the motor system at quite different levels of precision. For the dentist or the surgeon, the motor system is involved at the finest degree of movement control (precision of the order of tenths of millilmeters) while for the truck driver or heavy equipment operator, the motor behavior is coarser (precision is of the order of centimeters or larger).

The starting point for a consideration of ability–performance relations regarding perceptual–motor skills is not with individual differences, but rather with general theories of learning. Fortunately, at the level of analysis needed for this discussion, most current theories of perceptual–motor learning are in agreement about the nature of the learning process. Although learning is typically thought of as a continuous process, without breaks or hierarchical plateaus (e.g. see Newell and Rosenbloom, 1981), theorists have often settled on a description of learning that is broken into phases or stages of skill acquisition. More details can be found in the respective descriptions of the theories, but we will consider the three major phases of skill acquisition in the same way as they are described by Fitts and Posner (1967), Anderson (1982, 1985), and Shiffrin and Schneider (1977). (See also the review by Annett in Chapter 2 of this volume for additional details.)

*Phase 1: Declarative knowledge*

The first phase of skill acquisition starts with the learner's initial confrontation with the task. During this phase, the learner begins to understand the basic task requirements, the rules for task engagement. In other words, the learner formulates a general idea of what is required of him or her. The term 'declarative knowledge' refers to 'knowledge about facts and things' (Anderson, 1985, p. 199). For a word processing operator, information that would have to be encoded as declarative knowledge would presumably include rules of starting the program, organization of commands (e.g. menu structure), effects of command implementation on the text (e.g. understanding the difference between 'single occurrence' and 'global' search and replace commands), location of command keys, and the use of macro (or multiple) commands. The essence of declarative knowledge is that it is represented in a form that generally allows conscious-mediated retrieval. Thus, a test of knowledge at this stage of skill acquisition could take the form of a written examination of facts and procedures. Typically, as the research of Schneider and his colleagues (e.g. for a review, see Fisk, Ackerman and Schneider, 1987) has pointed out, performance at this phase of skill acquisition is slow, attentionally effortful, and error prone.

*Phase 2: Knowledge compilation*

Once the learner has developed the necessary declarative knowledge base that is required to move beyond a trial-and-error task engagement, the learner can proceed to the next phase of skill acquisition. This phase has been termed the 'associative' stage of skill acquisition by Fitts and Posner (1967) because the key element of performance improvements that takes place during this phase of skill acquisition comes about through increasing the strength and efficiency of associations between stimulus conditions and appropriate response patterns. In this sense the 'associations' are formed in the first phase of skill acquisition, but are strengthened in the second phase of skill acquisition. Anderson has coined the term 'knowledge compilation' from a computer programming analogy. That is, performance at the first phase of skill acquisition can be thought of as writing a computer program interactively. As each line of code is written, the system indicates whether the code is syntactically correct or incorrect. However, at the 'compilation' phase, the program has been completed and is compiled to be run more quickly and efficiently. Regardless of the analogy adopted, this phase of skill acquisition is typically marked by substantial increases in the speed of task accomplishment, with a concomitant increase in the accuracy of performance. While conscious mediation often takes place during the early part of this phase, with additional practice, the conscious mediation often becomes an epiphenomenon—it no longer plays a role in determining the speed and accuracy of performance.

*Phase 3: Procedural knowledge*

When the learner has reached a level of skill such that performance is characterized as requiring minimal attentional effort, but at the same time is fast and accurate, the knowledge required to perform the task has become 'automatized' (Shiffrin and Schneider, 1977). Anderson chose the term 'proceduralized knowledge' to refer to 'knowledge about how to perform various cognitive activities' (Anderson, 1985, p. 199). In contrast to declarative knowledge, proceduralized knowledge does not require conscious mediation. In fact, if the task is sufficiently proceduralized, so that declarative knowledge is no longer involved in task accomplishment, declarative knowledge of 'how' the task is performed can be forgotten, with no decrement to task performance. Numerous common examples of such situations can be found, from the person who can effortlessly dial a familiar phone number sequence (but has difficulty writing down the actual number), to a person who operates a complex piece of industrial machinery (but has incredible difficulty in reporting what it is that he or she does to a knowledge engineer). Although there is little empirical evidence to support or contradict the adage, there is a possible theoretical justification behind the idea that 'those who can, do; those who cannot, teach'. That is, if skills have *not* been developed to the level of proceduralized knowledge (as for experts), the learner is likely to have much easier access to the declarative knowledge so critical to training during early stages of skill acquisition.

### Structure of cognitive/intellectual abilities

In order to discuss individual differences in skill acquisition, and particularly the role of abilities in predicting performance at the three phases of skill acquisition, it is necessary to explicate a structure of cognitive/intellectual abilities. Although the literature is scattered with numerous competing theories of the structure of human intellectual abilities (e.g. Guilford, 1967; Horn and Cattell, 1966; Vernon, 1961), there is a familial similarity among most current perspectives that allows a similar degree of commonality found in theories of skill learning. These theories have been termed 'hierarchical'.

Explicit in most of these theories is a general intellectual ability factor (or *g*). The theories agree, further, that other ability factors are important components of intelligence. The *g* ability factor represents the highest node in a hierarchy of ability factors. The influence of such a factor has been estimated by Vernon as reflecting anywhere from roughly 20–40% of the variance in a population of 'all human abilities'. Typically, theories diverge when it comes to identification of factors that constitute the nodes below *g*. However, all theories appear to be in agreement about the nature of the hierarchy. That is, the general factor represents the broadest ability, and factors at the next level represent broad, or major group factors (e.g. Verbal: Educational, Practical: Mechanical, as in Vernon's theory). Each of the abilities at this broad group factor node may be fragmented to reveal their constituent abilities. For example, at the next node, the Verbal ability factor might fragment into Vocabulary, Reading Comprehension, Associational Fluency, and so forth. These lower ability nodes may, in turn, be further subdivided to allow representation of the different test formats for assessing the specific abilities, and so on.

A particularly useful heuristic approach to describing the structure of abilities that is also consistent with the hierarchical approach is one developed by Marshalek, Lohman and Snow (1983; see also Snow, Kyllonen and Marshalek, 1984) called the radex. The graphic representation of the structure of abilities is with a circle, as shown in Figure 7.1.

Two salient characteristics of this structure should be noted. First, the proximity of a test or measure to the center of the circle is determined by the 'complexity' of the material being tested. As complexity of material increases,

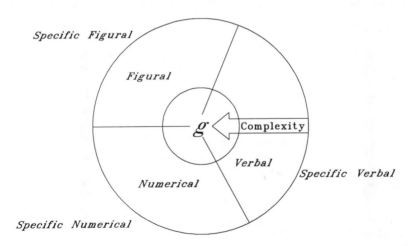

**Figure 7.1.** A radex-based model of cognitive abilities. The construct of complexity/specificity is represented as the proximity to the center of the circle. Content abilities are represented as different segments of the circle. From Marshalek, Lohman and Snow, 1983. 'The complexity continuum in the radex and hierarchical models of intelligence,' *Intelligence*, **7**, 107–127. Copyright, Ablex Publishing Corporation. Reproduced by permission.

the measure shares more in common with *g* or with tests of general intellectual abilities (e.g. reasoning). As the complexity of test material decreases, the measure has less in common with *g*, and indeed, more in common with narrower abilities and skills. The second salient characteristic of this model is that 'content' abilities represent different segments, or slices of the circle. This particular aspect of the structure illustrates the nature of so-called 'group' factors of spatial, verbal, numerical (and, perhaps, mechanical) abilities. That is, tests that share the same or similar contents, also have an increased degree of common variance. Thus, the location of a particular test in this structure is a function of the test's complexity of required information processing *and* the type of content upon which the test is constructed.

While the Marshalek *et al.* (1983) model is useful for capturing the relations among a great many ability tests, a shortcoming of the structure is that it does not take the speed of processing into account. Ackerman (1988) has proposed a modification of this structure that adds speed of processing as a third dimension, orthogonal to the dimensions described by content and complexity. This model is illustrated in Figure 7.2.

As shown in the Ackerman model, adding the speed dimension has the advantage of delineating unspeeded types of information processing (such as are required in power tests), from speeded information processing that is required in prototypical perceptual speed and psychomotor ability tests. While the Marshalek *et al.* model would relegate both highly speeded tests and tests that involve specific content (e.g. narrow tests of spatial or verbal

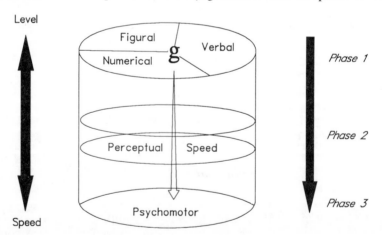

**Figure 7.2.** A modified radex-based model of cognitive abilities. Complexity is represented as in the Marshalak *et al.* model. However, the dimension of level/speed is added to represent perceptual speed and psychomotor abilities. From Ackerman, 1988, 'Determinants of individual differences during skill acquisition: Cognitive abilities and information processing,' *Journal of Experimental Psychology: General*, **117**, 288–318. Copyright, American Psychological Association. Reprinted by permission.

knowledge) to the periphery of the circle, there is now an explicit separation of these two classes of ability measures. As will be discussed below, this particular structure is quite useful in linking ability constructs with phases of perceptual–motor skill acquisition. However, it is also important to keep in mind that the structure of abilities discussed here is also, by and large, consistent with the Marshalek theory, and thus is consistent with the broad hierarchical theories of intelligence offered by numerous ability theorists.

## The dynamic relations between abilities and skills

Using the basic outline of skill acquisition briefly reviewed above, in conjunction with the ability structure offered here, it is possible to build a representation of the determinants of individual differences in performance during skill acquisition. The structure adopted here is based on the theory proposed by Ackerman (1988) that maps classes of cognitive/intellectual abilities to the phases of skill acquisition. The theory states that a direct mapping of ability classes and phases of skill acquisition can be established. From this mapping it then becomes possible to predict the association between individual differences in abilities and individual differences in task performance during skill acquisition. The principles are as follow:

### Phase 1

Given the fact that the first phase of skill acquisition has substantial demands on the cognitive system (mostly in the domain of attention, memory, and reasoning; but also in the area of broad content knowledge), this phase of skill acquisition closely represents the types of information processing that are sampled in tests of high complexity and minimal speed demands. Thus, general and broad content abilities (namely, spatial, verbal and numerical) illustrated at the top of the ability cylinder shown in Figure 7.2 are implicated in predicting individual differences at the declarative knowledge phase of skill acquisition.

### Phase 2

Once the learner has developed appropriate strategies for successful task accomplishment, and moves to the knowledge compilation (or associative) phase of skill acquisition, the demands on the general and broad content abilities are reduced in a fashion analogous to the reduction in demands on the attentional and declarative knowledge systems. Superior performance at this phase of practice is indicated when learners can efficiently develop streamlined productions for task accomplishment, those that improve speed and accuracy. Similarly, as one moves forward on the speed dimension of the proposed ability structure, from general and broad content abilities to perceptual speed abilities, marker measures require fewer demands on attention and memory and greater demands on the refinement of relatively simple productions (as in a digit-symbol test, or a clerical checking test—both such tests are prototypical exemplars of Perceptual Speed ability). In fact, perceptual speed ability can be thought of as 'the capacity to automatize, by means of practice' (Werdelin and Stjernberg, 1969, p. 192). Thus, individual differences in performance at the second phase of skill acquisition will be well-predicted by individual differences in the perceptual speed ability.

*Phase 3*

When the final phase of skill acquisition, procedural knowledge, is reached, the learner can often effectively meet the task demands with little or no attentional effort (e.g. see Schneider and Fisk, 1982). Performance limitations at this phase, especially when the task is critically dependent on motor operations, are primarily determined by differences in the speed of encoding and responding, with very little involvement of declarative knowledge. The phenomenological essence of such levels of skill acquisition is that task performance is 'automatic'. The highly deterministic nature of the task has a number of striking similarities to ability measures at the extreme level of speededness, that is, the family of psychomotor tests (such as simple reaction time, or tapping speed). In both task and test scenarios, the individual knows exactly what response (or response sequence) needs to be made once the stimulus is detected. As such, the theory specifies that individual differences in psychomotor abilities will well-predict individual differences in performance at this last phase of skill acquisition.

The overall implication of the theory is that the determinants of individual differences in performance are *dynamic*, that is, different classes of abilities are most highly correlated with performance at each phase of skill acquisition. Across a sequence of task practice, leading to proceduralized knowledge, the anticipated pattern of ability–performance correlations is illustrated in Figure 7.3. As indicated in the figure, individual differences in performance at Phase 1 are best predicted by general and broad content abilities; at Phase 2, the best predictions come from measures of perceptual speed ability; and at Phase 3, the most salient correlations are found for psychomotor abilities. From an applied viewpoint, the question of 'what is the appropriate ability test for selection of job applicants' does not have a single answer. Rather, the investigator must assess which phase or phases of skill acquisition are to be predicted (e.g. training success versus success after substantial tenure-on-the-job). From this information, an appropriate battery might be constructed that is optimal for the selection application at hand.

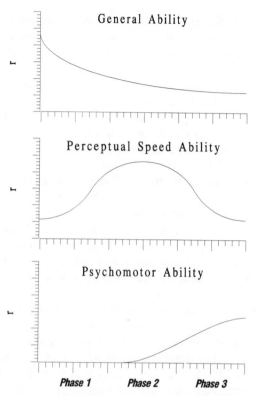

**Figure 7.3.** Hypothetical ability/skill relations over the course of practice on a perceptual–motor task. From Ackerman (1988), 'Determinants of individual differences during skill acquisition: Cognitive abilities and information processing,' *Journal of Experimental Psychology: General,* **117**, 288–318, Copyright, American Psychological Association. Reprinted by permission.

## A brief review of empirical studies

Research concerned with individual differences in skill acquisition, and especially with the relations between ability-performance has a lengthy, if not especially extensive, history (for reviews, see Ackerman, 1987; Adams, 1987). Early correlational work was performed by Anastasi (1934), but the first series of systematic investigations of learning and intellectual abilities was conducted by Woodrow (see Woodrow, 1946, for a review). Woodrow's main conclusion was that there was little shared variance between measures of intellectual abilities and measures of individual differences in learning. However, Woodrow's analysis of the issues was predicated mostly on the use of gain scores, which have been more recently criticized on both conceptual and psychometric bases (see Cronbach and Snow, 1977, for an extended discussion).

A later series of studies using direct performance measures, as opposed to gain scores, was reported by Fleishman and his colleagues (see Fleishman, 1972, for a review). Although Fleishman's data seemed to indicate a diminishing association between broad content abilities and task performance during skill acquisition, other conclusions about the nature of ability–performance relations were clouded by the use of particular factor analytic methods that have also been criticized on psychometric grounds (e.g. see Bechtoldt, 1962; Humphreys, 1960; Adams, 1987; Ackerman, 1987). Reanalyses of some of the extant literature (namely, three of the Fleishman *et al.* studies) have been conducted towards evaluating the Ackerman theory. When these data were analyzed with current psychometric techniques, the data were found to be generally supportive of the theory proposed by Ackerman (1988).

The initial empirical work behind the theory was based on a series of eight experiments (Ackerman, 1988) that examined the role of task factors of consistency and complexity/novelty in moderating ability–performance relations during skill acquisition. The following conclusions were supported from the basic exposition of the theory, and from the empirical results:

1. The novelty and complexity of a task both determine the initial degree of association between general/broad content abilities and individual differences in task performance. (The complexity finding has been previously demonstrated by other researchers, most notably by Kyllonen, 1985.) Tasks which have little in the way of complexity, or those that allow positive transfer of training from other tasks, may bypass the first phase of skill acquisition, and thus be more highly associated with perceptual speed abilities than general/broad content abilities.
2. The consistency of task components, a requirement for transition from declarative to procedural knowledge, is also a requirement for the transition of general/broad content ability determinants of individual differences in performance to perceptual speed and psychomotor abilities. When consistent information-processing components are not the dominant elements of the task, performance will continue to have substantial associations with these broad abilities, regardless of the amount of task practice.
3. For novel, moderately complex, but consistent tasks that importantly depend on motor behavior, ability–performance relations are well described by the theory. That is, initial performance is best predicted by general and broad content abilities, intermediate levels of skilled performance are best predicted by perceptual speed abilities, and late, asymptotic performance levels are best predicted by psychomotor abilities.

A subsequent investigation (Ackerman, 1990) has demonstrated that some prototypical perceptual speed and psychomotor ability tests are best thought of as microcosms of skill acquisition, in agreement with the theory described above. That is, the critical determinants of individual differences in performance on perceptual speed tests in their canonical instantiation are associated with rapid and efficient development of proceduralized knowledge. However, if examinees are given substantial *practice* on the perceptual speed tests themselves, performance on such tests after practice has more in common with psychomotor abilities than with perceptual speed. A similar effect is found with some predominantly psychomotor tests. That is, post-practice performance on psychomotor tests has less in common with perceptual speed abilities and is increasingly determined by individual differences in asymptotic psychomotor abilities. It was further found that there is a great deal of underlying heterogeneity to the nature of validity changes associated with practice on prototypical perceptual speed ability tests. Tests that were contingent on proceduralization of rules that were somewhat novel, and mostly consistent, showed the predicted shift in predictive validities with practice (i.e. post-practice test performance is more highly associated with post-practice performance on the criterion task). Tests that lacked consistency of information processing components (e.g. number checking), or those that had high initial memory demands (e.g. digit-symbol substitution), showed quite different patterns of initial performance and post-practice validities for a criterion task.

The results from this preliminary investigation show that there is still much work to be done in delineating the predictor space, especially when the additional dimension of test practice (familiarity) is included. Although single administrations of perceptual speed ability tests often show sufficient communality to 'hang together' in factor solutions, the dynamic properties of predictive validity of such tests show too much diversity to provide a coherent taxonomic identification of such tests. Similarly, it has become clear that a distinction between perceptual speed ability and psychomotor abilities can only be drawn in an arbitrary fashion. The dimension of speededness, as with the dimension of complexity, is continuous and multifaceted.

This research has been predominantly laboratory-based, but there appear to be at least two major applications to be considered. The first application is a method for assessing the skill learning referents of predictor measures. That is, by examining the practice-based validity changes of predictor tests, the current predictor space can be better mapped out, and modified, when the result of such an analysis is an indication of a more cost-effective stage of skills to be predicted (e.g. training success versus on-the-job performance). The second application concerns the increased predictive power that might be obtained by using predictor measures that are administered in a repeated fashion. In this way, both intermediate levels of skilled performance might be well predicted (from initial performance on the predictor measures), and late, asymptotic performance levels on the criteriton might be well predicted (from later, post-practice performance on the predictor measures).

One last point is to be made about the predictability of skilled performance on perceptual–motor tasks. Fleishman and his colleagues have claimed that as practice proceeds on a perceptual–motor task, 'the predictability of advanced performance levels from external measures may become increasingly difficult to accomplish' (Fleishman, 1962, p. 147). This conclusion has become increasingly controversial in recent years, and the subject of more than a few discussions and data reanalyses (e.g. see Ackerman, 1987; Adams, 1987). However, the empirical results discussed above have pointedly demonstrated that it is, indeed, possible to validly predict performance at *all* three stages of skill acquisition, from measures that are administered prior to engagement of the criterion task. Discovering the *particular* predictors for skilled criterion task performance is of paramount importance to applying ability theory to selection of trainees for optimizing post-training on-the-job performance.

## ACQUISITION OF KNOWLEDGE AND COGNITIVE SKILLS

Ideally, a model of individual differences in the acquisition of knowledge and cognitive skills would be based on a widely, if not universally, agreed upon theory of cognition. Unfortunately, as with the perceptual–motor domain, no such theory exists. Researchers who have scanned the contents of and citations in cognitive textbooks have argued that there is not even a consensus on what the topics of such a theory should be, let alone an agreement on the details. But, specified at a general enough level, there is a consensus by many of at least the broad outlines of cognition. Most researchers would not object strenuously to the general model of cognition depicted in Figure 7.4, for example, which is largely inspired by Anderson's ACT* theory and similar production-system models of the architecture of human cognition. And it is this kind of model that has served as the basis for Kyllonen and Christal's 'four-source' model of individual differences in cognition.

Figure 7.4 depicts the flow of information through the human processing system. Information is presented to a learner (or performer), perhaps in the form of a problem to be solved. That information is deposited in a limited-capacity working memory capable of holding only a few facts or procedures at a time. The knowledge a learner has that is related to that information is then retrieved from either of two long-term memories: a declarative memory that contains factual knowledge, and a procedural (skills) memory that contains procedural and strategic-type knowledge. After a series of knowledge-retrieval acts, the answer to the problem occurs to the learner, who then executes a motor response (such as pressing a button on the computer, or filling in an answer sheet), and the problem-solving episode is complete.

Given this general model, in what ways might individuals differ? Kyllonen and Christal (1989) suggest four possible 'sources' of individual differences:

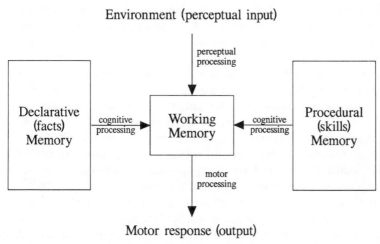

Figure 7.4. General information processing model. Flow of information through human memory systems [working (short-term), procedural/skill (long-term), and de-clarative (long-term)] is depicted by arrows.

(1) breadth of declarative knowledge; (2) breadth of procedural skills; (3) capacity of the working memory; and (4) speed of processing (encoding infor-mation into working memory, retrieving knowledge from the long-term memories, and executing a motor response). This, of course, is an over-simplification, because individuals differ in infinite ways. But it does represent a first cut at defining the broad categories into which individual differences dimensions might be sorted. We now consider evidence for the importance of these sources as determinants of learning.

## Knowledge

Individuals certainly differ with respect to what they already know, and it is just as certain that such differences are generally prognostic of future success in instructional and training situations. A student with five years of program-ming experience is a better bet to succeed in a programming course than the student with no programming background. This statement seems quite ob-vious on the surface, and hardly needs research support. However, there are more subtle questions on the role of declarative (factual) knowledge in learn-ing that warrant study. For example, what is the role of general knowledge in learning a particular topic? More specifically, can the person who comes to a particular learning task with a broad storehouse of factual knowledge use that knowledge to assist him or her in learning the particulars being addressed, even if the particulars are novel?

The answer appears to be yes. Studies of paired-associates learning

(Kyllonen and Tirre, 1988; Kyllonen *et al.*, in press) have shown that breadth of declarative knowledge, as indicated by performance on vocabulary tests and general knowledge surveys, predicts the speed with which a person will learn new facts or associations. Probably, the reason for this is that learning novel concepts is essentially a matter of integrating those concepts into an existing knowledge base. It has long been known that novel concepts that do not fit into existing knowledge schemata are quickly forgotten (Bartlett, 1932). Thus, low-knowledge students have more difficulty than high-knowledge students integrating a new concept by virtue of their lack of knowledge (see also the discussion of aptitude–treatment interactions below).

A second question is this. How much does domain-relevant knowledge help over the long run? If a trainee comes to a learning task already knowing lots of the particulars, how much of an edge does that give him or her when it comes to learning how to put those particulars into action, for example, to acquire a complex cognitive skill? Consider a programming course. Will the trainee who already knows what is meant by 'integer', 'string', 'real', and so on, learn how to program faster than the trainee who has to be taught those things? To answer this question it is useful to recall the declarative–procedural distinction. Studies of cognitive skill acquisition suggest that declarative knowledge, either general or domain specific, affects declarative learning, but has no additional affect on procedural learning (Kyllonen and Stephens, in press; Shute and Kyllonen, 1990). That is, having declarative knowledge gives the learner an initial edge, but that advantage does not necessarily maintain over the duration of the training experience.

### Skills

Individuals differ in what they know about *how* to solve problems. That is, they differ in their procedural knowledge. This is different from knowing particular facts in the domain (declarative knowledge). Good learners have internalized useful and general problem-solving heuristics, such as using analogies to the current problem, working backwards from the solution to the givens, drawing the problem to understand it, searching for counter examples, and so on. In fact, college courses teaching these kinds of skills have been developed to make people better problem solvers (Hayes, 1981; Wickelgren, 1974; Schoenfeld, 1980). The central question concerning individual differences may be stated as follows: How important is this kind of procedural knowledge, or these kinds of skills, to learning?

Before addressing this question, it is necessary to develop a way for measuring procedural knowledge. Unfortunately, it is not entirely obvious how to do so. One cannot simply ask a learner whether he or she knows how to work backwards from the solution to the givens. Procedural knowledge is by its nature *tacit*, that is, not necessarily amenable to articulation. A person can report that he or she knows a particular problem-solving heuristic, yet not be able to apply that heuristic in actual problem solving. Alternatively, a person can quite expertly apply heuristics in problem solving without being apparently aware that he or she is doing so.

Two approaches have been used to get around this problem in trying to assess the role of procedural knowledge in learning. One is, rather than developing a test of procedural knowledge, use the cognitive training approach (discussed earlier): Teach procedural knowledge then observe its effect on subsequent learning. This approach has been applied in showing the importance of strategic knowledge in associative learning (Kyllonen *et al.*, in press). A second approach is to develop tests that require general procedural knowledge, even if such knowledge cannot be measured directly. For example, Kyllonen and Stephens (in press) developed tests that required subjects to learn simple novel rules to solve problems. The idea was that learners with a rich repertoire of procedural skill would be at a distinct advantage in learning the novel rules, which would then show up as high scores on the tests. There was some evidence that the tests did tap procedural skill in that the novel rules tests were factorially distinct from other measures of cognitive ability. However, Kyllonen and Stephens did not find that the procedural knowledge factor uniquely predicted learning. A problem uncovered in that study is that procedural knowlege is highly related to, and consequently hard to differentiate from, working memory capacity. This point is discussed in detail in the following section.

## Processing capacity

Individuals differ in how much information they can attend to at one time, that is, in the capacity of their working memory. Working memory is the basic bottleneck of cognition, and for some people the neck is wider than it is for others. There is considerable evidence that limitations in working memory capacity are responsible for limitations in how much and how quickly we can learn (Anderson and Jeffries, 1985; Baddeley, 1986). Correspondingly, there is considerable evidence that individual variation in working memory capacity to a large extent determines individual differences in learning. This relationship has been demonstrated on numerous and quite diverse learning tasks, including paired-associates (Tirre, 1990), logic-gates (Christal, 1990; Kyllonen and Stephens, in press), if–then rules (Woltz, 1988), and programming skill (Shute and Kyllonen, 1990), to name a few.

Working memory capacity is apparently most important during the initial stages of learning, corresponding to that point where the learner feels overwhelmed and overloaded. An informal observation we have made is that subjects (ourselves included) do not like taking working memory capacity tests; they consider them 'hard work'. By report (and again by our own experiences), it is much easier and more enjoyable to take a knowledge test. Part of the motivation for learning, and much of the satisfaction derived therefrom, is moving cognitively from the point where the task is hard work to the point where the task feels like a knowledge test. There is a relationship between knowledge and working memory capacity such that having specific knowledge can replace having to exercise working memory. Thus, it is important in measuring working memory capacity to make the task essentially non-learnable, which can be accomplished by varied-mapping techniques (see Shiffrin and Schneider, 1977, for a discussion of such techniques). This is a key way in which working memory capacity tests differ from procedural knowledge tests, where changes in performance with practice are expected.

## Processing speed

Individuals differ in the speed with which they process information. Considering the model depicted in Figure 7.4, there are in fact a variety of processing speeds. For instance, there is: (a) encoding speed, the speed with which information makes its way from an initial percept to a representation in working memory; (b) retrieval speed, the speed with which information from one of the long-term memories is deposited in working memory; and (c) response speed, the speed of executing a motor response. Theoretically, these are separable components of processing speed, but they have proven to be fairly highly correlated in empirical work to date (e.g. Kyllonen, 1985), suggesting that in many applications it may be useful to speak of general information processing speed.

Processing speed has proven to be correlated with learning, and not surprisingly, primarily under conditions when study time is quite limited (Kyllonen et al., in press). With liberal study time, other variables, such as working memory capacity, tend to become more relevant to learning success. Still, there are many contexts in which study time is limited, and thus processing speed cannot be dismissed as an unimportant variable. It also appears to be the case that general processing speed becomes the key limitation of performance during the later stages of learning, after domain concepts and rules are memorized, and the learner is moving toward the point of being able to execute task steps automatically (Ackerman, 1988; Woltz, 1988).

## Evaluation of four-source framework

The four-sources framework represents a starting point for the development of a new kind of aptitude battery (Kyllonen, 1990). We do not expect such efforts to lead to an overhaul of existing conceptions of aptitude. Indeed, there is considerable overlap between conventional aptitude batteries (e.g. the *Kit of Factor-Referenced Cognitive Tests*, Ekstrom et al., 1976) and batteries based on the four-sources framework (Kyllonen, 1990). The important point, though, is that the four-sources framework does correspond better with current conceptions of cognition, and thus is likely to evolve with developments in cognitive theory. Presumably, one of the advantages of such an intertwining is that it will lead to the identification of aptitudes not measured in conventional aptitude batteries.

A major challenge to differential psychology was issued by Schmidt and Hunter (1977) who argued for the 'validity generalization' hypothesis, which stipulates that (a) all tests are equally valid, and (b) criteria are interchangeable. This runs in contrast with the generally accepted position that (a) different aptitude tests will differentially predict success, and (b) criterion settings differ in which aptitude test predictors are most valid. Surprisingly, it has proven remarkably difficult to garner data inconsistent with Schmidt and Hunter's strong thesis. A possible explanation for the lack of differential validity is that the space of aptitudes sampled by conventional batteries is limited. Possibly, efforts inspired by information processing psychology, such as those discussed here, will result in the identification of truly unique aptitudes.

Another possibility is that the space of criterion performances thus far tapped has been limited. Schmidt and Hunter are correct because researchers re-employ the same criteria in study after study. For example, differential validity studies in the military services almost invariably use technical school grade point average as criteria. But perhaps it is necessary to consider alternative indications of learning or training success. This is a topic to which we now turn.

# LEARNER CHARACTERISTICS IN THE CONTEXT OF A 'TAXONOMY OF LEARNING SKILLS'

Individuals differ in their ability to learn new concepts and acquire new skills. An important psychological question is whether learning ability is unidimensional or multidimensional. That is, are there simply fast learners and slow learners, or are there those who quickly learn some kinds of tasks but have difficulty with others? If so, what are the dimensions of learning ability? How can learning tasks be classified? Answers to these questions have implications for the development of aptitude batteries and personnel selection systems.

With general cognitive abilities, we found it useful to borrow from cognitive theory in an attempt to develop a tentative taxonomy of cognitive abilities. Similarly, with learning abilities it may be useful to consider cognitive models of the acquisition of knowledge and skill. Earlier we reviewed a three-phase model of the develoment of cognitive skill that has received widespread support in the cognitive and psychometric literature.

Kyllonen and Shute (1989) elaborated this three-phase model to a taxonomy of learning skills (cf. Gagné, 1965). The two major dimensions of the taxonomy are *knowledge type* and *instructional environment*. The idea is that any learning act can be characterized in terms of the environment in which it occurs and the nature of the knowledge that results from the learning experience. These learning acts could potentially represent multiple dimensions of learning ability.

The simplest knowledge type is the *proposition*, such as 'programs have statements', and 'the first statement is BEGIN, and 'BEGIN is followed by functions', and so on. A set of related propositions such as these constitutes a *schema*. Another knowledge type is the if–then *rule*, such as 'IF the goal is to write a program, THEN write BEGIN and code the rest of the program'. Knowing a large set of related rules constitutes *skill*, for example, skill in being able to write programs that add a column of numbers. (There is conceptual overlap between the Kyllonen and Shute notion of skill and that of Adams (1987).) A characteristic of rules and skills is that they vary in generality, that is, in their domain of applicability. Presumably, practice on a rule generalizes to the point where the learner can be said to possess a *general rule*, and similarly with *general skill*. Further, when such a skill is well practiced it becomes an *automatic skill*. Finally, having large amounts of related, structured knowledge, that is, possessing domain-relevant schemata and skills, is synonymous with possessing a *mental model* of some domain, such as programming. Propositions, schemata, rules, skills, general rules, general skills, automatic skills, and mental models are the eight knowledge types in Kyllonen and Shute's learning taxonomy.

The conditions under which one acquires knowledge of these types (learns a rule, for example) might affect the learning. For example, being told a rule by a teacher might well be a different psychological experience from learning the rule by observing programs written by others. Each may differ from the experience of practicing the rule over and over. Thus, the second key dimension in Kyllonen and Shute's taxonomy is the instructional environment, that is, the conditions under which a person learns. The taxonomy specifies six categories of instructional environments, which vary according to the degree of control of the instruction from teacher to student:

1. *Rote*: Learning is memorizing what a teacher says;
2. *Didactic*: Learning is a matter of integrating or assimilating a concept taught by a teacher into one's existing knowledge base;
3. *Practice*: Learning occurs as a result of using the knowledge repeatedly;
4. *Analogies*: Learning results from inducing a rule or concept by analogy to already known rules or concepts;
5. *Example*: Learning results from inducing a rule or concept by observing examples of that rule or concept provided by a teacher; and
6. *Discovery*: Learning results from inducing a rule or concept by noting the

effects of those rules or concepts based on one's own initiative, for example in a computer 'microworld'.

Presumably, any of the eight knowledge types could be taught in any of the six environments, which yields 48 different categories of learning experiences. The hypothesis, not yet evaluated in any single study, is that there thus could be as many as 48 different learning abilities. Some of these categories might not be psychologically plausible—learning a mental model in a rote environment does not seem likely, for example. Still, this taxonomy provides a starting point for thinking about the potential multidimensional nature of learning.

The empirical database relevant to evaluating this taxonomy as a framework for individual differences in learning ability is thus far quite modest. There does seem to be considerable support for the separation of declarative (proposition and schema) from procedural (rule and skill) knowledge acquisition processes. Studies of skill acquisition in learning to solve logic gate problems (Kyllonen and Stephens, in press) and computer programming (Shute and Kyllonen, 1990) have demonstrated a discontinuity between declarative and procedural learning. In these studies, declarative learning proficiency is related to, but far from perfectly predictive of, procedural learning proficiency, and the two learning abilities are predicted by different underlying cognitive abilities. For example, knowledge level predicts declarative but not procedural learning; and working memory capacity seems to be more predictive of procedural learning than of declarative learning (Kyllonen and Woltz, 1989). However, it is too early to tell whether further distinctions among the various knowledge types suggested by the taxonomy will turn out to be warranted by the data.

There also is some support for the differentiation of instructional environments. High structure environments (i.e. teacher controlled, such as rote and assimilation) have been shown to be better for certain students than for others; and conversely low structure environments (i.e. student controlled, such as the inductive environments) seem to be better for other students. (This work is reviewed in more detail in the next section.) This suggests that different learning abilities may be tapped in the different kinds of environments, but again, the corpus of data on these issues is too spotty to permit statements on whether the elaborate differentiation of environments posed by the taxonomy is warranted.

In any event, an important feature of the taxonomy as a model of individual differences in learning is that it suggests hypotheses for different possible dimensions of learning. Undoubtedly some of the cells in the taxonomy will be found to overlap extensively with others; that is, they will be found to be factorially similar (possibly identical) with other cells. But the possibility remains that some differentiation can be found; that is, multiple learning dimensions will emerge. Then we should expect that different cognitive abilities will underlie the various distinguishable learning dimensions. A criticism of the validity generalization hypothesis is that studies have employed inadequate learning criteria (Cronbach, 1970, p. 436; Humphreys, 1986, p. 429). A goal for the taxonomy is that it will inspire the collection of extensive and diversive indicators of learning success.

## APTITUDE–TREATMENT INTERACTION THEORY AND RESEARCH

First, let us recall our earlier identification of an 'aptitude', as any characteristic of trainees that determines their ability to profit from instruction (Cronbach and Snow, 1977). Second, let us expand our consideration for this section, to include not just *cognitive* aptitudes, but also *conative* (volitional) and *affective* (personality) aptitudes. With this delineation of aptitudes, an *aptitude–treatment interaction* (ATI) can be defined as any situation when two (or more) treatments have differential impact on individuals of differing levels on some trait (see Cronbach, 1957, 1975). The notion that there is no single training approach that is optimal for every trainee is one potential implication from the ATI perspective. This is illustrated by the ATI portrayed in Figure 7.5, Panel A. In this example, persons of low levels of the hypothetical aptitude benefit most when given training Method 1, and those of high levels of the same hypothetical aptitude benefit most when given training Method 2. Given the arrangement of the respective regressions between aptitude level and training proficiency, this type of ATI has been called a 'crossover' or 'disordinal' interaction. A less striking, but also potentially important ATI is illustrated in Figure 7.5, Panel B. This type of 'ordinal' interaction is important when the more effective training program (training Method 1) comes at a higher cost of implementation than the less effective training program (Method 2). That is, when the more expensive training program (Method 1) cannot be universally used, it would be the most cost-effective to administer that training to those persons who are low on the hypothetical aptitude (Cronbach and Snow, 1977).

From a research and theoretical perspective, the existence of ATIs was seen as revolutionary when Cronbach originally proposed an interactionist perspective in 1957. As subsequent empirical findings have illustrated, the ATI approach has been a fruitful one (for extensive reviews, see Cronbach, 1975; Cronbach and Snow, 1977; Snow, 1989a, 1989b; Snow and Yalow, 1982). Although empirical research in this area is still formative, several repeated demonstrations of ATIs have been established. Two of these ATIs, high versus low structure, and anxiety and achievement motivation are discussed in turn, along with some provocative results concerning transfer of training and of higher-order interactions during learning.

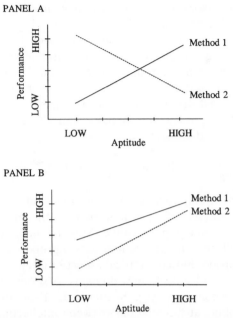

**Figure 7.5.** Hypothetical regressions of aptitude on performance under two training methods (1 and 2). Panel A shows a disordinal interaction, Panel B shows an ordinal interaction. See text for further discussion.

## Two illustrative ATIs

Reviews of the ATI literature have often pointed to two ATIs as particularly salient in multiple investigations (e.g. see Snow and Yalow, 1982). The first of these interactions concerns general intellectual ability as the aptitude and degree of instructional structure as the treatment variable. The interactions found in such studies is that high-ability learners seem to benefit most when placed in low-structure learning environments (e.g. independent reading, discovery), while low-ability learners seem to benefit most when given high-structure learning environments (e.g. lecture, drill-and-practice).

Another frequently demonstrated ATI, with affective/conative constructs, also relates to high- and low-structure treatments. According to Snow (1989a), for learners with achievement motivation oriented towards 'achievement via *independence*' or with low levels of anxiety, low-structure learning environments are most effective; whereas for learners oriented towards 'achievement via *conformance*' or having high levels of anxiety, high-structure learning environments are most effective.

In both cases, the degree of structure in the learning environment determines which persons will benefit most from instruction. However, in the first case, a selection procedure that allowed only high-ability applicants to enter the training program is not sufficient for establishing a single *best* learning environment, because affective and motivational variables also interact with structure to determine learning outcomes. These two different sources of ATIs suggest that a maximally effective training technology must be predicated on a multifaceted perspective—one that incorporates knowledge about the interactions between training methods and all three types of aptitudes: cognitive, conative, and affective.

## Transfer of training

Although most of the empirical research on ATIs and transfer of training has involved primary- and secondary-school students, the implications for training technology are nonetheless provocative. Most of the empirical work in this area has been built on a theoretical foundation proposed by Ferguson (1954, 1956). Ferguson proposed that a critical aspect of intelligence is the ability to transfer knowledge and skills to new domains. A series of studies conducted by Sullivan and his colleagues (e.g. Skanes *et al.*, 1974; Sullivan, 1964) tested this theory by looking at the relations between intellectual abilities and performance on two types of transfer tasks: those that involved material that was close in content to the original training task (i.e. a 'near' transfer condition), and those tasks that involved relevant material that was less similar to the trianing task (a 'far' transfer condition). What these researchers determined was that when transfer is near, the influence of general intellectual abilities in determining transfer task performance is reduced (from a control condition). However, when transfer is far, the influence of general abilities on transfer task performance increases.

Given that near transfer situations concomitantly involve higher degrees of positive transfer, the findings can be summarized as follows: as the overall average level of transfer increases, the correlation between general abilities and transfer task performance decline. One interpretation of this finding is that 'near' transfer conditions constitute a high-structure learning environment. With such an interpretation, the transfer finding appears to be related to the previously mentioned ATI findings. However, the transfer-of-training issue seems to be more general. Furthermore, the presence of this ATI concretizes, for the training technologist, the implications of using particular training methods. In the case of modularized training, of classroom/ hands-on training, or of analogous types of part-task training, choices made regarding the structure of the training sequence may have a direct effect of increasing or decreasing the ability (predictor)–performance (criterion) relationship.

**Higher-order interactions**

A recent investigation by Kanfer and Ackerman (1989) examined the effectiveness of different training approaches, goal-setting interventions, and general intellectual ability as they affected learning of a simulated air traffic controller task. These authors postulated that goal-setting, while a generally effective intervention for increasing task/job performance, was likely either to interfere with performance or to enhance performance, depending on the degree of attentional resource demands of the learning task. Kanfer and Ackerman developed two pretraining approaches, prior to task engagement. The first was a 'declarative' pretraining program, which sought to teach learners the knowledge base for task accomplishment (essentially the rules of the task). The second was a 'procedural' pretraining program, which sought to teach learners the procedures of the task, without direct instruction on the declarative knowledge portion of the task. The idea behind the declarative pretraining was to move the learners from the initial, cognitively demanding phase of skill acquisition to the associative phase of skill acquisition, thus reducing attentional resource demands when the learners were transferred to the full task. On the other hand, the procedural pretraining method was designed to enhance performance at the full task, without reducing the cognitive demands on the learner.

Although both the declarative and procedural pretraining procedures improved performance at transfer to the full task, the goal-setting procedure resulted in a classic crossover ATI. When learners were under high attentional demands (transfer after procedural pretraining, plus a performance goal), the lower-ability learners were impeded in acquiring skills in the full task. However, when learners were under lowered attentional demands (transfer after declarative pretraining, plus the performance goal), low-ability learners performed almost as well as their high-ability counterparts. That is, the type of pretraining, coupled with the presence or absence of a goal jointly interacted with general intellectual ability. Thus, goal setting was found to be optimal for high-ability learners under high attentional demands or for low-ability learners under low attentional demands. Conversely, goal setting was found to be detrimental for low-ability learners when they were already occupied with high attentional demands. Given the dynamic nature of attentional demands during the course of learning (see the three-phase learning perspective presented earlier), this research supports a dynamic perspective that indicates a trade-off between the influences of ability and motivational aptitudes, even during the course of a single training situation.

**Implications for design of training programs**

The prevalence of the types of ATIs discussed above, along with recent successful applications of intelligent computer-aided instruction (where individualized instruction implicitly capitalizes on ATIs) suggests the relevance of an interactionist perspective for training technology applications. While simple ATIs may prompt trainers to adopt two or perhaps a few different approaches to particular training situations, higher-order ATIs (those that involve more than one aptitude or even classes of aptitudes) call for a highly individualized approach to training. With an increased dependance on sophisticated computer-aided training technology, it will be increasingly feasible to incorporate ATI theory into training practice. Furthermore, in the world of changing demographics for job applicants—especially when trainees cannot be easily selected to *fit* a fixed training program, the successful training program of the future will have to *adapt* in ways that will maximize the range of aptitudes that can be accommodated. The ATI perspective provides the impetus and the corpus of empirical research that can meet this challenge.

## SUMMARY AND CONCLUSIONS

The theory and research described in this chapter highlighted three fundamental issues in delineating trainee characteristics. The first of these issues concerned establishing linkages between ability theory and learning theory in the acquisition of perceptual–motor skills, and in the acquisition of knowledge and cognitive skills. The second issue concerned mapping learning skills to task and training program characteristics. The third issue focused on applying an interactionist approach to training: one that particularly includes cognitive, conative, and affective aptitudes as they interact with one another and with various types of training programs. Traditionally, there has been a tension between training technology and selection technology. The material in this chapter, though, has pointed to approaches that merge these two technologies. The focus of individual-differences research is no longer just incrementing correlations between predictor and criterion. Instead, we believe that current efforts in unifying ability theory and learning theory will ultimately allow training designers to ask 'what if' questions regarding the applicant pool, the task to be trained, and the training environment, and be able to formulate answers regarding training success and wash-out rates, training time, and possible sources for remediation. In this way, individual-differences approaches and training technology approaches can cooperate in ways that are maximally beneficial to the outcome of training programs. Progress made in the past decade has brought us closer to this goal, and the near future holds promise for validation of the approaches to building a functional taxonomy of aptitudes for learning.

# ACKNOWLEDGEMENTS

Preparation of this chapter was made possible through the support of the Office of Naval Research, Cognitive Science Program—Contract N00014–89–J–1974, Phillip L. Ackerman, principal investigator, and by the Air Force Human Resources Laboratory. The opinions expressed in this chapter are those of the authors, and do not necessarily reflect those of the US Navy or the US Air Force.

# REFERENCES

Ackerman, P. L. (1987). Individual differences in skill learning: An integration of psychometric and information processing perspectives, *Psychological Bulletin*, **102**, 3–27.

Ackerman, P. L. (1988). Determinants of individual differences during skill acquisition: Cognitive abilities and information processing, *Journal of Experimental Psychology: General*, **117**, 288–318.

Ackerman, P. L. (1990). A correlational analysis of skill specificity: Learning, abilities, and individual differences, *Journal of Experimental Psychology: Learning, Memory, and Cognition*, **16**, 883–901.

Adams, J. A. (1987). Historical review and appraisal of research on the learning, retention, and transfer of human motor skills, *Psychological Bulletin*, **101**, 41–74.

Anastasi, A. (1934). Practice and variability: A study in psychological method, *Psychological Monographs*, **45**, (Whole No. 204).

Anderson, J. R. (1982). Acquisition of cognitive skill, *Psychological Review*, **89**, 369–406.

Anderson, J. R. (1983). *The Architecture of Cognition*. Cambridge, MA: Harvard University Press.

Anderson, J. R. (1985). *Cognitive Psychology and its Implications*, 2nd edn. New York: W. H. Freeman.

Anderson, J. R. and Jeffries, R. (1985). Novice LISP errors: Undetected losses of information from working memory, *Human–Computer Interaction*, **1**, 107–131.

Baddeley, A. D. (1986). *Working Memory*. Oxford: Clarendon Press.

Bartlett, F. C. (1932). *Remembering: A study in experimental and social psychology*. New York: Macmillan.

Bechtoldt, H. P. (1962). Factor analysis and the investigation of hypotheses, *Perceptual and Motor Skills*, **14**, 319–342.

Binet, A. and Henri, V. (1895). La psychologie individuelle, *L'Anee Psychologique*, **2**(81).

Carpenter, P. and Just, M. A. (1988). The role of working memory in language comprehension. In D. Klahr and K. Kotovsky (eds). *Complex Information Processing: The impact of Herbert Simon*. Hillsdale, NJ: Erlbaum.

Carroll, J. B. (1989). Factor analysis since Spearman: Where do we stand? What do we know? In R. Kanfer, P. L. Ackerman and R. Cudeck (eds). *Abilities, Motivation, & Methodology: The Minnesota Symposium on Learning and Individual Differences*, pp. 43–67. Hillsdale, NJ: Erlbaum.

Cattell, J. McK. (1890). Mental tests and measurements, *Mind*, **15**.

Chase, W. G. and Ericsson, K. A. (1982). Skill and working memory. In G. H. Bower (ed.). *The Psychology of Learning and Motivation*, Vol. 16. New York: Academic Press.

Christal, R. E. (1990). *Correlates of Logic-Gate Learning*. Unpublished manuscript.

Cronbach, L. J. (1957). The two disciplines of scientific psychology, *American Psychologist*, **12**, 671–684.

Cronbach, L. J. (1970/1990). *Essentials of Psychological Testing*, 3rd/5th edn. New York: Harper & Row.

Cronbach, L. J. (1975). Beyond the two disciplines of scientific psychology, *American Psychologist*, **30**, 116–127.

Cronbach, L. J. and Snow, R. E. (1977). *Aptitudes and Instructional Methods: A handbook for research on interactions*. New York: Irvington Publishers.

Deary, I. J., Head, B. and Egan, V. (1989). Auditory inspection time, intelligence, and pitch discrimination, *Intelligence*, **13**, 135–148.

Ekstrom, R. B., French, J. W., Harman, H. H. and Dermen, D. (1976). *Kit of Factor-Referenced Cognitive Tests*. Princeton, NJ: Educational Testing Service.

Ericsson, K. A. and Simon, H. (1980). Verbal reports as data, *Psychological Review*, **87**, 215–251.

Ferguson, G. A. (1954). On learning and human ability, *Canadian Journal of Psychology*, **8**, 95–112.

Ferguson, G. A. (1956). On transfer and the abilities of man, *Canadian Journal of Psychology*, **10**, 121–131.

Fisk, A. D., Ackerman, P. L. and Schneider, W. (1987). Automatic and controlled processing theory and its application to human factors problems. In P. A. Hancock (ed.). *Human Factors Psychology*, pp. 159–197. New York: North Holland.

Fitts, P. and Posner, M. I. (1967). *Human Performance*. Belmont, CA: Brooks/Cole.

Fleishman, E. A. (1962). The description and prediction of perceptual–motor skill learning. In R. Glaser (ed.), *Training Research and Education*. Pittsburgh: University of Pittsburgh Press.

Fleishman, E. A. (1972). On the relation between abilities, learning, and human performance, *American Psychologist*, **27**, 1017–1032.

Frederiksen, J. R. (1982). A componential theory of reading skills and their interactions. In R. J. Sternberg (ed.), *Advances in the Psychology of Human Intelligence*, pp. 125–180. Hillsdale, NJ: Erlbaum.

Frederiksen, J. R., Warren, B. M. and Rosebery, A. S. (1985a). A coponential approach to training reading skills: Part 1. Perceptual units training, *Cognition and Instruction*, **2**, 91–130.

Frederiksen, J. R., Warren, B. M. and Rosebery, A. S. (1985b). A componential approach to training reading skills: Part 2. Decoding and use of context, *Cognition and Instruction*, **2**, 271–338.

Gagné, R. M. (1965). *The Conditions of Learning*. New York: Holt, Rinehart, and Winston.

Galton, F. (1869). *Hereditary Genius: An inquiry into its laws and consequences*. London: Macmillan.

Galton, F. (1883). *Inquiries into Human Faculty and its Development*. New York: Macmillan.

Gitomer, D. (1984). *A Cognitive Analysis of a Complex Troubleshooting Task*. Unpublished doctoral dissertation, University of Pittsburgh.

Gough, H. (1976). Personality and personality assessment. In M. D. Dunnette (ed.). *Handbook of Industrial and Organizational Psychology*, pp. 571–607. Chicago: Rand McNally.

Guilford, J. P. (1967). *The Nature of Human Intelligence.* New York: McGraw-Hill.

Gustafsson, J.-E. (1988). Hierarchical models of individual differences in cognitive abilities. In R. J. Sternberg (ed.). *Advances in the Psychology of Human Intelligence,* Vol. 4, pp. 35–71. Hillsdale, NJ: Erlbaum.

Haier, R. J. (in press). Cerebral glucose metabolism and intelligence. In A. Vernon (ed.), *The Biological Basis of Intelligence.* Hillsdale, NJ: Ablex.

Haier, R. J., Siegel, B. V., Jr, Nuechterlein, K. H., Hazlett, E., Wu, J. C., Paek, J., Browning, H. L. and Buchsbaum, M. S. (1988). Cortical glucose metabolic rate correlates of abstract reasoning and attention studied with positron emission tomography, *Intelligence,* **12,** 199–217.

Hayes, J. R. (1981). *The complete Problem Solver.* Philadelphia: Franklin Institute Press.

Hayes, J. R. (1984). Three problems in teaching general skills. In J. Segal, S. Chipman and R. Glaser (eds). *Thinking and Learning Skills,* Vol. 2. Hillsdale, NJ: Erlbaum.

Hayes, J. R. (1985). Three problems in teaching general skils. In S. F. Chipman and J. W. Segal (eds). *Thinking and Learning Skills,* Vol. 2. *Research and Open Questions,* pp. 391–407. Hillsdale, NJ: Erlbaum.

Horn, J. L. (1968). Organization of abilities and the development of intelligence, *Psychological Review,* **75,** 242–259.

Horn, J. L. and Cattell, R. B. (1966). Refinement and test of the theory of fluid and crystallized general intelligences, *Journal of Educational Psychology,* **57,** 253–270.

Humphreys, L. G. (1960). Investigations of the simplex, *Psychometrika,* **25,** 313–323.

Humphreys, L. G. (1986). Commentary (The g factor in employment: A special issue of the *Journal of Vocational Behavior*). *Journal of Vocational Behavior,* **29,** 421–437.

Hunt, E., Frost, N. and Lunneborg, C. (1973). Individual differences in cognition: A new approach to intelligence. In G. Bower (ed.). *Advances in Learning and Motivation,* Vol. 7, pp. 87–122. New York: Academic Press.

Hunter, J. E. (1986). Cognitive ability, cognitive aptitudes, job knowledge, and job performance, *Journal of Vocational Behavior,* **29,** 340–362.

Jackson, M. D. and McClelland, J. L. (1979). Processing determinants of reading speed, *Journal of Experimental Psychology: General,* **108,** 151–181.

Jensen, A. R. (1982). Reaction time and psychometric g. In H. J. Eysenck (ed.). *A Model for Intelligence.* Heidelberg: Springer-Verlag.

Kanfer, R. (1990). Motivation theory and industrial and organizational psychology. In M. D. Dunnett and L. M. Hough (eds). *Handbook of Industrial and Organizational Psychology,* Vol. 1, pp. 75–170. Palo Alto, CA: Consulting Psychologists Press.

Kanfer, R. and Ackerman, P. L. (1989). Motivation and cognitive abilities: An integrative/aptitude-treatment interaction approach to skill acquisition, *Journal of Applied Psychology—Monograph,* **74,** 657–690.

Kranzler, J. H. and Jensen, A. R. (1989). Inspection time and intelligence: A meta-analysis, *Ingelligence,* **13,** 329–348.

Kyllonen, P. C. (1985). *Dimensions of Information Processing Speed* (AFHRL–TP–85–57). Brooks Air Force Base, TX: Air Force Systems Command.

Kyllonen, P. C. (1990, April). A taxonomy of cognitive abilities. In R. Ekstrom and I. Bejar (chairs). *New Directions for the Kit of Cognitive Referenced Tests.* Symposium conducted at American Educational Research Association Annual Convention, Boston, MA.

Kyllonen, P. C. and Christal, R. E. (1989). Cognitive modeling of learning abilities: A status report of LAMP. In R. Dillon and J. W. Pellegrino (eds). *Testing: Theoretical and applied issues,* San Francisco: Freeman.

Kyllonen, P. C. and Christal, R. E. (in press). Reasoning ability is (little more than) working memory capacity?! *Intelligence*.

Kyllonen, P. C. and Shute, V. J. (1989). A taxonomy of learning skills. In P. L. Ackerman, R. J. Sternberg and R. Glaser (eds). *Learning and Individual differences: Advances in Theory and Research*, pp. 117–163. New York: W. H. Freeman.

Kyllonen P. C. and Stephens, D. L. (in press). Cognitive abilities as determinants of success in acquiring logic skill, *Learning and Individual Differences*.

Kyllonen, P. C. and Tirre, W. C. (1988). Individual differences in associative learning and forgetting, *Intelligence*, **12**, 393–421.

Kyllonen, P. C., Tirre, W. C. and Christal, R. E. (in press). Knowledge and processing speed as determinants of associative learning proficiency, *Journal of Experimental Psychology: General*.

Kyllonen, P. C. and Woltz, D. J. (1989). Role of cognitive factors in the acquisition of cognitive skill. In R. Kanfer, P. L. Ackerman and R. Cudeck (eds.). *Abilities, Motivation, and Methodology: The Minnesota Symposium on Learning and Individual Differences*, pp. 239–280. Hillsdale, NJ: Erlbaum.

Marshalek, B., Lohman, D. F. and Snow, R. E. (1983). The complexity continuum in the radex and hierarchical models of intelligence, *Intelligence*, **7**, 107–127.

Newell, A. and Rosenbloom, P. S. (1981). Mechanisms of skill acquisition and the law of practice. In J. R. Anderson (ed.). *Cognitive Skills and their Acquisition*. Hillsdale, NJ: Erlbaum.

Pellegrino, J. W., Mumaw, R. J. and Shute, V. J. (1984). Analyses of spatial aptitude and expertise. In S. Embretson (ed.). *Test Design: Contributions from Psychology, education, and psychometrics*, pp. 45–76. New York: Academic Press.

Ree, M. J. (1989). *The Differential Validity of a Differential Aptitude Test* (Tech. Paper AFHRL–TP–89–59). Brooks AFB, TX: Manpower and Personnel Division, Air Force Human Resources Laboratory.

Salthouse, T. A., Babcock, R. L., Mitchell, D. R. D., Palmon, R. and Skovronek, E. (in press). Sources of individual differences in spatial visualization ability, *Intelligence*.

Schmidt, F. L. and Hunter, J. E. (1977). Development of a general solution to the problem of validity generalization, *Journal of Applied Psychology*, **62**, 529–540.

Schneider, W. and Fisk, A. D. (1982). Dual task automatic and control processing, can it occur without resource cost? *Journal of Experimental Psychology: Learning, Memory, and Cognition*, **8**, 261–278.

Schoenfeld, A. H. (1980). Heuristics in the classroom. In S. Krulik and R. E. Reys (eds). *Problem Solving in School Mathematics*, pp. 9–22. Reston, VA: Council of Teachers of Mathematics.

Shepard, R. N. and Metzler, J. (1971). Mental rotation of three-dimensional objects, *Science*, **171**, 701–703.

Shiffrin, R. M. and Schneider, W. (1977). Controlled and autommatic human information processing: II. Perceptual learning, automatic attending, and a general theory, *Psychological Review*, **84**, 127–190.

Shute, V. J. and Kyllonen, P. C. (1990). *Modelling the Acquisition of Programming Skill*. Unpublished manuscript.

Skanes, G. R., Sullivan, A. M., Rowe, E. J. and Shannon, E. (1974). Intelligence and transfer: Aptitude by treatment interactions, *Journal of Educational Psychology*, **66**, 563–568.

Snow, R. E. (1989a). Aptitude–treatment interaction as a framework for research on individual differences in learning. In P. L. Ackerman, R. J. Sternberg and R. Glaser (eds.). *Learning and Individual Differences: Advances in theory and research*, pp. 13–59. New York: Freeman.

Snow, R. E. (1989b). Cognitive–conative aptitude interactions in learning. In R. Kanfer, P. L. Ackerman and R. Cudeck (eds.). *Abilities, Motivation, & Methodology: The Minnesota Symposium on Learning and Individual Differences*, pp. 435–474. Hillsdale, NJ: Erlbaum.

Snow, R. E., Kyllonen, P. C. and Marshalek, B. (1984). The topography of ability and learning correlations. In R. J. Sternberg (ed.). *Advances in the Psychology of Human Intelligence* Vol. 2, pp. 47–103. Hillsdale, NJ: Erlbaum.

Snow, R. E. and Yalow, E. (1982). Education and intelligence. In R. J. Sternberg (ed.). *Handbook of Human Intelligence*, pp. 493–585. Cambridge: Cambridge University Press.

Spearman, C. (1904). 'General intelligence', objectively determined and measured, *American Journal of Psychology*, **15**, 201–293.

Spearman, C. (1927). *The Abilities of Man*. New York: Macmillan.

Sternberg, R. J. (1977). *Intelligence, Information Processing, and Analogical Reasoning: The componential analysis of human abilities*. Hillsdale, NJ: Erlbaum.

Sternberg, R. J. (1984). Testing and cognitive psychology, *American Psychologist*, **36**, 1181–1189.

Sullivan, A. M. (1964). *The Relation between Intelligence and Transfer*. Unpublished doctoral dissertation, McGill University, Montreal.

Thurstone, L. L. (1935). *The Vectors of Mind*. Chicago: University of Chicago Press.

Thurstone, L. L. (1938). Primary mental abilities, *Psychometric Monographs*, **1**.

Thurstone, L. L. and Thurstone, T. G. (1941). Factorial studies of intelligence, *Psychometric Monograph*, **2**.

Tirre, W. C. (1990). *Reading Correlates*. Unpublished manuscript.

Tirre, W. C. (in press). Knowledge and ability factors underlying simple learning by accretion. *Genetic, Social, and General Psychology Monographs* (Also, 1989, (Tech. paper AFHRL–TP–89–48) Brooks AFB, TX: Manpower and Personnel Division, Air Force Human Resources Laboratory.)

Vernon, P. E. (1961). *The Structure of Human Abilities*. New York: Wiley.

Warner, R. (1958). *The Greek Philosophers*. New York: New American Library.

Werdelin, I. and Stjernberg, G. (1969). On the nature of the perceptual speed factor, *Scandinavian Journal of Psychology*, **10**, 185–192.

Wickelgren, W. A. (1974). *How to Solve Problems: Elements of a Theory of Problems and Problem Solving*. San Francisco: Freeman.

Wissler, C. (1901). The correlation of mental and physical tests, *Psychological Review Monograph Supplements*, **3**, *No. 6* (Whole No. 16).

Woltz, D. J. (1988). An investigation of the role of working memory in procedural skill acquisition, *Journal of Experimental Psychology: General*, **117**, 319–331.

Woodrow, H. (1946). The ability to learn, *Psychological Review*, **53**, 147–158.

Young, R. K. and Chaiken, S. R. (1990). *The Inspection Time Paradigm: An exploration of tactics to eliminate the apparent-movement strategy*. (Tech. Paper AFHRL–TP–90–40). Brooks AFB, TX: Manpower and Personnel Division, Air Force Human Resources Laboratory.

# Chapter 8

# Training media and technology

**Greg Kearsley**
*George Washington University*

This chapter examines the role and significance of media and technology in the training domain. It begins with a discussion of the major issues associated with training media and an explanation of what technology is, and is not. Different types of technology are then described including audio/visual media, computer-based systems, and simulators. The next section addresses the topic of choosing technologies based on media selection models, cost-effectiveness analyses, and human factors considerations. This is followed by an overview of implementation issues including feasibility studies, management, and socio-political concerns. The final section provides a summary and conclusions in the context of future trends, research questions, and practical guidelines.

This chapter is a selective rather than comprehensive overview of training media and technology. It presents a certain perspective, namely, that technology, when used properly, amplifies our ability to learn and teach. For more complete reviews, see Ellis (1986), Heinich, Molenda and Russell (1982), Reiser (1986), or Saettler (1968). For further elaboration of the theme outlined in this chapter, see Kearsley (1984).

## INTRODUCTION

A good place to begin is with a definition of the terms 'media' and 'technology'. Media is understood as a way of conveying or communicating ideas. We are all familiar with print, radio, and television as vehicles for news and entertainment. We are also familiar with correspondence and telephones for personal or business communication. Training media serve the same role—to convey and communicate ideas in an instructional setting.

Technology is the practical application of science. It can take the form of inventions (new devices) or innovation (new methods). While we tend to associate technology with physical things, it is important to realize that technology can be intangible in nature (e.g. when it takes the form of procedures

*Training for Performance: Principles of Applied Human Learning.* Edited by J. E. Morrison
© 1991 John Wiley & Sons Ltd

or techniques). For example, when we talk about automobile technology, we refer to much more than simply cars or trucks. It also includes assembly lines, car dealerships, auto insurance, the United Automobile Workers (UAW), gas stations, drivers' licenses, speeding tickets, emission control regulations, and so on. In the training realm, technology refers to the devices and methods used to facilitate learning.

As defined, technology is a broader term than media. When we focus on print or television as media, we are primarily concerned with how specific books or programs convey information. As technologies, we are interested in the ways print and television materials are created, distributed, and evaluated. Used loosely, both terms refer to the physical device used in training. But, in more precise usage, training media denotes how instructional messages are delivered; training technology covers the entire delivery system.

There are two fundamental issues underlying the use of technology for training: (1) Does it matter?, and (2) Does it matter which medium is used? Almost all of the research literature about technology deals with one or both of these questions. Unless you believe that the answer to the first question is affirmative, there is no justification for using technology in training. If you fail to accept a 'yes' to the second question, the selection of one medium over another is essentially arbitrary. Let us examine each of these two issues in more detail.


**Impact on learning**

The first issue is a question of effectiveness or impact on learning. When we deliver instruction using technology, does it facilitate learning? This question is almost always posed in a relative sense. The baseline for comparison is a teacher using no media other than his or her own voice and actual equipment for demonstrations. (In practice, the baseline teaching setting usually includes a blackboard, flipchart, or overhead projector and hence is already 'contaminated' by some media usage.) The effectiveness of a given medium is measured in terms of any improvement in achievement or performances shown by the media-using group over the baseline group.

Results of such studies often show that various media do have positive effects on student learning (e.g. Howe, 1983; Kulick, Bangert and Williams, 1983). This research also shows that subtle differences in the design of materials and teaching style can alter the effectiveness of media. The real issue underlying these studies is whether the effects of instruction can be measured at all, regardless of what media are involved. For this reason, the best baseline would be a comparison with a group who receives no instruction. However, for a variety of reasons, this baseline is rarely used in effectiveness studies.

## Media comparisons

The second issue focuses on the question of whether one medium results in more effective learning than another for a given learning situation. Studies conducted on this theme use the same paradigm as mentioned above, except the comparison is now between the same subject-matter taught via different media instead of a baseline comparison. Some paradigms explore the additional variable of individual differences confounded with the media such as the Aptitude × Treatment Interaction (ATI) studies (Cronbach and Snow 1977).

Hundreds, if not thousands, of media comparison studies have been conducted over the decades (e.g. Allen, 1971; Clark, 1983; Cuban, 1986) with the same general outcome: no significant differences. Actually, what the studies show is that to the extent design and delivery variables are controlled, there is no difference in using one medium versus another to present the same information. Only a naive view of media would expect any differences in such a study.

To exploit properly the powert of any medium, we know that the information to be presented must be specifically suited to and designed for that medium. Each medium has its unique features that training designers and managers should try to exploit fully. For example, video/television is a dynamic and attention-getting medium. It is highly suitable for depicting action sequences or arousing emotion. Print is a 'cool' medium, superb for presenting detailed information or long arguments. The unique characteristic of computers is their interactivity—appropriate for any form of practice activity. To the extent that a medium is used properly it would not be used to present the same information in the same way as another medium.

This is the reason why comparison studies rarely show any differences—if all media were used to their full advantage they would not teach the same material and hence could not be compared. When they are used to teach the same material in the same way, the power of the media are essentially stripped away leaving only the underlying content. McLuhan (1964) summarized the point in his famous expression: 'the medium is the message'. Rather than trying to show that one medium is better or worse than another, we need to understand how to use each one optimally for learning activities. This is the purpose of media selection models discussed latter in this chapter.

So what can we conclude about the two fundamental issues associated with the use of media in training? First if any medium is used properly it can facilitate learning. Secondly, no medium is inherently better than any other—it just conveys information differently. What really matters is that the power of a medium is fully exploited when used. In other words, both these issues boil down to the same thing: a thorough understanding of a technology is needed in order to make effective use for teaching purposes. In the rest of this chapter, we concentrate on the critical features of three broad technologies: audiovisual media, computer-based systems, and simulators.

# AUDIOVISUAL MEDIA

Audiovisual media include print, transparencies, slides, radio/television, audio/videotapes, videodisc, and compact disc. Print, transparencies, slide/ tape, and video are the most commonly used technologies in training. All of these technologies share one common characteristic—passive information delivery. They can present information in various ways but cannot interact with the student. This lack of interactivity is the major characteristic that differentiates audiovisual media from computer-based training and simulators to be discussed later in this chapter.

## Print

Print media (texts, manuals, notes) comprise the oldest and most pervasive instructional technology. In developed countries, almost everyone can read and hence make use of printed materials. The writing skills needed to create print materials are possessed by almost all teachers. Printing equipment and services are easily obtained and inexpensive. Indeed, the advent of desktop publishing has made it even easier for people to produce professional quality documents. Printed materials are compact, reliable, and inexpensive.

Even though print technology has been in use for a long time, it is only within the last two decades that serious attention has been given to the optimal design of text starting with the legibility of print (Tinker, 1969) and elaborated by subsequent research (e.g. Hartley, 1980; Jonassen, 1982). Based upon this work, a number of techniques and guidelines for effective text design have emerged (see Table 8.1).

## Transparencies

Overhead transparencies are widely used for classroom instruction. The popularity of overheads can probably be attributed to the ease of operation of the projector and the ease of making transparencies. Despite their widespread use, however, they are not always used effectively. The most common problems are overheads that are illegible (usually because the text is too small), contain too much information, or are uninteresting. Table 8.2 lists some rules that determine effective use of overheads.

There are two major benefits of using transparencies: better organization and time savings during delivery. The preparation of overheads forces the instructor to do some degree of planning and think through the structure and

**Table 8.1.** Guidelines for text design.

---

Principles for organizing text
- Put sentences and paragraphs in logical order
- Give an overview of the main ideas
- Use short informative headings
- Make a table of contents for long documents

Principles for writing sentences
- Use the active voice
- Use personal pronouns
- Write short sentences
- List conditions separately
- Avoid unnecessary and difficult words
- Avoid multiple negatives

Typographical principles
- Avoid lines of text that are too long or too short
- Use white space in margins and between sections
- Use ragged right margins
- Avoid using all caps
- Use highlighting techniques sparingly

---

sequencing of a presentation. Because the content of the presentation is already prepared, the information can be delivered more quickly than if it had to be created during the session (i.e. by using a blackboard or flipchart). If handouts of the overheads are provided, students do not need to be preoccupied with note taking and can listen to the presentation.

### Radio/television

The broadcast media of radio and television have a long history of use as an instructional technology but neither medium has ever achieved sustained use in training settings. Radio was used for military training during the 1940s and

**Table 8.2.** Guidelines for transparencies.

---

Preparation
- Present one major idea or concept per transparency
- Use only a few key words or phrases on each transparency
- Make sure letters and graphics are large and legible
- Make your overheads visually interesting

Presentation
- Start with an outline
- Emphasize information by pointing
- Control the pace by progressive disclosure
- Turn the projector off to make a point or for discussion
- Use two projectors for increased effect
- Obtain group involvement by writing on a blank transparency

---

1950s and television has been used by many corporations for business training. These media seem more suitable for information delivery or entertainment purposes than for instruction because of their lack of permanence. On the other hand instructional television has proven to be an effective learning tool in elementary and adult education (e.g. Lesser 1974; Howe, 1983).

Instructional television has received a new lease on life in the context of teleconferencing. In a typical teleconference, a group of experts give a presentation that is broadcast via satellite and can be viewed at many sites. Participants at the receiving sites can ask questions any time via phone links. In the case of videoconferencing a two-way video link exists so that all parties can see and hear each other. Teleconferencing adds an interactive component to television thus moving it into the same category as interactive videodisc, computer-based training, and simulators. If teleconferencing becomes popular as a method of training delivery, instructional television will become a mainstream instructional technology.

### Slides/tapes

Slides and tapes (audio or video) are widely used in training settings, although not to the same extent as print or transparencies. Slides are most commonly used in group presentations although they can be used in self-study carrels. Most of the considerations mentioned for transparencies also apply to the preparation and use of slides. The major advantage of slides relative to overheads is that they can present photographic and graphic information more effectively and they can be duplicated easier. Audiotapes are most often used for self-study in conjunction with print materials. On the other hand, videotapes (now usually in the form of videocassettes) are primarily used for group-based learning, although their popularity for self-study learning has increased as VCRs become ubiquitous. Videotapes carry on the tradition of using films for training purposes begun during the Second World War.

### Video

Video has the unique property of being able to present dynamic information (i.e. sequences of events) as well as conveying effect. This makes it very suitable for teaching procedures, processes, and interpersonal skills. It has the potential to be more attention getting than static media such as print or slides and hence can achieve a higher level of student involvement. Of course, this potential can be thwarted by misuse of the medium as anyone who has sat through a boring 'talking head' lecture on tape or television can attest.

Video can be used in two different ways for training: (a) as a medium for presenting pre-recorded content and (b) as a tool to record and play back learning situations such as role plays or practice sequences. It is more commonly used in the former mode, although the latter offers some unique opportunities for feedback and diagnostics. While there are thousands of pre-recorded tapes available for training on every conceivable topic, most organizations create the majority of the video materials they use for training. Video production equipment and expertise are widely available, although making professional quality videotapes is not inexpensive.

### Videodiscs/CDs

Videodiscs and compact discs represent a new era in audiovisual media since they introduce the digital storage of information. Digital storage means that information can be packed much more densely and can be randomly accessed. Together, these two factors add up to a lot of information in compact form that can be displayed or searched very quickly. For example, a standard 12 inch videodisc can store 54000 frames of text, photographs, or audio that all take about the same time to access. Compact discs can store about 600 megabytes of data; equivalent to about 300000 pages of text.

More importantly, videodiscs and CDs marry audiovisual and computer technology since presentation can be controlled by software. This means that audiovisual media can now be made interactive and take advantage of the benefits of being able to branch and provide feedback to input. It also means that audiovisual materials can be produced and edited electronically which can speed up development and allow new computer-generated effects.

For the moment, use of videodiscs or CDs in training is limited since the delivery and development technology is not widely available or affordable. There have been plenty of studies and projects involving the use of videodiscs for training and they seem to show that videodiscs work well when developed and used properly (e.g. DeBloois, 1988; Fletcher, 1989; Kearsley and Frost, 1985). There will probably be a similar spate of studies focused on CD (or subsequent forms of digital storage media). However, videodisc/CD technology is not likely to have a major impact on training until the hardware become less expensive and hence more widely available. One of the well-established lessons of the educational technology field is that a medium will not have much impact until it is affordable and easily accessible to most trainers. Affordable means that it can fit into current training budgets. Accessible means that the necessary hardware and software are already present in the training center. Neither of these conditions currently obtains for videodisc/CD technology.

# COMPUTER-BASED LEARNING

The use of computers for learning activities began in the late 1950s (e.g Coulson, 1962; Galanter 1959) as an outgrowth of the programmec instruction (PI) movement. Initial applications simply implemented the branching structure of PI materials in the form of tutorial materials. Eventually drill and simulation strategies emerged that involved more complex feedback and branching structures. Today, computer-based training is widely used in all types of organizations (Gery 1987; Kearsley, 1983; Seidel and Weddle, 1987).

The increase in the use of computer-based training is closely tied to the broad use of computers for all applications. As more and more jobs involve the use of computers, there is a natural tendency to deliver training via computers too. With the advent of microcomputers, the use of computers for instruction became much more affordable. In addition, microcomputers provide color graphics and better resolution screen displays that allow for more interesting instructional presentations.

## Traditional strategies

There are many ways that computers can be used for training. Tutorials probably represent the most common form of computer-based instruction. Questions or problems can be interspersed throughout a lesson to allow students to check their understanding of the material as they progress. Since the feedback provided is immediate the student can discover any misconceptions during the lesson, not afterwards. Furthermore, the system can provide remedial or enrichment sequences based upon the student's performance. The capability to tailor the instructional presentation based upon the detailed performance of the student is one of the major benefits of tutorials.

Drills, simulations, and games are other common forms of computer-based instruction. These strategies are primarily practice activities since they do not present new information like tutorials. Drills simply present problems and then provide feedback on the answers. Simulations present a situation and one or more parameters that can be set by the student. Based upon the student's input or selection, a new event is presented that reflects the choice made. Games are similar in nature to simulations, but add fantasy, scoring, and competition.

Online testing is another important form of computer-based training. Like drills, simulations, and games, testing does not involve the presentation of new information. Thus, online testing (as well as drills, simulations, and games) must be used in conjunction with some other medium that presents the concepts or procedures to be learned. The value of online testing is that it provides immediate feedback to students and automatically grades the tests. In any training setting where a lot of testing is involved, considerable time can be saved by automatic grading capabilities.

## Embedded training

A new type of computer-based instruction is embedded training. Embedded training refers to the inclusion of instruction in a computer-based system, typically in the form of an online help capability (Kearsley, 1988). The system might be an accounting program or a fire control program; the embedded training explains how to use the program when the user asks for information. Embedded training represents a new direction in computer-based instruction because the instruction is presented in the context of specific problems when requested by the student—in contrast to the usual pedagogical model of presenting information via lessons under the control of the instructor. Embedded training can also eliminate the difference between instruction and documentation by providing a range of online options some of which explain and others that only present information. Table 8.3 outlines some of the types of information that a help system could address.

**Table 8.3.**  Types of online help information.

* Current location or status
* Description of current options
* Explanation of what things do
* Description of format for input
* Explanation of output displays
* Explanation of error messages/conditions
* Information about how the program works
* Explanation of terms (glossary)
* Explanation of help options

## Intelligent tutors/expert systems

Another new type of computer-based training is intelligent tutors and expert system advisers (Kearsley, 1987; McFarland and Parker, 1990; Poulson and Richardson, 1988). These systems utilize artificial intelligence techniques to develop programs that 'understand' what they teach. The programs consist of knowledge networks and sets of rules that specify how concepts are related to each other. Because these programs can reason and make inferences about the subject-matter, they are capable of answering student questions and making fine-grained diagnostic decisions about student misconceptions. However, tutors and expert advisers take considerable time to develop and this has limited their availability to date.

In fact, most forms of computer-based training take a long time to develop. The essence of computer-based training is interactivity—which means complex response analysis and branching structures must be designed, programmed, and tested. This is a lengthy process and requires specialized skills and knowledge (e.g. Allessi and Trollip, 1954; Hannafin and Peck, 1988). The long development times and high costs are two of the reasons why computer-based instruction has taken a long time to become established. On the other hand, the development of computer-based learning materials is no more involved or expensive than professional video productions yet they seem harder to justify than video.

**Personal tools**

All of the forms of computer-based training discussed so far have been cast from the original perspective of providing individualized instruction. In this perspective, the main argument for using computers is that each student can receive a uniquely tailored instructional sequence based upon his or her pattern of responses or selections. However in recent years a different side of computer-based learning has become prevalent, namely the use of the computer by the student as a personal learning tool. In this perspective, the emphasis is placed on using applications software such as word processing, spreadsheet, database, and telecommunications programs to acquire information and solve problems. The instructional value of computers is not to convey content but to provide the student with better learning tools.

This new approach to computer-based learning de-emphasizes individualized instruction and focuses more on group interaction. Indeed, instructors are being encouraged to use computers to structure group activities. The use of electronic mail and conferencing via networks supports this approach. Students use the computer to exchange ideas and solve problems with other students and their instructor. They may also have access to online databases or data collection programs. In general, this new approach to computer-based learning is much more closely aligned to the way people use computers in their jobs and hence has more immediate relevance to work than the traditional form of computer-based training.

**Computer learning strategies**

Finally, it should be mentioned that teaching employees how to use computers for their job duties is a far more important concern of most training managers than using the computer to provide training. As more and more jobs come to rely on the use of a computer, teaching people how to use computers is quickly becoming a dominant aspect of training. What we have learned through research and experience is that this is often a difficult task and one which is not very well suited to the traditional forms of classroom instruction or training materials design (Carroll, 1982).

When most people learn how to do a task involving a computer they tend to be very 'action oriented'. They do not want to sit through lectures or read manuals. Instead they want to try out the program and get as much accomplished with the minimum learning effort. This learning approach can be accommodated by a 'minimalist' teaching style (Carroll, 1990) that involves presenting only the essential information needed at any given moment. Embedded training, discussed above, is another way to meet this need.

# SIMULATORS

Simulators (also called training devices) have a long history with the first flight simulators appearing prior to the Second World War. A simulator is a device intended to teach someone how to operate or maintain a piece of equipment such as an airplane, weapon, ship, or nuclear power plant. The primary benefit of the simulator is that it can train less expensively, faster and more safely than through the use of the actual equipment. In some cases (such as space vehicles), the simulator is used to train for equipment that is not yet built or operational. In almost all cases, safety is an overriding concern since students can make mistakes while learning with the simulator that would be catastrophic if performed using the actual equipment.

## Types of simulators

While there are many different types of simulators, the most common is the flight simulator used to train military or commercial pilots and aircrews. Indeed, most pilots today spend a large portion of their training in simulators. These simulators may be used to train cockpit familiarization, normal and emergency flight procedures, or combat tactics. Types of simulators range from part-task trainers, which may be simple mock-ups or computer displays, to full-motion platforms with elaborate visual displays that duplicate the look and feel of flying (see Rolfe and Staples, 1987; Taylor and Stokes, 1986).

Another important category of simulator is the maintenance trainer. In the military, as well as the manufacturing, transportation, and telecommunication industries, a great deal of time and money is lost due to improper maintenance as a consequence of poor training. Simulators can provide a means to improve the effectiveness of training by providing hands-on experience in diagnosing and repairing equipment problems. One of the particular strengths of using simulators for maintenance training is that the trainee can be exposed to a wide variety of problems in a short time that might not occur often on the job. Furthermore, faults can be programmed in a systematic way so that an instructional sequence can be followed. Of course, maintenance trainers also provide the standard benefits of simulators: reduced costs, increased safety, and better availability.

The effectiveness of simulators is well documented, particularly in their most common application—flight training. Orlansky (1986) summarizes the results of numerous studies of flight simulators in military settings and concludes that with few exceptions training time in a simulator saved training time in the actual aircraft. The median per cent transfer was 31%; that is, use of the simulator reduced the amount of equipment time required by 31%. Effectiveness results are more clear-cut for simulators than for other training media because the transfer of training can be measured directly (i.e. successful operation or repair of the equipment). In most other areas of training the job performance measure is not so easy to identify. Furthermore, the transfer of training paradigm provides a means of making decisions about the relative merits of different alternatives in simulator design and use.

## Fidelity

Apart from questions of cost effectiveness (which will be addressed in the next section), there are two major issues in the design and use of simulators: fidelity and instructional features. The fidelity issue concerns how closely the simulator needs to resemble the actual equipment it simulates. Simulators can have physical fidelity which means that they resemble the equipment in terms of appearance; psychological fidelity which means that the simulator is perceived to behave in the same way as the equipment in terms of perceptual sensory–motor, or cognitive cues; and instructional fidelity which means that it produces the same skills and competencies as training in the actual equipment.

The type of fidelity desired strongly influences the design and use of the simulator. For example, if physical fidelity is considered important, the design of the simulator is primarily an engineering task—to replicate the equipment as closely as possible. On the other hand, if psychological fidelity is desired, the design must include the work of human factors psychologists who measure and specify the behavioral parameters. To obtain instructional fidelity, training specialists must be involved to determine the skills and competencies that need to be learned. Over the years, the focus of attention in simulator design has shifted from physical fidelity to behavioral and instructional fidelity (Adams, 1979; Andrews, 1988; Caro, 1979; Cream, Eggemeier and Klein, 1978).

The fidelity issue is closely related to the part-task versus full-task consideration. Part-task trainers are built and used to train a certain competency or part of the job. For example, non-functional cockpit mock-ups are often used to familiarize aircrews with the physical arrangement and location of controls and instruments. Such a part-task trainer could have high fidelity even though it does not operate. On the other hand, a computer display of equipment could be used to practice procedures. While this simulator would have low physical fidelity, it could have high behavioral or instructional fidelity. The whole idea of part-task trainers is to use the least expensive instructional medium (simulator or otherwise) to achieve the greatest training results. Many aspects of a complex job can be learned from simulators with low physical fidelity.

## Instructional features

The issue of instructional features concerns what capabilities a simulator should have in order to produce the desired training results. Some of the common features include freeze action, automated demonstrations, record and replay, automated cuing and coaching, reset/position initialization, malfunction insertion, automated performance measurement, and programmed mission scenarios. Some of these features appear to be useful while others are not. For example, freeze action allows the instructor to stop the simulation at any point and provide the student with feedback and demonstration mode allows procedures to be shown to the trainee. Research shows that neither of these two options seems to be very worth while. On the other hand, replay and reset features are often used by instructors to review performance or retry a procedure (see Taylor and Stokes, 1986, for a review of this research).

## Team training

So far, we have focused on simulators used to train specific equipment. However, simulators can have broader objectives such as team or mission training. In a team or mission simulator, a set of interacting job positions is simulated such as a cockpit, submarine, or tank crew. One of the earliest attempts to use mission simulators was the SAGE simulations developed in the 1960s to simulate air defense installations. The SAGE simulations were nationwide exercises involving many radar and command centers including ground, airborne, and ship-based facilities (Parsons, 1972). Air traffic control is another team-based activity that has used simulators for training. One of the interesting aspects of the simulators used for this application is the experimentation with speech input/output to simulate voice traffic (Grady 1982).

Another interesting use of simulators for team/mission training is the use of the MILES (Multiple Integrated Laser Engagement System) for battlefield tactical exercises. The MILES system consists of low-power lasers and detectors mounted on actual weapons systems (including small arms, canons, and missiles). The detectors (mounted on soldiers as well as all weapons) register direct and near misses when blank rounds are fired. This allows the results of the exercise to be tracked precisely by computer and analyzed for performance deficiencies and training needs (Freeble, Hannaman and Sulzen, 1982).

The most sophisticated use of simulators for team training is the SIMNET project sponsored by DARPA (Orlansky and Thorpe, 1989). SIMNET involves the use of networks to link together many simulators representing a variety of different tactical weapons including tanks, helicopters, artillery, close air support, and operations centers. The simulators can be located in the same building or thousands of miles away. SIMNET allows battalion size teams to practice their tactical skills in real-time combat simulation. The same kind of instructional capabilities possible with one-person or crew simulators (e.g. playback, programmed missions) can now be used at the team training level.

Clearly, simulators provide a diverse range of alternatives for training equipment-related jobs or tasks. Even though simulators reduce operational costs over the use of the actual equipment they are still expensive to design and build. For this reason, simulator use needs to be limited to those training situations where it is most beneficial. This means that audiovisual media and computer-based instruction (especially simulations) still have a major role to play in equipment training programs even when simulators are used. Deciding which medium to select for a particular learning activity is the purpose of media selection models to which we turn our attention in the next section.

# CHOOSING MEDIA AND TECHNOLOGIES

Looking over the discussion of the previous three sections, the reader should be struck by the large number of alternatives possible for training activities. Even in those cases where it is obvious that a certain medium/technology should be used (such as simulators for hands-on equipment training) it is not always clear what specific technology should be used, when, where or how. There are three basic sets of criteria that are taken into account when making such choices: pedagogic, economic, and ergonomic. Pedagogic criteria are based on what instructional features are needed; economic factors have to do with what can be afforded or cost justified; and ergonomic considerations concern the acceptability and usability of the technology.

### Pedagogical factors

Media selection models are intended to help instructional developers choose the most appropriate medium for a given training situation (e.g. Allen, 1971; Bretz, 1971; Diamond, 1977; Reiser and Gagné, 1983; Romiszowski, 1988). While each model differs, they share some common characteristics. In most models, media attributes are identified on the basis of the instructional objectives or skills to be learned. Student aptitudes and situational variables are also taken into account in favoring or precluding certain media. Some models also include economic or organizational factors.

The fundamental idea underlying media selection models is that the type of behavior or skills to be learned should dictate what kind of medium is appropriate. For example, if the behavior to be learned calls for an auditory stimulus or response, then a medium with audio capability is needed. Similarly, if the knowledge to be acquired involves visual images, then a medium capable of presenting pictures or graphics is required. If the learning involves procedures, the use of a dynamic medium such as video or computer simulation is suggested. By and large the basic logic of media selection models is based on the common-sense notion of matching the characteristics of the learning situation with those provided by the media.

The other aspects of media selection models have to do with constraining the choices according to student or situational attributes. For example if the students are known to have poor reading skills, an emphasis would be placed on visual rather than textual presentations. If the students are known to have low motivation, then a more stimulating medium such as video or computers might be favored. The most important characteristic of the learning situation to be taken into account is whether the instruction involves group-based or individual study. Some media (such as overheads or text) are more suited to one type of study than the other. On the other hand some media such as audio/videotape can be used equally well in both contexts.

Media selection models may also take into account economic or organizational factors. Some technologies are simply too expensive for an organization to afford (no matter how effective). For example, video and computer technology require that a sufficient number of VCRs or terminals is available for students to use; if they are not available, the instruction cannot be provided. A more subtle factor is the availability of the specialized skills needed to implement or develop materials for a particular medium. If these skills are not available or affordable, then the medium is not a viable candidate. In many cases, the training developers (or managers) who make a choice of media may not be aware of the need for such special skills and make a poor selection because of this.

Many media selection models provide a decision-making process for weighing the factors just discussed. Typically this process includes the following steps: (1) list all media that are possible candidates; (2) for each objective or task, rate each medium's possibility based upon the learning attributes involved; (3) select the medium for each lesson or course that has the highest total rating; and (4) rank the media in terms of economic or organizational factors. A decision matrix such as that shown in Table 8.4 is often used to implement the decision process. The table shows the ratings of different media for a set of lessons that comprise a course (a score of 5 is most desirable) and the totals are given in the right-hand column.

The simple decision matrix shown in Table 8.4 reveals one of the major problems with media selection models. While the totals suggest the best overall media to be used in the course, it is clear that different media would be best

**Table 8.4.** Example of a media selection matrix.

| | Lesson/Module | | | | | | | | | |
| | A | | | | B | | | C | | |
| Media option | 1 | 2 | 3 | 4 | 1 | 2 | 3 | 1 | 2 | |
|---|---|---|---|---|---|---|---|---|---|---|
| Workbook | 5 | 5 | 3 | 5 | 5 | 5 | 3 | 4 | 3 | 38 |
| Workbook with photos | 4 | 4 | 3 | 5 | 4 | 4 | 2 | 3 | 4 | 33 |
| Lecture | 5 | 5 | 3 | 3 | 5 | 5 | 5 | 3 | 3 | 37 |
| Lecture with overheads | 4 | 4 | 3 | 4 | 4 | 4 | 5 | 4 | 4 | 36 |
| Lecture with slides | 4 | 4 | 3 | 4 | 4 | 4 | 5 | 5 | 4 | 37 |
| Slide/tape | 4 | 4 | 3 | 5 | 3 | 3 | 4 | 5 | 5 | 36 |
| Slide/tape with workbook | 4 | 4 | 3 | 5 | 3 | 3 | 2 | 4 | 4 | 32 |
| Videotape | 3 | 3 | 4 | 5 | 1 | 1 | 5 | 4 | 5 | 31 |
| Videotape with workbook | 3 | 3 | 4 | 5 | 1 | 1 | 2 | 3 | 4 | 26 |
| Simulation | 3 | 3 | 4 | 3 | 2 | 2 | 1 | 5 | 5 | 28 |
| Simulation with workbook | 3 | 3 | 4 | 4 | 1 | 1 | 5 | 3 | 4 | 28 |

suited for particular lessons. The attempt to select a single medium for the whole course results in an overall compromise that is not optimal for every lesson. A better 'media fit' would be achieved by using a combination of different media for different lessons. However, a multi-media solution makes the development and implementation of a course complicated and hence the 'single best' medium solution is preferred by most training developers.

**Cost effectiveness**

So far we have been discussing the choice of media on the basis of instructional considerations. Another major dimension to selection is cost effectiveness. Cost-effectiveness models address the question: What is the least expensive way to deliver the desired level of training proficiency? Note that the most cost-effective means may not be the most desirable from an instructional perspective. For example, one-on-one training is probably the most effective form of instruction in most cases but rarely very cost effective. On the other hand, some media, such as simulators, may not only be the most cost-effective method but also the best approach from an instructional point of view.

Cost-effectiveness models have a broader function than media selection models since they are often used in planning and evaluating training programs. They are commonly used to justify one training approach over another or to compare the relative merits of different approaches. As such, cost-effectiveness studies have an empirical (i.e. data collection) aspect that media selection models do not. A variety of different cost-effectiveness models and techniques have been developed and used in training settings (e.g. Kearsley, 1982; Seidel and Wagner, 1979; Van der Drift, 1980). Some cost-effectiveness models have been developed to predict the optimal use of a single medium such as CBT or simulators (e.g. Sticha *et al.*, 1986). When applied to training media and technology, cost-effectiveness models tend to be used to analyze the life cycle payoffs. As a general rule of thumb, the more complex a medium, the longer it takes for the benefits to be realized. For example, video- or computer-based materials take longer to develop (and hence cost more) than text materials or overheads. However the video or computer materials may do a more effective job with less instructor support than the print materials and, over a suitable period, the reduced costs of delivering the training may justify the additional expense of development. Note, however, this argument rests on the assumption that the video or computer materials reduce the amount of instructor time needed; if this is not the case then the basis for the cost effectiveness is eliminated. On the other hand, if the basis of the justification had been that the video or commputer materials teach more effectively, and this can be proved, then the value of improved job performance (instead of reduced instructor support) becomes the cost savings that add up to a better training approach.

While there are cost-effectiveness studies that purport to justify the use of almost all training media, simulators are the best documented technology. Orlansky (1986) reviews many studies of flight and maintenance simulators in military training and concludes that the use of simulators rather than the actual equipment saves student time, equipment acquisition costs, and operating costs. For example, the data on flight simulators showed that one hour in a simulator saved about half an hour of aircraft training and that operational costs of simulators were about 10% of the operating costs of aircraft. Coupled with the results that simulator training produces satisfactory transfer of training to aircraft operation the data from these studies establish a strong case for the cost effectiveness of simulators.

In a study of computer-based instruction in military training, Orlansky and String (1981) found strong evidence that the use of computers reduced student completion times with an average reduction of 30%. They did not find any evidence that computer-based instruction improved student achievement overall, although there was no evidence that it resulted in poorer results. This leads to the conclusion that computer-based instruction can be more cost effective than other approaches if the time savings can be taken advantage of (i.e. getting students on the job faster). On the other hand, if there are no economic advantages to getting students through training faster, computer-based instruction is not more cost-effective than other media.

The major problem with most cost-effectiveness studies is that the results and conclusions are highly dependent upon the validity of the assumptions made in the model. For example, many studies assume that training equipment or courses will have a lifetime of at least 5 years. In reality, a lot of training programs and devices have much shorter operational lifetimes, often

2 years or less. Another common fallacy of cost-effectiveness studies is that technology will displace the need for instructors or training administration staff. However, this rarely happens since, to succeed, effective applications typically depend upon good instructors and administrators. In fact, technology-based systems usually require additional personnel with specialized skills to design and implement them.

**Ergonomic factors**

Beyond media selection and cost-effectiveness models are human factors or ergonomic considerations. Human factors concerns include the usability, reliability, and flexibility of a technology. Usability refers to how easy or difficult it is for people to operate a device. If it takes a long time to learn or if it results in a lot of errors, people will avoid using it. Similarly, a device must be very reliable or people will not use it routinely. Finally, to be widely accepted, a device must be adaptable to different situations. Training media that can only be used in a narrow instructional context are not likely to become very popular.

Because ergonomic factors determine the acceptability of a technology to students or instructors, they often tend to override the results of media selection or cost-effectiveness studies. For example, for many years computers were not an acceptable medium for group-based instruction because people could not see the monitor screen unless they were sitting in front of it. Attempts to display the screen on large monitors were usually not very successful. However, with the advent of video projectors and more recently LCD tablets, the computer became a more viable media for classroom use.

Reliability and flexibility are important ergonomic factors that determine the use of a particular medium. If a device is not highly dependable, neither students nor instructors will be willing to adopt it as a regular instructional method. One of the reasons why the textbook and the blackboard have come to be the dominant instructional media is because they almost never fail. On the other hand, electrical/electronic devices do fail and users must learn the concept of 'backups'. Makers of overhead projectors who provide a spare bulb in their projectors understand this concept. Most regular users of technology learn that they need to have two of everything if they want to count on reliability.

Flexibility refers to the ability to adapt a technology to different instructional settings or uses. Media in which the students or instructors can modify the content or create their own material are always more popular than materials that cannot be changed. Consider, for example, how popular overhead projectors would be if it was not possible for teachers to make up their own materials. This holds true for video and computers as well—they are much more readily accepted when the capability to create or modify materials is available. Even in the domain of simulators, flexibility is important. Simulators that are generic in nature and can simulate a range of different equipment are more desirable than those specific to only one piece of equipment.

Pedagogic, cost-effectiveness, and ergonomic factors are different criteria used to determine what media are most suited to a particular training situation. However, even the most astute determination does not guarantee that the technology will succeed. Indeed, there is good reason to believe that a poorly selected medium can work if it is well implemented. In other words, how a medium is used is far more important than which one is selected. The next section discusses a series of implementation issues that make the difference between successful or unsuccessful use of technology.

# IMPLEMENTATION ISSUES

Findings from many studies of instructional technology support the conclusion that how a technology is used is more important than the particular medium involved. In this section we examine some of the most important issues in implementation including instructor training, feasibility studies, management considerations, and socio-political concerns. (A more general discussion of the organization issues relevant to training is provided by Latham and Crandall in Chapter 9 of this volume.)

### Instructor role

One of the most consistent findings about the success or failure of technology in training is the significance of the instructor. If an instructor is enthusiastic about the use of technology and proficient in its use, the training usually works well. Conversely, if the instructor is uncomfortable with or does not understand how to use the technology involved, it is very likely that the training will be ineffectual. To the extent that instructors play the main role in the delivery of training, their competency with the technology will be a critical factor. This means that proper training of instructors about technology is one of the single most important implementation steps.

What about self-study training programs in which an instructor plays no role? First of all, instructors do play a role in the design and development of such materials, building in all their teaching experience beforehand. Secondly, most students are likely to need some sort of help during the course provided by telephone, electronic mail, or one-on-one tutoring. Thirdly, few self-study programs work unless someone monitors and reviews the progress of the student on an ongoing basis. Finally, self-study materials typically need a lot of 'tuning' to fill gaps and add examples or elaboration. This is usually done by an instructor. In short, the effectiveness of self-study materials is heavily dependent upon instructor involvement too, even though the instructor may do little conventional teaching. This is true regardless of whether the medium used is print, video, computers, or simulators.

### Feasibility studies

Feasibility studies are conducted to determine if a new or different training approach will work prior to implementation. Because the use of technology almost always represents an innovation in training methods and practices, it is important to determine ahead of time what changes are likely to result or may be needed when a new technology is used. For example, as the previous discussion has indicated, training staff are likely to need training and new skills. This raises questions about who will provide and receive this training, when, where, and how much it will cost. The use of technology may involve new staff and new facilities. Development of technology based materials can take a long time—will they be ready when needed? And, finally, there is the question of equipment costs—can the organization afford the initial and ongoing expenses of the technology?

Pilot studies or field tests are an important aspect of a feasibility study. While consultants and experts will be able to make judgements about the general effects and impact of a technology in an organization, there are too many variables involved to make exact predictions. The best way to assess the detailed effects of implementing a new technology is to try it out on a small scale with a representative sample of employees. This will provide the data needed to determine budgets and procedures for full-scale implementation. It also provides a low profile opportunity to abandon an approach if it does not work.

### Management considerations

One of the especially weak areas of most implementations of technology is management. This includes both training management as well as operational management. Technology-based training requires a great deal more planning than conventional training approaches because longer lead times and long-term budgets are necessary. Staff or consultants with specialized skills will probably be needed for development of materials and they take time to recruit. Media selection, cost effectiveness, or feasibility studies must be planned and conducted. Instructor training must also be planned and conducted. Furthermore, just as instructors must understand how to use technology in their teaching activities, training managers must understand how to administer training activities that involve technology.

In addition to the extra tasks and complexity that technology introduces for training managers, it also brings new challenges for operational managers. If the technology is used as part of a decentralized training approach in which training activities are conducted in the field or on the job, managers are likely to be involved in some aspects of administering or evaluating the training. Since managers are ultimately responsible for the performance of their employees, they have a big stake in how training is conducted and how well it works. They need to know what possibilities a technology offers and how it can be used to remediate job deficiencies. For example if a manager observes that many employees are weak in a certain procedural skill, the manager can request a video demonstration or a computer-based simulation that focuses on that specific skill. This is likely to be more effective than additional lecture or print materials on the subject. In general managers need to have an accurate idea of what training can (and cannot) accomplish in terms of employee competencies and job skills.

## Socio-political issues

This brings us to a discussion of socio-political issues in the implementation of technology. One of the most critical factors in achieving the successful use of a new technology is to be sure that all individuals who will be affected by the technology are involved in the planning, design, and implementation stages. If people are going to accept something new, they must feel some sense of ownership. Attempts to introduce technology into a training system in which there has been no significant involvement of training staff or operational managers is a sure formula for rejection of the technology—no matter how good or effective it is. The consequences of widespread participation in the planning and design of a program are that it takes longer to implement, and that political conflicts over control and power are likely to surface. However, the extra time required and the resolution of political conflicts are part of the process of implementing technology successfully.

It is common for people to be uncomfortable with things that are new and to resist change. Change requires learning new procedures, new roles, and new traditions. To bring about change it is necessary to provide motivation or incentives that make it worth while for people to change. Every individual affected by an innovation must perceive some personal gain that will result. In the case of training, most people are familiar with classroom instruction and text materials. The use of video, computer-based instruction, or simulators—especially in the context of self-study or decentralized learning—represents something new and hence gives rise to resistance. This resistance can only be overcome by providing employees, training staff, and managers with some form of incentive to try the new approach. Possible incentives include better job performance, faster training, more enjoyable training, improved status during or after training, or less expensive training. Peer pressure is also a powerful incentive — once one group of employees uses a technology and likes it, it is much easier to get everyone else to try it.

The last set of socio-political issues has to do with expectations. People often expect technology to produce magical results (sometimes it does). In the context of training, there are often unrealistic expectations about what technology can accomplish. For example, there are many developers and managers who naively believe that if video- or computer-based instruction is used to deliver a course, it will automatically make that course effective. Of course, if the materials are poorly designed or fail to take advantage of the media (e.g. the classic 'talking head' video or 'electronic page turner' computer lesson), no instructional miracles result. Furthermore, training staff and managers often have no concept of how long it takes to develop technology-based materials resulting in unrealistic expectations about availability and completion dates. The only way to overcome these and other unrealistic expectations is to ensure that everyone involved in a training technology project has a good understanding of what the technology can accomplish and how it is developed.

One clear-cut theme emerges in this discussion of implementation issues: the importance of making sure that everyone involved in the use of training media is well informed about those media. To succeed with technology, it is essential to: (a) properly train the instructors and managers who will use it; (b) provide incentives for people to use it; (c) include everyone in the planning and implementation; and (d) cultivate realistic expectations about its use.

## SUMMARY AND CONCLUSIONS

This final section discusses future trends in training media, outlines research issues that need to be adressed, and provides a set of guidelilnes for the practitioner. It also serves to summarize the conclusions presented in the previous sections.

### Future trends

In the first three sections of this chapter, a diverse range of audiovisual, computer, and simulator alternatives were described. One clear-cut trend is the increased use of computer-based tools to develop materials for all of those media. Thus, computers are used to edit audio or video, create computer-animated graphics or synthesized music, and store the results in digital form. Desktop publishing and graphics software are used to produce text and overhead materials. Word processing is used across the entire spectrum of development activities from writing scripts to evaluation questionnaires. Authoring programs allow instructors and subject-matter experts to create computer-based instruction materials without any programming background.

Even more interesting is the emergence of automated instructional development systems that help training designers to conduct task analysis, develop objectives, write storyboards, and perform other such tasks (Kearsley, 1986). This is an area where expert systems can be put to good use in terms of packaging the knowledge of training experts and making this expertise available to all training developers when needed in a specific project (Merrill, 1987). Computer-based systems for media selection and cost-effectiveness analysis have been in the research stages for a number of years (e.g. Brecke and Blaiwes 1981; Kribs, Simpson and Mark, 1983) and are likely to come into regular use in the next decade.

Because of the pervasiveness of computer technology across all media, new developments in hardware and software will have significant impact on the training technology field. New forms of digital storage beyond present CDs will make it even easier and cheaper to deliver multimedia instruction. Hypertext will make it easier to access large databases for instructional purposes. Developments in networking and telecommunications will also make it easier to transmit multimedia information. In the not too distant future, we may be able to buy small satellite receivers that hook up to a personal computer and allow two-way transmission of video, audio, text, and graphics to any other suitably equipped computer. Such a technology would essentially combine the capabilities of all existing media.

There is a general trend in the education and training world towards increasing decentralization of instruction and the use of self-study materials. The major benefit of decentralized training is that it can provide 'on-demand' training—instruction that is available when and where it is needed by the employee. Technology can play a major role in making such distributerd training work by providing interactive learning experiences and the necessary student–instructor interaction via telecommunications. However, all of the media selection and implementation issues discussed above apply to distributed learning as well as to issues having to do with maintaining student motivation (Kearsley, 1985).

## Research issues

Current research issues derive from unresolved problems of the past as well as new problems raised by the emerging developments just mentioned. In the discussion of choosing media, three different sets of considerations were outlined: media selection models, cost-effectiveness models, and human factors guidelines. However, these techniques do not account adequately for the interplay among the different sets of considerations and they certainly do not take into account the implementation issues discussed in the preceding section. We need much more sophisticated decision tools that include these interactions.

The point was also made that media utilization guidelines are probably far more important than media selection models. Instead of worrying so much about choosing the theoretically perfect medium, perhaps more attention should be given to how to use most effectively whatever medium has been selected. Such guidelines would cover how to design, develop, and deploy a given medium (or more realistically, a set of media) for a specific training program. The automated instructional development tools mentioned above could play a major role in providing this kind of help.

Attempts to develop automated instructional development systems have revealed that we have a very rudimentary understanding of the cognitive processes underlying instructional development. For example, when attempts are made to develop systems that automate the steps in completing a task analysis or creating objectives, we discover that the procedures available for even these routine development activities do not specify the detailed processes. Research studies are needed that identify exactly what developers do when they perform these activities and the differences between expert and novice developers.

Demographic data clearly indicate that we are moving into a more multi-cultural, multi-lingual world. Training programs need to adapt to and accommodate this trend. Technology should provide us with a means to present instruction in multiple languages and formats simultaneously. However, we do not see many procedures or guidelines to help instructional designers develop such materials. We also need more research on inter-cultural communication and how technology can facilitate such communication.

Finally, we have the eternal bugaboo of individual differences. We know from research and practical experience that people learn differently. Despite this, we do a poor job dealing with such differences. Computer-based instruction holds the potential to accommodate differences in aptitudes and styles but it has never been fully realized due to a lack of clear-cut theory. Ironically, such theory may eventually emerge from the study of artificial intelligence and attempts to build tutoring systems. Through the development of internal student models and detailed diagnostic strategies tutoring systems force a proceduralization of how individuals differ while learning. Computer-based training and other interactive technologies can provide a vehicle to operationalize theories and models of individual differences such as those presented by Ackerman and Kyllonen in Chapter 7 of this volume.

### Guidelines

The considerations associated with using technology in training can be boiled down to a relatively small set of guidelines listed in Table 8.5. The first important rule of thumb is to select media first on the basis of learning requirements and then take into consideration economic, ergonomic, and organizational factors. This means that it is critical to know what the learning needs are prior to selecting media. The second rule points out that a typical training program will involve a number of different learning activities and hence will probably require a mix of different media. The idea that there is one best medium for a course does not make a lot of sense. The third rule that all instructors and managers should be properly trained to use a technology, comes from the common finding that technology most often fails because the training staff do not know how to take advantage of it. Finally, the last rule addresses the need to have people involved in the planning and implementation of training if they are to accept it.

**Table 8.5.** Practical guidelines for training media.

- Since different media facilitate different learning activities, it is essential to know what kind of learning is involved
- Because most training programs are likely to involve a variety of different learning activities, a combination of media will probably be needed
- Be sure that instructors and managers have been properly trained in a technology before it is used with students
- Involve everyone who will be affected by technology in the planning and implementation process

Note that these guidelines do not deal with the prospective merits of one medium versus another. This should not be the primary concern of training professionals. Instead, they should have an understanding of each different medium and how it can facilitate learning. The real task is to match a given technology to a particular learning activity and then implement it in a way that ensures that the medium works as it should. Media are the tools of training; we need a toolbox with lots of different tools for different jobs. Just as nobody would try to build a house with only a hammer, we should not think we can build a training program with a single medium.

# REFERENCES

Adams, J. A. (1979). On the evaluation of training devices, *Human Factors, 21*, 711–720.

Allen W. H. (1971). Instructional media research: Past, present and future, *Audiovisual Communications Review* 1, 5–8.

Allessi, S. and Trollip, S. (1985). *Computer Based Instruction: Methods and development*. New York: Prentice-Hall.

Andrews, D. H. (1988). Relationships among simulators, training devices and learning: A behavioral view, *Educational Technology,* January, 48–52.

Brecke, F. and Blaiwes, A. (1981). CASDAT: An innovative approach to more efficient ISD, *Journal of Educational Technology Systems, 10*(3), 271–283.

Bretz, R. A. (1971). *A Taxonomy of Communications Media.* Englewood Cliffs, NJ: Prentice-Hall.

Caro, P. W. (1979). The relationship between flight simulator motion and training requirements, *Human Factors,* **21**, 493–501.

Carroll, J. M. (1982). The adventure of getting to know a computer, *IEEE Computer,* **15**, 49–58.

Carroll, J. M. (1990). *The Nurnberg Funnel.* Cambridge, MA: MIT Press.

Clarke, R. (1983). Reconsidering research on learning from media, *Review of Educational Research,* **53**, 445–459.

Coulson, J. E. (1962). *Programmed Learning and Computer-based Instruction.* New York: Wiley.

Cream, B. W., Eggemeier, F. and Klein, G. A. (1978). A strategy for the development of training devices, *Human Factors,* **20**, 145–158.

Cronbach, L. and Snow, R. (1977). *Aptitudes and Instructional Methods.* New York: Irvington.

Cuban, L. (1986). *Teachers and Machines.* New York: Teachers College Press.

DeBloois, M. (1988). *Use and Effectiveness of Videodisc Training: A status report.* Arlington, VA: Future Systems, Inc.

Diamond, R. M. (1977). Piecing together the media selection jigsaw, *Audiovisual Instruction,* **42**, January, 344–69.

Ellis, J. A. (1986). *Military Contributions to Instructional Technology.* New York: Praeger.

Fletcher, J. D. (1989). *Report on the Potential of Interactive Videodisc Technology for Defense Training and Education.* Alexandria, VA: Institute for Defense Analyses.

Freeble, J. D., Hannaman, D. L. and Sulzen, R. H. (1982). One on one infantry training, *Infantry,* May/June, 30–34.

Galanter, E. (1959). *Automatic Teaching: The state of the art.* New York: Wiley.

Gery, G. (1987). *CBT: Making it happen.* Boston, MA: Weingarten Publications.

Grady, M. (1982). *Air Intercept Controller Prototype Training System* (NAVTRAE-QUIPCENT 78–C–0182–14). Orlando, FL: Naval Training Equipment Center.

Hannafin, N. J. and Peck, K. (1988). *The Design, Development and Evaluation of Instructional Software.* New York: Macmillan Publishing Co.

Hartley, J. (1980). *Designing Instructional Text.* New York: Nichols Publishing Co.

Heinich, R., Molenda, M. and Russell, J. D. (1982). *Instructional Media and the New Technologies of Instruction.* New York: Wiley & Sons.

Howe, M. J. A. (1983). *Learning from Television: Psychological and educational research.* New York: Academic Press.

Jonassen, D. H. (1982). *The Technology of Text.* Englewood Cliffs: Educational Technology Publications.

Kearsley, G. (1982). *Costs, Benefits, and Productivity in Training Systems.* Reading, MA: Addison-Wesley.

Kearsley, G. (1983). *Computer Based Training.* Reading, MA: Addison-Wesley.

Kearsley, G. (1984). *Training and Technology.* Reading, MA: Addison-Wesley.

Kearsley, G. (1985). *Training for Tomorrow.* Reading, MA: Addison-Wesley.

Kearsley, G. (1986). Automated instructional development using personal computers: Research issues, *Journal of Instructional Development,* **9**(1), 9–15.

Kearsley, G. (1987). *Artificial Intelligence and Instruction.* Reading, MA: Addison-Wesley.

Kearsley, G. (1988). *Online Help Systems.* Norwood, NJ: Ablex.

Kearsley, G. and Frost, J. (1985). Design factors for successful videodisc-based instruction, *Educational Technology,* March, 7–13.

Kribs, H. D., Simpson, A. C. and Mark, L. J. (1983). *Automated Instructional Media Selection* (NAVTRAEQUIPCEN 79-C-0104-1). Orlando, FL: Naval Training Equipment Center.

Kulick, J. A., Bangert, R. L. and Williams, G. W. (1983). Effects of computer-based teaching on secondary school students. *Journal of Educational Psychology,* **75**(1), 19–26.

Lesser, G. (1974). *Children and Television: Lessons from Sesame Street.* New York: Random House.

McFarland, T. and Parker, O. R. (1990). *Expert Systems in Education and Training.* Englewood Cliffs, NJ: Educational Technology Publications.

McLuhan, M. (1964). *Understanding Media: The extensions of man.* New York: McGraw-Hill.

Merrill, M. D. (1987). Expert system for instructional design, *IEEE Expert,* **2**(2), 3–9.

Orlansky, J. (1986). The productivity of training. In J. Zeidner (ed.). *Human Productivity Enhancement,* Vol. 1. New York: Praeger.

Orlansky, J. and String, J. (1981). Computer-based instruction for military training, *Defense Management Journal,* 46–54.

Orlansky, J. and Thorpe, J. (1989). SIMNET—An engagement training system for tactical warfare, *Journal of Defense Research,* 1989, 95–94.

Parsons, H. M. (1972). *The Design of Man–Machine Systems.* Baltimore, MD: Johns Hopkins Press.

Poulson, M. C. and Richardson, J. J. (1988). *Foundations of Intelligent Tutoring Systems.* Hillsdale, NJ: Lawrence Erlbaum.

Reiser, R. (1986). Instructional technology: A history. In R. M. Gagné (ed.). *Instructional Technology: Foundations.* Hillsdale, NJ: Lawrence Erlbaum.

Reiser, R. A. and Gagné, R. M. (1983). *Selecting Media for Instruction.* Englewood Cliffs, NJ: Educational Technology Publications.

Rolfe, J. and Staples, K. J. (1987). *Flight Simulation.* Cambridge, UK: Cambridge University Press.

Romiszowski, A. J. (1988). *The Selection and Use of Instructional Media, 2nd edn.* New York: Nichols Publishing.

Saettler, P. (1968). *A History of Instructional Technology.* New York: McGraw-Hill.

Seidel, R. and Wagner, H. (1979). A cost-effectiveness specifcation. In H. O'Neil (ed.). *Procedures for Instructional Systems Development.* New York: Academic Press.

Seidel, R. and Weddle, P. (1987). *Computer-based Instruction in Military Environments.* New York: Plenum Press.

Sticha, P. J., Blacksten, H., Knerr, C., Morrison, J. and Cross, K. (July 1986). *Optimization of Simulation-based Training Systems* (HumRRO Report 86–13). Alexandria, VA: Human Resources Research Organization.

Taylor, H. L. and Stokes, A. (1986). Flight simulators and training devices. In: J. Zeidner (ed.). *Human Productivity Enhancement, Vol. 1.* New York: Praeger.

Tinker, M. A. (1969). *Legibility of Print.* Ames, IA: Iowa State University Press.

Van der Drift, K. (1980). Cost effectiveness of audiovisual media in higher education. *Instructional Science,* **6**, 355–364.

# Chapter 9

# Organizational and social factors

**Gary P. Latham[1] and Susan R. Crandall[2]**
[1]University of Toronto, [2]University of Washington

Training effectiveness can be defined as the systematic development of the attitude, knowledge, and skill patterns required by an individual in order to perform a given task or job (Latham, 1988). Cost estimates indicate that only 10% of the $100 billion dollars spent annually on training and development programs resulted in an enduring behavioral change (Georgenson, 1982; Kelly, 1982). One reason for the failure of training to transfer to the workplace is the failure to take into account organizational and social factors when designing and implementing training programs.

The purpose of this chapter is to specify organizational and social factors that should be taken into account in order to increase training effectiveness. The identification of these factors is based on inferences drawn from the human resource management and organizational psychology literature. The chapter is organized around three themes. First, organizational culture is examined in terms of its ideology, demographics, corporate strategy, and the values placed on theory on developing training programs. These factors influence not only the composition of training programs, but also the extent to which the organization even offers formal training to its employees. Second, the effect of organization-wide factors such as pay and promotion policies, and environmental constraints such as the financial health of the organization on training effectiveness are discussed. Finally, the importance of three social variables that can affect training effectiveness is described, namely, trainee interactions with the trainer, the peer group, and the supervisor. These social variables, if applied correctly, should facilitate training effectiveness.

## ORGANIZATION CULTURE

Culture may be defined simply as that which is valued in the organization. It is the values that differentiate one organization from another that, in part, give an organization its uniqueness. When one speaks of the effect of an organization's culture on the individual, one is generally referring to the formal as well

*Training for Performance: Principles of Applied Human Learning.* Edited by J. E. Morrison
© 1991 John Wiley & Sons Ltd

as the informal training in accepted behaviors within an organization, which the employee acquires through social interaction.

The culture of an organization consists, in part, of a particular set of accepted actions for solving problems. A problem confronting most, if not all, organizations is ensuring that their employees can perform organizational tasks effectively. Two solutions to this problem are the use of valid selection and training systems.

### Ideology: selection versus training

An organization's ideology can be characterized by the emphasis that is placed on selection versus training for ensuring that employees perform their jobs effectively. For example, the prevalent ideology in organizations in the eighteenth and nineteenth centuries regarding the workforce was that 'the lower orders are innately idle and depraved except when they are goaded by the spur' (Downs, 1983). Such ingrained attitudes, which still exist in some organizations, discourage formal training activities.

In North America, in particular, there has been a push–pull philosophy between selection and training advocates (Howard and Bray, 1988; Hinrichs, 1970). The selection or early identification philosophy stresses identifying people with strong potential so that the expense of training can be minimized. In the case of a training philosophy, the organization is primarily interested in identifying and overcoming existing performance deficiencies in employees in their present jobs. This latter position is becoming the dominant philosophy of organizations in Canada and the United States (Mealiea and Duffy, 1985). This is due in part to the legislation in both countries which encourages the recruitment and training of a culturally diverse workforce.

### Demographics

Demographic changes in the workforce composition are forcing organizations to re-evaluate their attitudes toward training and selection. The shrinking labor pool has made the selection of skilled workers difficult, and has compelled organizations to invest in training and re-education programs (Offermann and Gowing, 1990). Four demographic changes, which are likely to affect training in organizations, include: (a) the shortage of skilled entry-level workers, and the increasing numbers of (b) minorities, (c) women, and (d) people over 40 years of age.

#### Entry-level workers

The labor pool from which organizations select their employees has declined. Whereas the 'baby-boom' generation (1946–61) produced a plentiful supply of workers for the North American economy, the 'baby-bust' generation (1964–75) will be unable to fill all the entry-level positions the baby-boom generation will be vacating within the next 20 years, let alone the millions of new jobs that will be created annually (Offerman and Gowing, 1990). It is predicted that by 1995 there will be about 1.3 million fewer workers in the 18–24 age group. Compounding this problem is the low level of literacy and lack of basic skills of many of these individuals. The high school dropout rate is 50%, and climbing, with one out of eight 17-year-olds leaving high school functionally illiterate (Sandroff, 1990; Kruger, 1990).

As a result of this labor shortage, an increasing number of industries are likely to place emphasis on research and development to bring about technological advances to minimize problems caused by a shortage of employees. This has been a dominant strategy in the logging industry since the 1960s where emphasis has been on mechanization in order to reduce the need for manpower. However, the increasingly complex nature of jobs is likely to exacerbate the problem of an undereducated workforce (Offermann and Gowing, 1990). For example, many entry-level jobs in the 1990s already require computer literacy and the ability to understand technical manuals.

To correct these problems, organizations will have to implement basic skills training programs (Wexley and Latham, 1991). These programs will have to be empirically evaluated if they are to be supported by the trainees, let alone senior management who must fund the development and implementation of them. For example, an empirical evaluation of a military training program found that skills in reading, writing, and arithmetic were learned efficiently when the practice material was integrated with relevant information from the job (Sticht et al., 1987). In the absence of this evaluation, trainees would likely to have become frustrated, and senior management would likely have become disillusioned with the need to continue their support of this training.

*Minorities*

Demographic trends suggest that about one-third of new entries into the workforce between now and the year 2000 will be non-white (Johnston and Packer 1987; Offermann and Gowing, 1990). This is likely to prove problematic for organizations as many of these people are currently underskilled.

An analysis of unemployed youth conducted by the Ford Foundation (Berlin, 1983) has distressing implications for society:

> Figures concerning youth indicated that in 1982, when the US unemployment rate was unusually high (10.8%), the comparable rates for teenagers who were high school graduates were 17% for whites, 53.5% for blacks and 28% for Hispanics. For high school dropouts, the rates rose to 29%, 71%, and 35%. When unemployment rates improved nationally to only 5.4% in 1985, the rates

for teenage youth were 16% for whites, 42% for blacks, and 23% for Hispanics. (Goldstein and Gilliam, 1990, p. 138).

The undereducation of minorities is likely to result in an increasing number of businesses forging partnerships with government agencies and high schools to institute training and re-education programs (Schuler and Huber, 1990). For example, the Insurance Society of Philadelphia has instituted a six-week summer internship for non-college-bound students which consists of on-the-job training as well as remedial instruction in mathematics, reading and analytical thinking (Kruger, 1990).

*Women*

Approximately 60% of entry-level workers between 1985 and the year 2000 will be women (Johnston and Packer, 1987). Much of the increase is due to women who have children entering the workforce. In 1987, 53% of mothers with children under age one were already in the workforce. This number is more than double the rate in 1970 (US Bureau of Labor Statistics, 1987).

The entrance of women into jobs traditionally performed by men may need to be taken into account when conducting a training needs analysis. This is because differences in the background of males and females may affect the type of training that each of them requires to perform their jobs effectively. For example, a study conducted by Berryman-Fink (1985) focused on male and female managers' views of the training needs of people in management. Both male and female managers identified four skills for which women managers needed training: assertiveness confidence building, public speaking, and dealing with males. Male managers needed training in listening, verbal skills, non-verbal communication, empathy, and sensitivity. However, in a survey of government workers, Tucker (1985) found no significant difference between female and male requests for training.

In support of Tucker's findings, Goldstein and Gilliam (1990) argued that there is currently minimal evidence that the task requirements of a managerial job for a female (or non-white) differ from those required for a white male. Second, there is little evidence that females need training which is not required for white males. Thus, they argued that managers should question the alleged effectiveness of training programs designed specifically for women. The importance of empirically evaluating the effectiveness of training programs is discussed later in this chapter.

*People over 40*

Between 1986 and the year 2000, the number of persons aged 35 to 47 will increase by 38%; the number between the ages of 48 and 53 will increase by

67%; while the overall population growth will be only 15% (Johnston and Packer, 1987: Offermann and Gowing, 1990). There is evidence to suggest that older workers are less willing to retrain for new jobs (Johnston and Packer, 1987). Tucker (1985) conducted a survey which focused on perceptions of older workers in order to determine their training needs in the technological and management areas within the US Geological Agency of the Department of the Interior. The younger age group (40–49) preferred management training; the middle age group (50–59) preferred training in technological areas; while the older group (age 60 and above) showed little interest in any kind of training. There are at least two explanations for the latter finding. First, the 60 and over group may be focusing on retirement rather than training issues. This explanation, if true, is troublesome because of the few people who will be entering the labor force. Second, these people may not believe they are trainable.

Observed negative relationships between age and performance may stem from employers withholding developmental resources from older employees (Fossum *et al.*, 1986: Goldstein and Gilliam, 1990). This underscores the need to garner full organizational support for older workers participating in training and retraining programs. When organizational support is absent, the self-efficacy of older workers regarding their ability to perform the to-be-trained task may be low (Bandura, 1977, 1986). When this occurs, it should not be surprising that they would be unwilling to volunteer for training programs to learn the necessary skills for mastering a new technology (Gist, Rosen and Schwoerer, 1988; Fossum *et al.*, 1986). The importance of self-efficacy to the success of training programs is explored in detail later in this chapter.

In summary, training processes need to take into account the demographic make-up of the organization's workforce if the organization is to have employees who will perform their jobs well. As the workforce becomes diverse in race, age, and sex, cross-cultural training programs traditionally applied to people before transferring them to a foreign country may, in the future, need to be adapted by organizations operating within their home country. Companies such as Ortho Pharmaceutical, Digital Equipment Corp., and US West have already implemented cultural diversity training programs. The purpose of this training is to make people aware of how subtle biases can decrease a minority person's chances for advancement; to allow people to express their feelings concerning inter-racial conflict; and to increase cross-cultural understanding among employees (Marby, 1990).

## Organizational analysis and corporate strategy

Organizational analysis is defined as identifying explicitly the organization's long- and short-range goals, and its strategy for attaining them (Wexley and Latham, 1991). An underlying theme that emerges from the training literature over the past decade is that training must be linked to an organization's strategy if it is to be viewed by higher management as effective (Latham, 1988). The importance of this step can be found in a paper by Brown and Read (1984). They argued that the productivity gap between UK and Japanese companies could be closed by UK companies taking a strategic view of their training policies. This should be done by ensuring that the training plan is constructed in the same context and by the same process as the business plan, and more importantly, that it be viewed in direct relationship to it. Thus, achievement of training goals should be regularly monitored and subjected to a thorough annual review alongside the business plan.

The need to make training objectives congruent with the organization's goals has also been recognized by the US military. The original Instructional Systems Development (ISD) approach to identifying training needs was based on a detailed analysis of input from job incumbents. In other words, training needs were defined on the basis of how often and how well job incumbents were performing their job tasks. The military concluded that this approach focused too narrowly on the job as it was defined and thus was less useful for analyses of jobs that were being redefined in accordance with new technology. More importantly, the traditional ISD approach did not ensure that military training was compatible with the long-term strategy of the military. The current approach to defining training needs is based on a thorough analysis of the training provider's mission. From this mission-based analysis, training objectives are now derived (John Morrison, personal communication).

Recently, researchers have begun to theorize on how corporate strategy should drive training content. For example, Jackson, Schuler and Rivero (1989) suggested that managers should adopt training programs which complement their competitive strategies so that the desired employee role behaviors are indicated.

Three types of competitive strategies are innovation strategy, quality-enhancement strategy, and cost-reduction strategy (Porter, 1980; Schuler and Jackson, 1987). Innovation strategy is used to develop products and services which are new and different from those of competitors. Quality-enhancement strategy focuses on improving the quality of an organization's products or services. Cost-reduction strategy is used as an attempt to gain competitive advantage by being the lowest cost producer.

Training programs in organizations with an innovation strategy should teach employees how to deal effectively with ambiguity and unpredictability. Moreover, training should focus on the skills required by existing jobs as well as future-oriented skills that are likely to be required when pursuing innovation strategies. Organizations with quality-enhancing strategies should focus on teaching employees to identify ways to improve the process by which goods and services are made or delivered. An organization pursuing a cost-reduction strategy should teach people how to implement tight controls without hurting morale. For example, these firms may wish to emphasize cross-training which enrich jobs so that fewer enployees can be used to achieve maximum efficiency (Schuler and Jackson, 19897).

Hussey (1985) has argued that training objectives, especially for management development, should be reviewed by top management whenever a major change in strategic emphasis is planned. However, his survey of UK companies revealed that only one-third of the respondents saw the necessity for doing so. Most managers felt that training objectives should be tailored to the individual rather than to corporate needs. Hussey argued for a shift in thinking regarding the purpose of training. Training should not be for the sole improvement of the individual with the hope that it will benefit the organization; training should also be for the benefit of the firm, knowing that this in turn will benefit the individual.

## Theory

Related to the topic of organization analysis and its ideology is the value, if any, that the organization's culture places on psychological theory in developing training programs. To the extent that theory is absent, there is an absence of understanding of why a training program worked or failed to work. Consequently, the steps that can be taken to increase training effectiveness are often difficult to discern. Thus, when theory is neglected, it is not surprising that training programs often waste an organization's time and money.

Social learning theory, more recently referred to as social cognitive theory (Bandura, 1977, 1986), provides a useful theoretical framework for predicting, understanding, and increasing training effectiveness. This theory posits reciprocal determinism among the person's cognitions, the environment, and overt behavior. In other words, behavior influences and is influenced by both cognitive thought processes and environmental (e.g. organizational) contingencies.

Training programs are often ineffective because they fail to take into account each of these three variables, let alone the interactions among them. Self-regulation plays an important role in social cognitive theory. Individuals regulate their behavior based on their performance goals, their beliefs about their ability to achieve these goals (self-efficacy), and their beliefs about the environmental consequences of their behavior (outcome expectancies). Thus, teaching self-regulation should be an important aspect of the training process.

Training effectiveness is enhanced when the organization takes steps to ensure that: (a) managers and trainees understand the relationship between training and the organization's goals; (b) the trainees perceive that desirable outcomes are attained as a result of completing the training program satisfactorily; (c) trainees perceive that environmental obstacles to applying what is learned in training are minimized; (d) trainees develop a strong sense of self-efficacy regarding the to-be-learned material; and (e) trainers, supervisors, and co-workers support what is learned during and after training. The first point, with regard to organizational goals and strategies, has been discussed. The remainder of this chapter focuses on the remaining four points. These four points are discussed under the rubric of organizational and social factors.

## ORGANIZATION-WIDE FACTORS

Organization-wide factors can be defined as those variables affecting the trainee which are primarily determined by persons or events external to the immediate work group. Under this rubric fall such factors as pay and promotion policies, and environmental constraints including the overall financial health of the organization. The relation of these organization-wide variables to trainee outcome expectancies is discussed separately.

### Pay and promotion

Outcome expectancies are trainee beliefs about whether particular behaviors will lead to desired outcomes (Bandura 1977, 1986). Trainees may believe that they are capable of performing a specific behavior, but may choose not to do so because they believe it will have little or no effect on their status in the organization. Thus, high outcome expectancies are critical to the transfer of training to the job setting.

Researchers in the behaviorist tradition have long known that the environment affects behavior. While this finding should be a platitude by the 1990s, there is evidence to suggest that our knowledge of environmental reinforcers such as pay and promotion practices is not being applied in the training context (Leifer and Newstrom, 1980; Robinson and Robinson 1985). For example, research strongly suggests that pay for performance systems are effective methods for bringing about and sustaining performance (Heneman, 1990; Latham and Huber, in press). Thus, newly acquired skills should be incorporated into merit pay plans in order to increase the probability that these skills will be used on the job.

Robinson and Robinson (1985) cited an example of the importance of incorporating newly learned skills into a merit pay plan. Customer relations representatives (CRRs) in an organization received training in customer relations. Prior to training the CRRs were provided incentives based on the dollar value of orders received each day but not on time spent handling customer complaints. When handling a customer complaint, however, the CRRs would spend twice as long on the phone compared with the time it took to take an order. Since management realized that the old plan failed to reward customer relations behavior, the incentive system was modified following training so that the newly learned customer relations skills would be utilized on the job.

Caplow (1983) described a study of clerical workers who, following training, were allowed to work without close supervision. The result was lower productivity and morale than those in a control group. Interviews with the clerks who had received the training disclosed that after they were given autonomy they thought themselves entitled to higher pay than the other clerks. They became so disgruntled at not receiving a pay increase that their output eventually declined to a much lower level than that of the control group. This study highlights the importance of making certain that the outcome expectancies of management and trainees are in alignment prior to implementing training.

As one progresses up the organizational hierarchy, the opportunities for promotion, remuneration, and honors increase over those of the organization's rank and file employees. Paradoxically, the opportunities for disappointment not only increase, but they are often more severe than they are lower in the organization. To have completed successfully an executive development program (e.g. Harvard's or Toronto's) and then to just miss becoming an executive vice-president is usually a greater disappointment than to have just missed a promotion to an assistant supervisor. Moreover, the likelihood that other managers will want to model this person's behavior by taking time away from the job to attend similar executive programs will likely decrease. The likelihood that the disaffected employee will leave the organization for another is increased.

In addition, the projected expansion of middle-aged workers may inhibit the outcome expectancies for promotional opportunities in large organizations. In 1987, one person in 20 was promoted into top management; in 2001, only one in 50 will be successful in achieving a top management position (Arnett, 1989; Offermann and Gowing, 1990). Clearly, the organization must carefully evaluate constraints to promotional opportunities before launching training programs.

**Environmental constraints**

Environmental constraints can obviously have a deleterious effect on a trainee's outcome expectancies. In the context of training, there are at least eight constraints which can hinder the transfer of training to the job setting: namely, the lack of job related information, tools and equipment, materials and supplies, required services and help from others, time availability, physical aspects of the work environment, job-relevant authority, and budgetary support (Peters, O'Connor and Eulberg, 1985).

For example, Peters *et al.* (1982) found that three types of situational constraints (completeness of task information, ease of use of materials and supplies, and similarity of work environment to the training environment) affected performance on a goal-setting task. When these situational constraints were low, goal level correlated significantly with performance ($r$ = 0.63); when these situational constraints were high, the correlation was reduced to non-significance.

To minimize the probability of low outcome expectancies, Robinson and Robinson (1985) suggested conducting a work environment assessment to identify barriers to transfer before training begins. This assessment should be made in addition to the traditional individual and organizational training needs assessment. For example, a survey can be distributed to supervisors and potential trainees where they are asked to identify perceived situational constraints. Barriers to performance should be corrected prior to training in order to facilitate high outcome expectancies and maximize transfer of training to the work setting.

Environmental constraints are often beyond the organization's control (e.g. noise levels, uncooperative customers). One way to overcome the difficulty of maintaining behavior following training is to teach trainees coping strategies. Based on clinical research on addictive behaviors, Marx (1982) proposed a relapse prevention model for use in managerial training. The goal of the model is to equip trainees with the cognitive (e.g. awareness of non-adaptive thought processes) and behavioral (e.g. anxiety reduction stress management) skills to prevent slips from becoming total relapses.

Acquiring coping skills can be an integral part of the entire training process in two ways (Marx, 1982). First, trainees should be made aware of the potential for relapse. Thus, trainers and trainees should discuss the possibility of such problems rather than focusing solely on training success. Participants should be encouraged to describe previous slips or relapses as these descriptions may become valued data for the prevention of future difficulties. Next, trainees should identify high risk situations which may prevent the use of the newly learned behavior. Trainees can then analyze their high risk situations according to problem type (e.g. social, situational, emotional, interpersonal).

Following high risk identification, coping strategies can be developed. Coping strategies might include time management, assertiveness training, negotiation skills, or interpersonal problem-solving training. The key point to emphasize is that trainees should perceive high risk situations as hurdles to be cleared through the appropriate development of coping skills. Knowing that one has the skills to overcome obstacles following training will enhance self-efficacy and decrease the chance of a relapse to the pretrained behavior. The importance of high self-efficacy for ensuring training effectiveness is emphasized in a subsequent section in this chapter.

Another potential environmental constraint is organization size. No studies to our knowledge have been conducted on the effect that size of the organization plays on training effectiveness. One could speculate that the relationship is curvilinear. In a very small organization, trainee outcome expectancies are likely to be low as the opportunities for pay and promotion are limited. On the other hand, the greater degree of impersonality brought on by the increased bureaucratization of very large organizations could also affect outcome expectancies adversely.

## Financial health

When there is a prolonged labor shortage, training activities increase as the number of job openings exceed the number of people to fill them. Such factors are often a function of the economic climate in which the organization is functioning. However, to reduce costs in a bad economy, organizations frequently decrease, or downsize, the number of people employed (Ropp, 1987). A survey of 1084 companies and non-profit organizations showed that in 1988, 39% reduced their workforces by cutting an average of 162 employees (Skrzycki, 1989).

The plight of displaced workers in the United States has exposed organizations to considerable political attack. In a *Business Week* editorial (1986). Randolph Hale, Vice-President of the National Association of Manufacturers, was quoted as stating that retraining workers is one way to cool down this issue. In addition to reducing political pressure, retraining workers should foster corporate loyalty and make the workforce flexible and adaptable.

The financial health of an organization is a key factor influencing the very existence, let alone success of, training programs. The norm in most organizations that are experiencing financial hardship is to reduce severely the number of trainers and training programs regardless of whether downsizing is implemented. This decrease in training activities, however, may worsen rather than improve the organization's performance. For example, the Swedish Government has argued that training should be emphasized rather than de-emphasized during an economic recession so that skilled employees are available during a recovery. In this way inflationary pressures are relieved and industries can be rapidly expanded (Haveman and Saks, 1985). The German Federal Employment Institute also carries out its activities countercyclically with the economy. They too argue that a primary objective in a weak labor market is to provide training for meeting probable skill bottlenecks when expansion again occurs.

The antidote to an incorrect decision is to provide feedback which will enable upper management to evaluate the success or failure of training programs. The current controversy in the scientific literature concerns the form that the feedback should take. Boudreau (1983) is among those who advocate utility analysis as a way of developing credible 'bottom line' estimates of the value of training programs that may soften the criticisms of those executives who view training as little more than the source of burdensome overhead expenses. Utility analysis examines the monetary contribution of a training program to a firm's performance.

A critical flaw in utility analysis models, however, is that the value of employees—the criterion variable—is estimated simply by asking the opinion of supervisors about how much a subordinate is worth relative to others (i.e. the standard deviation dollar of performance) (Hanlon, 1990). As Dreher and Sackett (1983) noted: (a) there is no evidence that a rational estimate approach to assessing the standard deviation of performance approximates the true value; (b) agreement among job experts is not a guarantee that the estimates are valid; and (c) the procedure lacks face validity in that the basis of each supervisor's judgment is unknown. Although advances in utility analyses for training programs have been made (cf. Cascio, 1989; Arvey and Cole, 1989), difficulties with estimating the standard deviation dollar of performance remain.

The appropriate question to ask is what executives take into account when determining whether training programs should be supported. Tenopyr (1987) reported that utility analysis has little effect on the decision making of executives at AT&T. As noted elsewhere (Latham, 1988), a major impediment to upper management support for training may be the failure of managers to see how training has had a positive effect on employee behavior with regard to the attainment of organizational objectives. Seeing a positive behavior change on the part of employees may result in upper management treating training seriously—more seriously than if presented with dollar estimates that justify time spent on training. Research is needed on managerial decisions regarding the continuation of training as a result of seeing observable job-related behavior change versus seeing dollar estimates.

# SOCIAL VARIABLES

Other environmental variables that influence training effectiveness are social in nature in that they stem from interactions with trainers, peers, and supervisors. These social variables, in turn, can have a positive or a deleterious effect on a cognitive variable that is crucial to training success, namely, self-efficacy. The steps to increasing self-efficacy and the ways trainers can incorporate these steps into training programs are described below. This is followed by a discussion of the role peers and supervisors play in the process.

Self-efficacy is defined as one's belief that he or she can perform a specific task (Bandura, 1986). When individuals believe they are capable of high performance, they are more likely to attempt the appropriate behavior in order to achieve their goals. Self-efficacy has been found to influence performance in a variety of organizational situations, including sales performance (Barling and Beattie, 1983), faculty research productivity (Taylor *et al.*, 1984), perceived career options (Lent, Brown and Larkin, 1986), and the job attendance of unionized workers (Frayne and Latham, 1987; Latham and Frayne, 1989). Low self-efficacy is so detrimental to training success that behavior will not change even when outcome expectancies are high (Frayne and Latham 1987).

## Trainer skills

The discussion of trainer skills is restricted to the trainer's knowledge and ability in taking the necessary steps to ensure high self-efficacy among trainees. Based on empirical findings in clinical and social psychology, Bandura (1982) identified four informational cues which trainers can use to enhance a trainee's self-efficacy beliefs. In descending order of infleunce, they are enactive mastery, vicarious experience, persuasion, and emotional arousal (Bandura, 1986).

### Enactive mastery

The first strategy trainers can use to increase self-efficacy is to focus on the trainee's experiences with the particular task. Positive experiences and success with the task tend to increase self-efficacy, while failures lead to a lowering of efficacy. For example, Bandura (1982) has found that self-efficacy increases when one's experiences fail to validate one's fears, and when the skills one acquires allow mastery over situations that the person once felt threatening. But if in the process of completing a task trainees encounter something that is unexpected and intimidating, or if the experience highlights limitations of their present skills, self-efficacy decreases even if performance was 'successful'. Only as people increase their ability to predict and manage perceived threats do they develop a robust self-assurance that enables them to master subsequent challenges. Thus, it is imperative that trainers arrange subject-matter in such a way that trainees know in advance what they will be taught and that they experience success with the task through active participation with the subject-matter.

### Vicarious experience

A second way self-efficacy can be increased is through vicarious experience, that is, by observing others and then modeling their behavior. Observing others exhibit successful performance increases one's own self-efficacy, particularly when the model is someone with whom the trainee can identify (Bandura, 1986). Behavioral modeling training programs have proven to be especially effective for inculcating supervisory skills (Latham and Saari, 1979; Burke and Day, 1986).

Gist, Schwoerer and Rosen (1989) found that behavioral modeling is an effective training technique because it operates through self-efficacy to influence performance. Observing a model perform specific computer software operations was shown to enhance individuals' beliefs about their own capabilities to use the software correctly.

### Persuasion

A third approach that trainers can use to increase a trainee's self-efficacy is through verbal persuasion. Trainers can focus on methods which teach self-persuasive techniques and take steps to ensure that supervisors and trainers convey to the trainee their confidence in the trainee's ability. One type of self-persuasive technique, cognitive modeling (Meichenbaum, 1975), involves visualizing one's thoughts as one performs an activity. This entails convincing the trainee of his or her competence on a particular task. For example, Gist (1989) has argued that self-censorship can stifle creativity through the cognitive process of self-judgment (e.g. 'my idea is no good'). Thus she argued that cognitive modeling may be more appropriate than behavioral modeling when the performance deficiency is due to inappropriate thoughts rather than overt behavior or skills.

To investigate the effects of cognitive modeling in a training context, Gist (1989) conducted a study on creativity training in a Federal research and development agency. The results of this study showed that, following training, subjects in the cognitive modeling condition had significantly higher self-efficacy than their lecture-trained counterparts. In addition, the cognitive-modeling subjects were superior to the lecture/practice group in generating divergent ideas (Gist, 1989). Thus, cognitive modeling, like the relapse prevention model (Marx, 1982) discussed earlier, encourages trainees to convince themselves of their ability to overcome obstacles by preventing them from acquiring and engaging in specific inappropriate behaviors.

The persuasive effect the trainer can have directly or indirectly influences a trainee's self-efficacy and hence behavior. This point has recently been documented under the rubric of the Pygmalion effect (Eden 1984). For example, Eden and Shani (1982) conducted a field experiment to investigate the Pygmalian effect on Israeli Defense Force trainees. Boot-camp trainees were randomly assigned to one of three conditions where they were described respectively to their instructors as having high, regular, or unknown command potential. The results of this study showed that those trainees who were designated as having high command potential performed significantly higher than the control group on an objective achievement test. Moreover, trainees in the high potential condition reported greater satisfaction with the course and more motivation to continue with the next training course than did their peers in the control group.

A follow-up study by Eden and Ravid (1982) replicated these results and provided further insight into the nature of the Pygmalion effect. Specifically, these authors tested the influence of the Pygmalion effect when manipulated independently on the trainee as well as the trainer. Trainees in clerical courses in the Israeli Defense Force were randomly assigned to one of three conditions where the instructors were informed that trainees had either high potential for success, or regular potential for success, or insufficient information prevented prediction of trainee success. The trainees in the insufficient information condition unbeknown to the trainers, were then randomly assigned to two groups. Specifically, one group was told that they had high potential for success, while the other was told they had regular potential for success. Success in training was subsequently measured by instructor performance appraisal ratings as well as by an objective performance examination.

The results of this study demonstrated highly significant Pygmalion effects for both the instructor-expectancy and trainee-expectancy conditions. Instructor expectancy accounted for 52% of the variance in mean performance ratings; trainee expectancy (i.e. self-efficacy) accounted for 35% of the variance. As for the objective performance exam, instructor expectancy accounted for 27% of the variance in scores; trainee-expectancy accounted for 30% of the variance. Interestingly these results persisted despite a change in instructors midway through the training course who were unaware of the Pygmalion manipulation. Thus, the effects of the initial expectancy induction 'carried over' to the relief instructors whose expectations had not been experimentally manipulated.

The results of these two studies show the effects of trainer beliefs on trainee beliefs and behavior. Trainers who have high expectations of trainees can communicate these expectations in a myriad of ways (e.g. attention, verbal persuasion). A trainee who believes that others think highly of his or her capabilities develops a strong sense of self-efficacy and thus exhibits high performance. Taking steps to persuade trainees that they have the capability to perform well would appear to serve as an antidote to a trainer or supervisor who does not think highly of a trainee's performance potential.

*Emotional arousal*

A fourth method of influencing self-efficacy is emotional arousal. Trainers, however, need to be aware that high levels of anxiety may debilitate one's sense of personal efficacy, and therefore lead to decreased levels of performance, especially on complex tasks (Huber, 1985). For this reason, goal setting can be a double-edged sword.

Empirical studies conducted in a wide variety of contexts have consistently shown that setting specific difficult, but attainable, goals leads to high performance (Locke and Latham, 1990). This is due in part to the fact that trainees' perception of their performance is measured against the goals that are set. Depressive reactions often arise from stringent standards of self-evaluation. Trainees who are prone to 'giving up' are often people who self-impose high performance demands and then devalue their accomplishments because they fall short of their exacting goals (Bandura and Cervone, 1983). Nevertheless, goal setting is important for increasing a trainee's self-efficacy because without specific goals people have little basis for judging how they are doing, or for gauging their capabilities. Self-motivation is sustained by adopting specific attainable subgoals that lead to large future goals (Bandura, 1982; Locke and Latham, 1990). Subgoal attainment provides clear markers of progress, which in turn verifies a growing sense of self-efficacy. Thus, it is important that the trainer should coach trainees to set specific goals that are difficult but attainable.

Trainers, however, must distinguish between process (i.e. behavioral) and outcome (i.e. result achieved) goals. Outcome goals (e.g. make 10 widgets) can be detrimental to the learning process if they are set in the early phases of skill acquisition. Learning theorists describe skill acquisition as a three-phase process: (a) declarative knowledge; (b) knowledge compilation; and (c) procedural knowledge (Adams, 1987; Anderson, 1982, 1983). Kanfer and Ackerman (1989) found that the effectiveness of outcome goals was moderated by the attentional demands of each specific learning stage. The higher the attentional demands of the learning stage, the less effective the setting of an outcome goal is on behavior.

In the first phase of learning (declarative knowledge), the trainee acquires a basic understanding (through lecture or observation of task performance) of what is required to perform the task. During the second phase of learning (knowledge compilation), the trainee integrates the sequences of cognitive and motor processes required to perform the task. Performance improvement results from task practice and trying out various methods of simplifying or reducing each task component. In the third phase of skill acquisition, procedural knowledge occurs when the learner has essentially automatized the skill.

The success of an outcome goal intervention may depend on the attentional demands of the learning phase (Kanfer and Ackerman, 1989). Because the declarative knowledge phase involves high attentional demands, it is difficult for trainees to concentrate on additional information-processing demands such as the strategies for attaining outcome goals. As performance stabilizes during knowledge compilation and procedural knowledge stages, attentional demands are reduced and attention may be shifted to other areas without substantial decrements in performance.

To test these propositions, Kanfer and Ackerman (1989) investigated the effects of performance outcome goals during different stages of the learning process. Since the self-regulation required in attaining a specific performance outcome requires attentional demands, the authors hypothesized that attentional resources would be diverted from the learning task. Kanfer and Ackerman tested this hypothesis using Air Force trainees who were learning an air traffic control computer simulation task. The task involved accepting and landing planes on appropriate runways based on specific rules (e.g. weather conditions, amount of fuel) over 10 trials. In a series of experiments, subjects received either no goal (do your best), or an outcome goal on early trials (achieve score of 2200 during trials 5, 6, and 7). The results showed that only outcome goals assigned after initial learning had taken place exerted a significant positive effect on task performance.

To summarize, trainers must ensure an optimal level of arousal by setting outcome goals only after the learning process is near completion. The setting of outcome goals during the later phases in the learning process directs trainees' attention toward effective performance strategies, and helps to create a robust sense of self-efficacy. Research is needed on the effects of setting process goals (e.g. goals which provide behavioral task strategies) during different phases of the learning process. Interactions with peers may provide trainees with appropriate behavioral goals for performance attainment.

**Peer group**

A potent force in the socialization process within an organization is the interactive dynamics between the individual and his or her peers. Such interaction can provide support and reinforcement for not only learning what is being taught in the training program, but also applying what was learned in training to the job. Conversely, failure to secure such support can result in alienation during training and/or on the job. For example, an early study by Lippitt (1949) on training for participation in community affairs found that those people who had been members of training teams were significantly more active in community affairs subsequent to training than those who had been trained alone. In addition, Evan (1963) found that avoidable terminations were significantly lower when a trainee was assigned to a department with two or more trainees than when the person was assigned to a department either alone or with only one other trainee. These findings suggest that a trainee who has the substantive support of other trainees will have higher self-efficacy and superior coping mechanisms to deal with the stresses created by a new or redesigned job than would be the case without such support.

Few studies to our knowledge have been conducted on the optimal peer-group size for training effectiveness. However, since it is known that enactive mastery is crucial for bringing about high self-efficacy, it would appear safe to conclude that the training class should be small enough to allow ample practice with the subject-matter that is being taught. For example, cooperative learning involves training in pairs or in small groups in which trainees help one another learn (Slavin, 1983).

In a review of 46 studies conducted in school settings, Slavin (1983) found that 63% showed cooperative learning methods to have significantly positive effects on student achievement, 33% found no differences between cooperative and individual methods, and 4% found higher achievement for individual methods. The advantages of cooperative learning are that: (a) it facilitates learning through discussion; (b) it builds rapport among trainees; (c) it cuts training time in half; and (d) group members share goals (Lookatch, 1989). As Lookatch pointed out 'cooperative learning leads to cooperative working' (p. 66). Pairing trainees from different departments provides an opportunity for an organization-wide idea exchange and encourages networking between employees in different departments.

Few empirical studies on cooperative learning have been conducted in an organizational context. An exception is a study by Saxe (1988) who investigated the effects of peer interaction and incentives on learning how to interpret a financial annual report. One hundred and six employees at a major California bank were randomly assigned to one of six conditions according to the degree of peer interaction (high interaction, moderate interaction, and no structured interaction) and type of monetary incentive (group or indidivual). The type of incentive offered had no effect on trainee performance. However, the people in groups with moderate levels of interaction performed significantly better on a written performance test than either the people in the high- or low-level interaction groups. These findings suggest that an excess of interaction may produce social loafing (Latane, Williams and Harkins, 1979). In other words, the high-level interaction subjects might have focused on pooling answers rather than concentrating on ensuring that all team members understood the material (Saxe, 1988).

No studies to our knowledge have been conducted on the optimal composition of the training group in terms of learning effectiveness. However, there is indirect evidence suggesting that the trainees should be comparable in attitude and skill prior to entering the training class. For example, Langer (1979) found that the mere presence of a highly confident person can sometimes undermine the effective use of routine skills. Related to the research on the Pygmalion effect, Langer found that when people were assigned inferior labels that implied limited competence, they performed activities at which they were skilled less well than when they were not so labelled.

With regard to the goal-setting process, there is evidence to suggest that trainees should make their goals known to peers as a way of increasing goal commitment. For example, Hayes et al.'s (1985) students set goals on the number of questions they would answer correctly on reading passages of the Graduate Record Examination (GRE). Students in the public condition handed their goals to the experimenter, who then read them aloud. Students in the private condition deposited their goals into an anonymous box. Although the goal difficulty levels of the public and private conditions were not significantly different, the public goal group performed significantly better than the private goal group.

In another study investigating the effects of public goal commitment, Hollenbeck, Williams and Klein's (1989) subjects set goals for the grade point average (GPA) they would obtain the following quarter. Subjects were randomly assigned to either a public goal or a private goal condition. In the public goal condition, students' GPA goals were distributed to other individuals within that condition and a copy of their respective goals was sent to a self-determined significant other. The results of this study revealed that subjects in the public goal condition had higher goal commitment than those in the private goal condition. Further, there was a significant effect for commitment on performance independent of goal level.

Taken together, these findings suggest that interactions with peers can facilitate learning through both the discussion of the subject matter and public commitment to performance goals. When designing training programs, trainers should consider both the composition of the trainee groups and the amount of peer interaction which will maximize trainee learning.

## Supervisory support

Another social factor critical to training effectiveness is supervisory support. To increase the probability of transfer of training to the workplace, supervisors need to reinforce the application of what was learned in training to the job. To do this effectively, the supervisors must be fully aware of the training objectives as well as the content of the training for attaining those objectives. Although we know of no research on the subject, it has been our experience that this can be done effectively when a supervisor serves as either the trainer or co-trainer. This not only increases supervisory understanding of and appreciation for the training, but it increases trainee outcome expectancies that demonstrating the learned skills will be valued by the organization.

When the trainee returns to the job, supervisors should adopt the same strategies as those used by trainers in the classroom. That is, early task assignments should be given to allow the employee to experience success in applying the newly acquired skills. The supervisor should continually model skills of exhibiting the verbal and non-verbal cues that connote a positive expectation that the employee will constantly apply the newly acquired knowledge and skills and that the trainee will be able to do this well. As discussed earlier, observational learning and verbal persuasion provided by the supervisor are critical for maintaining high employee self-efficacy. Moreover, the supervisor should coach the employee to set specific difficult but attainable goals. These goals should be made public.

One way to publicize commitment to training objectives is for both the supervisor and the trainee to sign a contract which explicitly lists the long-term goals of the training program and the conditions under which the learned behavior will occur on the job (Leifer and Newstrom, 1980). By setting goals in advance, the trainee can focus his or her attention on the important components of the training program content. In addition, having supervisors publicly commit to the objectives of the training program helps to increase their investment to the outcome of training. The contracted goals should be specific and measurable so that progress toward the goals can be evaluated through the use of behavioral-based performance appraisals such as behavioral observation scales (Latham and Wexley, 1991).

## FINAL REMARKS

The underlying theme of this chapter is that if training is to be effective, it cannot be viewed as an isolated set of activities within an organization. It must affect and be affected by the organization's culture, strategy, structure, and human resource systems.

Culture refers to the values, often unwritten, that senior level management wish to infuse throughout the organization. Included in this culture are written statements regarding the organization's vision and mission. For training to be viewed as effective by senior management, training programs must be tied directly to the vision and mission statements. In short, training objectives must be tied to 'business purpose'. Values are not always easily articulated: vision and mission statements are often expressed at high levels of abstraction. Training departments, through an organizational analysis, can be invaluable in developing strategies for clearly communicating and instilling these values throughout a diverse workforce.

The processes for attaining training objectives must be imbedded in the corporate strategy. These processes must take into account ways of maximizing trainee learning that reflect demographic and individual differences so as to maximize the transfer of what is learned to the job. The extent to which the latter is accomplished is affected directly by other human resources systems such as staffing, performance appraisal, and compensation.

Staffing can have an adverse effect on training if the people hired and placed in an organization lack the aptitude to learn what is required of them. Training affects staffing in two ways. First, it often serves as the criterion for ascertaining whether the right person or persons were hired in terms of trainability. Second, it develops and facilitates the growth of the aptitudes that the person brings to the organization. Thus, staffing and training are interconnected in that both are designed to increase the probability that employees will be able to execute the role behaviors needed for the attainment of the organization's goals.

The late Mason Haire, an industrial psychologist who served on the faculties of Berkeley and MIT, is credited with the maxim 'that which gets measured gets done'. Of importance to training is the fact that that which gets appraised and rewarded gets performed on the job. Thus, appraisal and compensation systems can facilitate or hinder the transfer of training. Training in turn, can affect these two systems by teaching managers to give constructive feedback, to set specific goals, and to reward their people properly. In addition, trainers can help develop appraisal instruments that reflect the organization's values as well as the behaviors that must be engaged in to implement the corporate strategy. As noted earlier in this chapter, organizations often spend too much time developing vision statements and strategy and far too little time on the systems that need to be put in place to ensure that the strategy is implemented.

It was Chandler (1962) who originally pointed out that structure usually follows strategy: in particular that a strategy of diversity fosters a decentralized structure. A decentralized structure characterizes many organizations of the 1990s. The result has been fragmented training programs and an inflation of training budgets to meet the needs of relatively autonomous businesses within the organization. Training departments can bring unity to such situations by retaining a focus on the overall culture and vision of the organization. This can be done by getting the key managers from each business to reach consensus on the commonalities among their different strategies for attaining the overall corporate mission, developing training processes for inculcating these commonalities in employees, ensuring that the appraisal and reward systems reinforce the acquisition and demonstration of knowledge and skills, and removing barriers in the environment to this demonstration.

## SUMMARY AND CONCLUSIONS

1. Choosing between selection versus training as a strategy for ensuring that employees can perform their jobs effectively is unnecessary. Both valid selection techniques and effective training programs should be used regardless of economic conditions.
2. As the workforce becomes diverse in race, age, and sex, cross-cultural training programs traditionally applied to people before transferring them to a foreign country may be adapted to organizations operating within their home country. Such training would appear especially applicable in Canada, the United States, and Israel where there is, respectively, a lack of understanding of values between French and English, Hispanic and English, and Arab and Jewish employees who are interacting with one another on the job. In addition, an increasing number of organizations will need to develop programs which train undereducated youth in basic

skills, as well as find ways to reduce skill obsolescence among older employees.

3. The definition of training effectiveness may need to be expanded beyond a sole focus on the individual's immediate job to include the attainment of an organization's strategy. A recent article on the front page of the *Wall Street Journal* bemoaned the overemphasis in developing corporate strategy and the under-emphasis on the training of people to achieve it. Training programs must be designed to complement the organization's competitive strategy.

4. The lack of training effectiveness and hence the waste of an organization's training dollars may be attributed in part to the lack of appreciation within organization cultures for the importance of theory to guide training programs. Social cognitive theory (Bandura, 1986) suggests that trainers should give equal emphasis to cognition, environment, and behavior, and the reciprocal determinism among them when developing and implementing training procedures.

5. The contingencies of reinforcement should be made clear to trainees prior to training. In this way high outcome expectancies can be created so that trainees are motivated to learn and demonstrate the acquired behavior. The reinforcement for desired behavior should be tied where possible to a merit pay play as well as to promotional opportunities. At a minimum, the organization needs to describe explicitly the positive consequences for the individual performing the learned behavior on the job so that outcome expectancies are high.

6. The organization should pay as much attention to ways of minimizing environmental constraints on exercising newly acquired behavior as it does to ensuring that the trainees learn the desired knowledge and skill. Conducting an environmental needs assessment and clearing barriers to skill transfer is critical to the success of the training program.

7. The financial health of the organization directly influences the amount of budgtetary support available for training. Executives are beginning to realize, however, that investment in training programs is critical to the achievement of the organization's long-range goals and financial well-being. Because utility analysis models used to evaluate training based on dollars are currently of questionable value, human resource specialists must learn to document success or failure of training programs in terms of observable changes in trainee behavior.

8. The extant research clearly demonstrates the importance of designing training programs which facilitate the development of self-efficacy, a key variable in social cognitive theory. If a robust sense of self-efficacy is developed during the training process, trainees are more likely to demonstrate the learned behavior on the job. Enactive mastery experience,

vicarious experiences, persuasion, and moderate arousal levels are four effective ways of increasing self-efficacy.

9. Trainers can use these strategies by arranging the subject-matter in such a way that trainees experience early success through active participation in the subject-matter. First, trainers must design training programs which incorporate positive enactive mastery experiences. Second, trainers can ensure that models who are similar to the trainees are used to demonstrate the desired behaviors. Third, trainers must convey positive expectations of trainee performance. Fourth, trainers need to coach trainees to set specific goals that are difficult but attainable.

10. With regard to goal setting, outcome goals are effective only when the trainee has the requisite skills to perform the task. During initial stages of learning, outcome goals may divert attention away from the task at hand. When performance stabilizes, trainees are able to devote adequate attention to the outcome goal and improve their performance through self-regulation. In the interim, only process goals should be set. The importance of goal setting in achieving high trainee performance and transfer to the work setting cannot be overemphasized.

11. Peers can also be used as a method for increasing a person's self-efficacy and commitment to training goals. This can be done by placing a trainee in a cooperative learning setting and providing opportunities for peer interaction on the job.

12. The influence of the supervisor can have a pivotal effect on the success or failure of a training program. First, supervisors must communicate with top management to ensure that training is consistent with the long-range strategy of the organization, and that financial incentives and promotional opportunities will be available to successful trainees. Second, the supervisor must attend to the removal of situational constraints, and to the design of a social environment that is conducive to the transfer of training. Finally, supervisors can directly motivate employee performance subsequent to training by setting goals, monitoring trainee progress through formal and informal feedback, and taking steps to maintain high employee self-efficacy on the learned-task.

# REFERENCES

Adams, J. A. (1987). Historical review and appraisal of research on the learning, retention, and transfer of human motor skills, *Psychological Bulletin*, **101**, 41–74.

Anderson, J. R. (1982). Acquisition of a cognitive skill, *Psychological Review*, **89**, 369–406.

Anderson, J. R. (1983). *The Architecture of Cognition*, Cambridge, MA: Harvard University Press.

Arnett, E. C. (1989). Futurists gaze into business's crystal ball, *Washington Post*, 20 July, F1–F2.

Arvey, R. D. and Cole, D. (1989). Evaluating change due to training. In I. L. Goldstein (ed.). *Training and Development in Work Organizations: Frontiers of industrial and organizational psychology*, pp. 89–118, San Francisco, LA: Josey Bass.

Bandura, A. (1977), *Social Learning Theory*. Englewood Cliffs, NJ: Prentice-Hall.

Bandura, A. (1982). Self-efficacy mechanism in human agency, *American Psychologist*, **37**, 122–147.

Bandura, A. (1986). *Social Foundations of Thought and Action*, Englewood Cliffs, NJ: Prentice-Hall.

Bandura, A. and Cervone, D. (1983). Self-evaluative and self-efficacy mechanisms governing the motivational effects of goal systems. *Journal of Personality and Social Psychology*, **45**, 1017–1028.

Barling, J. and Beattie, R. (1983). Self-efficacy beliefs and sales performance, *Journal of Organizational Behavior Management*, **5**, 41–51.

Berlin, G. B. (1983). *Not Working: Unskilled youth and displaced adults*. New York: Ford Foundation.

Berryman-Fink, C. (1985). Male and female managers' views of the communication skills and training needs of women in management. *Public Personnel Management*, **14**, 307–313.

Boudreau, J. W. (1983). Economic considerations in estimating the utility of human resource productivity programs, *Personnel Psychology*, **3**, 551–576.

Brown, G. F. and Read, A. R. (1984). Personnel and training policies—some lessons for Western companies, *Long Range Planning*, **17**(2), 48–57.

Burke, M. J. and Day, R. R. (1986). A cumulative study of the effectiveness of managerial training, *Journal of Applied Psychology*, **71**, 232–246.

*Business Week* editorial (1986). Automation needs a speedup and so does retraining. *Business Week*, 29 September, 132.

Caplow, T. (1983). *Managing an Organization*, New York: Holt, Rinehart and Winston.

Cascio, W. F. (1989). The use of utility approaches as an evaluation model. In I. L. Goldstein (ed.). *Training and Development in Work Organizations: Frontiers of Industrial and Organizational Psychology*, pp. 63–88. San Francisco. CA: Jossey Bass.

Chandler, A. D. (1962). *Strategy and Structure: Chapters in the History of the American Industrial Enterprise*. Cambridge, Mass: MIT Press.

Downs, B. (1983). Industrial training. In A. P. O. Williams (ed.). *Using Personnel Research*. Aldershot Hants, England: Gower.

Dreher, G. F. and Sackett, P. R. (eds) (1983). *Perspectives on Employee Staffing and Selection*. Homewood, Ill.: Irwin.

Eden, D. (1984). Self-fulfilling prophecy as a management tool: Harnessing Pygmalion, *Academy of Management Journal*, **9**, 64–73.

Eden, D. and Ravid, G. (1982). Pygmalion v. self-expectancy: Effects of instructor and self-expectancy on trainee performance, *Organizational Behavior and Human Performance*, **30**, 351–364.

Eden, D. and Shani, A. B. (1982). Pygmalion goes to boot camp: Expectancy, leadership, and trainee performance, *Journal of Applied Psychology*, **67**, 194–199.

Evan, W. M. (1963). Peer-groups interaction and organizational socialization: A study of employee turnover, *American Sociological Review*, **28**, 436–440.

Fossum, J. A., Arvey, R. D., Paradise, C. A. and Robbins, N. E. (1986). Modeling the skills obsolescence process, *Academy of Management Review*, **11**, 362–374.

Frayne, C. A. and Latham, G. P. (1987). Application of social learning theory to employee self-management of attendance, *Journal of Applied Psychology*, **72**, 387–392.

Georgenson, D. L. (1982). The problem of transfer calls for partnership, *Training and Development Journal*, **36**, 75–78.

Gist, M. E. (1989). The influence of training method on self-efficacy and idea generation among managers, *Personnel Psychology*, **42**, 787–806.

Gist, M. E., Rosen, B. and Schwoerer, C. (1988). The influence of training methods and trainee age on the acquisition of computer skills, *Personnel Psychology*, **41**, 255–265.

Gist, M. E., Schwoerer, C. and Rosen, B. (1989). Effects of alternative training methods on self-efficacy and performance in computer software training, *Journal of Applied Psychology*, **74**, 884–891.

Goldstein, I. L. and Gilliam, P. (1990). Trianing system issues in the year 2000. *American Psychologist*, **45**, 134–143.

Hayes, S. C., Rosenfarb, I., Wulfert, E., Munt, E. D., Korn, Z. and Zettle, R. D. (1985). Self-reinforcement effects: An artifact of social standard setting? *Journal of Behavior Analysis*, **18**, 201–214.

Hanlon, M. H. (1990). Review of L. Dyer, 'Human Resource Management', *Personnel Psychology*, **43**, 166–168.

Haveman, R. H. and Saks, D. H. (1985). Transatlantic lessons for employment and training policy, *Industrial Relations*, **24**, 20–36.

Heneman, R. (1990). Merit pay research. In K. M. Rowland and G. R. Ferris (eds). *Research in Personnel and Human Resourcesa Management*, Vol. 8, Greenwich, CT: JAI Press.

Hinrichs, J. R. (1970). Two approaches to filling the management gap, *Personnel Journal*, **49**, 1008–1014.

Hollenbeck, J. R., Williams, C. R. and Klein, H. J. (1989). An empirical examination of the antecedents to commitment to difficult goals, *Journal of Applied Psychology*, **74**, 18–23.

Howard, A. and Bray, D. (1988). *Managerial Lines in Transition*, New York: Guilford Press.

Huber, V. L. (1985). Effects of task difficulty, goal setting, and strategy on performance of a heuristic task, *Journal of Applied Psychology*, **70**, 492–504.

Hussey, D. E. (1985). Implementing corporate strategy: Using management education and training, *Long Range Planning*, **18**(5), 28–37.

Jackson, S. E., Schuler, R. S., and Rivero, J. C. (1989). Organizational characteristics as predictors of personnel practices, *Personnel Psychology*, **42**, 727–785.

Johnston, W. B. and Packer, A. H. (1987). *Workforce 2000: Work and Workers for the Twenty-first Century*. Indianapolis, IN: Hudson Institute.

Kanfer, R. and Ackerman, P. (1989). Motivation and cognitive abilities: An integrative/aptitude-treatment interaction approach to skill acquisition, *Journal of Applied Psychology*, **74**, 657–690.

Kelly, H. B. (1982). The problem of transfer calls for partnership, *Training and Development Journal*, **36**, 102–106.

Kruger, P. (1990). A game plan for the future, *Working Women*, supplement, January.

Langer, E. J. (1979). The illusion of incompetence. In L. C. Perlmutter and R. A. Monty (eds). *Choice and Perceived Control*. Hillsdale, NJ: Erlbaum.

Latane, B., Williams, K. and Harkins, S. (1979). Many hands make light the work: The causes and consequences of social loafing, *Journal of Personality and Social Psychology*, **37** 823–832.

Latham, G. P. (1988). Human resource training and development, *Annual Review of Psychology*, **39**, 545–582.

Latham, G. P. and Frayne, C. A. (1989). Self-management training for increasing job attendance: A follow-up and a replication, *Journal of Applied Psychology*, **74**, 411–416.

Latham, G. P. and Huber, V. L. (in press). Schedules of reinforcement: Lessons from the past and issues for the future, *Journal of Organizational Behavior Management*.

Latham, G. P. and Saari, L. M. (1979). Application of social-learning theory to training supervisors through behavioral modeling, *Journal of Applied Psychology*, **64**, 239–246.

Latham, G. P. and Wexley, K. N. (1991). *Increasing Productivity Through Performance Appraisal*. Reading, MA: Addison-Wesley Publishing Co.

Leifer, M. and Newstrom, J. W. (1980). Solving the transfer of training problem, *Training and Development Journal*, August 34–42.

Lent, R. W., Brown, B. D. and Larkin, K. C. (1987). Comparison of three theoretically derived variables in predicting career and academic behavior: Self-efficacy, interest congruence, and consequence thinking, *Journal of Counseling Psychology*, **34**, 293–298.

Lippitt, R. (1949). *Training in Community Relations: A Research Exploration toward new group skills*. New York: Harper.

Locke, E. A. and Latham, G. P. (1990). *A Theory of Goal Setting and Task Performance*, Prentice-Hall: Englewood Cliffs, NJ.

Lookatch, R. P. (1989). Options for interactive video, *Training and Development Journal*, December, 65–67.

Marby, M. (1990). Past tokenism, *Newsweek*, **115**(20), 37–43.

Marx, R. D. (1982). Relapse prevention for managerial training: A model for maintenance of behavior change, *Academy of Management Review*, **7**, 433–441.

Mealiea, L. W. and Duffy, J. (1985). Contemporary training and development practices in Canadian firms. Presented at Annual Meeting Atlantic School of Business, Halifax.

Meichenbaum, D. (1975). Enhancing creativity by modifying what subjects say to themselves, *American Educational Research Journal*, **12**, 129–145.

Offermann, L. R. and Gowing, M. K. (1990). Organizations of the future: Changes and challenges, *American Psychologist*, **45**, 95–108.

Peters, L. H., Chassie, M. B., Lindholm, H. R., O'Connor, E. J. and Kline, C. R. (1982). The joint influence of situational constraints and goal setting on performance and affective outcomes *Journal of Management* **8**, 7–20.

Peters, L. H., O'Connor, E. J. and Eulberg, J. R. (1985). Situational constraints: Sources, consequences, and future considerations. In G. Ferris and K. Rowland (eds). *Research in Personnel and Human Resources Management*, Vol. 3, pp. 79–114.

Porter, M. E. (1980). *Competitive Strategy*. New York: Free Press.

Robinson, D. G. and Robinson, J. C. (1985). Breaking barriers to skill transfer, *Training and Development Journal*, **39**, 82–83.

Ropp, K. (1987). Restructuring: Survival of the fittest. *Personnel Administrator*, February, 45–47.

Sandroff, R. (1990). Why it won't be business as usual, *Working Woman*, supplement, January.

Saxe, S. (1988). Peer influence and learning, *Training and Development Journal*, **42**, 40–53.

Schuler, R. S. and Huber, V. L. (1990). *Personnel and Human Resource Management*, St Paul, MN: West.

Schuler, R. S. and Jackson, S. E. (1987). Linking competitive strategies with human resource management practices, *Academy of Management Executive*, **1**, 207–219.

Skryzycki, C. (1989). The drive to downsize, *Washington Post*, 20 August, B1.

Slavin, R. (1983). When does cooperative learning increase student achievement? *Psychological Bulletin*, **94**, 429–445.

Sticht, T. G., Armstrong, W. B., Hickey, D. T. and Caylor, J. S. (1987). *Cast Off Youth*. New York: Praeger.

Taylor, M. S., Locke, E. A., Lee, C. and Gist, M. E. (1984). Type A behavior and faculty research productivity: What are the mechanisms? *Organizational Behavior and Human Decision Processes*, **34**, 402–418.

Tenopyr, M. L. (1987). Policies and Strategies Underlying a Personnel Research Operation. Paper presented at the Annual Meeting of the Society for Industrial—Organizational Psychology, Atlanta.

Tucker, F. D. (1985). A study of the training needs of older workers: Implications for human resources development planning, *Public Personnel Management*, **14**, 85–95.

US Bureau of Labour Statistics (1987). *Press Release* (No. 87–345, August). Washington, DC: US Department of Labor.

Wexley, K. N. and Latham, G. P. (1991). *Developing and Training Human Resources in Organizations*. New York: Harper and Row.

# Chapter 10

# Review and outlook

**Dennis H. Holding[1] and John E. Morrison[2]**
[1]*University of Louisville,* [2]*Human Resources Research Organization*

At this point it seems appropriate to reconsider, at least in outline, some of the principal issues that have emerged in the preceding chapters. There are many different considerations that bear on the efficiency with which trainees can be moved from an initial lack of competence to a final level of acceptable performance. The book began by describing the basic theory and research on acquisition, retention, and transfer of skill, and the manner in which practice may be arranged to facilitate learning. After considering the complex taxonomies needed to describe task and trainee characteristics, the focus shifted to the essential background issues of training media and organizational variables. There is clearly a need to review some of these topics, in order both to provide an overall perspective on training issues and to reinforce some of the more important points that have been raised by the earlier contributors. At the same time, it has seemed incumbent upon us to attempt some brief forecasts of the directions likely to be taken in training research, and to draw attention to further changes that might be expected in training practice.

## REVIEW

As the introductory discussion by Morrison (Chapter 1) made clear, research and practice in training have undergone tremendous changes in the past 25 years. For one, the theoretical basis for training research has changed from a behavioristic conception of learning to a more cognitive explanation. Morrison argues that whereas cognitive theory has deepened our understanding of training processes, we must not discard useful training technologies and methods derived from the earlier behavioristic conception of learning. During the past 25 years, there have also been changes in the workplace, particularly those caused by increasing automation. These changes have focused new or revived interest toward topics such as the learning and retention of procedures, the identification of cognitive training requirements, and the performance of time-shared tasks. Despite these changes, training research must

*Training for Performance: Principles of Applied Human Learning.* Edited by J. E. Morrison
© 1991 John Wiley & Sons Ltd

still be concerned with basic issues such as the acquisition, retention, and transfer of skills.

Since the purpose of training is to impart necessary skills, it is obvious that training research must be based on an understanding of the mechanisms involved in the acquisition of skill. Writing on skill acquisition has undergone fundamental changes during the last decades, resulting in the cognitive approach described by Annett (Chapter 2). From this perspective, the theory of skill acquisition must distinguish between declarative and procedural knowledge, that is, between facts and their application. Acquisition seems to proceed by stages and, although it is not clear exactly how these stages are to be characterized, it seems that either the three-stage progression originally advanced by Fitts (1964), or at least a progression from more controlled to more automatic processing, must be reckoned as staple components of skill acquisition. However, Annett cautions against the proposal put forth by Anderson (1982) and others that learning is defined as the conversion of declarative (verbal) knowledge into procedural (motor) knowledge. Annett proposes instead a composite model of motor skill acquisition and performance wherein motor and verbal components may develop in parallel. He marshalled both behavioral and physiological data in support of his two-process theory.

Once acquired, skills must be retained, often for very long periods. As Schendel and Hagman explain in Chapter 3, there is a surprisingly large amount of research on the retention problem. In some cases, the research literature shows similar findings for verbal and motor retention; for instance, the test trials have similar effects on the retention of verbal and motor performance. Unfortunately, the results of much research, most of which is concerned with applied problems, show a rather poor fit with the results emanating from verbal learning. Because motor skill and verbal learning impose rather different information loads, typically have different rehearsal characteristics, and differ in other ways, it remains difficult to compare directly verbal and skill retention. Indeed, it is difficult to fit the existing findings into any neat theoretical mold. One difficulty in skill retention research is that skill acquisition processes are frequently discussed apart from retention processes. Schendel and Hagman object to the arbitrary separation of the two concepts arguing that many variables that increase acquisition (e.g. number of repetitions) also elevate retention levels. Interestingly, a functional dissociation of acquisition and retention effects can be attained with certain variables such as the schedule of repetitions. For instance, a massed training schedule facilitates the acquisition of skill whereas spaced training promotes its retention. Schendel and Hagman maintain that these dissociations are important because they point to training variables that have a lasting effect on performance as opposed to those whose effect is only transitory.

The transfer of training is a perennial problem, since training is virtually always conducted in conditions different from those obtaining in the real, target activity. In Chapter 4, Holding shows how one-shot transfer studies differ from those measuring extended savings, and discusses the measurement issues that often confuse interpretations of transfer results. The principles of transfer are simple enough in outline, because people tend to do the same thing in the same circumstances, as when current conditions resemble those of original learning. However, exact predictions are difficult to make in many practical situations. Transfer seems to diminish when the similarities between conditions are relatively abstract, and cases of asymmetrical transfer are difficult to handle except by pitting inclusion effects against the effects of differing performance standards. Negative transfer, where not artifactual, can be viewed as increasing with similarity, but is usually a temporary phenomenon arising from intrusion errors. Recent studies have concentrated on positive transfer, attempting to identify underlying cognitive mechanisms such as schemata, mental models, or production systems.

Although learning, retention, and transfer processes can be discussed in the abstract, the purpose of training is to provide specific instructional events to facilitate those processes. Patrick (Chapter 5) describes task analysis as a process that is the essential prerequisite to the development of such instructional events. He discusses two general types of analytic methods that can be used to define training objectives. The first is non-psychological and task oriented in nature and is used to specify training needs, objectives, and content. The second type of analysis is psychological in nature and is used to select trainees, design training, and elaborate on the content of tasks. Patrick discusses examples of both types of analyses, although clearly the effectiveness of any classification scheme depends on the purpose for which it is adopted. He notes that a particular problem is posed by the analysis of complex tasks. Although some ingenious analyses have been performed on individual cognitive tasks, no codified set of analytic procedures exists to apply across tasks. Such procedures would seem to provide a fruitful area for future research.

Chapter 6 provides examples of how the results from careful task analyses can provide the basis for effective learning strategies. Lintern defines a learning strategy as the systematic arrangement of practice events for training. The issues here include those arising from the use of part-task training techniques, which have recently experienced a resurgence of interest. In this area of research, the most promising findings usually occur in conditions of segmentation, where training is given on contiguous subsections of an entire task (e.g. Ash and Holding, 1990). Heretofore, much less success has been obtained from part-task training using fragmentation procedures, in which training is targeted to task components that are performed simultaneously. In contrast to these findings, Lintern reviews new research wherein a complex task (Space Fortress) is successfully trained by fragmenting the task into meaningful skill components. In addition to part-task training, Lintern examines the issues related to adaptive training, in which the level of demand is linked to the performance of the trainee. Despite some tremendous initial interest, adaptive training principles have apparently failed to yield successful training techniques. A more promising technique is adaptive augmented feedback, wherein the trainee is provided cues for off-target performance. Careful analyses of flight tasks have also identified situations in which skills can be learned and effectively transferred under low-fidelity simulation conditions. The latter findings are especially important to the design of effective, yet lower cost training devices.

Whereas Chapter 6 is more directly concerned with the responsibilities of the trainer, Chapter 7 shifts focus to the aptitudes and abilities of the trainee. It should be obvious that the effectiveness of different methods of training must depend on the interactions between the techniques selected and the characteristics of the trainees using them, although the contribution of individual differences is often neglected. This occurs in part because the possibility of personnel selection exists as an alternative to training, or as a supplementary technique that produces training groups more homogeneous than would otherwise be the case. In Chapter 7, Ackerman and Kyllonen effectively integrate training and selection by interpreting individual differences in ability in the context of theoretical processes of learning. This integrated approach has allowed them to address a variety of training problems. For instance, previous research (e.g. Fleishman and Hempel, 1954) has indicated that performance becomes increasingly less predictable from abilities as a function of practice.

Using the three-stage learning model similar to that described by Annett (Chapter 1), Ackerman and Kyllonen describe a model that is successful in predicting performance at beginning, intermediate, and even late stages of learning. They also discuss individual differences in learning abilities in terms of their interaction with types of knowledge and learning environments and their interactions with various training interventions. The goal of this sort of research is to match more closely the content and context of training to differences among trainees in learning aptitudes and abilities. The decreases in skill level of job applicant abilities and skills make it more difficult for employers to select the most desirable trainees. Consequently it will become increasingly important for the trainer to be able to adapt training to individual differences.

A different kind of complexity arises in connection with the impact of different training media. As Kearsley points out in Chapter 8, the manner in which information and skills are imparted to the trainee has a definite impact on what is learned and retained. Different media of communication vary in their efficiency when put to different training purposes. For example, video is especially effective for the presentation of dynamic information about task sequences, and is therefore suitable for training specific procedures. In addition, it seems possible that the form taken by training media introduces an element of context dependency. There is at least suggestive evidence that what is learned, and later remembered and applied, by one method constitutes a functionally different form of knowledge than what is learned by another method. Clearly, the nature of the material to be learned will often determine the medium to be employed. The process of systematically selecting media should be based on these pedagogic factors as well as cost-effectiveness and ergonomic considerations. As Kearsley points out, however, even a well-selected medium will not be successful if it is not implemented effectively. The key factor in implementation appears to be that everyone in the training organization should be well informed about the new training medium.

To a large extent, the implementation problems discussed by Kearsley in Chapter 8 relate to social and organizational issues, which are discussed in a wider context by Latham and Crandall in Chapter 9. They point out that the importance of any particular training scheme can only be appreciated within the wider background of a system of organizational goals and values—that is, the corporate culture. The process of explicitly identifying this system is known as organizational analysis whose purpose is to ensure that training is congruent with the goals of the organization. In other words, Latham and Crandall do not view training as an end in itself; rather, they see training as an integral component of the overall corporate strategy. Despite the importance of training, several organizational and social factors potentially impede the implementation of effective training programs. If the various managers in an organization are brought together to address these problems, the corporate training strategy can serve as a focal point for defining more precise statements of corporate goals.

## OUTLOOK

It is evident that a great deal is known about the detailed conduct of training. A great deal is also known about the process of learning, which might be regarded as a separate issue. Like the literature it reports, the present volume does not maintain a clear distinction between training and learning, between the functions of the trainer and the progress of the learner, between applied work on training and basic research on learning. As discussed in the introduction, the book was organized to start with basic learning issues (acquisition, retention, and transfer) and to transition to more applied training issues on task characteristics, learning strategies, trainee differences, and comparisons of training media. However, it is impractical and unprofitable to attempt any rigid separation between learning and training issues. Training practices are bound to learning principles, and advances in learning theory dictate changes in training procedures. However, it might be forecast that future work on training will concentrate more specifically on functions available to, and learning variables manipulable by, the trainer.

Unfortunately, future research on training is likely to be reduced in volume. Much of the information we possess has been gleaned from three types of sources: academic, industrial, and defense related. Academic researchers have provided a large amount of basic work on learning issues, and a surprisingly large proportion of the research on more applied problems. There seems to be no doubt that academic sources will continue to be active at the present level, perhaps with even greater emphasis on applied contributions. Applied cognitive psychology, for example, continues to make very promising progress. In contrast, industrial sources of research have always been limited, except perhaps in areas related to personnel selection and training systems, and it seems unlikely that the volume of information from these sources will show any appreciable upturn.

The biggest changes may be expected in defense research which, for the best of political reasons, is undergoing severe cuts. Defense funds have hitherto made possible a wide spectrum of research covering basic issues of learning and complex practical issues of training. However, applied research that shows how basic principles of learning relate directly and specifically to demonstrable training needs (e.g. Morrison and Holding, 1990; Wells and Hagman, 1989) is likely to become extremely scarce. Defense cuts in training research are probably misguided, because efficiency in training should be expected to ensure the optimal utilization of limited personnel and equipment resources, but these cuts are unlikely to be reversed in the near future. It is to be hoped that some of the funds lost to defense will eventually be rerouted to research through other agencies, but there is no immediate sign that this is taking place.

With regard to specific training issues, an examination of the previous chapters indicates several overlapping areas of interest. Because of the demonstrable interest in these areas of overlap, we think they point to areas of research that are likely to be fruitful topics in the future. None of these issues is really new; rather, some of these research topics are of continuing interest and require further development, while others are older topics that have been revived recently by looking at them in the light of new theoretical concepts or emerging training problems.

One continuing topic of research is the role of task analysis in determining training requirements. It should be noted that significant progress has already been made in the technology of task analysis. As argued in Chapter 1, traditional task analyses that relied on S–R concepts of learning have been successfully used to determine behavioral training objectives for knowledge-lean procedural tasks. Furthermore, information-processing models, such as

Hierarchical Task Analysis described by Patrick (Chapter 5), have been useful in specifying more complicated, decisional tasks. The new challenge is to describe complex, knowledge-rich domains. The value of detailed analyses of complex tasks is certainly made clear by the success of the learning strategies program described by Lintern (Chapter 6). One problem with 'cognitive' task analysis methods is that they are typically applied to narrow domains of performance. Notable exceptions are some recent attempts to codify cognitive analysis methods for more extensive job domains such as troubleshooting (Glaser et al., 1986) and for air traffic controller skills (Means et al., 1988). Both of these examples of 'cognitive' analyses have theoretical as well as face validity; as suggested in both Chapters 5 and 6, however, the value of such task analytic techniques is in the effectiveness of training interventions derived from them. Evaluation of such training interventions provides an appropriate topic for future research.

Another noticeable trend in the present volume was a continuing interest in the qualitative changes in performance that occur as a function of practice. As noted earlier, Fitts (e.g. 1964) was the first to describe learning as a discontinuous process consisting of three phases. In the first phase, cognitive processes dominate as the learner seeks to understand instruction and learn how to perform the required motor responses. During the second phase, the learner associates responses with specific cues. Verbal mediation is required in the early stages of this phase but may drop out with practice. Finally, the third phase of learning is characterized by gradual but continued increase in performance without any evidence of verbal mediation at all. In a now-classic article, Anderson (1982) interpreted the three phases of skill acquisition observed by Fitts as the conversion of verbally based declarative knowledge into non-verbal procedural knowledge. This point of view is sanctioned by Ackerman and Kyllonen (Chapter 7) and by Latham and Crandall (Chapter 9), and tacitly assumed by other contributors. Annett (Chapter 2) agrees that learning does qualitatively change over practice trials; however, he does not agree that learning is the conversion of declarative into procedural knowledge. His model of performance holds that verbal and non-verbal components of perforance coexist in interconnected but independent systems. Clearly, future research should be designed to clarify the theoretical mechanisms that underlie the qualitative changes in knowledge and performance that occur with practice.

Another future research topic suggested by the present volume is the further explication of the mechanisms of mental practice. The effectiveness of such internal rehearsal was recognized by Holding (1965) as having practical utility in the review of training principles, although its rationale was poorly understood at the time. The military has more recently recognized that mental practice is reliably associated with increases in motor performance and that its utility in military training should be systematically investigated (Druckman and Swets, 1988). Indeed, such work has already been performed in the context of rifle marksmanship (Heller, in preparation) and tank gunnery (Morrison and Walker, 1990). In the present volume, Schendel and Hagman (Chapter 3) speculate that mental practice may be a cost-effective method for sustaining motor performance. Furthermore, Annett (Chapter 2) points out that the phenomenon is important not only as a technique for performance enhancement, but also as a paradigm for the more general issues of how thoughts are translated into actions. Modern cognitive psychology and modern physiological studies might be expected to clarify further the nature of the underlying mechanisms. Further developments of this topic are to be expected.

Team training was a research topic generating much interest in the 1960s (e.g. Boguslaw and Porter, 1962; Briggs and Naylor, 1965; Klaus and Glaser, 1968). The present volume indicates that interest in this topic may be revived in the near future. In Chapter 3, Schendel and Hagman propose that team training should have a beneficial effect on skill retention. Kearsley (Chapter 8) indicates how group interactions can be facilitated by computer-based training and communication. Finally, Latham and Crandall (Chapter 9) describe the social benefits of training in small groups. These discussions indicate that there are two separate rationales for team training. One reason for training individuals in teams is simply because their job is performed in a team context. The implied rationale for team training in this case is that training in a team context maintains the similarity between training and job performance and therefore promotes skill transfer. The second reason individuals are trained in groups is to facilitate learning: although the exact mechanism for this effect is unknown, the beneficial effects of training in small teams is well documented in the literature on cooperative learning (e.g. Slavin, 1983). Future research on team training should focus on the interaction of these two approaches. For instance, should the make-up of a small training group consist of those in job teams only, or should teams be comprised of those whose characteristics would enhance cooperative learning effects?

Another new emphasis in training research is an increasing reliance on physiological theorizing. For instance Annett (Chapter 2) uses physiological evidence to support the dissociation of cognitive and more purely motor aspects of motor learning and retention. Some of this evidence is based on new brain scanning techniques for measuring blood flow, which in turn is taken as an indicant of local neural activity. The findings from these techniques are used to support his model of the relationships between verbal and non-verbal systems in training. In another context Ackerman and Kyllonen (Chapter 7) cite physiological variables, such as glucose metabolization rates, which correlate with performance on intelligence tests. The latter findings have occurred as a direct consequence of a new physiological technique (i.e. positron emission tomography) that has the capability to locate effects anatomically that heretofore have not been possible using earlier techniques. Such new physiological techniques may help to identify the underpinnings of learning and retention processes, thereby deepening our understanding of the effects of training.

Our review of possible research trends therefore indicates that there are plenty of new and fruitful areas of research in training. In addition, it can be assumed that research must continue in the basic areas of skill acquisition, retention, and transfer as well as the applied topics of training design, development, and evaluation. An implicit assumption of this volume is that training is valuable to an organization, and is cost effective if it is executed properly. The problem is that training methods are continually evolving as a function of theoretical and technological developments. Hence, research must continue to be performed to ensure that the training methods used in practice conform to the current state of knowledge.

# REFERENCES

Anderson, J. R. (1982). Acquisition of cognitive skill, *Psychological Bulletin*, **89**, 369–406.

Ash, D. W. and Holding, D. H. (1990). Backward versus forward chaining in the acquisition of a keyboard skill, *Human Factors*, **32**, 139–146.

Boguslaw, R. and Porter, E. H. (1962). Team functions and training. In R. M. Gagné (ed.). *Psychological Principles in System Development*. New York: Holt, Rinehart, and Winston.

Briggs, G. W. and Naylor, J. C. (1965). Team versus individual training, training task fidelity, and task organization effects on transfer performance by three-man teams, *Journal of Applied Psychology*, **49**, 387–392.

Druckman, D. and Swets, J. A. (1988). *Enhancing Human Performance: Issues, Theories, and Techniques*. Washington, DC: National Academy Press.

Fitts, P. M. (1964). Perceptual–motor skill learning. In A. W. Melton (ed.). *Categories of Human Learning*, pp. 243–285. New York: Academic Press.

Fleishman, E. A. and Hempel, W. E., Jr (1954). Changes in factor structure of a complex psychomotor test as a function of practice. *Psychometrika*, **19**, 239–252.

Glaser, R., Lesgold, A., Lajoie, S., Eastman, R., Greenberg, L., Logan, D., Magone, M., Weiner, A., Wolf, R. and Yengo, L. (1986). *Cognitive Task Analysis to Enhance Technical Skills Training and Assessment* (Contract No. F41689–83–C–0029). Learning Research and Development Center, University of Pittsburgh.

Heller, F. H. (in preparation). *Effects of Mental Practice on Rifle Marksmanship Training* (ARI Draft Technical Report). Alexandria, VA: US Army Research Institute for the Behavioral and Social Sciences.

Holding, D. H. (1965). *Principles of Training*. London: Pergamon Press.

Klaus, D. J. and Glaser, R. (1968). *Increasing Team Proficiency Through Training: 8. Final Summary Report*, (AIR E 1–6/68–FR). Pittsburgh, PA: American Institutes for Research.

Means, B., Mumaw, R., Roth, C., Schlager, M., McWilliams, E., Gagné, E., Rice, V., Rosenthal, D. and Heon, S. (1988). *ATC Training Analysis Study: Design of the*

*Next-Generation ATC Training System* (OPM Work Order 342–036). Alexandria, VA: HumRRO International, Inc.

Morrison, J. E. and Holding, D. H. (1990). *Designing a Gunnery Training Strategy* (HumRRO Final Report FR–PRD–90–12). Alexandria, VA: Human Resources Research Organization.

Morrison, J. E. and Walker, S. A. (1990). *The Effects of Mental Practice on Tank Gunnery Performance* (ARI Technical Report 873). Alexandria, VA: US Army Research Institute for the Behavioral and Social Sciences.

Slavin, R. E. (1983). When does cooperative learning increase student achievement? *Psychological Bulletin,* **94,** 429–445.

Wells, R. and Hagman, J. D. (1989). *Training Procedures for Enhancing Reserve Component Learning, Retention, and Transfer* (ARI Technical Report 860). Alexandria, VA: US Army Research Institute for the Behavioral and Social Sciences.

# Author Index

Page numbers in **bold** type are in reference sections of the chapters.

# Subject Index

Ability
  effects on retention, 55, 77
  general, 207–212
  see also general ability (g)factor
  psychomotor, 207–212
  relation to skill, 207
ACT* theory, 119, 212
Action-language bridge, 22–3
Adaptive training
  augmented feedback in, 179
  by simplification, 180–1, 184
Air defense tasks, 243
Air traffic control, 223, 243, 275
Analogical reasoning, 199
Anxiety, 273–4
Aptitude, 195–6
Aptitude-treatment interaction (ATI),
  130, 195, 220–4, 233
Artificial intelligence, 239
  see also intelligent computer assisted
  instruction
Assembly/disassembly of machine guns,
  60-2
Associative phase of skill acquisition,
  see knowledge compilation
Asymmetrical transfer, 110–13
  principle of inclusion, 111–13
  principle of performance standards,
  111–13
Audiovisual media
  print, 234
  radio/television, 235–6
  slides/tapes, 236
  transparencies, 234–5
  video, 236–7
  videodiscs/CDs, 237

Balancing, 64
Basic skills training, 261–2
Battlefield tactics, 243–4
Behavioral modeling, 271–2
Behavioral objectives, 2, 3–4, 136
Bicycle riding, 14–15

Bilateral transfer, 103–4, 110
Blocked-order training, see practice,
  variability and variety in
Bow tying, 23, 25

Cerebellum, 42–4
Chess playing, 26
Chunking, 18, 28–9
Clerical work, 267, 273
Closed-loop processing
  theory, 36
  versus open-loop processing, 39
Cognitive modeling, 272
Cognitive skills, 193
Cognitive strategies, see learning
  strategies
Cognitive task analysis, 132, 152–160,
  201–2, 272
Component Display Theory (CDT),
  137–9, 150
Computer-based training, 237–41
  in military training, 247
Controlled versus automated
  processing, 38–9
  automatisation, 37–41
Cooperative learning, 275–6
Coping strategies, 268
Corporate strategy, see Organizational
  analysis
Critical Incident Technique, 139–40
Cross-cultural training, 263
Cross-education, see bilateral transfer
Crosstraining, 265
Customer relations training, 266–7

Dart throwing, 108
Decision making task, 156–60
Declarative knowledge, 23–4, 118–19,
  152–3, 203, 213–14, 274
Demographic changes in working
  population, 260–3
Demonstration, 21, 24–7
Discrimination, 28, 29